ISLE OF
HOKKAIDO

Sapporo

Hakodate

Aomori

Akita

E OF SADO

Niigata

Sendai

Nikko

MAIN
ISLAND
(HONSHU)

NAKASENDO

TOKYO

YOKOHAMA

BŌSŌ
PENINSULA

FUJI

KAIDO

IZU
PENINSULA

NSULA

P A C I F I C   O C E A N

Japan

1:1,750,000

(showing the author's itinerary)

0   100   200   300   miles

Meeting with Japan

BY THE SAME AUTHOR

SECRET TIBET

FOSCO MARAINI

Meeting with Japan

Translated from the Italian by Eric Mosbacher

NEW YORK: THE VIKING PRESS

L'Europe, à diverses reprises—avec Alexandre le Grand, avec Marco Polo, au seizième siècle,—a découvert l'Asie orientale, et chaque fois ce fut une surprise nouvelle, comme s'il s'agissait d'une planète différente. Chaque fois, en effet, nos classicismes méditerranéens avaient l'impression de se trouver en présence de classicismes analogues, quoique formés d'éléments à première vue incompréhensibles. Dans l'Inde, en Chine, pour ne citer que les foyers originaux, s'etaient constituées des 'sociétés parfaites' avec des philosophies, des littératures, des arts formant un tout en soi.

RENÉ GROUSSET: *Bilan de l'Histoire*

Photographs by the author, except Nos. 28, 33, 81, 82, which are from Japanese sources. Drawings by Makino Yone, Moriya Tadashi, S. Pannuti. Original ideograms by Moriya Tadashi and others. Japanese title: *Zuihitsu Nippon,* 'Japan, following the brush on the paper, letting memories write themselves'. Ideograms on cover by Hasegawa Luca.

Contents

Author's Preface

This book deals with the experiences of several years spent in a civilization profoundly different from our own during a period of revolutionary change and transformation.

A prolonged stay in a country which belongs to the same great family of nations as that in which the traveller was born and grew up differs from a shorter stay only in that it furnishes the mind with a larger number of facts, a clearer vision of the details of the total picture. But, if we cross the borders within which the influence and traditions of the classical world, Christianity, the European Renaissance, have been at work for centuries, there may also be a qualitative difference between a mere visit and long residence; we may succeed in entering another order of ideas, a world governed by different dimensions. The special correspondent comes and goes; he sees things through the eyes of his place of origin, recognizes the exotic, and enjoys it. But he who spends a substantial part of his life among people whose history might have taken place on another planet ends by undergoing a subtle trans-formation. What at first sight seemed strange becomes normal; exotic beings become real men, women, and children. On the one hand you realize the great identity of man's terrestrial adventure, on the other the validity of looking at life and the world through eyes entirely different from our own. Both are vital in an age of shrinking distances and multiplying populations. How are we to live together if we do not know and understand each other?

The travels which are the subject of these pages took me to the sources of Japanese civilization: to Ise, the scene of its earliest flowering; to Nara, which flourished when the first contacts were made with China and Buddhism; to Kyoto, where Japanese institutions, literature, and arts reached their zenith; to Nagoya, the city of the Tokugawa Shoguns who governed Japan from 1600 to 1868; to Tokyo, marvel and horror of our century. This journey prompted me to recapitulate, stage by stage, the most important elements in Japanese history in the broadest sense of the term—politics, economics, religion, literature, the arts. I have deliberately avoided the pedantic aim of trying to include everything. Many things have been left in the shade; those mentioned arose out of visits, meetings, memories. But I believe I have not omitted essentials, and hope I have given the reader a true total picture.

I propose in two shorter subsequent volumes, if I am able, to describe my impressions and experiences in north Japan, with its bearded aborigines who are now disappearing, and in south Japan, now famous principally for the ominous name of Hiroshima.

I wish to mention the names of a few persons who were closely connected with the writing of this book, to whom it is therefore dedicated; first of all, my daughters Dacia, Yuki, and Toni, and my wife Topazia, for whom, poor things, the Far East in war-time meant more pain and suffering than joys and pleasures. Without my daughters, how much more superficial would have been my approach to a country which is so difficult to understand! Through them, legends, myths, fables, penetrated into our blood as if we grown-ups had breathed them ourselves in our childhood. Nor shall I ever forget the courage with which Topazia held to her chosen path in September, 1943, in the face of the miseries, humiliations, hunger, perils, of a long internment.

Nor must I omit the name of Miyazawa Hiroyuki, one of my dearest Japanese friends, a companion of my studies and mountain climbs, whose life was cut short with blind and subtle cruelty by the militarist régime of his country. Hiroyuki represented the noblest aspect of the Japanese mind, the aspect of greatest value to the world; its exquisite sensibility to beauty, understood in a religious sense that is perhaps closer to that of the ancient Greeks than to that of the contempory west; its passionate engagement in life; its deep sense of brotherhood, not only with men, but with everything 'possessed of mind' (as the Tibetans say) and 'not possessed of mind'. Opposed to him there was another facet, the crude, violent, obscurantist facet of the Japanese personality, which has been in continual conflict with itself for centuries. I hope that the fact that it was this latter which got the upper hand in Hiroyuki's case was only an absurd mischance of fate.

Finally, there are two persons to whom I owe a huge debt of intellectual gratitude: Professor Giorgio Pasquali (1885–1952) and Dr. N. G. Munro (1864–1941), a philologist and a doctor, an Italian and a Scotsman, two brilliant embodiments of that western spirit whose supreme gifts to the world have been science and music. In all other fields the east can unquestionably claim equality or superiority, whether it be in philosophy, religion, the arts, or ways of life. But science and music are creations which are absolutely our own, gifts which we shall leave the world even if we disappear from it. Both Pasquali and Munro, though scientists, were devoted to music.

Meeting with Japan

SEA OF
OKHOTSK

Hokkaido
Abashiri
Asahigawa
Mount Asahi
Akan

Otaru
Sapporo
Mt. Sap-
poro-dake
Chitose
Shiraoi
Noboribetsu

Hakodate

Aomori

Akita

Hiraizumi

Matsushima
Sendai
Fukushima
Haramachi

Isle of
Sado
Isle of Hekura
Niigata

Yumoto
Nikko

Noto
Peninsula
Nagano

Kanazawa
Mount Hodaka
10,466 ft.
Suwa

Shirakawa
River Hida
TOKYO

Oki
Islands
Kuzu'ryu
Yokohama
Bōsō
Peninsula
Onjuku.

Amanohashi-
date
Tsuruga
Mount Fuji
12,395 ft.
Kamakura
Kakone

Kinosaki
Biwa
NAGOYA
Kasayi
Mishima
Odawara
Atami

Tottori
Iwami
Wadoyama
Maibara
Okazaki
Shizuoka
Yaizu
Oshima

Izumo
Hanase
Yokkaichi
Okrome
Kyoto
Otsu
Ouji
Hamamatsu
Izu
Peninsula

Akana
Himeji
Kobe
OSAKA
Nameyama
Fuji
Toyohashi

Joge
Okayama
Nara
Iso
Toba

Hiroshima
Kurashiki
Muró-ji
Yamato

INLAND SEA
Koya
Yoshino

Tsushima
Myajima
Tokushima
Kii
Peninsula

Hakata
Bay
Shimonoseki
Shikoku
Hachijō-jima

Hirado
Moji
Fukuoka

Aso Volcano
Kumamoto

Nagasaki

Amakusa
Kyushu

Kagoshima

Tane-ga-shima

JAPAN, showing places mentioned in text and captions

SEA OF JAPAN

PACIFIC OCEAN

Japanese Alps

River Tenryu

I

Three Tokyos in a Century

Flowering Fields of Light

FOR a long time, I could not say how long, the aircraft, like a bird resting on the wind, seemed to be gliding down from an indeterminate height over a carpet of coloured lights which suddenly flowered in the night. Patches of rich, tangible blackness appeared, surrounded and intersected by silver daisies. By reason of our movement, which alternately concealed and disclosed them, they seemed to light up and go out again, pulsating like living things. From time to time more fantastically illuminated areas or concentrations appeared, festoons and clusters of red, green, or orange.

The weather was bad; the sky was filled with clouds and patches of mist; every now and then we vanished into a vaporous void (which made the aircraft bump) and emerged a moment or two later. But down below the soft, voluptuous carpet of flowering lights was still there; there was a touch of unreality about it which made it seem the work of a magician. We were flying over Tokyo by night. What a marvellous sight! And what a strange surprise!

For the reader to appreciate why I was so captivated it is necessary to explain that Japanese towns, seen from ground-level and by daylight, are indescribably ugly. This applies both to big towns, like Tokyo, Osaka, Nagoya, and to small ones, like Hiroshima, Sendai, or Sapporo; it applies to them all, I should say without exception. Even Kyoto, which ends by turning out to be one of the most fascinating places in the world, is at first sight a bitter disappointment.

What is the explanation of this fact in a country so sensitive to all forms of beauty? To find the answer it is necessary for a moment to note some of the basic differences in the outlook of east and west. With us there is something essentially sunny and radiant about beauty, which would make it absurd to want to conceal it; it is almost necessarily accompanied by a certain need of bright light. When Hegel says that '*das Schöne ist wesentlich das Geistige, das sich sinnlich äussert*' (beauty is essentially a material manifestation of mind) he is expressing a profound belief of the west.

Keats's 'beauty is truth, truth beauty' illustrates another aspect of our western attitude. Not only must beauty shine out in the world, but it is linked by subtle, ancient, and deep subterranean veins with truth. All our aesthetic thinking, from Aristotle to Croce, turns in the last analysis on the relations between truth and beauty. Thus our cities declare themselves in squares and avenues, colonnades and cathedrals. Their beauty is spread out in the sun, is constructed, organic. They are the children of the social order and technique, but also the children of dialectics and geometry.

In Japan, however, beauty is something that has to be worked for, earned; it is the reward for a long and sometimes painful search, it is the final attainment of insight, a jealously guarded possession; there is a great deal of vulgarity about beauty that is immediately perceptible. The historical links of this aesthetic approach are not so much with truth and understanding; they take us at once into the fields of intuition-illumination *(satori),* taste *(shumi),* and the heart *(kokoro).* In one way it can be called a romantic attitude to beauty; from another angle it can be said that, as the beautiful is always recondite, it is an aristocratic attitude.

Hence it follows that to associate a town, the place where everybody comes and goes, the public domain *par excellence,* with beauty would be absurd. Japanese towns are always mere tools for working and living in, impermanent entities serving mere practical ends. They contain beauty, of course, but first of all you must desire it and seek it out, and then, perhaps, in the end it may be granted you to find it. Then, if you find it, it will offer you subtleties unimagined elsewhere, among secluded gardens and temples, or villas where the most perfect communion between man and his environment is achieved. In Japan beauty is like

an island, a whispered word, a moment of pure intoxication to be
retained in the memory for ever.

It is noteworthy, for example, that Japanese towns are almost
entirely lacking in 'smart' streets; places such as the Via Veneto in
Rome, the Via Tornabuoni in Florence, the neighbourhood of the
Place Vendôme in Paris, Bond Street in London, or Fifth Avenue in
New York. Tokyo has a big commercial street, the Ginza, 'the Silver-
smith's',[1] with its satellites the Nishi and the Higashi Ginza, Kyoto has
its Kawara-machi, between San-jo and Shi-jo, but they cannot really be
said to be 'smart' streets in the western sense, however obvious it may
be that in the course of time they will tend to become that. In Japan
there are residential quarters, with quiet avenues where walls and gates
barely allow you to guess the existence within of an elegant luxury that
refrains from the slightest hint of display; and there are smart amusement quarters which suggest and hint rather than say and show. But
the streets are mere traffic arteries, a part of the urban physiology, not
a complement and continuation of the drawing-room and the theatre,
or sometimes of the alcove. All this opens unexpected glimpses into
habits of secrecy, exclusion, withdrawal, and also of aristocratic contempt for luxury; a world of private gatherings of persons to whom
the public gaze is abhorrent; a life lived in isolated cliques and groups;
small coteries of initiates, the elect, those favoured with special privileges.
The street? Why, it belongs to everybody, and hence by definition
cannot be elegant, delicate, civilized.

No one will ever convince me that the Japanese do not take an
involuntary pleasure in the slovenliness with which they build their
towns, as if to surround and protect their real treasures with a thick
layer of ugliness. The ugliness of their streets, which are indiscriminate
jumbles of huge hideous structures of reinforced concrete and of huts,
revolting hovels, and houses of every conceivable style, covered with
advertising slogans and invariably disfigured by huge telegraph posts
with untidy tangles of wire, has to be seen to be believed.

Tonight, however, I discovered in a Japanese town beauty which
nobody could conceal; beauty that rises from the earth into the sky
when dark sets in; interminable fields of flowering lights, deep meadows

---

[1] Also 'Mint'. The name is derived from the fact that silver coins were minted in the immediate
neighbourhood from 1636 onwards.

which are the scene of secret carnivals. What a delightful surprise!
Thank you, Japan, for this first welcome.

Temple-River; Eels

We landed to the accompaniment of a terrific splashing of water, which
was illuminated by the aircraft's headlights and crashed against its
metallic structure. Frankly, it was a relief. In spite of all the confidence
that one may have in electronics and its mysteries, it is always slightly
uncomfortable to feel oneself at the mercy of night and storm in several
tons of mechanism suspended in the sky.

But now we were on *terra firma*. They opened the door, and we got
out; and here were the first Japanese sounds, smells, voices. After so
many years' absence, it was very evocative. I felt very moved, though
afraid of being disappointed. So many people had told me that Japan
was spoilt, that the young had 'gone American' and chewed gum, and
that the old were disillusioned and no longer thought about anything
but money. Would this turn out to be true or false? I took deep breaths
of the air of my second country, the country in which I had lived and
suffered for so long, where my daughters were born, the air of this
eastern Hellas which has the gift of putting those who have once loved
her under a permanent spell.

I quickly completed the customs and passport formalities. How
smoothly they went! Times seem to have changed greatly; in a few
moments it was all over. Even my collection of photographic apparatus,
my cine-camera, the many boxes of film I had brought with me, passed
without question, almost without a glance. How different it was the
first time I arrived in Japan, in distant 1938! Then you were subjected to
interminable inspections, interrogations, the most minute customs and
medical examinations—even your faeces were examined; you had to
give the names of all your close and distant relatives, and if it turned
out that you had, or had had, a connection with any army or political
party or international organization, it was just too bad. Finally you had
to make a complete list of all the books and other printed matter you
had with you.

Half an hour later—that is the time it takes from Haneda ('the field
of wings') to the centre of the city—we stopped outside a Japanese
restaurant. The old man who opened the door looked as small and

twisted as a 500-year-old dwarf tree. '*Irasshai*' (Come in, welcome), he said.
Most Japanese restaurants serve only one or two specialities, with various
accompaniments. Here we were in a *kabayaki-ya* where the speciality was
roast eels on rice with soya sauce. Actually it was the most famous
and venerable *kabayaki-ya* in Tokyo; there was something subtly rural
about the entrance (though we were in the centre of the city), almost as
if we were in a Tuscan villa. One side of the paper-and-bamboo lamp
displayed the two ideograms for the word *Miyagawa* (palace-river)
written with faultless calligraphy; they are among the most harmonious
of all ideograms, because of the balance between the brush-strokes and
the empty spaces.

Outside the dark wooden fence which bounded the area occupied
by the restaurant and its garden there was the infernal
din of motor traffic and the clanging of trams, but
here it was quiet and still; there was a mere penumbra
of sound, and everything was small, delicate, exquisite.
Everything that might suggest unpleasing, violent sensations was rigorously excluded; all that remained was
wood, paper, old stone made shiny by much polishing.

Miya-
Palace
Shrine
Prince

gawa
River

Inside the gate we had found ourselves in a small
garden, contrived with such cunning irregularity that it
seemed possible to lose one's way among the shrubs and
the dwarf, twisted pine-trees. Dotted along the paths, as
if by chance, were six or seven little one-room wooden
huts, each ready for a party of guests. Each was a little above ground-
level, and before entering you had to remove your shoes; the floor was
covered with *tatami,* soft mats made of shiny, regularly laid straw.
Tatamu in Japanese means to roll up, and in ancient times *tatami* were
undoubtedly mats which were simply unrolled and laid on the floor,
but in the course of time they developed into a kind of shiny, polished,
perfumed vegetable mattress, fixed to the floor.

It was late, and few customers remained; in one of the huts only
did I see a party of young men, singing cheerfully. The *jochu-san* ('Miss
Waitress') came hurrying towards us, and led us towards a pavilion at
the bottom of the garden. We slipped off our shoes and squatted on the
floor.

'Maraini-san, sit here, I insist on your taking the seat of honour.'

'Certainly not, Bamba-san, the seat of honour is yours, and you must take it.'

It was necessary to get used to the exchange of such compliments again. In Japan the place of honour has a special meaning. In every room there is an alcove, a *tokonoma*, reserved for one or two beautiful things—a painting, a poem written in delicate hieroglyphics, an old piece of sculpture, a vase—and a few cunningly arranged flowers. When the master or mistress of the house are persons of taste the whole is bound by subtle harmonies; work of art and flowers are often so arranged as to suggest or comment on some event, experience, or emotion, *e.g.*, arrival, pleasure, spring, parting, love, nature, sadness, mountains, congratulations. The occupant of the place of honour sits with his back to the *tokonoma*, so that to the other guests he is framed by it. After a brief struggle of smiles and bows I had to give in.

While we talked, sipping our *saké* (rice wine), I looked round. Everything about me was wood, paper, straw, smooth, planed, unadulterated surfaces; no paint, nothing that concealed the grain of the vegetable matter; and no metal. Silence. Every now and then you could hear the rustle of the *fusuma* (fragile doors of wood and paper) being opened or shut. The cheerful singing of the young men had stopped; probably we were now alone in the Palace-River house.

After days and days of noise in the belly of an aircraft, after offices, airports, customs, hotels, conversations in all languages and storms in all skies, it seemed like living in a dream.

One of my friends helped me to translate the big ideograms displayed on a flag hanging in the *tokonoma* (there was nothing in the alcove but this and a thistle flower). There were four characters, and they were difficult to decipher at first sight. They read *Hoge jaku*; perhaps the best translation is: 'Free yourself from attachment to useless things.' A supremely Buddhist maxim. The thistle was not put in the *tokonoma* by chance.

When we had finished drinking our *saké* (in Japan one drinks before rather than with or after a meal), our eels arrived, arranged in slices on white rice in three rectangular black lacquer boxes. We removed the odorous wooden chopsticks from their paper wrappings and started to eat.

Giorgio and I got back very late last night. Our dinner of eels lasted a long time, we drank more *saké*, and reached that happy state of vagueness about the exact relations of spatial co-ordinates that leads to the opening of hearts.

This morning I was awakened late by a thin ray of sunshine which penetrated into the dark room. Air travel is tiring to the nerves; you notice only afterwards the unexpected bill you have to pay in the form of physical exhaustion. Giorgio's housekeeper, Abe-san (in Japan everybody is san, *i.e.*, Mr., Mrs., Miss), came and opened the *amado*, the wooden doors of Japanese houses which are shut at night, and brought me a cup of tea. '*O-furo dekita yo*,' she said (The honourable bath is ready), and then knelt beside my *futon* (bed-clothes, Photograph 118) and opened a fusillade of questions about my health, my journey, my family in Italy, etc., etc. All this was part of Japanese politeness; questions which strike us as unpardonably inquisitive, such as 'How old are you?' or 'Are you sorry you have no sons?' are the most ordinary thing in the world in Japan, and are meant to demonstrate the respectful interest that the inquirer is taking in you. Etiquette does not, however, require a precise answer. An acquaintance you meet in the street, for instance, is almost certain to ask you where you are going, but the requirements of politeness are fully met if you answer: '*Eh chotto*' (Just over there!)

After a final stretch and yawn I got up, put on a *yukata* (light cotton kimono), and went to the bathroom. The bath is another domestic feature in which the Japanese have the advantage over us. In the first place a Japanese bathroom is not, as it is too often with us, a cold, metallic, tiled place containing a bath; rather is it a kind of extension of the bath itself, in which everything possible is made of that warm, comforting, restful substance, wood. The bath itself is usually wooden, and when warm gives off a delightful scent of pines; and you do not lie in it, you sit; it is a kind of miniature swimming pool. It seems impossible that such a minor detail should make such a big difference. Can lying in warm water and sitting in it have different effects on the circulation and therefore on the general sense of well being? The fact remains that nearly all westerners in Japan infinitely prefer the Japanese bath to the European. You emerge from it rested, refreshed, at peace with the world.

Moreover, the Japanese approach the bath in an entirely different spirit. In the west, after nearly two thousand years of opposition from the various churches, the bath was reduced, not long before the present age, to its mere hygienic or medical function, *i.e.,* the removal of the surface dirt of the body when its effluvia became offensive to the nostrils of others; and it was used as a cure for certain affections. Am I wrong in suggesting that the western custom of lying in the bath was medical in origin? True, for a century we have been reacting against old prejudices, but in these things fundamental attitudes change slowly, and everything connected with the body touches fundamental attitudes at their most sensitive spot. Nowadays the bath has resumed importance in our lives, but as a barely tolerated concession, a challenge to deep emotional attitudes. It is surrounded with bolts and locks and glazed windows, and is only too often hidden in the least sunny and attractive room in the house. Bathrooms are still designed on the assumption that you enter them with your clothes on and keep them on, taking them off only for the brief time necessary for immersing yourself in a tiled or metal coffin in which you simmer for a few minutes in a brew of your own dirt.

In Japan, however, the ultimate origins of the bath are religious. The bath is a domestic aspect of ancient purificatory rites *(yuami, misogi)* which from the earliest times were an essential element of the Shinto cult.[1] Now, in the last analysis, every expression of religious feeling is a joyful thing; when man feels, however indirectly and remotely from his conscious, that he is in harmony with God, with the gods, the invisible, he is happy, at peace with himself and with others.

The Japanese bathroom is consequently an inviting, welcoming place, in which it would be bad taste to hurry, or to hide oneself, or in any way to inhibit restful relaxation. The water is heated simply and ingeniously, in a middle-class house generally by a small stove outside the room, but in more modest or poor houses by a stove that is partly in the bath itself. Finally, the floor is always so constructed that the water flows rapidly away; and you wash yourself outside the bath, using a bucket or basin to pour warm water over your shoulders and your head 'without fear of wetting the furniture'; thus you wash all the dirt

[1] 'Actual personal dirt was considered disrespectful towards the gods.'—W. G. ASTON, *Shinto,* London, 1905, p. 248.

away with the soap (Photograph 119). Then, when you are perfectly clean, you enter the bath to warm yourself, relax, meditate, sing, or perhaps to resume your conversation through the thin walls with those in neighbouring rooms.

A thing that always and with good reason shocks the Japanese is having bath and lavatory in the same room—another thing which points to our purely material, hygienic, medical attitude towards the bath. The Japanese always separate lavatory and bathroom; they never indulge in our deplorable confusion of essentially different functions. In Japan the bath originated with ritual purification, hence it is a positive, pleasurable act, an essential ingredient in the rest and refreshment which a man takes after the toil of the day, a function as important and vital as sleep or meals.

It is characteristic, for instance, that with us no time of the day is by immemorial usage consecrated to the bath; you generally take it in a hurry, in the morning or in the evening, and plenty of people only take it every so often. When you say someone is having a bath there is generally an implied apology in the statement. Our eating customs, which go back for many generations, are far more sacrosanct and universal. In Japan the time between five and seven in the evening is sacred to the bath, as, indeed, it was in ancient Greece and Rome. You go home, take your bath in comfort, change into your ample oriental robes, and then you have your evening meal. This applies universally to rich and poor alike. In my Japanese travels I have seen dwellings of every conceivable type; even the huts of the most poverty-stricken peasants or labourers had their *o-furo* (honourable bath); in the worst cases there would be a big basin in which you washed as best you could. But there was never a complete lack of facilities.

It is also worth mentioning that while with us there are no traditional popular customs, I believe, connected with the bath, Japan is rich in them. A typical example is the Boys' Festival *(Tango no sekku)*, celebrated annually on May 5. On this occasion a long pole is erected outside houses blessed with male children, and to this there are attached one or more huge carp made of brightly coloured material *(koi-nobori)* which swell in the wind and seem to be vigorously swimming against the invisible current; the carp is a universally recognized symbol of strength, energy, and will-power, to say nothing of long life. Inside the house miniature armour and swords, or dolls representing armed Samurai ready for action, presents to the children, are displayed on shelves specially put up for the occasion. Special sweets called *shimaki* are eaten to the accompaniment of *saké*, to which *shobu*, a medicinal herb, is added; and leaves of *shobu*, which is a kind of Florentine iris, are added to the bath, because of the strengthening and purificatory virtues traditionally attributed to them. Similarly on December 23, on the occasion of *toji*, the winter solstice, every good housewife prepares a bath with *yasu*, the juice of a small, scented orange which is said to bring fortune, purify mind and body, and be beneficial to health in various ways.

The Japanese system of immersion in the bath after cleaning one-self also has the advantage of economy, for it enables the whole family to use the same hot water. Normally the first to enter the bath is the head of the family, followed by his wife and the young children, fol-lowed by the other children, followed by the servants. The bath is also naturally a social occasion. I do not refer here to the innumerable public baths which round about five o'clock in the afternoon take the place that is taken at different times of the day with us by the café or the inn, but it is worth mentioning that the very common sharing of the daily bath by persons of the same age and sex often has about it the quality of a fraternal *agape*.

Naturally all this assumes an attitude to nudity that is different from ours, a healthier, serener, less morbid attitude. That is a subject to which I shall return later. Here I shall mention only that, while in the west the nude generally awakens responses connected with sex, in Japan nudity is accepted with fewer complications.

After my bath I went back to my room. What a delicious house it was! A pavilion of wood and paper, with shiny, nearly black tiles, set among gardens and woods at the foot of a hill, reminiscent of old Chinese paintings. The arrangement of the rooms round the little garden was perfectly worked out. The whole house was turned out-wards towards nature (Photograph 96). There was no trace here of the dividing line which the western house draws so firmly, seeming to tell nature that she is all very fine, but must stay outside, for it is the business of the house, with its solid walls, its locks on the windows and bars on the doors, to protect its occupants. Here it was different. In the warm season the wooden outside doors (*amado*) and the inside wooden and paper doors *(shoji)* could be entirely removed, and then the rooms opened straight on to the surrounding foliage, flowers, and trees.

We were near the centre of Tokyo but, thanks to the fortunate disposition of the surrounding hills, the noise of traffic hardly reached us. Tokyo is not only one of the most populous cities in the world, it is also one of the most extensive. Twenty miles separate the outermost suburbs of Kawasaki and Kawaguchi; that is because the Japanese, though they consent to work in concrete boxes many storeys high, wisely decline to live in them.

The garden in front of me was typical of thousands of others. What do we do when we make a garden? First of all we fill the whole space with geometry—here a path, there a flower-bed, there a bench or fountain—until every square inch is composed and regimented. Here architect and gardener have expended just as much time and energy to attain a diametrically opposite effect. At first sight you might be in the clearing of a wood. Then you realize that you are surrounded by the work of man, but that the artist's aim was the unobtrusive recreation of nature. There is no geometry here; or rather there is a secret, infinitely non-Euclidian and subtle geometry, a secret harmony that the mind seizes before the intelligence. Everything is irregular; the shape of the central lawn, as soft and green as the strange skin of a sea monster, the shape of the flat blocks of granite taken from the bed of a mountain stream, the arrangement of the azaleas, the jasmin, the gardenias, the clumps of bushes that rise gently towards the pines and maples which hide the boundary wall and the neighbouring houses and form a framework for the sky. The harmony of the whole strikes one immediately.

The interior of Giorgio's house is almost entirely Japanese. There are *tatami* in every room. In my room there is a handsome *tokonoma* with an ancient Korean vase and a view of mountains rising over a bamboo wood. A special concession to the west is a small table and chair for working at. I confess that this gives me pleasure, for with all my love of eastern things I have never succeeded in writing or reading for a long time while squatting cross-legged on the floor. Domestic utensils and furniture, as well as the many *objets d'art* of Giorgio's collection, are enclosed in wall cupboards, as is the custom. The Japanese home (Photographs 93–98, 116–119) is distinguished by simplicity, elegance, a slight touch of asceticism—the living, century-old expression of many ideas which we imagine we have only just discovered, which we think still belong to the future.[1]

Plain of Green Stones

Today I walked about Tokyo for the first time. As soon as I got out of the *shosen* (underground) I was surprised at the number of new houses and new concrete buildings, at the speed with which Japanese reconstruction had taken place, at the liveliness of the streets and, at any rate superficially and at first sight, the general impression of prosperity.

I was unable, however, to efface from my mind the picture of Tokyo as I saw it immediately after the end of the war. I arrived there at the beginning of September, 1945, from Nagoya, shortly after my release from two years' internment. It was a desolate sight indeed. Around Marunouchi, the financial centre of the city, a few big concrete buildings were still intact (the allies seemed deliberately to have spared them in order to have offices from which to govern the country efficiently after their arrival), but the huge expanses of dwelling-houses, little shops, and stores of upper and lower Tokyo were razed to the ground; there were not even the mountains of rubble which were to be seen in the bombed towns of Germany; the wooden Japanese houses had gone up in flame and smoke, leaving the ground strewn with black dust and spent embers. The eye wandered over acres and acres of grey desert, with here and there some broken crocks, strange green stones (piles of melted bottles), pieces of twisted metal barely covered by rampant vegetation which had managed to germinate between one air-raid and the next.

In all this desolation only three things stood out: the surviving *kura,* or strong-boxes, shaped like little houses and made of brick or concrete and therefore resistant to fire, used by the Japanese to keep their valuables in; the many empty, rusty safes, with doors removed from their hinges, looking like imperfectly fossilized monsters, which marked the sites of former shops and offices; and, finally, the innumer-

[1] Professor Walter Gropius remarked in an interview in the *Asahi Evening News* (Tokyo, June 16, 1954) that all the elements in the design of the modern house for which he and his fellow-architects had fought—close correlation between interior and exterior, movable partitions between the rooms, and other things as well—were present in the Japanese house.

able concrete troughs, which were supposed by the government of the time to hold enough water to put out the fires caused by the bombs. Here and there charred trees raised their crippled branches towards the sky. In the distance a tram, visible as if it were in open country, crossed the devastated plain.

Tokyo was devastated by fire in 1601, 1657, and 1772, and in the twentieth century has been almost completely destroyed twice: in 1923 by one of the most violent earthquakes recorded in history, and then again by the air-raids of 1945. Buildings that date from before 1923 and have survived both cataclysms are rare enough for tourists to go and look at them.

Much has been written about the 1923 earthquake; it is sufficient to recall that 60,000 persons died; most of them were burnt alive, not crushed by falling masonry.[1] The earthquake struck the city exactly at midday on September 1, when the fire to cook the rice was alight in every house. Within two hours the city was blazing like a great funeral pyre. How often have I heard people who experienced that catastrophe talking about it! Here I shall mention only one episode. At Yokohama somebody noticed a woman's hair apparently growing out of the ground like grass. The explanation was that a great crack had suddenly appeared in the roadway, into which a child had fallen; the child's mother jumped in after it to try and save it, and the crack then closed.

As for the destruction of 1945, few are aware that the carpet bombing between March and May of that year worked more havoc and claimed more victims than the atomic bomb at Hiroshima. The raid of March 9–10, for instance, started at about 10.30 p.m. and went on all night. Several hundred B.29s dropped thousands of tons of incendiary and high-explosive bombs on the lower quarters of the city.[2] The fire, fanned by a gale, was infernal; next day what had been the most populous part of Tokyo, a hive of houses, shops, workshops, public buildings, light industrial establishments, was a charred, smoking plain. Counting the dead was always difficult on these occasions, for it was impossible to tell

[1] If the whole area affected, including places outside Tokyo, is included, the total number of dead and missing as a result of the earthquake was 142,807. *See* A. IMAMURA, 'The Great Earthquake of S.E. Japan of Sept. 1, 1923', in *Scientific Japan*, Tokyo, 1926, p. 141.

[2] R. J. C. Butow (*Japan's Decision to Surrender*, Stanford University Press, p. 141), says that 130 aircraft took part, but eye-witnesses spoke of at least 300.

how many bodies had been reduced to a mere patch of grease by the terrific heat. Official documents speak of 124,711 dead and missing, a figure much higher than that of the Hiroshima hecatomb.[1]

Between November 24, 1944, and August 15, 1945, Tokyo was raided seventy times; the total number of dead and missing was 136,698, and about 760,000 houses were destroyed out of 1,377,000; in other words a great part of the metropolis was wiped out. It must, of course, be borne in mind that the ordinary Japanese house is a small wooden structure (the Japanese builder is a carpenter rather than a bricklayer) with windows and doors covered with paper; a flimsy thing compared with a house of brick or masonry. It has the advantage of cheapness (it costs about a tenth of a modern urban house in Italy); its fragile intimacy provides a charming home for a man and his family; and, because of its elasticity, it stands up magnificently to earthquakes—only the most violent shock will cause it to collapse. But it is also true that it is as combustible as a dry leaf in summer. The fire bogy (Photograph 28) is ever present in the Japanese mind, and the stranger notes alarm bells, watchtowers, fire stations, everywhere, in town and country alike.[2]

As soon as the Americans had established themselves in the Pacific islands nearest to Japan, within bomber range of her big cities, the methodical work of destruction began, countered with diminishing effectiveness by a steadily disintegrating defence. The Americans knew well enough that a box of matches was sufficient to start a blaze among those acres of flimsy wood and paper, and they concentrated on dropping showers of incendiaries. The mule-headedness of the governing militarists imposed indescribable suffering on the civil population. They refused to admit that the war was going badly and, on the pretext that nothing must be done to spread despondency and alarm, they evacuated women and children extremely slowly. Only after the infernal night of March 10 were energetic measures taken for the evacuation of civilians from Tokyo. In the meantime countless women, children, and old people had met an unnecessary and horrible death.

When I reached Tokyo from Nagoya life had started again. Many

---

[1] R. Guillain, who was present at the disaster and gives an impressive description of it in his *Le Peuple Japonais et la Guerre* (Paris, 1947, p. 205), speaks of 197,000, according to Japanese secret documents, and of 300 bombers.

[2] In old Tokyo fires were so frequent that they were called *yedo no hana* (Yedo flowers); Tokyo was called Yedo until 1868.

people had built themselves hutments on the site of their former dwellings, sometimes even with pretensions to taste, making ingenious use of pieces of twisted, rusty metal, half-charred wood, wire, sandbags, incendiary-bomb cases, old petrol cans. Grass and flowers followed, and everyone planted a few *satsuma-imo* (sweet potatoes), which send up vigorous shoots with leaves of a bright and cheerful green.

Hundreds of street vendors spread their wares on the pavement; the more enterprising had already set themselves up in little wooden shops the size of a seaside bathing cabin. People were still in a daze; the nightmare of war had lasted so long that they found it hard to believe that they could move about freely again, buy an ounce of unrationed sweets, talk without looking over their shoulder, or simply sit in the sun and do nothing. The crowd still looked pretty wretched—old women with dishevelled hair led whining children by the hand, men of all ages were dressed in ragged bits of old uniform, bare-footed and half-naked, there were many wounded still wearing their bandages or with disfiguring scars. But on the whole it was an orderly, dignified crowd and, as I said, it seemed to be moving in a daze.

In this crowd it would have been impossible to discover a young woman. Even girls of twelve or thirteen were rare; there was an absolute void up to the middle-aged and the old, and even these, with the ostentatious wretchedness of their clothing, their untidy hair, their lifeless expression, seemed to be deliberately cultivating as unprepossessing an appearance as possible. The Japanese were experiencing the relief of a sudden peace, but they were also experiencing the last hours of a fear that was perhaps deeper, more primitive, more fundamental, than the fear of air-raids—the fear of the vanquished at the approach of their conquerors.

For years their propaganda had painted the Americans as bloodthirsty wild beasts, red devils with huge hands made for throttling children, incomprehensible beings with the thick skin of Buddhist demons and rapacious eyes that lit up only at the sight of rapine and destruction. For months the wireless, the newspapers, group leaders, street leaders, had been preaching that, if the Americans landed, they would behead ex-service men, rape women, and abduct children. Now they had landed. The Emperor had called on the Japanese to welcome the victor's troops, and the expression on Japanese faces was one of

readiness to face one last and even more terrible ordeal, an ordeal calling
for their ultimate resources of will-power.

The first Americans had set foot on Japanese soil on August 28,
a few days before my arrival in Tokyo; every now and then small parties,
still armed and in full equipment, were to be seen in the streets. The
Japanese, with the anguished expression of a schoolboy looking out of
the window, hoping that the master will not ask him any questions
because he has not done his homework, pretended not to see; they
were waiting for the last bomb to drop, for the threatened *furor americanus*
to break out. But nothing happened. How extraordinary! Were the
Americans perhaps preparing their revenge quietly and in secret? It
passed understanding.

I too wore khaki fatigues, which had been dropped on our camp
by the Americans at the end of August. I walked through the crowd
in Kyobashi, along the Ginza, and was able to study in detail this historic
encounter of two peoples. The Americans were thinking: *What the hell
are these Japs up to? So quiet, so sullen. When are the hidden nationalists going to start
their last banzai charge?* The Japanese were saying to themselves: *Hen desu
né! Ada wo utanai no ka?* (How strange! Are they not going to take their
revenge?) Actually the Americans had landed with the firm intention
of giving a memorable lesson in civilization to a people who had been
governed for so many years by a set of gangsters, and the Japanese were
now convinced that they had been led astray and were determined to
rely on the Emperor's wisdom. But neither knew that the other was
sincere.

I felt like shouting from the house-tops, telling them not to be silly
but to drop their mutual suspicions, for peace, real peace, had come.
But shyness forced me to continue my walk in silence, watching what
was happening all round me. I noticed that the crowd insensibly grew
thinner at my approach, as might happen at the approach of someone
with an infectious illness, or perhaps a personage of great importance.
As long as I held my peace everybody's expression was that called
shiran-kao ('the face of once who knows nothing'). But, when I stopped
for a brief conversation about their wares with one or other of the
street vendors, after the first few words in Japanese their faces lit up in
a smile—a slightly too obsequious smile, alas!—and their breath came
in nervous, short pants, rather like a dog not sure whether he is

going to be stroked or given a bone, or whether he is going to get the whip.

'Oh! You speak Japanese? Have you been in Japan before?'

'Yes, but I'm not an American. I was imprisoned here during the war.'

'*Ah so desu ka! Ah so desu ka!* But you must know the Americans. What will they do to us now?'

'Don't be silly, what do you expect them to do? They'll execute Tojo if he doesn't commit suicide. . . .'

'Of course, of course, but what will they do to us poor people?'

'Don't worry, they won't do anything at all; they may even help to set you on your feet again. The war wasn't against you, but against the *gunbatsu*, the military clique!'

'Yes, so they say, but can you believe them?'

'Of course; *dai-jobu sa!*'

When I walked on, a crowd closed round the man immediately. They wanted to know what the 'American' had said, and he told them. I was happy to make my small contribution to reassuring them.

There was the same scene in reverse when I met some Americans.

'Hey, you, what unit do you belong to?'

'None, I'm a civilian internee. You freed me three weeks ago.'

They wanted me to explain what these Japs were up to, as I presumably knew them. For years the Americans had fought them all the way across the Pacific; they had fought like devils incarnate, and when there was no way out they flung themselves at you with their pockets full of bombs, preferring death to being taken alive. But now they were behaving like lambs. 'It just doesn't make sense, you see!' Weren't they preparing to stab the Americans in the back as soon as they discarded their arms? What did I think?

I did my best to explain that it was no good trying to judge the oriental mind by our own standards, that to the Japanese the Emperor's word was sacred, that he was like Pope and President in one. When the Emperor had told the people to fight, they had fought; now he had told them that they had lost, and that they must behave with respect towards their conqueror, and they obeyed him implicitly.

With the passing of the days the Americans and the Japanese, like puppies who were still suspicious but wanted to play with each other, started sniffing each other a little more closely. Finally, I cannot remember exactly when, but I think it was at the end of September or the beginning of October, the magic spark struck, and confidence started returning on both sides. Women and girls reappeared in the streets, at first in dull, dark clothes like penitents, then in brighter colours, and finally in the full glory of their gayest kimonos, which had somehow survived the air-raids and the fires and all the other hazards of war.

The ordeal had lasted for so long that the sudden return to normality was the richer and the more delightful. The summer ripened slowly, and autumn was at the gates. Autumn is the most delightful period of the year in Japan; the sky is nearly always blue, the heat is not disagreeable, the chrysanthemums bloom in a hundred extraordinary shapes, the leaves of the *momiji,* the maples, begin to redden. Wounds started to heal; the human race seemed to be emerging from an age of torment that had lasted for centuries. In a short time Tokyo became animated, gay, even festive. The streets filled with jeeps and allied vehicles; the first American soldiers fraternized with Japanese girls. It would not be long before legions of black marketeers and other unsavoury gentry sprang up to exploit a victor who was unprepared and too easy-going, before prostitution grew rampant and brothel-keepers bought up girls left homeless by the war to offer them to the American troops, before monstrous cities of black marketeering and vice rose around the American camps. But for a brief moment we enjoyed a peace and serenity such as we could not remember for years past and would remember for years to come. It was peace in the fullest sense of the word. Victors and vanquished met in their common humanity and looked to the future like children returned to health.

Unsigned Statement

During this period a telegram announced the arrival of Miki, the *nēsan,* 'elder sister' of our daughters, their former nurse. She came to visit us, loaded with cheap but precious gifts, after a long and difficult journey from her village in the province of Hiroshima. Her husband had had the misfortune to be at Hiroshima when the atomic bomb was dropped and, though not in the direct path of the radiation, was still very ill. He had lost all his hair, his teeth were falling out, and he was suffering from an alarming prostration. Miki therefore proposed to stay with us and the children for only a few days and to take Yuki (our second child, born in Hokkaido) back with her, 'to give her good country air to breathe and to feed her up', as indeed she did.

I do not remember exactly how the Uriu, that is to say Miki and her husband, entered our lives. I only know that one day we found them in our house at Kyoto, and that they remained our neighbours for years. They were childless; he was a man of about forty, an attractive idler, a ne'er-do-well with a latent capacity for intrigue which was the result more of a romantic temperament than anything else. Some years earlier he had inherited a considerable sum of money, but had drunk, sung, and gambled it away. Then he had tried his hand at journalism, but journalists have to work by the clock, 'and if the sun comes out and I want to lie down in a field, what am I to do?' He had ended up as a sort of assistant odd-job man in an office of Kyoto University.

Among the various jobs he had done in his time had been that of *omuko-san* ('honourable shouter of cries from the gallery'). He set great store by his memories of this theatrical, almost professional, period of his career, and used to talk about it on every possible occasion, particularly to strangers. It should be noted that in the Japanese *kabuki* theatre, which, because of the undisputed favour which it enjoys with all classes of the population, might be compared with the opera in Italy, the success of a performance is demonstrated, not only by applause, but by exclamations of encouragement, praise, or admiration which generally come from the gallery. It is apparently exceedingly difficult to judge the correct moment for making them, and much experience and sensitivity is needed; the *omuko-san* have thus become almost professionals, and are members of a club, or 'craft', to whom the management sends free seats. Moreover a certain amount of education is required; the *omuko-san* are generally small business men, sons of prosperous families, known and popular figures in the neighbourhood. The players say they act better if they are well supported by the *omuko-san*, and rumours of collusion between the two are always rife. One of the favourite cries is '*Matte imashita!*' (I was waiting for you!) Another is '*umai-zo!*' (bravo!) Sometimes, when an actor makes a mistake or stumbles over his lines, the terrible cry '*daikon*' is heard.

I write at this length about the worthy Uriu because he is a specimen of a fairly common type of Japanese that is the direct opposite of the stereotyped picture that many people have in their minds. It is true that in general the Japanese are industrious, methodical, obedient to every conceivable kind of authority, provided that it is properly constituted authority, which always has a numinous quality in their eyes. It is these characteristics which in nobler and more generous (and rarer) natures leads to heroism and self-sacrifice and in meaner and pettier natures (which are so much more common) leads to pedantry, police stupidity, conformism. But there are many other aspects of the Japanese character. One of the commonest and most agreeable of what I might perhaps call the unstandardized Japanese types is the improvident idler, wastrel, and misfit, who loves nature, cherry blossom, the red leaves of the maples, outings in boats, *saké,* women, and cheerful companionship, and every day makes good resolutions to change his ways but ends by dying in poverty, still with a song on his lips.

It is in fact this side of the Japanese character which gives Japanese literature its special charm, the charm of rich human experience and irrepressible vitality. If it were not for the diaries and caprices of exquisite court ladies, the love romances, the miscellanies of hermit poets, the poetry of great vagabonds like Bashō, the satires of Ibara, Jisho, and Kiseki, Japanese literature would largely be reduced to intolerable heroic rhetoric, pompous and stifling semi-philosophical treatises copied and re-copied from the Chinese, and cold and courtly historical apologias. Bashō, an eighteenth-century Buddhist monk and one of the greatest Japanese lyric poets, has rendered full poetical and there-fore social justice to the life of the carefree vagabond, who wanders from palace to palace and hut to hut and temple to temple, writing poems when the mood seizes him, giving his poems away, losing them, drinking, giving vent to his emotions, and in the last resort showing the life of the body to be a trifling, ephemeral incident in the real, true, eternal life of the mind.

As soon as we were able to sit down and drink a cup of *o-cha,* honour-able tea, Miki told us that on the morning in October, 1943, when we had been taken away by the *junsa,* the police, troubles had begun for her, and her husband too. They had been summoned to the Kyoto *keisatsusho* (police station), they had been separated, and an attempt had been made to make them sign a statement saying that we were spies.

At that time all foreigners were thought to be spies; it was a positive obsession. We were very much moved at the discovery that we owed our salvation to the Uriu. If they had signed that statement to get themselves out of trouble, the police could have done what they liked with me, and, because of the well-known oriental principle according to which the family of a guilty man must be punished too . . . Better not think about it.

Miki described how she and her husband had been beaten and kept locked up for many days. They had even been told that I had already confessed to espionage on behalf of the Emperor's enemies, so it was useless to continue with their denials. But Miki and her husband had been convinced that I had never meddled in such things. She had just been losing hope, particularly as she did not know what was happening to her husband, when the police had suddenly let them go. 'What strange people!' she remarked. But all that was over now. People might be poor, but at least they no longer had to live like wild beasts tearing each other to pieces. 'What do you think?' she concluded.

A few days later she left for her village in the south, carrying Yuki on her back in the country fashion.

2

Tokyo, World Melting-pot

Religions, Pleasures, Industries

Now I have been here for several weeks, and have had the opportunity of exploring the city from end to end. With its 8,253,339 inhabitants (August, 1956)[1] it is one of the most populous in the world, and it is certainly the most extensive, because nearly all the houses are of one or two storeys only and most of them are surrounded by gardens. I have been able to confirm my first impression. What rapid reconstruction, and what prosperity! True, just as in Italy, wealth is badly distributed, and side by side with luxury there is poverty and want, but at least there is a foundation on which it should be possible to build. The shops are full of goods, the traffic is dense to the point of chaos, the people are well dressed, and they look cheerful and unmindful of past years. In comparison with the state in which it emerged from the war the city seems indeed a new creation, invented only yesterday, that had floated up into the light of summer from the mysterious depths of the Pacific. *Keredomo,* but . . .

Those with eyes to see can see the old behind the chromium surface, the cares behind the smile. On the one hand past centuries, like the stumps of huge felled trees from which until yesterday all life seemed to have departed, are sprouting and throwing up new shoots; on the other hand the city is like some unfortunate person who has decided to confront courageously, with a song, the difficulties that are pressing upon him from all sides. The fascination of Tokyo, the cross-roads of the world, lies in its taste for life, however confused and disoriented it may be. 'Chicago,' it has been said, 'is stupefying . . . an Olympian freak, a fable, an allegory, an incomprehensible phenomenon . . . monstrous, multifarious, unnatural, indomitable, puissant, preposterous, transcendent . . . throw the dictionary at it!'[2] All that, and more, could be said

---

[1] According to the statistical department of the Prime Minister's office, in 1945 the population had shrunk to about three millions.

[2] J. STREET, quoted by J. GUNTHER, *Inside U.S.A.,* New York, 1947.

of Tokyo. Chicago is, after all, the product of a single civilization, that
of the west, and the vocabulary with which it confronts you is fundamentally Indo-European. But here we are confronted with a world
synthesis. Here there meet and mingle the twenty-six civilizations of
Toynbee, the eighteen religions of Turchi, the five *kalpas* (Buddhist
cosmic eras), von Eickstedt's thirty-eight races and sub-races of mankind,
the fifty-six ways of making love of the Kama-sutra, the seventy styles
of cooking, the six perfumes, the eighty-two smells, the 120,000 stinks,
the twelve dozen kinds of dirt, the seven wonders, the thousand lights,
the 2,600 tongues, the thirty-four vices (with the exception of opium
smoking), all the fantasies, and the two great principles of *yin* and *yang*
which, according to Chinese magical ideas, generate the infinite variety
of the world. Not for nothing has another American called it a 'wonderful, hybrid, dissolute, noisy, quiet, brooding, garish, simpering, silly,
contemplative, cultured, absurd city'.[1]

Nowhere else in the world can you see in the streets girls and
women in kimonos, either vividly coloured or subdued according to their
age, young women in Paris models, girls in jeans, or Indian saris, or neat
Chinese dresses; mothers leading their children by the hand, or carrying
them on their back, or pushing them in prams; men in shirts, in work
happi, in the uniform of ten different armies, with their sons on their
back (Photographs 126, 127), in straw sandals, gumboots, overalls, eighth-
century costume, in shorts, rags, smart white suits (Photograph 128), in
yukata, in *haori, hakama* and bowler hats (Photograph 125), or in *montsuki*;
with black, red, or fair, hair; with almond-shaped eyes or blue eyes;
men who drag their feet (Japanese), gesticulate (Latins), walk stiffly and
inexorably (Teutons) or loosely and smilingly (Americans); Buddhist
monks, Roman Catholic priests, Orthodox archimandrites, Protestant
pastors, Shinto *kannushi,* Indian sadhus, huge men with long hair knotted
on top of their heads (*sumō* wrestlers), martial and agile Sikhs in pink
turbans, human relics of Hiroshima or Nagasaki; white-shirted disabled
ex-servicemen begging and pathetically playing some instrument while
the victors pass with girls on their arms (Photographs 152, 153); boys on
bicycles demonstrating their virtuosity by threading their way through
the traffic with one hand on the handlebar and the other holding aloft
two or three layers of trays full of food; men-horses pulling perfumed,

[1] O. D. RUSSELL, *Here's Tokyo,* Tokyo, 1953.

heavily made-up geishas; people terrified of infection wearing surgeon's masks over their faces; students in uniform, railwaymen in uniform, postmen in uniform, firemen in uniform, nurses in uniform; itinerant flute-players who hide their heads in baskets *(komusō)*; men disguised as insects or corpses who dance, cut capers, or beat drums or do whatever else may be required to advertise some product or other *(chindon-ya)*; sellers of red-fish *(kingyo-ya),* or of roasted sweet potatoes *(yaki-imo)*, or a special bean paste *(tofu)* made up in beautiful wooden boxes; baseball players returning from a game; pipe-cleaners *(rao-ya)* pushing carts on which a tiny kettle is perpetually whistling; Coca-Cola sellers wearing the uniform and device of the firm; masseurs, who are generally blind; aged widows with their hair cut short; Buddhist nuns with shaved heads; scowling colonels of the reserve in kimono and bowler hat; and frivolous girls, often in wooden sandals, who probably belong to the reserve of another army, that of Tokyo's 80,000 prostitutes, for that is the number that the city is said to muster.

Only here do you see signs in so many different languages. Roman characters are often used with curious results, such as 'flolist' for 'florist', or 'dearer' for 'dealer', because the Japanese have difficulty in distinguishing 'l' from 'r'. 'Long "r" or short "r"?' is the question that they continually ask when trying to write down a western name. Once upon a time extraordinary things were to be seen, such as the sign 'Ladies have fits upstairs' outside a tailor's, or 'Every client promptly executed' outside a barber's. Now, however, linguistic knowledge has progressed. . . . And everywhere, of course, there are cascades and festoons of ideograms.

Nowhere else but in Tokyo are there to be seen in the shop windows dwarf trees 200 years old, as twisted and strange as the 1,000-year-old giants of the forest, growing in tiny porcelain pots *(bonsai)*; ancient lacquer boxes *(inrō),* exquisitely decorated with pictures in gold, formerly used for keeping medicines, side by side with high-precision optical instruments (f 1.1 lenses, for instance) or the latest models of the American, European, and Japanese motor industries; displays of sandals for men and women *(zori, geta),* umbrellas made of paper and bamboo *(kasa),* wigs *(katsura)* for wives or geishas, stone lanterns (Photograph 53), stamps with complicated ideograms, side by side with typewriters, refrigerators, wireless sets, calculating machines, cultivated pearls, plastic goods, travel agencies; big department stores—Mitsukoshi, Takashimaya, Matsuya, Shirokiya, Matsuzakaya—where you can buy anything from four ounces of seaweed for your evening meal to a yacht for your next summer's cruise—stand cheek by jowl with the tiny shops of craftsmen each specializing in one single article, which he often makes himself with the aid of his family, using agile fingers which have inherited the skill of many generations. A *kampogaku-ya*, the hair-raising, sinister, old-fashioned, 'Chinese-style' chemist's shop, displays in the window mummified snakes, asps, vipers, tortoises, monkeys, big bottles of yellow liquid containing terrifying worms that look like embryonic dragons, while next door the modern Japanese chemical industry is busy manufacturing for the markets of Asia ever new synthetic products, the result of the pioneering work of the Kagaku-Kenkyo-sho, for instance, the Institute for Scientific Research, or the various laboratories of the seventy-eight Tokyo universities.

The most popular of these products are pushed by furious, strident, publicity methods behind which there are inexhaustible imagination and fanatical persistence. Balloons hold aloft cascades of ideograms extolling this or that brand of toothpaste, electric lamp, or alcoholic beverage. Close to the key cross-roads of the city there rises over an old concrete building the Morinaga Kyarameru ('Morinaga Caramel') globe (Photograph 135), slowly rotating like a small celestial body which for some inscrutable reason had selected this particular spot in the universe for itself; and there is no lack of towers advertising this or that brand of butter, or *saké*, or rejuvenating pastilles, or beer which abolishes all griefs; and acres of hoardings announce forthcoming films or revues, often with luscious nudes spread across the space of half a dozen windows.

Meanwhile there suddenly passes in front of your nose a solemn procession of priests in their elegant coloured robes (Photographs 56, 57), some on horseback accompanied by a servant holding aloft a huge red umbrella, others seated in little carriages drawn by gnomes dressed in blue and with handkerchiefs round their heads, all preceding the ceremonial vehicle containing the presence of the deity who is being honoured and preceded or accompanied by turbulent, masked devils, whose purpose is either to provide additional protection against the forces of evil or to amuse the children, nobody knows for certain which.

You may also chance on one of these processions while passing under the Mansei-bashi iron bridge; overhead the electric trains rumble and roar, and the ancient, traditional procession passes underneath, with its thin musical accompaniment like wind in the reeds.

But these are calm and quiet processions, consisting chiefly of old men; the district elders never fail to attend in *haori* and *hakama,* that is to say in their ceremonial clothes, long silk robes with the family crest in miniature in the middle and high up on their backs, and in big straw hats decorated with small pink paper flowers. In the afternoon far livelier processions take place with youths carrying the deity's palanquins (*mikoshi*) on their backs to bring a blessing to all the streets of the neighbourhood. As the palanquins are extremely heavy, not infrequently weighing more than a ton, frequent stops are necessary, and wooden trestles are placed every hundred or two hundred yards along the street, in front of improvised altars covered with offerings. The owners of neighbouring houses and shops make liberal distributions of sweets and wine to refresh the tired porters. It will be readily understood that after five or six of these stops they are often very merry indeed.

Sometimes, for instance, at the festival of Sanja-sai, the Three Protectors, or Guardians, in June, revelry invades the city centre, the Ginza, Kyobashi, Yurakucho, Nihombashi; and the long, shiny Buicks, the squat Volkswagen, the little Toyopets, have to draw into the side and stop, or take refuge in side-streets. Even the trams come to a standstill. The police do what they can to keep the traffic moving, but they too are carried away by the occasion; everyone wants to see, even if they cannot take part in it. A mob of half-naked young men, all in transports of excitement and egging each other on with shouts of '*washio! washio!*' suddenly appear from round a corner. They debouch into the street, then suddenly stop, turn in their tracks, revolve, agitate the palanquin, and then start off again, panting, shoving, shouting, putting their whole heart and soul into it. It is like a tornado, a boiling sea, of perspiring heads and shoulders (Photographs 62–66). According to an ancient belief it is the *kami,* the god himself, who guides his palanquin, and it therefore has to go where the *kami* wants it to. Does he want to run? Come on, then! Does he want it to rotate like a maniac? The palanquin rotates until the bearers nearly lose their balance. From time to time the *kami's* sense of mischief causes a window to be broken or a shop to be smashed up. Then there is a great commotion—the noise of things being broken, shouts, screams, laughter, curses, threats. Closer inquiry always reveals that the victims of these misfortunes failed to make a sufficiently generous contribution to the expenses of the festival. The palanquins are numerous. The biggest and heaviest are carried by young men, but lighter ones (*onna mikoshi*) are carried by parties of girls; and children have their own miniature toy palanquins.

At such times the Ginza is transformed from an ugly commercial street into an enchanted village square; you almost expect to see jovial contented gods descending among people who are so devoted to them. It also helps you to understand many things about the Japanese, the strength that comes from loyalty to their ancient traditions.

After the revelry has died away you are left alone with the background, the buildings, and the monuments. What a chaotic jungle of styles! I believe Tokyo possesses everything required to illustrate an all-inclusive history of every conceived and conceivable style of building. There is no big Gothic cathedral (though there is a small one), but there is an Indian temple not far from some impressive modern buildings, pagodas stand cheek by jowl with railway stations (at Ueno, for example), impressive ancient gateways (such as the Sammon of the temples of Shiba) stand next to nineteenth century classic architecture, Greek colonnades, of which there are several, Russian churches, the Nikolai Cathedral, miniature palaces of Versailles (the Akasaka Palace), and it would not be surprising to see at one and the same glance the gentle curves of a concrete Buddhist temple and the Martian outline of a huge gasometer. Towering over everything else is the Parliament building, built in a vaguely rationalized Babylonian style. In the end the eye grows fond of this structure; so much so that it has ended by becoming what the Eiffel Tower and the Statue of Liberty have become for Paris and New York—a symbol. Among other things it is the tallest building in Japan; in a country so liable to violent earthquakes, a height in excess of 200 feet represents the extreme limit of daring.

Moreover, nothing in Tokyo is very old. Before 1456, when for the first time a fortress was built in these parts, the great plain of Musashi, as it was called, was noted only because, in the words of an ancient poem, 'the moon rises, the moon sets, in an ocean of grass'. It was Tokugawa Iyeyasu, the founder of the line of military governors who held the monopoly of power from 1603 to 1868, who chose this spot as the site of his administrative capital. (Kyoto remained the country's spiritual capital, the seat of the mystical, and almost mythical, imperial power.) It is known that in 1787 Yedo, as Tokyo was called until 1868, had 1,367,900 inhabitants; in other words, it was already one of the world's biggest towns.

東   *To-*
      East

京   *Kyo*
      Capital

  The town plan of Tokyo is fundamentally radiocentric; irregular circular avenues are cut by roads—irregular too—that radiate outwards to subsidiary centres, such as Shinagawa, Shibuya, Shinjuku, Ueno, to the suburbs and the country. The nucleus, the centre, the heart of it all, is the Imperial Palace.[1] Do not imagine this to be an imposing edifice, a turreted mausoleum, a fantastic Asian dream in marble and gold; a Palazzo Pitti, a Windsor Castle, a Neuschwanstein in terms of dragons and pagodas. The Japanese taste for sobriety here offers the world a memorable lesson in style and restraint. The palace as such can in fact be said not to exist; it seems that it consists of a series of modest villas. These, however, are not visible to the public; the imperial majesty is, however, powerfully suggested by the rustic and impressive inclined walls which, on the other side of a stream in which tranquil green waters run, mark the limits of the Chiyoda-jo, 'the castle-field of the thousand ages'. All that is to be seen are a few gates, bridges, *yagura* (corner towers). Strangely twisted pines crown the glacis; for the Japanese the pine-tree, the symbol of eternally youthful vigour, speaks with the vividness of a human voice. The task of suggesting, rather than celebrating, the imperial presence is left to nature.

  It is round the glacis, the canals, the bridges, the entrance gates of the palace, that the finest views of the metropolis are to be obtained. Of the walls Mousset well says:

    'Confronted with the masterly fashion with which the special- ists of the period piled one on top of another these millions of

---

[1] In Japanese Kyu-jo, Chiyoda-jo, *i.e.*, 'castle' rather than 'palace'.

colossal blocks, all different, which form mass and shape without any cement, and curve in movements of such purity that the mind, when it succeeds in diverting the eyes from one of the corners, tends to consider a simple straight line barbarous, we are filled with the admiration that we have for the builders of the pyramids.'[1]

It appears, moreover, from contemporary documents that the curvature of the glacis of the fortesses was calculated according to mathematical formulae which the master-builders kept secret. The vast expanse between Niju-bashi and Babasaki-mon has the breadth and space worthy of a great capital; in the evening, when the sun sets behind the gardens, some of the corner towers, with their slightly curving roofs, in particular that called Fuji-mi Hagura, 'the See-Fuji Watch-Tower', stand out against the reddening sky, together with the silhouettes of strange conifers, laden from birth with the weight of ages. Then the light pales, the colours fade from pink to blue, car lamps light up like great fireflies searching for a way out of a dark forest.

Some years ago a number of skeletons were discovered by workmen in the foundations of one of the bridges near the Imperial Palace, the Niju-bashi, which dates back to the time when the fortress was built for the Tokugawa Shoguns. Some of the skeletons were standing, others were reclining in various positions. In all probability they were the remains of *hito-bashira* (human columns), men who volunteered to be buried alive to pacify some spirit or dragon or water-god, particularly when building difficulties arose because of the nature of the site. Was this savage, barbarous? Such customs and beliefs have in one form or another been practically universal. Many old buildings in Europe have yielded up skeletons of animals, particularly cats, which were buried alive in the foundations to give the structure 'strength'. Human sacrifices, particularly of young children, were at one time frequent enough, particularly in northern countries, and the practice continued till the seventeenth century. E. B. Tylor, in his celebrated work on primitive culture, gives a long list of historically certified cases: the Nogat dyke in East Prussia (1463), Liebenstein Castle in Thuringia, the walls of Copenhagen, etc., etc. It seems that as late as 1843, when a big bridge was to be built at Halle, in Germany, search was made for a baby to sacrifice on

[1] P. MOUSSET, *Le Japon*, Paris, 1954.

the first stone. The only difference, and it is in the Japanese favour, is that the unfortunate *hito-bashira* were volunteers, whose relatives were granted special privileges.[1]

Looking in the direction of the Ginza from the entrance to the Imperial Palace, you see an almost uninterrupted row of big modern buildings. As I have already remarked, the general architectural effect of the city is indescribably wretched and shoddy, and often vulgar. Very rarely you may chance on some corner that is coloured with memories and has a less commercial flavour than the rest, such as a gate that miraculously survived when the rest of the temple was destroyed (*e.g.*, the Zozo-ji at Shiba), or one of those stone columns that were used 'for finding children lost in the crowd'—names and dates were inscribed on them out of gratitude—or an absurd monument to some nineteenth-century general on horseback. You have to leave the commercial quarters and the traffic to find a restful atmosphere among gardens and villas and many of the 215 parks which the city possesses, in a semi-rural area that stretches for dozens of miles.

Areas of green and tranquillity, not without some fine views, are to be found near the great shrine—itself hidden in greenery—dedicated to the memory of the Emperor Meiji (1852–1912), the father of modern Japan. In this neighbourhood there are stadiums and playing fields. Apart from the traditional sports handed down from antiquity, some practised by small groups, others enjoying enormous popularity[2] such as *kendo* (fencing), the various types of wrestling (judo, *karate, sumo*), and archery, the people of Tokyo take a great interest in *yakyu* (baseball) and in cycle- and horse-racing. In winter snow is sometimes brought down from the mountains for exhibitions of ski-jumping; and in summer everybody swims.

Kanda, the students' quarter, is another in which there are corners of peace and tranquillity; it also possesses some interesting examples of modern architecture. Tokyo, though not specialized in this way as Kyoto, is an important cultural centre. Its State University is the supreme scientific institution in the country, while entrance to the Waseda, Meiji, or Keio private universities, and a few others, represents the

[1] HASTINGS, *Encyclopedia of Religion and Ethics,* New York, 1914; E. B. TYLOR, *Primitive Culture,* London 1873, Vol. I, p. 104.

[2] C. BONACOSSA, *Lo Sport nasce in Asia,* Milan, 1956.

supreme goal of the country's studious youth. Frequently only one
candidate in fifteen, and sometimes fewer, succeeds in gaining entrance
to the State University. On the other hand, for those who succeed in
surmounting this obstacle the way is open, not only to a degree, but to
future employment and a career. Another internationally known
university is the Sophia Daigaku, which was founded and is run by
Jesuits. There are 78 universities in Tokyo (13 national, 64 private, 1 municipal), but it must be pointed out that in accordance with recent changes
nearly all the training colleges in the most diverse fields were granted the
rank of *daigaku*, institution of higher education, *i.e.*, university, and that
there are therefore included in this category a number of institutions
of limited importance. However, the number of educational establishments, particularly at the higher level, is remarkably high; the capital
attracts students from all over the country, there are 975 schools at the
secondary level *(chugakko, kotogakko)* and 936 at the primary level, including
nursery schools *(yochien, shogakko)*. School-children and students all wear
uniform.

A striking feature is the respect for knowledge that prevails among
Japanese at all levels of the economic and social scale from peasants and
clerks to bureaucrats and technocrats. Personalities like the great
bacteriologist H. Noguchi (1876–1928), whose monument, paid for by
popular subscription, stands outside the National Science Museum, or
that of H. Yukawa, the physicist and Nobel prizewinner of 1949, are much
nearer the firmament of *kami* than to the earth trodden by ordinary
mortals, particularly in the estimation of youth. In spite of the supreme
difficulty, the diabolical complexity, of learning to read and write
Japanese, the illiteracy rate is low.[1] The circulation of the big Tokyo
newspapers *(Asahi, Mainichi, Yomiuri, Tokyo Shimbun)* is impressive; more
than five million newspapers, morning and evening, are sold daily in
the metropolitan area. The circulation of magazines and reviews is
relatively equally high, especially when the number of pages (often
more than 300) and the seriousness of the subjects dealt with are taken
into account. Besides this there is the huge output of books; more than
20,000 titles are published annually at an average price of 312 yen, or about
6s. or 85¢. Everybody reads (and therefore many wear spectacles);

---

[1] In 1950 it was 7·2 per cent for the whole country, including the backward agricultural and
afforested areas in the north.

curiosity is not limited by age or time (Photographs 128, 129, 131, 132). A tacit convention permits you to browse for as long as you like over any book displayed in a bookshop, or even to read it from cover to cover, provided you do not sit down; poverty-stricken but determined students often take advantage of this to acquire what might be called an apatetic culture, attained while motionless. I was once told the story of a prostitute who, between one client and the next, managed in this way to get through the whole of Tolstoy.

At Kanda, the students' quarter, which is also full of hospitals and publishing houses, there is one of the most fascinating streets in the world, the Jimbo-cho, with its dozens and dozens of second-hand bookshops next door to one another. If Tokyo is the meeting-place of the world, it is here that you must come to savour the full implications of the description. The whole, or almost the whole, of human knowledge is displayed before the eyes of the passer-by. I do not just refer to the hundreds of categories and sub-categories of knowledge as classified in the world's great libraries, but to the joint presence of at least two of the world's great civilizations with their fundamental outlook on life which gives meaning to man's existence here on earth; I mean the outlook of the western world and that of the Far East. London has its Charing Cross Road, but there the western predominance is almost complete; for Far Eastern books you have to go to the few specialist shops in Great Russell Street; the same applies to Paris and New York (Rome does not even exist from this point of view). But the Jimbo-cho presents a scene of sublime impartiality. The classics of German philosophy rub shoulders with their Indian counterparts, American engineering or medical manuals stand cheek by jowl with French or Swiss illustrated histories of art, Buddhist encyclopaedias, English nineteenth-century novels, volumes of Chinese poetry or *belles lettres,* or Russian archaeology. All this, incidentally, reflects a people profoundly inquisitive about all things of the mind.

Other important sanctuaries of knowledge are the big museums and exhibition buildings that rise on the woody hill of Ueno: the fine National Museum, the Metropolitan Gallery of Fine Arts, the University of the Arts; there are also bookshops, Buddhist temples, a padoga dating back to 1651, the Science Museum, the Zoo. It is here that the big art exhibitions take place and the traditionalists and innovators of many races look askance at each other. The public interest in these exhibitions is phenomenal; on big occasions you have to use your elbows to get in, and then it is difficult to get sufficiently far away from a painting or piece of sculpture to be able to look at it properly.

Not far from here a sudden change takes place in the metropolitan landscape. There is a vast lower section of the city, along the harbour and the mouth of the Sumida river, where canals run alongside the streets, or sometimes take their place. There are 1,345 miles of canal, and no fewer than 5,824 bridges. It is this area which forms the city's capacious belly; through its innumerable warehouses and markets there pass most of the 1,850 tons of rice, the 450 tons of fish, the 100 tons of meat (the proportion of fish to meat—more than four to one—throws much light on the Japanese diet), the 30 tons of seaweed, the 1,500,000 eggs, the nearly 1,000 tons of vegetables and fruit that Tokyo consumes daily.[1] Here, too, an apocalyptic fire spectacle (*ryogoku kawabiraki*) takes place annually on the third Saturday in July; fires released from barges moored in mid-stream light up the black and oily waters in a fantastic manner.

If we next follow the Sumida, which is wide and always crowded with boats, lighters, sailing boats, sporting boats, small steamers, tugs towing long loads of floating tree-trunks, after crossing various parks and pleasure quarters, we end by approaching Arakawa-ku and Adachi-ku (*ku* means district), and finding ourselves among forests of smoke-stacks. Tokyo-to, the metropolitan area of Tokyo, is incidentally a curious administrative unit. It is the size of a province and includes twenty-three urban *ku*, five *shi* (satellite towns), but not Yokohama, which is a provincial capital on its own account, three *gun* (rural districts), one of which includes among other things some mountains of great beauty which form part of the national park of Chichibu-Tama and at Mount Kumotori ('Cloud-Bird') reach a height of more than 6,000 feet, to say nothing of some islets in the Pacific extending to Hachijojima, 260 nautical miles away. But Tokyo is fundamentally an industrial city, and its huge size is the result of very definite economic reasons. Of the two millions and more employed in the city, 10 per cent are employed in state offices, 18 per cent in commerce, and 26 per cent in industry, not including construction (6 per cent).

In the midst of this hideous landscape—or is it a kind of landscape

[1] *Tokyo, Dai Tokai no Kao* ('Tokyo, Aspect of a Metropolis'), Tokyo, 1953.

the beauty of which men have not yet discovered?—among coal dumps, factories, corrugated-iron roofs, high-tension wires, steel fencing, oil tanks, smoke-stacks of all shapes and colours, and the sound of whistles and steam-hammers, the blaze of furnaces and sudden clouds of steam, after crossing an old iron bridge, which incidentally is by no means easy to find, we come upon a delightful little restaurant dating back to Yedo times, beside which, on the banks of an irregular little lake, thousands of Florentine irises bloom in June. This is the Horikiri-en, which was once in open country but was then overtaken and surrounded by the metropolis; its survival seems to me to be characteristic of this surprising city. The restaurant is of a kind of which the Japanese are particularly fond. The offices and kitchens are all in the main building near the entrance, and you eat in one of the numerous little pavilions (*bekkan*) scattered about the garden, which is now surrounded by walls and houses; there is the 'plum hut' (*ume no ma*), for instance, or the 'wistaria hut' (*fuji-mi*), or the 'hut under the mountain' (*yama-shita*), or the 'white hut' (*shiro-ma*), or the 'western hut' (*nishi-yama*). Each one of these is like a little hut lost in the woods. It seems that once upon a time (fifteenth century?) the garden belonged to a Samurai of the name of Isogai; another characteristic feature is that Isogai is still the name of the family that runs the place.

When you have exhausted all that the culinary traditions lovingly preserved here have to offer you, you may care to sample some first-class French cooking, which is to be found at some of the bigger hotels and at one or two well-known little restaurants. Or would you prefer the wealth and imagination of a Chinese menu, with its 300, 400, 500, different dishes? There is an endless list of *shina-ryorya,* one noted for its sharks' fins, another for its bird's nest soup, another for its carp. On the other hand you may desire an American meal, in which case there are at your disposal innumerable grills, where they serve steak, soft, medium, or rare, iced water, and shrimp cocktails. If, however, none of these interest you, why not try one of the innumerable little Japanese taverns each of which has its own speciality? *Tempura,* for instance, prawns fried in pea-nut oil; or *sushi,* raw fish and rice; or *sukiyaki,* fried sliced beef with vegetables, including bamboo-shoots; or *uzura,* roast quail, or *hanpen,* a cunning preparation of dogfish, or *suppon,* tortoises cooked in various ways, or *fugu,* roast fish which is poisonous if cooked the wrong way but is said to be a powerful aphrodisiac. Of course there are always *kabayaki,* eels; and the list could be prolonged indefinitely. There is also a Mongolian *yurta,* where they serve mutton, a Russian restaurant where they serve excellent vodka, several Italian-American restaurants with rivers of tomato *purée*; and you would certainly have no difficulty in finding places where you could get Korean, Formosan, or Indonesian dishes. But what is perhaps from every point of view the most delightful experience, both gastronomic and because of the elegance of service and delicacy of presentation, is to dine in one of those vegetarian restaurants *(shojin-ryoriya)* often to be found near the big Buddhist temples. There you can get such things as fried chrysanthe-mums as light as air, soup in which rare seaweeds float served in a delicately lacquered cup, herbs with poetic names in tiny porcelain vessels; the whole is like delicate communion with fields and leaves, or a wood by moonlight.

Tokyo is also the city in which all, or nearly all, the religions ever invented by man to explain the mystery of his existence are represented in one way or another. When the sun rises in Tokyo it is greeted by Shintoists praying with joined hands and Muslims bowing towards Mecca. Later, in the temples belonging to eighty-seven Buddhist sects or sub-sects, the scriptures are read, and services, either solemn and splendid or simple and intimate, are held; mass is celebrated in the Roman Catholic chapels and services take place in the churches and chapels of the numerous Protestant congregations (at least thirteen are recognized by the Government.[1] Apart from these, there are in Tokyo the temples or chapels or shrines of more than twenty little-known or recently invented religions. You could, for instance, make obeisance before the Four Luminaries of Wisdom in the Tetsugaku-do, the Temple of Philosophy, founded forty years ago, on whose altar Confucius, Buddha, Socrates, and Kant are seated in serene harmony.

Side by side with the homage of the learned to the heroes of science goes the homage of the people to the unseen powers. The latter is expressed in innumerable ways, some moving and pathetic, some savage and cruel, some childish and ridiculous, some surprising and fantastic, some poetical in the extreme. I have already mentioned some of the more spectacular occasions, but all over Tokyo on every day of

[1] W. K. BUNCE, *Religions in Japan,* Tokyo, 1955.

the year ceremonies, services, offerings, rites, dances, gestures, prayers, silences, testify to the most extraordinary variety of beliefs about the nature of the universe and the ways of influencing the mysterious powers that govern it.

Every phase in the cultivation of rice is of course solemnized. In February the Emperor himself officiates in the Kashiko Dokoro, the palace chapel, imploring divine benevolence for the peasants when they begin the sowing; there are more ceremonies in May, when the seedlings are planted out; and finally, in the autumn, there are two important events, the *kanname-sai*, on October 17, when the first offering of the new crop is made to the gods, and the *niiname-sai*, on November 23, the first tasting of the new crop by Emperor and people. At Tokyo, as everywhere else in Japan, the five traditional festivals are celebrated, that of the Seven Herbs (January 7), girls' day (March 3), boys' day (May   5), stars' day *(tanabata)* (July 7), and chrysanthemum day (September 9). On April 8 the nativity of the Buddha is celebrated with processions, flowers, the dipping of holy statues in *ama-cha* (sweet tea). Finally, in July according to the new calendar,[1] and in August according to the old, there are the three-day celebrations of the return of the dead to the homes of the living *(o-bon)*.

This takes no account of all the occasions on which the sea is blessed, local celebrations, from 'the day of lances' *(yari-matsuri)* in August to 'the day of rakes to gather in good fortune' *(tori no ichi)* in November. There are dozens of them. One of the most extraordinary is the so-called walking on fire *(hiwatari)*, which takes place at various Shinto shrines and some Buddhist temples, generally at the end of September. I have never witnessed one of these, but it appears that numerous worshippers succeed in walking barefoot over burning embers without burning themselves. In February people drive devils from their homes by scattering previously blessed beans everywhere, paying particular attention to the dark corners. In September fruit, *saké*, sweets and flowers are offered to the Honourable Lady Moon, the finest full moon of the year, and people meet to compose, recite, and sing. When a little girl dies at any season of the year her mother takes her dolls to the Kiyomizu temple in Ueno park and places them in the arms of a big statue of the Buddha.

In August Buddhist monks and laymen go down the river Sumida

[1] Japan adopted the Gregorian calendar on November 9, 1872.

in boats, both to say prayers for the drowned and to apologize to the fish of river and sea for having taken their lives with rod and line, spear, and net. At the Oizumi cemetery, and in many other places, impressive services are held for the souls of dead cats and dogs and other animals, sometimes including insects. On such occasions many people visit the graves of cats who became famous for saving their master's lives, often in highly dramatic circumstances; the celebrated Gokoku-ji and Eko-in cats, for instance. There is actually a bridge in Tokyo, the Nekomata-bashi, dedicated to a cat which, with a somewhat under-developed sense of private property, tried to relieve the poverty of its sick mistress by stealing small gold objects from a neighbouring moneylender. Then there is the more straightforward story of the dog Hachiko which, I do not remember for how many years, went every evening to Shibuya station in the hope of meeting its dead master returning from work. The neighbours were so touched by this example of canine fidelity that they erected a monument to it.

The sense of brotherhood between men and all living things extends also to non-living things; the east is monist *à outrance*. It is possible to chance on a full-blown service for the souls of old hats ('during their life-time of service many hats have acquired personality and all should be treated with due reverence'[1]), for broken dolls, broken needles, or for the rich people who are 'tormented by hairdressers to give their girls a Hepburn hair cut'.[2] Or you might chance to enter a telephone exchange just at the time of the staff's brief ceremony of 'thanksgiving' for the loyal service given by the apparatus which they had harassed by so much work.

The whole city is full of such phenomena, sometimes inspired by genuine faith, most often based on mere superstition or exhibitionism. Apart from the big Buddhist temples and Shinto shrines, the Christian churches, the synagogue, the mosque, the sanctuaries of Confucian or universal wisdom, there is hardly a street or alley without its little shrine, dedicated either to some well-known or to some purely local god. You continually come across statuettes of Jizō, the protector of children; he is often covered with the clothes of children who have

[1] Statement by a hatter. *See* F. DE GARIS, *Their Japan*, Yokohama, 1936, p. 176.

[2] *Asahi Evening News*, June 22, 1954. The newspapers pointed out, however, that the service had been arranged by hairdressers and may therefore have had a publicity aspect.

died. Another very common sight in front of these shrines is two foxes, the emissaries of Inari, the goddess of the rice crop, of commercial success, and of success in worldly affairs. Shopkeepers, particularly in the popular quarters, prudently insure themselves by displaying signs of reverence for every conceivable deity. You will invariably see one or two small Shinto shrines, with offerings, *gohei* and *shimenawa,* probably beside the wireless or television set, the telephone, and a rotogravure magazine open at the photograph of the latest Hollywood film star or the world table-tennis championship. Special popularity is enjoyed by the Seven Gods of Good Luck *(shichi-fuku-jin)* arriving in a ship, the *takara-bune* or treasure ship, with a heavy cargo of good things—wealth, smiles, music, youth, a secure and well-nourished old age. One of these gods, Hotei, is the slightly vulgar individual with a huge fat belly who in the west is often mistaken for a Buddha. Two other members of this ship-borne party who are often seen alone are Ebisu (with a huge carp) and Daikoku (standing on bales of rice and carrying a miraculous hammer which produces wealth where it strikes). No less popular are the Maneki-neko, 'the cat that calls' customer and money, a smiling, porcelain creature with raised paw, and Daruma-san, a famous Buddhist patriarch of the sixth century A.D. who lost the use of his legs as the result of remaining motionless for eight years while engaged in meditation. He is represented in the shape of an almost egg-shaped doll; you buy him 'blind', that is to say, without eyes. If business is good, you paint in one eye, and later you paint in the other. If business is bad, you leave him blind as a punishment.

At the living centre of this realm of beliefs and practices there is true religious feeling and poetry, but towards the edges it degenerates into magic and superstition, occult medicine, and fraud. Even in this respect Tokyo is full of surprises. In the centre of the city, along the Ginza and its immediate neighbourhood, at Nihombashi, a few yards from the tall pylons of a wireless transmitter, in the shadow of buildings which house the headquarters of financial, industrial, commercial firms of international importance—Mitsui, Mitsubishi, Sumitomo, Asano Bussan—innumerable *tsuji-uranai* have their booths, ready for a few coppers to advise you on how to behave when buying that piece of land, or during the forthcoming visit of your parents-in-law, or when you next meet the girl you are in love with. The whole of Babylonian, Tantric and Taoist wisdom is distilled into the words and gestures of these sages, in whom the Japanese have the greatest confidence. There are also mind-readers *(ninsō-mi)*, astrologers who prepare horoscopes *(ekisha)*, hand-readers and graphologists *(teso-mi)*. The life of less-educated, and even of many well-educated, Japanese is governed by innumerable superstitions, based on beliefs at which they would probably laugh if they were able to look at them rationally; but they keep them intact by the tacit consent of that subterranean level of the mind where infantile emotions and memories, attitudes of reverence, vague fears, vague hopes, hold sway. In this the Japanese are no less human than their brothers in other continents. Superstition is the same everywhere; only the details vary. In Japan there are, for instance, good and bad days for beginning any enterprise, and these are carefully worked out on the basis of a combination of the twelve animals and the five elements. Before building a house attention has to be paid to the good and bad influences of directions and surroundings, and this makes the work of the geomancer sometimes more important than that of the engineer; and many people when ill have recourse to practitioners of acupuncture or moxa treatment, to snake-charmers and faith-healers of all kinds. As these sometimes succeed where orthodox medicine fails, belief in them persists.

The richest concentration of these human parasites is to be found in such neighbourhoods as that of the Ueno station, for instance, with its vagabonds *(rumpen)*, its strange shops (it has a 'sex station', for instance), its old-clothes merchants, abortionists, beggars, women bootblacks, mahjong saloons; and at Asakusa where, next to the venerable Kwannon shrine, which was founded in the seventh century but has recently been rebuilt in concrete, haunts of amusement, pleasure, and vice flourish—just as they did near certain temples of the pagan Mediterranean world; there are public baths, cinemas, *pachinko* (amusement arcades), *storippu* (strip-tease establishments, Photograph 140), theatres and booths where all kinds of entertainers perform and all the pleasures of the fair-ground are to be found, besides some more doubtful establishments; and the area extends all the way to the Yoshiwara, the city of sin which scandalized the respectable by being the first to rise from the ashes after the earthquake and fire of 1923, and, like a recidivist phoenix, repeating the performance in 1945, before even the funds had been provided for rebuilding essential public buildings, hospitals, and schools.

Tokyo by night! Perhaps no city in the world offers such a wealth of ephemeral things, such a volume of perfumed nothing, such guarantees of perdition. It is the capital of *samsara,* 'the vortex of becoming', to use a Sanskrit phrase, a Buddhist concept which the centuries have enriched with a wealth of subtle meaning. It is the capital of *uki-yo,* 'the floating world'—a Japanese phrase for the unsubstantial and the fleeting, suggesting clouds at dawn, floating between the void out of which they were born and the warmth of day which will disperse them. Not that Tokyo is a city of late hours. On the contrary, people keep even earlier hours than in America. Work stops at four or five, followed by the bath and the evening meal, and at half past six, seven, or eight at the latest, the evening begins. Nearly everyone is home by eleven; at midnight only sleepwalkers are abroad. At one o'clock, save for a rare, occasional taxi driven by a maniac, Tokyo is like a city of the dead.

At sunset, as soon as the light begins to fade, ugly, shoddy, chaotic Tokyo starts clothing itself in lights and dreams; knowing itself not to be beautiful, it insists at least on being fantastic. One by one the lamps are lit, lamps in an infinite variety of shape and colour, made of paper, glass, cloth, plastics, each with its own inscription and its own hieroglyphics. The lights dance, explode, cascade in a thousand fascinating patterns, the product of a bold, strange, fantastic imagination, like that of Japanese artists in their moments of happiest inspiration (Photograph 135). For a brief magic moment this electric dawn shines against the last pallor of the sky, and you do not know whether the display is the work of man or whether a lot of fantastic wiry monsters have descended from space, still vibrating with cosmic light, to rest among the trees and houses.

With the coming of night Tokyo yawns and stretches, and prepares itself for pleasure. For those who desire pleasures of the mind, there is music both of east and west; opera, and frequent symphony concerts, conducted by world celebrities, and performances by famous soloists, at the Hibiya, Teigeki, Korakuen, and Dai-ichi Seimei halls; or concerts of complicated Japanese instruments, *ga-gaku,* ancient court music which has been preserved intact through the centuries, or symphonies for groups of *koto,* the works of the great Miyagi, a blind and modest genius still unknown in the west, who died recently.

The theatre ranges from traditional performances of the *Kabuki* type (Photograph 111), in which the talent of the actors and the tremendous tradition behind them are reinforced by every modern technical aid in lighting and scenery, to the archaic, severe, sublime mysteries of the *Nō* plays (Photograph 110) which border on the sacred; or to the magic of the *bunraku,* where the most exciting puppets in the world laugh, weep, make love, fight, seduce, kill, flee, their movements and expressions guided by the hands of masters who have inherited the skill, taste, and experience of generations. All this is purely eastern. But Tokyo would not be Tokyo if the west were not represented too. There are half a dozen theatres which present modern, often the latest, plays; translations, adaptations, and new works by Japanese. The passion for *imamekashi,* the very latest thing, to use an old Japanese expression, is almost infuriatingly alive. No sooner is a new voice raised in Paris, New York, Oxford, Rome, Moscow, than its echo is heard among the *interi* (intellectuals) of Tokyo. Often no more is involved than a fleeting phase of fashion which leaves no trace but a paragraph or so in the newspapers or a few articles in 'high-brow' magazines.

Cinemas, as can well be imagined, are numerous; from the luxurious establishments in the city centre, with air conditioning and films from many countries in the original language, with sub-titles, to suburban flea-pits which stink of urine and offer a four- or five-hour programme—two full-length films, with news-reel, etc.—for a few dozen yen; also there are many revues, jazz bands, and ballets; typical are the performances of the Takarazuka troupe, which consists only of women, who play male parts too, incidentally very well.

As for society life, in our sense of the word it can be said not to exist, or, if at all, only in embryo. The foreign world of diplomatists, statesmen, American senior officers, is a closed circle which few Japanese enter, and at heart enter reluctantly. The differences in customs, language, and tastes are too great for social intercourse to go much beyond the exchange of formal courtesies. Dinners, dances, parties, receptions, succeed each other in an unending stream, particularly in autumn and winter and at the beginning of spring, but these things are a matter of relative concern to ten thousand among the millions of the city's inhabitants.

Japanese life, based on the separation of the sexes and, since the

Middle Ages (thirteenth to sixteenth centuries), on the absolute predominance of the male, offers a solid obstacle to the western habit of
enjoying the pleasures of life in common with wives, fiancées, sisters.
The night is therefore essentially the domain of the male, who plunges
into it like an agile, silent, uncommunicative, aggressive cat, with
bristling fur and shining eyes, looking for female companionship; and
it is unanimously agreed that of all female cats the Japanese are by a long
way the sweetest, most charming, most tender. One thing is certain: no
woman is able to sell herself with such grace as a Japanese woman; and
I do not mean selling herself in the cruder, sexual sense, but granting
a man her company in return for pay; it may be only the smile with
which she pours *saké* into the tiny porcelain cup, but she does it as if you
were the only man in the world and she your sweet and humble slave.
Many of these characteristics, which, from the selfish male point of
view, are unquestionably so delightful, are now disappearing. But one
thing may be noted: women here are capable of passing from the most
exquisite delicacy to the most appalling and barbarous crudity of
behaviour, voice, gesture, and speech. They plunge, not from one
tradition to another, from that of the east to that of Europe or America,
but from civilization to zero, to the most complete barbarism. Fortunately this phenomenon seems restricted to those circles most violently
affected by *apuré (après guerre)* circumstances. The great majority of
Japanese women change clothes, language, hair style, and dietetic,
sexual and religious customs without losing the humility, the grace, the
sweetness, the capacity for understanding and that look of a fledgling
just fallen from the nest that is capable of making a man ready for
anything, even to be diabolically deceived.

One of the ways in which the bristling male cats may begin their
evening is by licking their fur. One of the most remarkable results of
the grafting of American commercialism on the Japanese cherry-tree is
provided by an establishment worthy of some Caracalla of the electronic
age, the Tokyo Onsen (Tokyo Baths), right in the middle of the town, only
a few paces from the Ginza. Here all the traditional and charming rites
that surround the Japanese bath, particularly at hot springs, have been
studied with an unprejudiced eye and adapted to the requirements of
the age of glamour and publicity. The place is open from 6 a.m. until
10 p.m. You can have a marble bath, a porcelain bath, a perfumed deal

bath, or a chromium bath. You can take your bath alone, or in couples, or in whole parties; you can have hot or cold water unadulterated, or you can have a sulphur, milk, lemon, or hormone bath, or it can be vitaminized, irradiated, rejuvenating, aphrodisiac, soporific, or electric. You can have a Japanese, Turkish, Finnish, or Roman bath, with or without massage, with or without attractive attendants, either in vest and shorts or semi-nude. Afterwards you may have inhalations, sprays, showers, or sunlamp treatment. The place is full of young men who would have delighted Petronius, but also of people just up from the country with their eyes popping out of their heads at all these marvels of civilization; and, of course, American soldiers, looking either embarrassed or truculent, depending on whether the Puritan or the orgiastic element in them is uppermost at the moment.

A bath implies nudity. Those unscrupulous Japanese who from the outset of the occupation set about trying to squeeze as many dollars as possible out of the Americans quickly realized that nudity, a thing of little concern in their own country, was much sought after abroad, particularly by these pure Christians whose repressed instincts were always ready to boil over. So you want nude women, the pimps exclaimed, astonished that it was possible to satisfy the new *nam-ban-jin* (southern barbarians), the new masters of the earth and the sea, and in sex (Photograph 139), with such a little thing, and they proceeded to supply it in torrents, in floods, in oceans; and throughout Tokyo, which was followed in the matter by other Japanese towns, there was heard the new word *nūdo,* which had not previously existed in the Japanese dictionary. Hoardings, bills, leaflets, rotogravure illustrations, newspapers, photographs, celebrated the discovery of the female form in all the moods of which it is capable; from retiring shyness to Bacchanalian frenzy, from repose and serenity to impudent invitation. Innumerable 'photographic studios' sprang up at which for a few shillings you were supplied with camera, lights, instructions about filters and exposures, and one or two nude models.

Spectacular revues were put on which vied with the Folies Bergère (the Nichikegi, the Kokusai at Asakusa), imitated in the suburbs by many poorer, more vulgar, more simply carnal imitations. At the same time, without exaggeration, hundreds of *naito* (night clubs) were opened at which brief floor-shows were given several times a night. These might sometimes contain an acrobatic or musical act, but the chief interest was normally the gradual and skilfully delayed revelation of the female form.

In short, the erotic aspect of nudity is something new in Japan, one of the many gifts to it of the west. Not that Japan has ever been a Puritan country; quite the reverse. But sex had hitherto always been accepted very frankly and naturally; everyone was accustomed from childhood to seeing the human form naked. The Japanese woman lay back on the *futon* and said: '*Hai,* I am ready'; there was no point in embroidering fantasies round the act. But then the west arrived with all its psychological complications and sense of guilt about sex, which avenged itself by turning into vice.

The more sensitive Japanese discern this, and avoid these spectacles, which at best border on vulgarity; their pleasures are wiser and more refined. They take them in places far removed from noise, the crowd, in the so-called *karyukai* (flower and willow) quarters at Shimbashi, Kudan, Akasaka, Atago-Yama, along the Sumida, in the realm of the geisha (Photograph 137) where bath, dinner, music, dance, witty and intelligent company, the garden, the moon, the sea, the beauty of the night, taste and refinement in every detail of the furnishings, prepare the mind, the body, and the senses.

If a Japanese desires less traditional pleasures, he will probably go to a bar (Photograph 148). Here the geisha is reduced to an aerodynamic shadow of herself; she is dressed in western fashion, with short hair, serves whisky or gin, sits on chairs at a table, and is willing to discuss the latest film, the latest exhibition of abstract art that has caused such a stir at Ueno, or even social problems or sport. Her essence, her secret, however, remains the same; the possibility she offers to a man tired after his work, perhaps with office or domestic worries, to refresh himself for a few hours talking, joking, drinking with a girl who is charming, gentle, smiling, *soignée,* without any commitment, but not without the possibility—the possibility which incidentally lends flavour to all relations between man and woman—of a more tender relationship, whether fleeting or lasting. Hence the great success of these places, of which Japanese towns are full; in the case of Tokyo they range from quiet, relatively luxurious places, like the Manhattan, where you may find yourself sitting next to a Minister's son or celebrities of the Japanese stage and screen, to infernal dens lit by the most revoltingly coloured neon lighting (the notorious Show Boat, for example) where hundreds of waitresses are called by number through a hoarse loudspeaker.

So the night advances over the crazy, wise, vulgar, industrious, learned, and illustrious city. The frogs croak in the moats round the Imperial Palace, the breeze moves the long branches of the willows along the canals, and slowly the lights begin to go out. The moon sets over Fuji and dawn comes creeping over the Pacific. The only sound is that of the *sobaya* in the distance, the seller of hot soup for early risers or late bed-goers, making his way through the streets, pushing his little cart and every now and then sounding a few long, piercing, melancholy notes on his pipe.

Zero Year and After

In Japan the spiritual upheaval caused by defeat was particularly severe. Its moral effects—like those of a great shock or a superhuman effort —are more apparent now than they were immediately after the war; and so they will remain for a long time.

The explanation is not far to seek; in 2,000 years of history Japan had never been invaded, and no Japanese army had ever been defeated by foreigners. So deeply rooted was the legend of their invincibility that losing the war was like discovering that a fundamental law of nature was wrong; it meant re-shaping their basic ideas. The only foreign ruler who made a serious attempt to invade Japan was Kublai Khan, the Mongol Emperor of China, the Great Khan of Marco Polo, but his first attempt in 1274 failed, and his second and more dangerous attempt in 1281 ended in disaster; a gale destroyed nearly the whole of the fleet that was taking the Chinese and Mongol troops to invade the 'land of dwarfs', as Japan was called on the mainland. On that occasion the Japanese spoke of the *kami-kaze,* the 'divine wind' that saved them from the disgrace of invasion; the term became familiar all over the world when it was adopted during the war by the Japanese suicide pilots.

In more recent ages neither Portuguese, Spaniards, Dutch, British, Chinese, or Russians had succeeded in getting the better of the little Empire. Thus it was natural that the myth of invincibility should prosper. After the setting up of the modern state (1868), which even in so-called liberal periods (1920–30, for example) remained profoundly militarist, the ruling classes deliberately encouraged the myth, inculcating it into the young, reinforcing it with official, imperial, divine sanction, elevating it into a dogma which no one dared to doubt. Never, except perhaps in the Muslim world, have politics been so crazily coloured with metaphysics. I could quote innumerable examples which would cause a smile or a shudder, I do not know which; one, taken at random from a newspaper, will suffice:

> 'We Japanese know that our god [*Amaterasu,* "she who shines in the sky", *i.e.,* the sun], from whom the Emperor is descended, watches over Japan. This deity and the Japanese are related by consanguinity. The whole world searches for God, but only Japan possesses Him; Japan is the divine country . . . therefore the Emperor's will is the only key to a new universal order.'[1]

It must not be forgotten that Japan is an isolated archipelago, that the Japanese speak a difficult language, that their written language is extraordinarily complex, that they are separated from their nearest neighbours by a formidable barrier of different customs and mental habits, and that it is therefore extremely difficult for Mr. Shimizu or Mr. Tanaka, the Japanese man in the street, to form an accurate idea of the world 'outside'. Japanese had been brought up and mentally conditioned in a void; the vast majority genuinely and honestly accepted at their face value these and other fantastic statements spread abroad daily by the Press, the wireless, and in the speeches of their leaders.

Bearing all this in mind, it is easy to understand that August 15, 1945, the day when the Emperor communicated to his subjects the decision to surrender, seemed, if not the end of the world, at any rate the end of a world. There were many suicides, fifty of them outside the Imperial Palace, but the overwhelming majority of Japanese adapted themselves to the new circumstances with a kind of dazed passivity. The Americans did not cease to marvel at the way in which these ferocious enemies of yesterday became the so willing collaborators of today. They were more like automata than men; in their minds they were still marching in military formation, not towards physical death, but towards spiritual

---

[1] *Hochi,* of October 6, 1941, over the signature of K. Kato.

annihilation. It is worth recording that at the beginning of the occupation not a single incident took place between the occupying troops and the population; the first took place only several months later, when an American soldier who had been drinking killed a passer-by at Nara, but even then the crowd behaved in the most orderly manner and handed the man over to the authorities without touching a hair of his head. War-time discipline, combined with the profound Japanese hierarchical sense, was still in command.

In the end, however, the breakdown came; but after the work of material reconstruction had begun, after the new products of revived industries had started taking the place of the old, after the devastated towns had been almost completely rebuilt. For those who love Japan, from certain points of view, in certain districts, at certain times of day, it still presents a painful spectacle today. Where, for instance, do the degraded young men come from who follow allied soldiers—particularly around Yuraku-cho—offering them doubtful deals of every kind? Or all the shameless *pam-pam,* painted like harridans, with high heels and mis-shapen legs, who shout, smoke, spit, chew gum, and call out 'Hey, Johnnie!' at passers-by? You cannot open a newspaper without reading of scandals in high places. If Italy had its Montesi case, Japan had its shipbuilding and Omi factories scandals, which opened unexpected glimpses into a world of corruption on the one hand and of incredible industrial feudalism on the other; to say nothing of such incidents as the battle-royal in Parliament (on June 3, 1954), when fisticuffs took the place of debate. You feel surrounded by the depravity of a casino in which people are ready to throw away a month's earnings for the sake of five minutes' debauch or to sell themselves to the first-comer for a handful of cigarettes. 'Nothing matters, nothing makes sense' seems to be written on young people's brows. The passing fever that in 1945–6 affected Italy, a country immunized by many disasters and therefore quick to recuperate, here infected a pure, virgin, uninoculated organism, and its ravages have been the greater.

Perhaps the worst is over; signs of improvement are to be seen, but the way back will be long; no country has ever been so touched to the quick by defeat. Those who know the Japanese, observing certain signs that seem to point to taking pleasure in humiliation, to wallowing in the misery of defeat, certainly tend to form a very adverse judgment of them; the disabled men begging for alms, for instance, or families willing to sell for a few shillings uniforms once held to be practically sacred, or an ancestral sword, 'the soul of the Samurai'.

All this is true enough; and it derives from a particular way of looking at life; the Japanese have such a sincere and deep sense of moral values that the shadow of a compromise, the slightest sullying of an ideal by contact with the weaknesses of everyday life, suffices for the star to fall in the mud and lose all its meaning. It is thus perfectly logical to pass from extremes of honour, heroism, delicacy, to the most complete immorality, the most complete unscrupulousness, the vilest cowardice, the most terrifying vulgarity. It is the phenomenon that Ruth Benedict calls 'the expendability of damaged goods',[1] the phenomenon known through the ages to Latin wisdom as *corruptio optimi pessima*.

This morning I was watching a small crowd of bootblacks engaged in illicit trafficking with some foreign soldiers just by the requisitioned theatre now known by the name of the noted war correspondent Ernie Pyle when a woman's voice called me.

'Maraini-san!'

I did not recognize her.

'*Watashi-ga! dare da-ka oboete imasu-ka?*' (Don't you recognize me?)

She was an attractive young woman of about twenty-five, poorly dressed in western style. An insistent smile hid the tired lines of her face.

'Don't you remember Hirano-san? At Kyoto, twelve or thirteen years ago? I'm his sister. I was a little girl then, you didn't even notice me. So you're back in Japan? When did you come back?'

Now I remembered. Hirano had been a friend of mine at Kyoto; he had been a student of western history, and was writing a thesis on the Renaissance for his degree. He belonged to an old Osaka family which had produced generations of judges, professors, industrialists. How often I had been to his parents' house, a villa between Kyoto and Osaka, where a warm and friendly atmosphere prevailed! So the little girl playing with her dolls whom I had hardly noticed was Akiyo. It made me feel a hundred years old.

'And your brother?'

'He was killed in the invasion of Kiska, in the Aleutians. . . . *Shika-taganai* [it can't be helped]. My husband is dead too; he was not killed in

---

[1] R. BENEDICT, *The Chrysanthemum and the Sword*, Boston, 1946.

the war, he died two years ago of tuberculosis, *shikataganai*. Now I'm married to a Chinese. He owns a *pachinko* saloon near here. Would you like to meet him? It's only just round the corner. A nasty *kinjo*, a nasty neighbourhood, isn't it? *Shikataganai, sensō ni maketa* [it can't be helped, we lost the war].' Japanese constantly use this last expression as comment, excuse, on any sad or displeasing aspect of present-day life, in order to bury it and put it out of sight.

Poor Akiyo-san, how she had come down in the world! We made towards her *pachinko* saloon. *Pachinko* is the most depressing sympton of the loss of bearings of at least a part of the Japanese people in recent years (Photographs 122, 136). It is a pin-table device; you press a lever which releases a small steel ball; if the ball enters the hole you win a small prize; ninety-nine times out of a hundred the ball does not enter the hole. The *pachinko* craze started at Nagoya and spread like wildfire. As money prizes are forbidden by law, winners get such things as sweets, fruit, toys, shaving soap, etc., etc. After 1948 *pachinko* establishments spread prodigiously throughout the whole of Japan. At first they were humble affairs in fair-grounds, but then the small, medium, and big sharks of Japanese business life got hold of them, and *pachinko* arcades *de luxe* invaded the principal streets and became one of the characteristics of contemporary Japan. It is difficult to give accurate figures because the owners, the appearance, and the addresses of these places are changed continually in order to avoid the attentions of the tax-collector, but, according to recent statistics, there are 3,348 with 197,819 pin-tables in Tokyo alone, an average of sixty-one pin-tables per saloon; in other words there is one pin-table for every thirty-seven persons, including women and children. In the whole of Japan there are said to be 26,000 such establishments with about a million pin-tables.[1]

Akiyo and I made our way with difficulty across the street, risking being run over by two taxis which, as usual, were racing each other without the slightest regard for pedestrians' life and limb, and went down a narrow alley which was all lanterns and neon signs. The innumerable bars of the Ginza neighbourhood were just opening their doors, and troops of the waitresses who work in them were just returning from their bath and dinner. As soon as I turned the corner I heard the characteristic *pachinko* noise, rather like that of a factory or printing

[1] According to the *Asahi Evening News* of December 3, 1954.

works, a factory in which nothing is made, a printing works in which nothing is made. Over the door of the establishment there was written in bright red letters: *C'est la vie.*

'No, not that one,' said Akiyo. 'That one belongs to a *gaijin* ['someone from outside'—at least 612 *pachinko* saloons belong to foreigners] whom my husband can't stand. He's dishonest and they say he's a deserter, I don't know. He does very well, because he surreptitiously gives *kyameru* [Camels] and *rakki* [Lucky Strike] as prizes.'

We went on. More factory or printing works noises, more *pachinko* saloons, two, three in a row, with crowds round the pin-tables, their eyes glued to the steel ball; pure schizophrenia. The last saloon but one was that of Akiyo's husband. We went in; it was a poor, dirty place, with about twenty pin-tables; two women attendants were sitting in a corner, eating rice out of bowls. Everything in the place was demoralizing and depressing. I was introduced to Akiyo's husband, a suave Chinese with clammy hands. He suggested that I should try his 'special' pin-table, that is to say the one that was honest. I worked the handle a number of times, and won a packet of sweets and said thank you; I was much more interested in watching the people. It must have been about six o'clock by now, and the place was already quite crowded; many had had their evening meal—you could tell from their clean, shaven faces and their *yukata,* the light summer kimonos that nearly everyone wears at home or for informal leisure activities; others had obviously not yet gone home or taken the evening bath, but were glued to the pin-tables like people obsessed. There were students in their mournful black uniforms, clerks in threadbare jackets, old men, respectable housewives, doubtful-looking hags of uncertain age, and there were even one or two pretty girls who, I should have thought, would have been happier walking out with their young men.

The *pachinko* craze is a form of collective mania. It has been calculated that in 1954 something like 240 thousand million yen, or about a quarter of the national budget, passed through the hands of these establishments. Most of the customers are casual, but there are a large number of addicts, people who spend every penny they have on *pachinko* and let their wives and children go hungry for its sake.

It is difficult to understand its fascination. It is obviously a flight from reality, a drug; but only a people which was fundamentally

Buddhist could develop such enthusiasm for this particular form of fugue. There are several Buddhist techniques for attaining illumination, but one of the principal consists of freeing the mind from all contingent thoughts so that the light may enter; and one of the ways of doing this is by repeating a phrase, a *mantra,* a brief ejaculatory, *ad infinitum*, until consciousness is annihilated. That is the unconscious soil in which the *pachinko* phenomenon took root. Poor Jiro Yamada, a clerk earning £15 a month, with a wife and three children to keep, bored by his work and a life that has nothing to offer him and, moreover, probably entirely ignorant of the philosophical foundations of the civilization in which he lives, finds a kind of narcotic salvation in the crazy, endless, absurd, repetitive movement.

On the other hand the *pachinko* is also a mechanical device, made of steel, almost scientific, because the calculation of probabilities enters into it; to say nothing of the fact that it makes a noise like a factory. Buddhism and industry, in other words a combination of past and future! A people spiritually reduced to zero, which has suffered destruction even in the secret places of the heart, faced with the huge task of finding new reasons for hoping and living, responds like an army of automata to these calls of the unconscious. It is the only possible explanation. Any other would be an insult to Japanese intelligence and sensibility.

Akiyo-san insisted on accompanying me back to the Ginza. We took tea in a little bar and ate two leaf-shaped sweets. She did not want to leave me; I reminded her of her obviously happy childhood, which had been only too different from the squalid present. She talked about the war years, and the day on which 'they told me the Emperor was no longer god', and her family.

'Only you, Maraini-san, know how I was born and brought up, and can understand that I don't belong to that filthy alley.'

She smiled, as she had been taught to smile from childhood, even when her eyes were shining because they were full of tears.

Individual and Society

My meeting with Akiyo sealed by personal experience my contact with this sad, ugly, squalid, post-war world. Similar features characterized other countries in the post-war period, but on nothing approaching the Japanese scale. But was it a general picture of a people, or only one aspect? Let us try to look at things dispassionately.

It is easy enough to paint a gloomy picture of present-day Japan. Its 90 million inhabitants are restricted to a territory of 142,000 square miles; in comparison with pre-war Japan a population that has increased by 20 million has to live in an area reduced by 45 per cent; the density of the population is 638 to the square mile. These figures are sufficient to indicate a present full of problems and a future full of uncertainties. It is true that in the last few years (from 1949 onwards) attempts have been made to restrict the growth of population by birth control (law of eugenic protection, of July 13, 1948), but the results have not been very happy, probably because of insufficient education of the public in this field; instead of planned conception the only result has been a disproportionate number of abortions (legal abortions numbered 1,143,059 in 1954). In the economic field Japan lost as a result of the war 25 per cent of her national wealth; 34 per cent of her industrial capacity was destroyed or made unusable, she lost 80·6 per cent of her shipping, and a quarter of all Japanese dwellings were reduced to dust and ashes. The newspapers are full of stories (though allowance should be made for journalistic distortion, exaggeration, or invention) of corruption in high places, juvenile delinquency, vast-scale smuggling, illegal foreign exchange deals, the drug traffic, and that festering sore which is most difficult to eradicate because it is a deeply rooted custom, the selling into prostitution of young girls, particularly by the poor peasants of north Japan (Tohoku and Hokkaido).[1] The death rate from tuberculosis is very high, particularly in the towns.[2] The suicide rate (23.4 per 100,000 inhabitants) is the highest in the world, and in the great majority of cases is attributed simply to *ensé* (tiredness with life).

The economic situation of the great majority of the population is sufficient to make one's hair stand on end. The average monthly pay in urban areas was recently (in 1955) increased to 18,608 yen (about £18 or $50) but half the industrial workers receive barely 12,000 yen. A Socialist

[1] *See*, for instance, 'Dealers in Human Flesh in Hokkaido', *Asahi Evening News*, December 17, 1956.
[2] An investigation by the Ministry of Public Health in 1954 showed that between four and five million persons were suffering from the disease.

Party proposal to establish a legal minimum of 8,000 yen monthly for adult workers was rejected as 'unrealistic'.[1] Innumerable women work long hours in bars and restaurants for 7,000 or 8,000 yen a month; the Kyushu coalminers have to manage on 250 yen (5s. or 70¢) a day. This is not a book of statistics or of economic studies; I merely quote facts to give some idea of a situation that is prickly with intractable problems.

On the other hand it is possible to argue, as many optimists do, that '*mo sengo de wa nai!*' (the post-war period is over!) Evidence for this is not lacking. From many points of view the Japanese recovery from the depths of the disaster of 1945, after losing a war on which they had staked everything, can be described as truly remarkable. The original impetus was given by the Americans, but it would not have been possible without the intelligence and industry of the Japanese. The fundamental virtues of this people explain the successes they have often wrung from adverse circumstances. *The Times* of London recently remarked that the discipline of the Japanese nation neutralized much indecision, and even intrigues and corruption, at government level. I repeat that this is not a book of statistics, but I cannot refrain from quoting some figures which illustrate the steady and continuous ascent from the depths of 1945. In 1955 the production of steel, pig iron, and steel products reached 15 million tons, less than half that of Germany, but double that of Italy. Production of electric power exceeded 63,000 million kilowatt hours (United Kingdom 80,000 million kilowatt hours), and huge dams for the production of electric power have recently been built, at Sakuma for instance. The merchant fleet, which was practically wiped out in 1945, is the fourth in the world in the number of ships and among the first eight in total tonnage, and shipbuilding is booming. The production, and in particular the export, of machinery of all kinds has increased in striking fashion, and Japan has invaded new fields—the manufacture of precision instruments, cameras, lenses, for instance, and has shaken the former hegemony of other nations; the United States, for instance, now imports more Japanese than German cameras. In 1956 Japanese exports had increased relatively more than those of any other country. Unemployment has remained practically constant at between one and two per cent. The mortality rate declined from 27 per 1,000 in 1945 to 7.8 per

[1] *See* articles by H. Tiltman in *Asahi Evening News, e.g.,* that of August 23, 1956.

1,000 in 1955. In 1955 there were 13 million wireless licences and 130,000 television licences. (In the United Kingdom in 1957 there were 14.5 million, of which nearly half were for television.) The newspapers are among the most prosperous in the world with 34 million copies sold daily, a figure unsurpassed except in Britain and the United States.

Institutions and political customs which assured a special place to the military and encouraged the trend to war have been abolished, notably the rule, explicit from 1911 onwards, that service ministers must be appointed from among serving officers selected by the general staff; this was adroitly used by the *gunbatsu,* the military clique, to enslave the country for its own purposes, and the Emperor has of course renounced the statutory declaration of his own heavenly ancestry and transformed himself into a symbol of the state and of national unity (Article I of the new constitution of 1946). Apart from these things, Japan has carried through an important programme of agrarian reform, the benefits of which are now beginning to be felt; has undertaken a huge social welfare programme; has carried out big reforms in the education system, with the result that every Japanese child has the right of free education from his sixth to his fifteenth year; and finally, political life is firmly on the rails of a two-party parliamentary system of the Anglo-American type. In certain directions reformist enthusiasm has gone ahead too quickly, *e.g.,* in the permanent renunciation of war enshrined in Article IX of the new constitution. Finally, here are some signs which tend to show that the invalid is feeling better and that his taste for life is returning: on May 8–11, 1956, a party of Japanese climbers, led by Maki Yo, twice reached the summit of Manaslu (26,658 feet), one of the highest hitherto unclimbed peaks in the Himalayas, and a strong Japanese expedition, financed chiefly by the newspaper *Asahi,* left for the Antarctic in connection with the International Geophysical Year. Thus there is no doubt that Japan, in spite of all the creaking of its old bones, in spite of the rheumatism that still racks its joints, is a fundamentally healthy organism.

During this period I had occasion to visit many factories, offices, workshops, hospitals; and again, as in previous years, I had occasion to wonder what was the secret of this people that has often enabled them to achieve extraordinary successes. At first sight—and this is something that has deceived many foreign observers—the offices seem full of confusion, the factories primitive and badly kept, the hospitals poor and badly organized, and even the workers along the railway line handle their tools with the slow solemnity of an archaic rite. But it is the old story; one civilization should never be judged by the standards of another. Because our western efficiency has a certain look it does not follow that Japanese efficiency must have an exactly similar look. Just as the Japanese reaction to death is a smile, so their reaction to work is a kind of relaxed tranquillity, which has, perhaps, the great advantage of involving less nervous tension.

Summing up the experience of many years in Japan, I should say that there are at least five important Japanese characteristics which throw light on their success in the world, the modern world which they did not help to create.

The first is their sense of communion with nature. As we shall see later, the relations between man and his environment in the Far East are profoundly different from our own. Matter is not regarded as something inert and passive to be dominated, but as life, to be understood, loved, possessed. This, of course, is not consciously present in the mind of an operator using a machine-tool in an engineering shop, and if you questioned him about it he would probably be at a loss for an answer, but, like all other men, he is much more than he is consciously aware of. In each one of us there lives the civilization in which we were brought up; behind that workman there are thousands of years of mystic relationship with things, the subtleties of a profoundly monist philosophy, all the poetry of a popular religion according to which the divine suffuses everything, of an art which regards matter as a sister, not as a slave. These realities, on the level of an entire people, count; they give the Japanese, whether designer, director, artist, or simply workman, a lead of several lengths over others.

The second characteristic, closely connected with the first, is the extraordinary manual skill, particularly in little things, widespread among Japanese of all regions and all classes. Examine an eighteenth-century *inrō* (medicine box), a sixteenth- or seventeenth-century *tsuba* (sword guard), a plate, any lacquered object, a wicker basket, above all a sword blade; consider the skill and care with which boats, wooden boxes, lanterns, cheap paper-and-bamboo umbrellas are made, and you will immediately appreciate that this standard of workmanship, when harnessed to modern industry, is equivalent to a fabulous gold-mine on which to draw. For centuries the level of excellence required for native products has been such that these skills have become second nature. Examining the work of western craftsmen after one has grown used to Japanese standards is like passing one's hand over articles of furniture chopped with an axe after caressing the work of a first-class cabinet-maker. To get some idea of Japanese standards, one must think of Swiss watches, Italian Renaissance armour, certain English furniture and clothing; bearing in mind, however, that in Japan the high standard of craftsmanship applies not only to expensive products, but also to cheap articles of everyday use.

The third characteristic is the traditional specialization of the classes. In Japan the feudal system was abolished in 1868; only the day before yesterday, so to speak. For three centuries Japanese society had been rigidly stratified. At one extreme were the 262 *daimyo* (great names) and their families; at the other the *eta*, social pariahs condemned to what in a society under Buddhist influence were such degrading tasks as tanning hides and butchery. In between, starting from the top, came the Samurai (warriors, about 7 per cent of the population), *hyakushō* (peasants, about 85 per cent), *shokunin* (craftsmen, about 2 per cent) and *shonin* (traders, about 3 per cent).[1] It should be noted that traders were at the bottom of the scale, only a little way above the pariahs; a fact which explains the low Japanese commercial morality which prevailed, particularly during the long period at the end of the nineteenth century and the beginning of the twentieth, when the descendants of the best families preferred the professions or state employment to commerce or industry. There is still something degrading associated with money in Japan, and this often leads to hypocritical behaviour of the kind which with us is associated with sex. To return to class divisions; being so close to a past of specialization imposed from birth leads to ready acceptance of the limitations imposed by the requirements of modern industry. In the brief space of three or four generations there has been no time to develop a complete human nature, a rounded personality; thus a working life confined to the perpetual repetition of a few movements tends less strongly to stimulate resentment; it harmonizes with the

[1] N. SKENE SMITH, *Tokugawa Japan*, Tokyo, 1937, p. 31.

atmosphere of family memories handed down by word of mouth; and that makes the condition seem more tolerable.

Some of the characteristics of the Japanese of which everyone has heard should also be remembered—their frugal and Spartan habits. These are favoured by the fact that life is organized in such a way that the fundamental human needs are satisfied both cheaply and pleasingly. Housing, food, clothes, baths, are all much cheaper than they are with us; a man can be surrounded by beautiful objects without much expense. Luxury, as I have already remarked, is regarded as vulgar. Even middle-class habits are Spartan. People get up early, put up patiently with cold, and are not demanding in such matters as food, dress, and entertainment.

Finally, there is a group of characteristics which I perhaps should have put first, characteristics that are to be noted in all fields of Japanese life; the lack of outstanding personalities, the natural need to collaborate, the docility of groups to their leader (Photograph 78). One of the things which strikes foreigners, particularly Latins, most vividly is that when you meet the Japanese you rarely have the impression of meeting an outstanding personality, with an above-average intelligence, though when you meet Japan (the product of some labour, a work of art, an event) you are so often carried away by the warmest admiration. With us it is nearly always individuals who are interesting, brilliant, or witty, while collectively they are a poor thing. In Japan the reverse is true, and the whole is superior to the sum of its parts. Japanese of real talent may perhaps be few, but evidently the system carries them to the top; the others follow and the organism works.

Month of Music on the Roof-tops

As I write the rainy season (nyu-bai), with its damp and stuffy heat, is ending, and July is advancing, bringing the first days of bright sunshine. With us the traditional enemy is winter; but here houses and domestic life are organized essentially to resist the humid and oppressive heat of the summer months. In the fourteenth century Kenkō-bōshi, in his delightful miscellany the Tsure-zure Gusa, includes, among his hundreds of observations about women and love, extravagance and the art of gardening, religion and wine, cats and philology, music and rural life,

nature and poetry, botanical curiosities and calligraphic styles, procrastination and tailoring, ancient times, recipes, games of chance, artistic
taste, hunting, the art of divination, the best position in which to sleep,
the best way of dealing with importunate beggars, cherry blossom,
humility, bamboos, married life, the correct way of lighting the fire in
the Emperor's presence, and the seven kinds of unpropitious friendship,
the following (Section 55): 'When building a house it should be designed
to suit the summer. In winter one can live anywhere, but in the hot
weather an uncomfortable house is indeed trying.'[1]

But, however troublesome and oppressive the humid heat, the
low, grey, drizzling sky of the rainy season may be, you discover that it
has its own subtle beauty. The rain becomes a song. In the silence of the
night the dripping on the roof sounds like armies of mysterious cats
scurrying who knows where; and everywhere you hear the music of
flowing water, now loud and strong, now quiet and subdued, now like
a love song or lament, now like the muttering of a venerable sage who
has had too much to drink, and is having the most glorious dreams. In
the daytime the plants gleam, because the sun often nearly shows itself
through the oceans of little drops suspended in the sky. In the country
the rice-fields shine like mirrors, and tremulous pearls of water gather
on the great leaves of the lotus (sato-imo); veils of mist get caught in the
foliage of the trees; and at night the frogs croak agitatedly among the
newly planted-out rice seedlings.

Early this morning there was an earthquake. In Japan earthquakes
are so common that normally you take no notice of them. According
to the statistics, there are more than 2,000 a year; of these at least two or
three a month on an average are strong enough to be noticed. Their
incidence is irregular, of course. Sometimes there are long periods of
tranquillity during which the great fish, on which, according to ancient
legend, the Japanese archipelago rests, sleeps quietly and peacefully;
there are other periods during which it is continually restless and
agitated.[2] I remember a period before the war when for many days on
end what came to be known as the 'five o'clock earthquake' occurred
regularly every afternoon. Earthquakes have so many different ways of

---

[1] W.N. PORTER, The Miscellany of a Japanese Priest, being a translation of the Tsure-zure Gusa, London
1914.

[2] Earthquakes are one of the four Japanese terrors; the others are fire, thunder, and father.

behaving that you can never hope to know them all. Sometimes they begin gently and mildly; the world is first rocked by a gentle hand, which then gets angry and shakes it violently; sometimes the first warning is a sudden, violent shock, succeeded by more gentle shocks which gradually fade away into nothing. The ordinary Japanese wooden houses are admirably constructed to resist them; they are built like a ship, or a big piece of furniture, held together internally by interlocking beams, and only the most exceptional shock is capable of wrecking them. At the first sign of an earthquake they start shaking, creaking and groaning, giving ample warning to those within to seek refuge in the open air. This morning's shock was of the nasty, sly, kind, which starts by making the house rock gently, as if it were nothing but an unusually strong gust of wind, then suddenly increases in violence and makes you seek refuge half-naked in the garden, and then stops equally suddenly, as if playing a practical joke on you.

Having been thus awakened, I did not get back to bed, but read and listened to the wireless. Everything in Japan happens much earlier than it does in the west. People get up early; the wireless starts at five-thirty, with vigorous instructions for early morning exercises, to the accompaniment of a march, which has not changed since the beginning of time, hammered out on a piano. Before and during the war these broadcast physical training instructions were a nightmare; they were to be heard at all times of the day, that is to say when anthems to *Hitora-kakka* and *Mussorini-kakka* (Hitler and Mussolini—*kakka* means 'excellency') were not being played. Nowadays, however, things are less grim; the reign of *giri* (duty, moral obligation) has been succeeded by that of *ninjo* (human feeling), and broadcast talks deal with such things as art, politics, culture, birth control, cosmetics, sport, and gardening. Some days ago there was a talk on the three supreme beauties of all time: Cleopatra, Ono-no-Komachi, and Yang Kuei-fei. For the benefit of readers who may not have heard of the last two, Ono-no-Komachi ('Little Village in Little Field') was a celebrated poetess of the ninth century (the Heian period). According to the legend she was extremely beautiful, fastidious, fond of luxury, proud, and haughty. In 868, when the priests called on the gods in vain for rain, her verses are said to have succeeded in causing them to relent. But even she must have had her share of

disappointments in life; one of her poems tells us with the most unbridled melancholy that

Iro miede	In this world
Utsuro mono wa	Only the hidden
Yo no naka no	And secret flower
Hito no kokoro no	Of the human heart
Hana ni zo ari keru.	Fades slowly
	Without changing colour.

As for Yang Kuei-fei,[1] hers is indeed a tragic story. She was the favourite concubine of the Chinese Emperor Ming Huang (*d. 756*), one of
the greatest emperors of the T'ang period, but was strangled when the
Emperor, having grown old and frightened, realized that only her
death could satisfy a powerful rebellious clique to whom she had
become odious as a result of court intrigues. The story was written in
letters of flame in Chinese history, and for more than a thousand years
was a favourite theme of poets, artists, novelists, and dramatists. The
Japanese recently made a film of it which was an international success.

I had despaired of tracking down the family of my friend Hiro when
one day by chance I met his sister in the city centre. To my great surprise
I learned that she was working at the Tokyo Onsen. Was this another
case of *apuré,* post-war demoralization? I soon saw that it was nothing of
the sort. She spoke English, was a receptionist, and merely directed
customers to what they wanted. It was a job like any other. Besides, it
was enough to have a look at her; she looked more like a healthy sports
mistress than a survivor of tragic events. She talked about Hiro as if he
were still alive, laughing at his student pranks, and the excuses he used
to make up at home in order to come ski-ing with me.

But those are distant memories, belonging almost to another age,
another life. More immediate, and more tragic, was my last meeting
with Hiro immediately after the end of the war. After my release from
internment I was employed by the Americans to interview Japanese
applicants for jobs with the American military government. The pay
was good and there was always a long queue. One cold January morning
I was sitting in my office when there appeared at the door what at first
sight I took for the shadow of an old man. I looked again, and saw that
the shadow was greeting me. Then I saw that there was something

[1] In Japanese Yo Ki-hi.

familiar about his features, though they had changed in a fashion that for the moment I was at a loss to explain. Then the man came forward hesitantly and said in a whisper:

'*Maraini-san desu-ka?*' (Are you not Mr. Maraini?)

'*Hai*' (Yes). '*Anata-wa?*' (And who are you?)

'Don't let me disturb you now,' the shadow said, looking nervously all round him. 'Later, later. I'll wait for you outside. I'm Hiro.'

'Hiro! Hiro!' I was too taken aback to do anything but repeat his name. Heavens, how he had changed! He could not be more than twenty-three or twenty-four, but he looked like fifty. He was toothless, and had the yellow skin, the puffy flesh, of one who has spent long years in prison, far from the light. There were many like him at that period, but I had never known any of them before their ordeal, and therefore had no point of comparison. But I had known Hiro well when he was a student at Sapporo, in Hokkaido; a sturdy, strong, warm-hearted, decisive young man, with an immense thirst for knowledge, and a mountain-climber into the bargain. He was one of the first friends I made in Hokkaido, and we had been on many ski-ing expeditions together in the northern winter of that remote island. It seemed impossible that this wreck of humanity could be he. . . . Even his eyes, his look, were those of another; he was a broken man; his hesitation and uncertainty were poles apart from the self-confidence that had been one of his most pleasing characteristics.

I asked permission to leave the office, and we went together to a café. I tried to conceal how shocked I was at seeing him like this, but he was only too well aware of the state to which he was reduced. He told me about his five years of imprisonment, the hunger, the cold and the beatings, which he had not expected to survive. During the first year, in the Arctic cold of Abashiri, he and his fellow-prisoners had been left for whole nights without heating at zero Fahrenheit. He had beri-beri and tuberculosis, and knew that he had not long to live, but was happy because perhaps the better Japan of which he had dreamt was now going to be born. He had been imprisoned because they had said he was a spy, but I knew better than he did that his only crime had been to associate with me and the few other foreigners at Sapporo, in order to learn our languages, English, French, and Italian, and to learn something of the outside world.

I asked him whether he had been given a formal trial. Yes, he said, but it had been a farce; witnesses had appeared whom he had never seen, all his statements had been falsified, and he had been sentenced to twenty years' imprisonment for subversive activity in the *dai-to-a sensō*, the 'war of great east Asia'.

Next day I took him to the head of the American office which dealt with the victims of political persecution; he was received with open arms, and we set in motion the steps to obtain compensation, to enable him to start life again and obtain proper medical attention. But not long afterwards he died of a haemorrhage; another victim of the militarist tyranny, and certainly a hero in his humble and quiet way.

His sister now took me to see his parents; his mother could scarcely restrain her tears. The new home of the Miyazawa was a modest, recently built house in one of the higher quarters of Tokyo, another of those where you almost seem to be in the country though you are near the heart of the city. The Miyazawa were a middle-class family, of the kind that with us would certainly have owned a car, but in Japan life is lived at a much more modest level, not only out of necessity, but out of taste and tradition. At every social level the Japanese are unquestionably more Spartan than we, but it is in the middle class that the difference is most striking. The Japanese still have in their blood three centuries of the sumptuary laws of the Tokugawa period (1600–1868), ancient religious and artistic traditions in which Franciscan ideals prevail, the remote but still living martial cult of the *bushi,* the warrior whose only possession is his sword. Luxury, particularly conspicuous luxury, is a thing to be ashamed of; it is sufficient to observe the modest way of life of million-aires such as the Mitsui, for instance. Of course there are families, and many of them—particularly at Osaka, Kobe, Yokohama—with villas, yachts, American cars, jewellery and furs, but in the general estimation they are surrounded with the odour of vulgarity. Few Japanese phrases are more contemptuous than *narikin—nouveau riche*. Innumerable little things made it easy to see that the Miyazawa were prospering, but their house, food, clothing, pleasures, were all subtly dominated by the ideals of Buddhist simplicity which are almost inseparable from all that is most worth while in Japan.

We went together to visit Hiro's grave, or rather his sepulchral pillar, because in Japan the dead are always cremated. Hiro's parents belong to a Buddhist sect which from some points of view can be said to be the most Japanese of them all; it is characterized by little doctrine but much good works, and was founded by Nichiren (1222–1282), a visionary, turbulent, intolerant monk, who desired to sweep away more than a thousand years of metaphysical interpretation and return to what he believed to be the Buddha's original teaching. The followers of Nichiren are Protestants, so to speak, within the orbit of Japanese Buddhism, and they live their faith with more fervour, if with fewer intellectual subtleties, than the others. The ceremony at the temple was brief and simple.

It was one of those white mornings so common here in summer; it was hard to say whether it was cloudy or not; the light was bright and dazzling, without casting shadows. We emerged from the temple on to an open space, surrounded by huts and shops, the white walls of which dazzlingly reflected the light. Hiro's mother led me through the maze of sepulchral pillars (sotōba), varied in shape, but all fundamentally derived from the stupa-chorten-pagoda pattern common to the whole of Buddhist Asia, and soon we came to a grey stone pillar on which Hiro's posthumous name was inscribed in solemn ideograms; a very difficult name, entirely different from that which he had borne in life, according to the usage here.

His mother repeatedly poured water over the stone, announcing aloud, in accordance with the custom, all the news that might be of interest to him, as if he were there to hear. First of all she told him about my return to Japan. 'Namu Amida Butsu [let us worship the Buddha Amida]. Namu myō-hō-renge-kyō [let us worship the doctrine of the good law]. Your friend Maraini-san has again returned to Japan from his country beyond the ocean; we all still remember you, we all still love you. . . .' I too poured water over the stone from a little wooden cup, and lit incense sticks. Then it started to rain and we went away. According to Japanese usage, I should have smiled, and behaved perfectly normally, but I could not manage it. To avoid appearing ill-bred, I said that I wanted to wash my hands and disappeared for a few moments into a dark corner of the temple.

Incidentally, while on the subject of death, there was recently celebrated here the o-bon festival, which corresponds to All Souls' Day in the western world. But what a contrast there is in the attitude of the two civilizations to the same phenomenon! Perhaps in no other matter is the difference in outlook more strikingly illustrated. With us in the west death is a supreme and unique occurrence, a sharp cut in the metaphysical biography, the irreversible end of a brief appearance on the stage of the world, an act of violence, not only to the emotions, but also to reason, fearful above all because it is succeeded by the unknown, a verdict from which there is no appeal. Death therefore calls for sadness, nocturnal colours, tears, repentance, sackcloth, and ashes. All Souls' Day is celebrated at the beginning of November, after summer has gone and before winter has truly arrived, a grey, gloomy, damp, and melancholy season of the year, which was perhaps not chosen at random for this purpose by our forefathers. But in Japan the festival of the dead takes place in the height of summer, when all is light and life, after the planting out of the rice, in the season of sunshine and lush foliage. Death, whether because of Buddhist philosophy or the simple Shinto faith, is not the fearful thing it is to those who believe that there is one life only, at the end of which there is a judgment which decides the individual destiny for ever. Reduced to its nucleus of painful physical experience and violence to the emotions, it is therefore infinitely more supportable. Both the Buddhist doctrine of rebirth and the vaguer and more poetical Shinto faith are fundamentally optimistic; evil—particularly according to Buddhist conceptions—is certainly punished, but that does not preclude the ultimate and necessary attainment of Buddhahood by every living thing.

The dead are therefore celebrated gaily and cheerfully, and the three days of *o-bon* are an occasion for happy parties, dancing, and song rather than for sadness and grief. According to the new solar calendar, *o-bon* occurs in mid-July; according to the old calendar, it is thirty days later. In towns the new calendar is generally followed in the matter, while the country sticks to the old, with the result that in many places, particularly on the outskirts of big towns, advantage is taken of the opportunity to celebrate the occasion twice. In mid-July I went with Giorgio to the Shinto shrine of Yasakuni, the centre of the Shinto cult in Tokyo.

The spirits of all who died for their country are held to reside there; it is a true national shrine. It was a warm summer evening, and the stars

Mount Fuji, from Mito

Rocks, sea, and pine-trees at Matsushima.

The pine is a great feature of the landscape. A wooded offshore islet.

Japan, archipelago of snow-covered mountains. Forest and volcano of Hokkaido in winter (4 & 5); Hodaka (10,466 ft.), the highest peak of the Japanese Alps, in summer (6).

One of the important aspects of life dependent on abundance of water is rice-growing. Paddy during the rainy month, with processions (9, 10).

Cloth spread out to dry in the sun to fix the colour after being washed in the clear waters of a river (11); *gathering in the rice near Kyoto* (12).

Autumn sets the woods ablaze. Momiji "in flower" and old stone lanterns at Takao, near Kyoto.

The forest is always fundamentally sacred; roofs of the great Shinto shrine of Izumo lost among the foliage of the pines in a remote mountain setting. Izumo, like Ise, is one of the most venerated places in Japan.

The Japanese countryside is civilised, ancient, serene. Peasants' houses in various provinces (16, 17, 18, 19), and (20) a small valley with many characteristic features: rice-fields on the flat land, unirrigated fields on the lower slopes, woods on the hillside; in the centre the home of a peasant family.

21

Hostility of the elements: (21) blizzard at Sapporo; (22) typhoon at night in Tokyo; (24) Gyushu volcano in eruption; (25) the earth boils at Noboribetsu; and (23) the anger of heaven embodied in Rai-jin, the god of thunder, as represented in a celebrated wooden statue of the Kamakura period (thirteenth century) at Kyoto.

22

23

24

25

Flood (26 and 27), fire (28), and earthquake (30) are among the hazards which continually test the character and ingenuity of a whole nation. Roads, like men, survive precariously (29, 30).

were scarcely to be seen through the haze so typical of Japan. The big park that surrounds the shrine was like a fair-ground, with the sound of music and singing; the trees were lit up by innumerable lanterns. We passed through the entrance (where disabled ex-servicemen in white shirts begged for alms) and plunged into the crowd. Nearly everyone, and particularly the girls walking about arm-in-arm in groups of three or four, wore light, gay, brightly coloured *yukata*. We walked all over the park, passed beneath the *torii* (monumental arches), and made our way past the big door with the golden sixteen-petalled chrysanthemum (standing for the sun, the symbol of the Emperor), along an avenue flanked by national exhibitions of painting, poetry, and the art of flower arrangement. The crowd consisted almost entirely of families, some young (father, mother, and child), some old, with chattering grandparents lagging behind and children running on ahead. There were also American soldiers and their families, but it was impossible to discern the slightest sign of anything remotely resembling hostility towards them, not a look, gesture, or shrug of the shoulders. Incidentally we were almost certainly taken for Americans ourselves; in Japan nowadays every westerner, in the absence of evidence to the contrary, is taken to be an American.

In front of the shrine itself—a simple, bare, and unadorned building in archaic style, the only outer sign to give it any importance being a silk awning displaying the imperial chrysanthemum—we stopped and watched the crowd. As people approached they gathered themselves into the position of attention (they did not spring to attention, which is different), bowed their heads, joined their hands in prayer for a moment, and then withdrew. Some clapped their hands in accordance with ancient custom, to attract the attention of the gods; others, also in accordance with custom, threw a coin into a big box outside the entrance as a contribution to the maintenance of the shrine.

After admiring the scenery for next day's *Nō* play we were attracted by the cheerful sound of a band and a babel of voices. Near the entrance we found an open pavilion where about fifty people in a circle were dancing the *bon-odori*, the *bon* dance, which is one of the most spontaneous outlets for the Japanese people's taste for music and rhythm. It reminded me of the many other, even more enchanting, occasions when I had seen the same dance in the country, by the light of a bonfire, the dancer's singing not amplified by the raucous notes of the loudspeakers that were installed here.

Next evening we went to Ueno, where the festival of the dead was being celebrated too. The park lake was surrounded by myriads of coloured lanterns, strung in garlands. The park was full to overflowing, but a sense of peace, freedom, relaxation—and cleanliness—prevailed; it was easy to tell that everyone had come straight from the honourable bath, after a light supper of cereals and herbs. In a western crowd (and, for that matter, a Chinese crowd too) there are always too many people walking about with decomposing pieces of meat inside them; they form a kind of peripatetic animal cemetery. All round the lake were *yomise*, miniature night-time markets, hundreds of stalls selling flowers, crickets in cages (their singing keeps you company), dwarf trees, red fish, ferns to keep your house fresh; in addition to the usual fortune-tellers, sellers of zodiacal talismans *(juni-shi)*, and face-readers.

Talking of faces, who was that poor disabled ex-serviceman in a white shirt, holding out his hand for alms while his companion played the organ? I looked at him and he looked at me, but I could not place him.

'*Maraini-san desu-ka?*' he said to me at last. 'I am Nishi, don't you remember me?' He smiled wretchedly; he was abject, he had lost all dignity. For a time he had been one of the police at our internment camp, the only human, sometimes even decent, one among them. He had been with us for two months, and then was sent away. 'I was called up,' he said. '*Shikataganai* [it cannot be helped]. I lost a leg without even being in action, in an air-raid at Okinawa.'

I called Giorgio, who was lagging behind. It was a painful moment; we did not know what to say. How many times had we cursed the police during the long months of cold and hunger in the camp! But now we felt ourselves to be in some way responsible for this man's present plight, and were full of a terrible remorse. And to think that he should be Nishi-san, the only tolerable one of the lot, 'the one who stank least', as Giorgio put it! We emptied our pockets for him, wrote him out addresses, wished him luck, and did not know how to say good-bye to him. But people started pushing, the festival dragged us back again into its vortex. For a moment we caught sight of him again, bowing towards us, and then he was swallowed up in the throng. Forgive us, Nishi-san, forgive us. . . .

The river of people carried us on to the little temple of Benzaiten, where a priest with a loudspeaker and an up-to-date projector was showing coloured slides illustrating the elementary ideas of Buddhism. Many people stopped and listened. The priest had a good voice, and was a simple and effective speaker. Death, he explained, would inevitably put an end to our brief life, which was as ephemeral as a wave of the sea; rebirth awaited us, but in what form? That depended on our actions in this life. . . . While he spoke, children stretched their hands up into the beam thrown by the projector, throwing the shapes of rabbits, cocks, and birds on to the screen beside the sacred pictures. The children laughed delightedly; nobody took any notice of them. One of the pictures showed a soul reborn as a pink babe on a bed of lotus flowers, while among the clouds in the distance Kwannon approved and gave his blessing.

The crowd still pressed on and took us with it. At the lakeside people were handing small coins to a number of priests and receiving in return little square paper lanterns each on a wooden base, rather like a little boat, to enable it to float on the black and silent water. Each contained a tiny candle, and on the paper was printed a lotus flower and the ideograms 'sankai banrei tsuizen-kuyo' (funeral service for the myriads of souls of the three worlds). People either added, or got a priest to add for them, the name of some dead person, and then went down to the water's edge and launched the lantern on the waters. Gradually the lake filled with floating lanterns, where they looked like thousands of enchanted glow-worms. The children cried out in delight at the spectacle; here and there a woman stood motionless, gazing fixedly at her lantern.

A month after the o-bon celebrations in Tokyo I had occasion to go into the country, to the Bōsō peninsula to the east of Tokyo, an area which possesses in miniature nearly all the beauties characteristic of the Japanese landscape: rich valleys with villages or farmhouses hidden by trees and surrounded by rice-fields rather like gardens (Photograph 20), wooded mountains, water-courses shining in the sun (Photograph 7), a sharply indented coastline, little islands on which strangely twisted pines strike root (Photographs 2, 3). Izu, another big peninsula not far from Tokyo, is extremely beautiful too, and because of its more striking beauties, because it is more dramatically broken up by the sea, because it has more impressive mountains, more terrifying valleys and gorges, and has hot springs and magnificent views of Fuji (Photograph 1), most Japanese and foreigners who make the excursion from Tokyo prefer it. Incidentally, in the same westerly direction there are Kamakura, with its temples and beaches, the pleasure resorts of Zushi and Enoshima, Atami and Hakone, with their hot springs, and Fuji with its 'sea of trees' (*ju-kai*) and its five lakes; it is easy to justify a much greater fame.

In the Bōsō peninsula, however, the roads are much freer of traffic and each village is more beautiful than the last; they have not yet begun to be disfigured by advertisement hoardings, the peasants and fishermen receive you with extraordinary charm and hospitality, and old customs survive which have changed or disappeared elsewhere. Here you frequently come across old houses which are half-way between farmhouse, villa, and castle, reminiscent of similar places in Tuscany or Venetia and suggesting an ancient, civilized, and loving communion between man and the soil.

Travelling after dusk in Bōsō while a huge, yellow moon rose over the rice-fields, we saw lamps flickering in front of all the houses (Photograph 50). *O-bon* is meticulously observed here, and none of its details has been lost. Here, unlike elsewhere, particular emphasis is given to the first *o-bon* after a relative's death. Neighbours and friends all present the bereaved family with a *chochin* (lantern), often of the fantastic Gifu kind; the most popular or most influential people therefore have the most lanterns. Outside some houses you see twenty to thirty tremulous little flames flickering inside their coloured paper prison, producing a most enchanting effect.

The belief that lies behind the pretty sight is perhaps even more enchanting. The lanterns, and sometimes fires (*ogara*), are intended to light the way for the dead returning to their homes for the three-day festival. It would be bad taste to receive a guest with sighs and long faces, and no effort is spared to make the house as clean, tidy, and welcoming as possible. Every house is open, and ready to receive guests both visible and invisible, and is filled with flowers, fruit, and offerings. The family stays on the *engawa,* the veranda, drinking tea and sometimes *saké,* in happy and peaceful relaxation and repose, the men nearly naked because of the heat, while the women stir the air with fans, and the girls run about in their best brightly coloured *yukata.*

The fiction is carried to the point of actually laying a table for the dead, and putting ready for their use things they were especially fond of during their life-time; some special dish, perhaps, or a pipe, a musical instrument, a book, a flower; and advantage is taken of the occasion to introduce new-born members of the family to them. Often a pail of water is put by the door 'so that they can wash their feet before coming in'. Priests go from house to house to say prayers and read sacred texts; and some people secretly send for soothsayers (not dissimilar to the shamans of Central Asia) to communicate with the dead and seek their counsel.

After touring the whole peninsula we reached the sea not far from Onjuku. Here the mountains plunged steeply into the sea, forming high, rocky headlands. The narrow road skirted precipitous places, now as black as pitch, now flooded with silvery moonlight, and we passed through innumerable tunnels. Nearly every inlet concealed a fishing village. The fishing boats—big ones, of up to twenty or thirty tons— were drawn up on the steep beach, and we saw the big capstans used to draw them up; nets and seaweed were spread out to dry, together with supplies of food, cables, anchors, buoys, hoes, and axes. We spent two days in these delightful parts. The hospitality of the people was touching; it was impossible to stop outside a house without being invited to enter (*'Dozo, o-agari kudasai'*[1]) and take tea, sweets, or *soba* (shell-fish). Here, too, many lanterns were lit for the dead. One more detail about *o-bon* in these parts: on the first day 'you go and meet the dead on the shore' and on the last 'you accompany them back to the water's edge'. In other words, the ultimate home is the sea.

On the way back to Tokyo, nearly at the gates of the city, near the great Chiba steelworks, we had a minor breakdown and had to stop outside a little cemetery. It was the last night of *o-bon*. Many people were laying offerings on the stones, but it could not be called a mournful occasion. The people were chattering and singing, relaxed and cheerful. Boys were chasing each other about and the young children were playing hide-and-seek between their parents' legs; all among clouds of incense, shining lanterns, and the glare from the bonfire on which faded flowers and foliage were thrown.

[1] 'Pray come up, honourable sir.' The fact that you are asked to 'come up' and not to 'come in' when you enter a Japanese house is a relic of the time when Japanese houses were built on piles; they are still built on piles, but only a foot or so high.

Apropos of flowers and foliage, I paid a visit to an exhibition by the great master of flower arrangement, Teshigahara Sofu.

Teshigahara, or Sofu, as he is invariably called here (like Michelangelo, omitting the Buonarroti), is the Schönberg of this ancient art, which in a way had been ossified by tyrannical traditions: the revolution that he introduced was as drastic as the introduction of the twelve-tone scale. His field is not restricted to flowers; he has extended his domain to the whole of nature. He uses mossy tree-trunks, fruit, cuttlefish bones, stones, rusty nails, bottles thrown up by the sea, and a hundred other things as the objects of his crazy and marvellous orchestration. He might well be called the sculptor of the ephemeral.

The exhibition was so crowded that it was difficult to make one's way through the throng; and the comments made by the crowd showed an extraordinary degree of appreciation and understanding. Indeed, the number and variety of exhibitions of all kinds held in Tokyo throughout the year testifies to the ardour of Japanese curiosity about all things of the mind and their passionate interest in all forms of art. At the beginning of June, for instance, there were eight different exhibitions at the Metropolitan Museum of Art at Ueno, ranging from *avant-garde* paintings and sculpture, traditional painting, water colours, drawings, and photography, to bamboo, wood, and metal work. At the National Museum of Modern Art there was an architectural exhibition—the work of Gropius and the Bauhaus. In the big stores in the centre of the town there was an exhibition of old glass (at Isetan's), of photographs of the national parks (at Matsuya's), painting and sculpture of various modern schools (at Matsuzakaya's, Shirokaya's, and Takashimaya's), of *Nō* masks (at Mitsukoshi's), of various schools of flower arrangement (at Shirokaya's and Matsuzakaya's). There were also exhibitions at about twenty galleries of abstract and non-abstract, traditionalist and non-traditionalist, art, of photography, lacquer work, porcelain, and collections of the popular arts of various regions and provinces of Japan.

It is to be noted that the public shows an extraordinarily keen interest in all this; that a large number of these exhibitions are held in the big stores or organized by the newspapers, whose activities range from the organization of Himalayan expeditions to the arrangement of retrospective exhibitions and concerts and the publication of art books. No pernicious distinction is made between major and minor arts, and an exhibition of flower arrangement, or lacquer work, or popular arts is capable of rousing just as much interest as an exhibition of painting or sculpture; and photography, as in America, France, or Germany, is now accepted on a plane of absolute equality with other means of expression.

Japonia capta ferum victorem coepit

The great area in front of the imperial residence, between Hibiya, Sakurada-mon and Babasaki-mon, cut up into avenues, lakes, stretches of ancient wall, lawns, and clumps of pine-trees, can really be said to mirror the mind and history of Japan. I remember how, before the war, when one reached a certain spot here in the tram, the ticket-collector stood to attention and announced: 'We have arrived in front of the honourable palace; gentlemen are requested to bow as a sign of respect.' Thereupon the passengers all rose to their feet—some even took off their overcoats as a sign of even greater respect—and bowed deeply and in solemn silence, trying not to lose their balance in the jolting vehicle, which would indeed have been absurd and inappropriate at such a solemn moment.

Then the war came, and what a war it was for the unfortunate Japanese people! It lasted so long that they must have ended by believing it to be the natural order of things. From 1931 (the occupation of Manchuria) to 1937 (the 'China incident') to 1941 (war in the Pacific) there was no relief, but merely a continual worsening. On December 8, 1941 (Pearl Harbour), things seemed to touch bottom (or top, depending on the point of view); Japan was at war with the world's greatest Powers. Long processions of people of both sexes and of every conceivable age and condition made their way more frequently than ever to the space outside the Imperial Palace; schoolgirls in uniform, housewives in *kappogi* (white dustcoats which became a kind of uniform too), old men in kimonos, railwaymen, schoolboys, wounded soldiers in white, each with his *Hinomaru-no-hata* (little sun flag), the leaders of each group bearing standards, many of them with robes over their shoulders bearing patriotic inscriptions; and they all went to the Niju-bashi, the bridge at the entrance to the palace, to pay homage to the sacred person of the Tenno, the 'king of heaven'. From afar there could be heard the echo of the famous songs *Roei* ('Bivouac'), *Shussei Heishi wo Okuru* ('For soldiers leaving for the front'), *Akatsuki ni Inoru* ('Prayer to the dawn') and others now forgotten. Then times grew bad; disasters began, the nights grew red with fire. And at last the Emperor spoke to his people (an unheard-of thing), announcing surrender. I still remember the photographs of the many Japanese who took their lives during those days, inevitably always in the same place, in sight of the Niju-bashi, the Double Bridge. Their bodies lay tidily in a row, face downwards; the requirements of etiquette must be scrupulously observed, even in death.

After the war the centre of interest and attraction appeared for a time to be displaced from the Emperor's invisible palace to the vast and extremely visible and impressive mass of the Dai Ichi Sōgō, chosen for his headquarters by the *aoi-me no shogun* ('the blue-eyed Shogun'), General Douglas MacArthur. I remember that at midday, when he left for lunch in his car with its five-starred pennant, a crowd of Japanese always turned up to see, admire, and even applaud their conqueror. This was something that never ceased astonishing Americans and foreigners in general. How explain that these enemies of yesterday, who preferred being burnt alive to surrender, who committed suicide rather than let themselves be taken prisoner, who had sworn to fight to the death, now gathered in orderly and spontaneous fashion to offer sincere and respectful applause to the principal author of their defeat? To find the answer it is again necessary to plunge into the deepest recesses of the Japanese mind, to remember the profound immanence of the Japanese vision of the universe, according to which all life, divine and human, is a single reality, in which there is no conflict between spirit and matter, between the ideal and the real. Consequently life can never be wrong. By his victory MacArthur had demonstrated the superiority of a certain order of things, and this necessarily abolished the preceding order. Apart from this, there was in the Japanese attitude a certain affinity with the sporting attitude; you fight like a demon to win, and then give the winnèr his due, whoever he may be. In addition, MacArthur understood extraordinarily well the emotional needs of the Japanese people, and in his appearance, manners, and gestures, reminiscent of some Renaissance hero, seemed an embodiment of the great captains of four centuries ago, Oda Nobunaga, for instance, or Toyotomi Hideyoshi, who made a united empire out of a chaos of conflicting war lords. I remember noting with surprise and admiration how General MacArthur descended into the throng unarmed, followed only by a singularly unmartial-looking bodyguard; anybody who had wanted to could have fired a revolver or thrown a bomb at him. But he had seen and understood; and the Japanese were grateful to him for his confidence in them.

Gradually, however, things changed; the understanding between victors and vanquished could not be expected to last for long on this idyllic plane. It is strange that MacArthur, who instinctively understood the Japanese so well, should have erred so grossly when he sat down at his desk to solve the numerous problems with which the occupation confronted him. One after the other directives flowed from his office, first to the Shidehara government, then to the Yoshida government, intended radically to reform a society with at least fifteen centuries of civilized tradition behind it. He ordered the breaking up of the mono-polies (*zaibatsu,* capitalist cliques), reform of the schools, a new consti-tution, the emancipation of women, trials for war criminals. It was obvious that a huge abstract scheme, lifted bodily from one civilization and imposed like a rigid framework on the living tissue of another, was destined to lead to failure, or at any rate to every possible sort of con-fusion. Then, on April 10, 1951, MacArthur was recalled by President Truman, and misunderstandings multiplied; and the resentment of a conquered people towards a conqueror who had acted with a mag-nanimity unique in the history of war was given an opportunity to consolidate.

During this period the focal point of interest shifted back to its point of origin, the Niju-bashi, the Imperial Palace. People started going there as they had done before, and even more than before. In the old days it had perhaps been possible to detect in the air the invisible pre-sence of the whip in the hands of the military leaders, and there was always the suspicion that the crowds who went to the palace might be motivated by fear. Now, however, no such suspicion was possible; the cheerfulness, serenity, orderliness, with which schools, clubs, trade unionists, delegations, families, approached the place of homage spoke its unmistakable language. Japanese feelings towards their Emperor, both as an individual and an institution, seem to me to be more alive today than ever.

After the war the big space opposite the Niju-bashi revealed other important changes in Japanese life. At the very beginning of the occupation, as I have mentioned, no young women were to be seen in the streets; then, when the Americans turned out to be decent fellows in spite of the prophecies of the rabid nationalists, there was a sudden blossoming forth of girls and young women from their hiding-places. For a short time there were strict rules against 'fraternization' on the American side, but, as was inevitable, these were eventually set aside, and the first American-Japanese couples were to be seen in the big space opposite the Emperor's palace; the men, tall, fair, and in uniform, with cameras slung from their shoulders, and the girls all smiles and bows, at first always in kimonos, but soon looking more self-possessed in *yōfuku* (western dress), with high-heeled shoes and handkerchiefs over their heads, rather like tourists enjoying the marvels of the Yellowstone National Park.

To say that American men and Japanese women got on well together is a gross understatement; they flung themselves into each other's arms as if they had been waiting for each other all their lives (Photographs 149, 150): *Japonia capta ferum victorem coepit*. Apart from the innumerable fleeting or clandestine relationships that were established, no fewer than 20,000 ended in marriage. Incidentally it should be noted that in practically 100 per cent of these cases the man was American and the woman Japanese; instances in which the man was Japanese and the woman American could be counted on the fingers of one hand. That was a phenomenon that anyone with a little familiarity with the contrasting psychologies of the two parties had no difficulty in explaining.

What the American male found in Japan was Woman, Woman with a capital W. American women undoubtedly make excellent wives and mothers, but not lovers. Japan brought the American male the revelation of Woman in a light that he had not hitherto believed possible; he discovered the most exquisite tenderness and abandon, a mind enriched by suffering, sensitive to poetry, desirous of dedication; for the first time in his life he discovered himself to be not half of a couple, but a whole man. True, he also discovered sinuous feline manœuvres, a language of looks, sighs, hints, a dangerous art of invisible scratches and sometimes insidious traps. But all this was exquisitely feminine and, above all, it was something entirely new. Also there was the attraction of Woman entirely lacking in a sense of original sin about the pleasures of life. It should be noted that by this I do not imply sensual refinements; on the contrary. The latter require repression of instincts, and westerners, both men and women, are actually much more sensual than the Japanese. What I mean rather is a serene acceptance of the good things that life has to offer (food, drink, rest, the bath, love, beauty, art) rather than the *carpere diem* spirit, the need anxiously to snatch a smile in the face of remorse and repentance to come. Finally there was the enchantment of an exotic little face and a perfect amber skin, indeed worthy of the daughters and granddaughters of marine deities.

On the other hand, the American male, groomed and tamed and made submissive by the American female, seemed to the Japanese female to be the fulfilment of her wildest dreams. Her tremulous, changeable mind, accustomed to having to conceal itself, to hold its peace, ever ready to resort to the most intricate and devious means to attain the most legitimate ends, to masquerade like one of those dwarf trees trained by the gardener to simulate a forest in two inches of earth, conditioned to obedience by centuries of submission or to the sadness of petty revolts promptly crushed between the paper of the *shōji* and the silk of the *tamoto,* now suddenly walked abroad in a heaven of understanding, gentle affection, and warm-hearted confidence. Here was a man who treated her like a queen! Not only did he open the door to let her pass, not only did he offer her his seat, not only did he hold her hand in the street, and help her up a step that was slightly steeper than usual, but he wanted to stay with her at all times and share his pleasures and amusements with her; and, finally, he opened his mind to her without restraint, not withholding anything of himself. He was an adorable big baby, strong, rich, powerful, kind, tender, and gentle.

No doubt the lovers, if left to themselves, would have been happy. But nobody ever marries just a woman or a man; you also inevitably marry an environment, a society; and societies, whether Japanese or American, have always been hard. As can be easily imagined, Japanese women who associated with foreigners immediately became the target of the jealousy of their compatriots, both male and female. Japanese women who were left out in the cold naturally loathed them; and

Japanese men who were left out in the cold too, unable to compete with these rich Americans, naturally loathed them even more. The kindest of the accusations that were flung at them was of 'selling themselves' to these foreigners, and this of course led to every kind of unpleasantness, and to the dragging of beautiful dreams in the mud. The Americans, however liberal their intentions were in principle, had to take account of the reactions of the Middle West and the Deep South, and the story did not, on the whole, have a happy ending. Most of the delightful little wives whom the Americans took home, rather like living souvenirs from the island at the other end of the world, ended by going back to Japan again, a little older and a little wiser.

This was the normal end of the affair at the most elevated and respectable level, but there was also the vast ocean of temporary associations and venal and degrading contacts (Photograph 147). Around the American camps there arose monstrous cities of vice, of which Chitose, in Hokkaido, and Tachikawa, near Tokyo, were perhaps the most fantastic examples. Things grew to such a pitch that no sooner was there talk of opening an American office or quartering foreign soldiers in any part of a Japanese town than people started writing indignant letters to the newspapers and defence committees were set up. For the public at large this was the blackest aspect of the occupation, and one of the deepest causes of anti-American feeling.

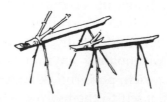

3

The Eastern Seaway

High Priest of the Rails

THE history of Japan has several times been described as a succession of periods in which the nation drinks eagerly at foreign sources and then withdraws into itself to digest and elaborate. In the fifth, sixth, and seventh centuries A.D. Japan absorbed Buddhism and Chinese civilization. In the fifteenth and sixteenth centuries there was a first, agitated, contact with the west; and finally, after 1854 and the visit of Commodore Perry, she abandoned her isolation and united her destiny with that of the rest of the world.

After several years of conflict between the advocates and opponents of modernization, the Emperor Meiji mounted the throne, and in 1868 the capital was transferred from Kyoto to Yedo, which was thereupon renamed Tokyo ('eastern capital'), and the country was seized with a mania for all western things; everything that came from Europe or America seemed precious, and the literature of the period is filled with pathetically naive hymns to progress, science, international amity, etc., etc. Everything traditional fell into such disrepute that for a time one of the loveliest Kyoto pagodas was up for sale at the price that it would fetch for firewood; fortunately no buyer appeared. One of the greatest poets of the period, Tachibana Akemi (1812–1868), expressed in verse the feelings of the traditionalists submerged by the tide of modernism:

Tanoshimi wa	It is a pleasure
Ebisu yorokobu	When, in these days of delight
Yo no naka ni	In all things foreign,
Mikuni wasurenu	I come across a man who
Hito wo miru toki.	Does not forget our Empire. [1]

In this atmosphere of passionate admiration for the *ebisu*, the western barbarians, the first railway line in Japan was opened in 1872; it covered the twenty miles from Tokyo to Yokohama, and was the

[1] D. KEENE, *Anthology of Japanese Literature*, George Allen & Unwin, Ltd., 1956

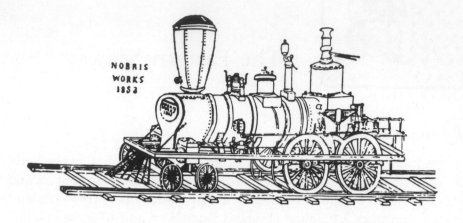

NOBRIS
WORKS
1853

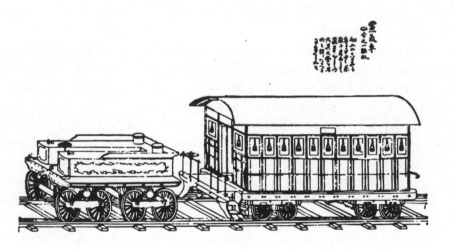

黒蒸車
四〇之二輛�
...

The first train ever seen by the Japanese; that presented by Commodore Perry to the Shogun Iyesada in 1854. The artist observes in his own handwriting: 'Steam vehicle . . ., faced with its complicated mechanisms, my power of observation fails; I fear I have made many errors in this sketch.'

(From *Contemporary Japan*, Tokyo, Vol. XXII, 1–3, 1953)

work of British engineers. The Emperor Meiji honoured the inaugural ceremony with his presence, wearing the ancient court costume called *naoshi* and attended by a suite also dressed in traditional robes, with long sabres denoting authority. The royal party mounted the train and were driven to Yokohama. Before the train drew out a message from the Emperor was read in which, among other things, he expressed the hope that 'the whole people will wish to use this means, thanks to which commerce will prosper and millions will obtain riches'. The Italian Count Alessandro Fea, doyen of the diplomatic corps, replied in the name of the foreign representatives.

The newspapers excelled themselves in honour of the occasion. *Nichi Nichi* (which means 'day by day') of September 6, 1872, said: 'In its rapid course the train will be like wind or the clouds. . . . History records no such event since the days of our first Emperor Jimmu' (*i.e.*, 2,000 years ago). The day naturally ended with fireworks and the sending up of coloured balloons.[1] Illustrations of the period show the marvellous toy puffing clouds of smoke, like a fundamentally benevolent monster, a living symbol of all that was new and therefore beautiful and right.

Perhaps because the railway came to the Japanese at such an important, such a profoundly lyrical, moment in their history, it has always remained particularly dear to them. In a few decades railways spread throughout the Japanese archipelago. Because of the mountainous nature of the country, nearly every mile of track represents an engineering feat. Though the longest tunnel does not exceed about six miles, the number of tunnels, bridges, viaducts, embankments per mile of track is among the highest in the world. The service is good, though the narrow gauge prevents high speeds. There has been little electrification, no doubt because of the ample coal supply, particularly in the northern isle (Hokkaido) and the southern (Kyushu).

One of the most characteristic personages of the Japanese railway world is the station-master. His elegant person, his violet uniform, his red, gold-laced cap seem to exude an ancient Confucian wisdom, to inspire a sense of awe and authority belonging to another age. Sometimes he is like an admiral skilfully manœuvring his terrestrial fleet, and he moves about the platforms solemnly, austerely, imposing universal

[1] NITOBE and others, *Western Influences in Modern Japan*, Chicago, 1931.

respect; sometimes he seems rather a high priest, a patriarch of travel, a pontiff of the time-table, particularly if you happen to catch him slowly, ceremoniously, and with immense dignity extracting his watch, a heavy silver affair on a chain, from his uniform pocket. His severe and sometimes exalted expression on these occasions is like that of one immersed in the music of the spheres.

For the westerner the Japanese station-master provides perhaps the simplest and most readily accessible illustration of the Far Eastern conception of authority, which differs so vastly from ours. In the west for the past 2,000 years spiritual and temporal authority have almost invariably been distinct. True, Charlemagne's new Roman Empire was called Holy, and the Kings of England since Henry VIII have also been heads of the Church of England. But these are exceptions, and until recent times all ordinary western monarchs have aspired to the sanction of the religious authority, which was universally recognized as being autonomous and distinct. The eastern approach is different, however; where the west distinguishes and differentiates, it tends instinctively to unify. Authority is one and indivisible, uniting the sacred and the profane, heaven and earth, the civil and the military, the visible and the invisible. The Emperor of China was the Son of Heaven, had a celestial mandate; the Emperor of Japan is the *Tenno,* the King of Heaven or Heavenly King, in whom all the lines of force of the nation converge.

Such fundamental differences of approach are reflected in details of everyday life; the whole river is coloured by the nature of the spring at its source. The attitude to the highest authority is in some measure reflected in the attitude to the most modest official. In the west civil authority is felt, both by those who exercise it and those subject to it, to be an eminently practical device, an answer to strictly practical problems. You wave the flag and send the train on its journey, I am responsible for the village water supply, he teaches the children. That, however, is not the situation in the Far East, where the aura of the unifying authority at the summit perceptibly descends into the field of ordinary life. In Japan a numinous quality surrounds in greater or lesser degree those who even in the most indirect manner represent the state, *i.e.,* the Emperor. When you are brought face to face with such a person you bow deeply, when you pass near him you cast down your eyes, or even draw in your breath in that characteristic sibilant manner that indicates embarrassment or reverence and was described by Pierre Loti as a viper's hiss.

Japanese station-masters almost invariably seem fully aware of their august position. True, in the course of years I have come across slovenly, rude, and hustling station-masters, but there are exceptions to every rule. The overwhelming majority seem to regard their work with an ancient dignity. Immediately after the war, when the country was in ruins, they were the only men in uniform who held their heads high. They seemed to be saying to the allied soldiers sitting on the blue velvet cushions in the second class: 'Those militarist rogues thought they were stronger than you and deceived the Emperor, and you rightly defeated them. Now the only true representatives of the Emperor are we, the soldiers of travel, the faithful servants of the people.' And they looked the blond travellers, their recent enemies, straight in the eye.

In Japan the railway is the means of communication *par excellence*.[1] The Japanese are always travelling, and they enjoy it; any excuse will do: to visit an aunt, a customer, a temple, to do business, to go on a pilgrimage, to visit dying relatives or new-born children. The railway corresponds to the Japanese way of life; it is paternalistic at the top and gregarious at the bottom. First-class compartments are rare, and are to be found only on the most important lines; second-class compartments are few, but the third-class compartments, with their green velvet seats, which are often torn, are as abundant as the sands of the sea. The trains are always full of people travelling in parties. Every school organizes one or two excursions a year, so that all or nearly all children who receive secondary education know the famous places of their country; young people travel in parties to the sea, to rivers and lakes, to fish, to the mountains to climb or ski; the old visit shrines and temples; trade and professional organizations hold congresses, trade unions arrange meetings and processions. Women, children, old people, big men, little men, the rich, the poor, runaway lovers, commercial travellers, everybody is always travelling everywhere by train.

[1] The number of traveller-miles is among the highest in the world. In 1954, in round figures, it was 87,000 million.

The Japanese roads, however, are grossly neglected.[1] It is true that for strategic reasons the militarist discouraged and at times actually prohibited their construction, but no people would submit to such absurd restrictions in the absence of a solid psychological background which made them acceptable. Bicycles are all right, and so are buses and lorries, but cars are a different matter. True, Japan is a poor country, and cars are still a great luxury, but, even apart from that, most Japanese would think twice or three times before buying a car even if it were well within their means.

A car implies individualism, independence, making sudden decisions, all things which go against the grain of the Japanese mentality. In a country of such close social texture individual initiative is fundamentally suspect; even the Japanese word for individual, private, *kojin-no,* and its derivatives, often have the connotation of selfishness. Independence for the Japanese implies helplessness, lack of support.

Cars as such are by no means despised; every Japanese would be delighted to *rouler en bagnole,* as the French put it in that delightfully untranslatable phrase; but he would want a driver at the wheel. Driving himself would imply revolutionizing several aspects of his life. In the first place, the sheer speed of driving involves sudden and unexpected meetings and situations, the full family, civic, and ceremonial implications of which there is no time to weigh up. You might meet people whom you wished discreetly to avoid, for instance, or find yourself suddenly faced with superiors or inferiors whom you would have to greet without being able to show them the exactly appropriate degree of respect, thus risking making irreparable errors, etc., etc. In other words, you would have to reveal yourself, a thing which the Japanese generally try to avoid. Then there is the grave question of responsibility *(sekinin).* On this point one must do the Japanese justice; they possess it to an outstanding degree. A Japanese is not an individual; he is a cog in a delicate social mechanism. His rights and duties are meticulously defined, and as a rule he takes them very seriously. Mentally he is always surrounded by superiors and inferiors, to both of whom he is

[1] *See* Photographs 29, 30.

bound by a sense of deeply felt moral obligation (*giri*) and responsibility. As all this constitutes a burden, no Japanese wishes to increase the share of *sekinin* imposed upon him by life. Now, supposing an accident happened while he was driving, apart altogether from the financial consequences, the result would be an upheaval in his tidy world of moral obligations. Supposing—which heaven forbid!—he ran over a man and killed him, he would obviously have to provide for his family. But the burden would not be financial only; a vast, almost unlimited, area of moral obligation, of a kind inconceivable in the west, would be involved. If, for instance, ten years later the dead man's son misbehaved himself and went to prison, the driver would be held responsible; or he might find himself under an obligation to find husbands for the deceased's daughters; driving, in other words, involves the risk of stirring up a wasp's nest of never-ending troubles. But if you employ a driver, all these things can be neatly settled with the aid of a set of elegant fictions; only the question of financial compensation remains.

The consequence of all this is that, while there are many motor-vehicles in Japan (in 1954 there were 1,338,313), private cars are few (81,893), *i.e.*, about one to every thousand inhabitants.

But to return to the roads, which we are to take to today, for we are leaving for Kyoto. With great difficulty I succeeded in hiring a car, and without Giorgio I should never have succeeded. I went to a number of garages, but the result was always the same; the owner was perfectly willing to hire me a car, but as soon as I explained that I wanted to drive he started scratching his neck and his head, and explained that he was very sorry indeed, but never in his life had he done such a thing as hire a car to a customer who wanted to drive himself, and he would not even know how to set about the necessary formalities. Finally I gave it up, and went to see Giorgio in his office over one of the many canals in lower Tokyo. I might have been in Venice, with reflections of the sun and the waves on the ceiling, and the sound of barges passing under the window, loaded with coal, cement, machinery. Giorgio was simultaneously telephoning to Hongkong, dictating a letter in English, and talking French to a South American seated by his desk. I waited a while, and looked at Giorgio's magnificent library of art history; it is one of the finest in the world. Not only does it contain everything that has been published in a dozen languages about Japanese art, but a large number

of ancient manuscripts, some of them rare. Meanwhile the inter-
continental storm continued behind me. '*Moshi moshi!* [Hallo!] *Motto hakkiri hanashite kudasai!* [Speak more distinctly, please!] Well, let's get on with the letter. I shall eventually return the samples, if . . . *Bien sur, je lui ai dit qu'il faut aller au Gaimusho, au Ministère des Affaires Étrangères. Moshi moshi, hai wakarimashita* [I understand]. . . .'

When the whirlwind subsided I dared to approach. I have always been greatly impressed at the sight of Giorgio at his desk; it is like being face to face with a deity who embodies at least eight of the ten ideals on which modern society lives; and at bottom I understand very well why he does not want to leave Japan. Here, at the heart of his empire, his mind sparks like an engine, a concentrated International Business Machine, he spreads his tentacles across the oceans, he defies the barriers of language, his eyes search out hearts, goods, grammars, philosophies, sensations. What would he be in Rome? Outside his own civilization he is a citizen of the moon, a most intoxicating experience.

'I know what you want and I've got the answer already,' he said to me, with the smile of the conjurer producing the rabbit out of the hat. 'Sit down and wait while I telephone.'

He dialled a number, and an American or English voice answered.

'Go to 356 Tamura cho, Icchomé, and ask for Jennings,' Giorgio finally announced. 'It's an old Chevrolet, but he'll let you have it cheap, 50,000 yen a month. It's a piece of luck. He's going to America, and is delighted to be able to earn something while he's away. Good-bye, good-bye, I'll see you this evening, I'm terribly busy now!'

Along the Tokaido

A short motor highway leading to Yokohama *via* Omori helps the traveller leaving Tokyo for the south; it is broad, the surface is excellent, and there is plenty of traffic. We passed many lorries, motorized tri-cycles, and miniature cars, and every now and then we were overtaken by big cars bearing the special number-plate 3A and containing American officers. Cars registered in Tokyo-to (the Tokyo metropolitan area) have no distinguishing sign; in the case of those registered elsewhere the number of the vehicle is preceded by the initial ideogram of the name of the province; it is also preceded by the figure 1 in the case of lorries, 2 in the case of cabs, 3 in the case of big private cars and 4 in the case of small private cars. Because of the shocking state of the roads you rarely see cars from another province. Just now we passed a car with an ideogram reading *hiroi,* obviously from Hiroshima. Needless to say, it was a 3A. Hardly anyone except the Americans undertakes a long journey by car; the Japanese, and I do not blame them, prefer the train. The distance by road from Tokyo to Hiroshima is about 550 miles, and any sensible person would allow at least three days for it.

You do not reach the country proper until you have left Yokohama behind; Tokyo–Kawasaki–Yokohama is a huge urban complex, more than forty miles across at its widest, with nearly 10 million inhabitants. It was a relief to escape from the factory chimneys at last. For several miles we proceeded at a short distance from the coast; occasionally the road climbed and then descended again. Every now and then we caught glimpses of blue sea framed between two promontories, and we passed through many long agricultural villages with old houses and beautifully thatched roofs. The asphalt road surface was still good. Sometimes we might have been travelling down an avenue in a park; tall, twisted pines lined both sides of the road. We were travelling along what for thousands of years has been the great artery of Japan, the Tokaido, the Eastern Seaway.

It was called this because the ancient Japanese looked at their islands from the Yamato area. A people's origins colour its life for many centuries. Why are the Italians, for instance, so little devoted to the sea? Because the Italian peninsula was for the most part populated from the continent; our ancestors crossed the Alps and continued south until they came to the sea; the sea was the end of the journey, a final, insuperable obstacle. The few groups with a strong maritime tradition, such as the Ligurians, the Neapolitans, and the Venetians, formed round nuclei of eastern Mediterranean origin, *i.e.,* arrived by sea. The slightness of the Italian knowledge of the water is shown by the relatively small proportion of the population that can swim,[1] their decided preference for meat to fish, their clothing, and other things as well. A people with true maritime traditions, like the Japanese, have a positive cult for swimming, prefer fish to meat, and use every imaginable product of the

[1] P. LUZZATTO-FEGIZ, *Il Volto Sconosciuto dell' Italia,* Milan, 1956, p. 225.

sea, including seaweed, which incidentally is rich in vitamins and is delicious.

But to return to the ancient Japanese. In the eighth and ninth centuries civilization in the Japanese archipelago barely reached the Kwanto, the area where Tokyo stands today. The area to the west and north of it was covered by the thick forests of Dewa and Mutsu, two remote territories inhabited by *emishi* (barbarians), the ancestors of the present-day Ainu, of whom we shall speak later. Here I shall mention only that they were stubborn enemies of the Japanese, who fought them in a war that lasted practically for a generation. A Japanese general, Ki no Kosami, was defeated by them at the battle of Morioka in 790; until 1945 this was technically the only defeat in Japanese history. The Tokaido was thus the road that led to the eastern sea, the sea beyond the Izu peninsula; the road to the Far East, using the term in the sense that Americans talk of the Far West, the road of the pioneers, of conquest, of advancing civilization.

After 1185, when Minamoto Yoritomo, the first of the long line of shoguns who governed Japan for centuries, leaving nothing but impressive court ceremonial to the Emperor, established his military government *(bakufu)* at Kamakura, a few miles from the site of present-day Tokyo, the Tokaido became very important indeed. Imagine England with a king in Edinburgh and a government in London; that was the situation that lasted in Japan for nearly 500 years. The road between the two became the nation's vital artery. The Tokaido, with its fifty-three stages, is a constant theme in Japanese literature, folklore, and art. Who has not seen at any rate some of the famous prints of Hiroshige (1797–1858) belonging to the series called the *Fifty-Three Stages on the Tokaido*?

But the most famous work, which keeps the Tokaido alive in the Japanese imagination—rather as Verona lives in ours because of Romeo and Juliet, and the hills of Settignano because of Boccaccio's tales—is the *Hizakurige,* a satirical novel in fifty-six parts by Jippensha Ikku (1766–1831), published between 1802 and 1822, describing the adventures of two attractive rogues named Yaji and Kita, who travel along the road on Shanks's pony. Western critics writing of Yaji and Kita recall Falstaff, Sancho Panza, Tartarin, the *Pickwick Papers,* and Mark Twain, but perhaps a better comparison would be with the *Satyricon* of Petronius.

Yaji's and Kita's travels consist of an endless series of imbroglios, amorous adventures, unexpected encounters, quarrels with creditors, flights, fisticuffs, jokes, and drinking bouts. The whole popular Japanese world of the period lives in these pages; noisy and amorous serving-maids, country samurai who become enraged over trifles and are regularly outwitted by humble townsmen; obsequious inn-keepers and greedy priests; *ronin* (masterless samurai), who are often rogues but sometimes strangely idealistic figures; porters, servants, thieves, horse-dealers, whores. Anyone who believes the Japanese to be humourless fanatics always ready to commit *hara-kiri* should read the *Hizakurige* to feel pulsating in every line the gay and irrepressible humanity of these people.

At Fujisawa we branched off to Kamakura. For more than a century this town was the residence of the shoguns, and of their deputies the Hojo *shikken,* and thus gave its name to a whole period of Japanese history, the Kamakura period (1185–1333), during which art, particularly sculpture, flourished.[1] Nowadays Kamakura is in a state of rapid development. Round the ancient centre, where a number of important temples with many works of art are preserved, a residential area has grown up where many artists and writers live. It is also a seaside resort, and once a year, in August, a tremendous American-style carnival is held, with drum majorettes leading a procession of floats. At Kamakura there is also a famous forty-foot-high statue of the Buddha; it was made in 1252 and stood inside a temple which was destroyed by a tidal wave in 1495; it now stands, huge and solitary, in the middle of a park. From the artistic point of view it is second-rate, but it is a great tourist attraction; everybody must have seen an illustration of it some time, whether in a book, or on a postcard, or on postage stamps which were in circulation for many years.

The Nude in Art and Life

We spent the night at a villa belonging to Giorgio at Atami, which is one of the famous Japanese *onsen*. Its name is written with the two characters for 'hot' and 'sea'. At Giorgio's villa, like all those at Atami, there is a bath which is filled twice daily with water from one of the many hot springs of the neighbourhood.

[1] *See* Photograph 23.

We were about to enter the *o-furo*, the honourable bath, when we heard Giorgio's voice. He had unexpectedly decided to join us, and invited us to bathe and dine with a party of friends in the village down below.

As we had taken off our western clothes, we put on *yukata*, light summer cotton kimonos, and accompanied him. As soon as we emerged from the quiet street in which the villa stood we found ourselves in the midst of the evening hubbub of Atami; a crowd of people, all in their *yukata*, were taking the air, boys were playing about, geishas were balancing on their *geta*, boys on bicycles were carrying trays full of food, girls were walking about in twos and threes, talking and laughing, there were even a few *riki-sha* (rickshaws); peaceful peasant families were taking the air before their evening rice, there were wealthy families, poor ones, clerks, allied soldiers with their *pam-pam, nouveaux riches* with their enormous American cars.

The gay, carefree crowd of strollers was contained between two rows of shops, restaurants, hotels, *pachinko* halls, shooting booths, with the usual phantasmagoria of neon lights. Gramophones and wireless sets filled the air with competing tunes. Here and there the lights and music faded, the crowd thinned, the houses for some reason were less close to one another. Then you noticed that the moon was rising, and that in a house standing almost invisible in its garden a woman was singing, accompanying herself on the *samisen*, the Japanese lute, the small box of which is always covered with cat's skin. The Japanese are at bottom a complicated, introverted, tense people, but one thing they thoroughly understand is the art of relaxation.

There are many restaurants-hotels-bathing establishments at Atami, ranging from huge affairs with a *roma-buro* (Roman bath), resplendent with marble columns, etc., to smaller and more elegant establishments on the one hand and cheaper and more popular ones on the other. At the place chosen by Giorgio we were shown to the pine room. Generally this is the best room in a Japanese hotel, followed by the bamboo and the plum rooms.

The pine room was big and opened on to the magnificent bay of Atami. Giorgio and his guests were already squatting round a low lacquer table. From his position in relation to the *tokonoma* it was easy to discern who was the most important guest, a young Japanese who had just returned from Europe. Next to Giorgio was a girl of striking beauty.

Introductions followed. It was strange to be wearing kimonos in the presence of Japanese dressed in *sebiro* (western style, from Savile Row).

The conversation was about France, from where Kotaki had just returned. He talked about the forthcoming exhibition of French art in Tokyo, of which he seemed to be one of the organizers. The French have a great reputation in Japan, a country which they take seriously instead of regarding it as the land of paper lanterns and *Madame Butterfly*. Interesting though the conversation was, I confess that I could not take my eyes off the girl. When Giorgio spoke to her, she bowed in the delightful manner peculiar to Japanese women, signifying assent, submission, affection.

There was a shining, morning, virginal quality about the beauty of Tamako ('Jewel'), for that seemed to be her name. If she had been a flower, she would have been a daffodil, if a stone an aquamarine. Though not small—seated she actually appeared to be rather tall—she might have come straight out of a miniature. There are women drawn by bold and charming strokes of nature's brush who are made to be looked at from a certain distance; they are the daughters of Renoir or Degas. Others are the daughters of Bronzino, Van Eyck, or Ku-Kaichi. Tama belonged to the latter type; her complexion, like that of so many Japanese women, reminded one of living porcelain. In a country of great racial uniformity it is difficult to be beautiful; there is little variety of type, of blonde, brunette, redhead, and all the intervening shades. Here things are more subtle, like music on a solo instrument. Tama could not have understood herself more perfectly; she could not have done better than tie her black hair back, like some strange, shining, tropical apple, at the back of her head, and wear that simple, tea-coloured *yukata* of plain country cloth, tied round the waist with an *obi* with bow at the back.

Indefinable details about her dress, her person, her gestures, made me conclude that she belonged to that vast Japanese world referred to by the name *karyu-kai* ('the world of flowers and willows')—the world of transient things; an expression deeply rooted in Buddhism, for which nothing is permanent, all is a fleeting illusion; it is also *par excellence* the world of the geisha, the stage, of affections that change with the season, of memory that fades, like the perfume of a flower pressed between the pages of a forgotten book.

In Japan there are on the one hand women brought up to be wives and mothers, on the other those brought up to be the repositories of the ancient arts, of everything which the Americans include under the term 'social graces'. It is a conception completely alien to our own. Present-day Japanese youth proposes to rebel against this order of things, but change in these matters is invariably very slow, and generations will be required.

'*Sa, o-furo e ikimashoka?*' (Shall we move towards the bath?)

Giorgio's question interrupted my contemplation of Tama, who was talking to the hotel proprietress. The old lady in her ash-coloured kimono must have been telling her something very funny, because she leant back on one arm and laughed, every now and then hiding her face behind her *tamoto*, the long wing of her sleeve.

We men got up, took our *tenugui* (small towels), and moved away.

Field
Strength
Nan, dan, otoko :
Man

The interior of a Japanese hotel is essentially a system of corridors. A basic principle of Far Eastern building is that you obtain increased space, not by increasing a building's size, but by duplicating or multiplying it by a number of pavilions, detached wings, or rooms, arranged in a casual manner on no fixed pattern, which you reach, perhaps, by way of a little bridge or veranda. We went down a little staircase, walked down a slightly sloping veranda, then down another staircase and another corridor, and then crossed a little bridge, where there were fountains, and some small maple trees, and came to the entrance to the big bath with its dressing-rooms. On the door of the first was the ideogram for Man, formed of the two roots 'field' and 'strength', work and soil; on the other was the ideogram for Woman, originally a bending figure attending to house-work.

Jo, onna :
Woman

We left our clothes in a wicker basket and went down to the bath-house, a big apse-shaped hall, in the middle of which was the pool, which was circular, about ten yards across and eighteen inches deep; in the centre warm water gurgled from a rough rock hewn into the shape of a pinnacle. On three sides of the pool there were taps, to enable you to wash before entering the pool, the water of which must always be kept scrupulously clean. There were already a few people in the bath, two men and three or four women, one accompanied by her children, who were splashing about and making an enormous noise.

In the west the nude is accepted in art, but not in ordinary life; in the east it is accepted in life, but not in art. Nowadays statues or paintings of the nude are often to be seen in Japan, but that is a recently imported innovation. The attitude towards the nude involves the deepest emotional levels. That of the west is exceedingly complex. On the one hand there is the result of 2,000 years of repression by the Church, not only in the interest of safeguarding chastity, but also as a consequence of the doctrine that the human body is sacred (the resurrection of the flesh) and therefore must not be exposed, either to desire or to mockery. To this there must be added our highly developed sensitivity to physical ugliness, due to the fact that classical art has accustomed the eye to very definite canons and ideals of beauty. Many westerners who have no moral objection to nudity are nevertheless distressed at the thought that only the young and healthy are beautiful. In Japan many factors weighed and still weigh in the opposite direction. In the first place the primary national religion, Shinto, has always attached the highest importance to ritual purity; hence ablutions (*misogi*) and the bath; secondly, Buddhism, though it holds life to be sacred because of the mysterious workings of *karma,* regards the body as nothing but an illusory outer covering; and finally, the Japanese have never had artistic canons of beauty about the human form; hence the naked human body, even if anything but young and healthy, is not felt to offend objective aesthetic values, and is accepted as naturally as a tree-trunk or the naked body of a horse. The equation nudity-lasciviousness is a purely cultural phenomenon which is to be found in certain civilizations and is typical of the west; there is no necessary link between the two.

'How delightful to be able to take a Japanese bath!' Kotaki exclaimed. 'In Europe I liked everything—the people, the life, the simplicity of relations between friends, even the cooking, to say nothing of the art! There was only one thing I really missed: our baths. In Europe you clean yourself; here you refresh yourself.'

At that moment a glass door opened and Tama appeared, naked, delightfully innocent, holding her *tenugui* in front of her in the gesture of I do not remember which famous Venus, but surely a minor deity of some sacred spring, born of the water, with the perfume of the entrails of the earth still lingering about her. As soon as she noticed that our western eyes were gazing upon her entranced, she vanished into the group of other women, turned her back on us, and started washing the back of her neck.

View of the Divine Mountain

Next morning we climbed the hill that in the course of a few miles mounts nearly 3,000 feet to the Hakone pass to rejoin the Tokaido. The road was abominable, little better than a mule-track. Below us Atami dwindled into the green of the woods, while the sea seemed to grow in size, as it does when one gains height, and the islands near and far assumed a proper place in the perspective. We could plainly see Oshima ('Big Island'), an active volcano rising directly from the waves. Many Japanese suicides jump into its crater.

The countries of the world can be divided into green and yellow. The yellow countries are those blinded with sunlight, with little foliage, like the islands and peninsulas of the Mediterranean, Mexico, Tibet, Australia; the green countries are those carpeted with chlorophyll. Perhaps it should be added that there are also grey countries (smoke, steel, coal) and white ones (ice). Japan belongs definitely to the green category. The climate is damp, and vegetation flourishes.[1] Beneath its mantle of fields and meadows, woods and forests, the bare earth or naked rock is hard to detect. Only in the high mountains (the Japanese Alps, parts of Hokkaido, the volcanoes), and along the coasts of the Inland Sea, where there is little rain, is it possible to see the framework, the skeleton, of the country (Photographs 6, 24).

Japan's wealth of forest is remarkable, as is the fact that man has not destroyed it, as he has in so many other parts of the world; instead, having created a whole civilization based on its products, he preserves it lovingly; a civilization of wood and paper—houses, temples, objects of everyday use, boats, umbrellas, windows, handkerchiefs, books, and newspapers, even clothes; wood and paper are intricately bound up with Japanese civilization in innumerable ways. The forests are mag-

---

[1] *See* Photographs 7 (valley in the Japanese Alps), 8 (Kegon waterfall at Nikko), 26 (Tenryu river in flood).

nificent, the coniferous and deciduous forests of Hokkaido and Tohoku ('the north-east'), the *sugi* (cryptomerias), and the strange, grassy forests of bamboo.

Still climbing, we came to the Atami *toge* (pass) at over 2,000 feet. From here the road continues more or less level for several miles along the flank of a wooded mountainside towards the Hakone pass. The road was asphalt here, and we had to pay a toll. The views change every minute, and they are all on a vast scale, which is rare in Japan, where everything, including mountains, valleys, and bays, is small. We left the gulf of Sagami behind, and ahead of us the gulf of Saruga opened up, with new promontories fading into the blue distance. Sagami and Suruga, Suruga and Kai are names that no longer appear in any official atlas, but are full of fascination to the Japanese ear. In the seventh century the poet Mushimaro wrote:

> Lo! There towers the lofty peak of Fuji
> From between Kai and wave-washed Suruga.
> The clouds of heaven dare not cross it,
> Nor the birds of the air soar above it.
> The snows quench the burning fires,
> The fires consume the falling snow.
> It baffles the tongue, it cannot be named,
> It is a god mysterious.[1]

And there, sure enough, was one of the most famous volcanoes in the world, and perhaps the most beautiful, Fuji.[2]

That delightful and fascinating poet Bashō, who came here to see Fuji on a winter's day towards the end of the seventeenth century, found the view obscured by cloud. In the absence of cars and asphalt roads, coming up here, whether on foot or on horseback, must have been an arduous enterprise, and he must have been grievously disappointed. But he wrote:

Kiri-shigure	A day when Fuji is unseen
Fuji wo minu hi zo	Veiled in misty winter shower—
Omoshiroki.	That day, too, is a joy.

[1] *Manyōshū*, III, 319 (English translation; Nippon Gakujutsu Shinkākai-Tokyo, 1941).
[2] Often called Fujiyama (*yama* means mountain). The Japanese, however, generally call it Fuji-san, reading the ideogram for *yama* in the Chinese fashion. (*See* Photograph 1.)

Apart from the fact that there enter into play here ancient and deep propensities of the Buddhist-nurtured oriental mind, which rates the suggestion of beauty higher than its possession by the senses; that there is a subtle play between appearance and non-appearance, between intangible realities and tangible illusions, how the poet's words hit the mark even if taken in the objective, western sense! Fuji is in fact one of those focal points of nature where things become endowed with personalities; its beauties are inexhaustible; it has its own beauty from every angle, at every time of day, in every light, even on a grey day, when it is hidden by rain. But today was a calm, serene, summer day, and the mountain rose from the haze that covers the endless plain like a being suspended in the sky, acquiring a deeper blue as its sides converged towards the summit.

In Japan there is always a miraculous quality about a fine summer day. The effect of the monsoons is that the clouds arrive laden with humidity from the huge pastures of the Pacific, and end by wheeling, merging with each other, stopping, and continually depositing their moisture over the Japanese archipelago. A fine summer day therefore always has about it a quality of magic, precarious equilibrium; it is like an old wine with a deposit at the bottom which the slightest movement will disturb, clouding the whole. It was one of those days today; before midday dark patches were to be seen on the horizon round which a ceiling of cloud would inevitably form later.

Certainly there are many other viewpoints from which the great mountain seems taller, more impressive, even more elegant, than from here. I think of winter evenings on the north side of the volcano, on the banks of the five lakes, when its summit reflected the last crimson light of the shy January sun and looked glassy and remote, like a mysterious and shining treasure buried in ice; or of spring days in the country at its foot, surrounded by cherry blossom, with the white summit glittering above; or summer days by the sea, with the waves of the Pacific breaking wearily on the sands of Miho-no-Matsubara after their long journey. Rows of twisted old pines followed the gentle curves of the coast; all the lines converged to a point on the horizon where other lines in another dimension took up the rhythm that led to the top of Fuji. Meanwhile every wave that broke created a momentary mirror on the beach in which Fuji appeared reflected upside down like a mirage.

So much for the physical Fuji, the mountain in its biological, mineral, atmospheric beauty, which would enchant even a Martian who had the good fortune to land in this part of the world. There is also another Fuji, the Fuji that lives in the hearts and minds, the history, of the Japanese. Whenever a Japanese looks at the mountain the two converge, producing an emotion the depth of which we spectators from a distant land can scarcely hope to understand. Italy, for instance, has nothing to compare with Fuji, that is to say, a meeting-place of heaven and earth, a place of supreme physical beauty which is at the same time a reminder of the invisible powers and of the nation's most ancient roots; Olympus may have had something of the same quality for the Greeks.

It is not difficult to imagine the sense of awe that must have filled the minds of the remote ancestors of the Japanese when they reached these shores and first set eyes on Fuji, then an active volcano. Surely from the first it must have seemed to them a divine thing, a god or the seat of a god. Eastern thought, so different from that of the west, dislikes subtle distinctions that kill the life and aura of sacred things. Sometimes the mountain is a god (*kami*), sometimes the seat of a god, or rather goddess, Konohana-Sakuya-Hime, the daughter of the god of mountains, to whom many shrines are dedicated, not only on Fuji, but elsewhere in Japan as well.

When the Japanese started populating the area round Fuji, probably about the beginning of our era, they found there the ancestors of the Ainu. The two peoples lived for centuries in a more or less permanent state of war, which can be said to be ending only now with the total extinction of the strange and mysterious aborigines of white race. Gradually the Japanese pushed the *emishi* or *ebisu*, as the Ainu were then called, northwards. These people, who for some obscure reason never succeeded in raising themselves above the most primitive level of civilization, left behind them traces of two kinds: pottery of the *jōmon-doki* (cord pattern) type, which is to be found everywhere in the south of the Japanese archipelago, and many place-names.

Just as the Celts in the course of centuries were pushed back to the western extremities and outlying islands of Europe, leaving behind them only certain place-names, such as London, Milan, Belgrade, so in the Japanese archipelago the former realm of the Ainu is testified to by a large number of place-names which have no meaning in Japanese, but a very definite meaning, and one often in perfect harmony with the nature of the site, in the aboriginal language. The name Fuji is part of this heritage. In Japanese it is written in various ways; sometimes with two characters standing for 'not-two', *i.e.,* 'no other like it', 'unparalleled', or 'not death', *i.e.,* 'immortal'. Normally, however, two characters are used meaning 'treasure' and 'samurai', but this is a case of what the Japanese call *ateji,* 'subsequently ascribed' ideograms, phonetical-etymological interpretations *a posteriori (prata quia sunt parata).* In Ainu Huchi, or Fuchi, is the name of the goddess of fire and of the hearth, an appropriate name for a volcano. Chamberlain points out that from the

Fu-
Prosperity,
riches

Ji
Warrior,
samurai

phonetic point of view it would be more logical to think of the Ainu word *push,* meaning 'to rise violently', referring, not to the mountain, but to the river Fujisawa, a swift and dangerous stream which rises from the volcano, cuts across the Tokaido, and in ancient times constituted a formidable obstacle to travellers. The Ainu in fact used to give names to rivers rather than to mountains, and the transformation from *push* to *Fuzi,* as Fuji seems to have been pronounced in ancient times in Japanese, would agree better with the phonetic mutations usual between the two languages. The question is not yet settled, but most scholars at any rate agree that the name Fuji is of Ainu origin.

The Japanese have not ceased to be fascinated by the mountain since their first encounter with it in the distant past. It runs like a golden thread through their literature and art, and through the ordinary life of the people. It is easy to compile anthologies of prose and verse devoted to Fuji, and it has often been done, from the eighth-century *Manyōshū* ('Collection of the Ten Thousand Leaves') to collections of modern times, ranging from the murmurs of courtly aesthetes to outpourings of the peasant mind. Similarly, in the field of art the gamut includes the delicate visions of Kano Tsunenobu and Maruyama Okyo (eighteenth century), the prints of Hokusai (1760–1849), with his *Fuji Hyakkei* ('A Hundred Views of Fuji'), those of Hiroshige, with his thirty-six views of the mountain, and the work of the photographers of the present day.

Fuji is one of the twenty national parks; the park includes the

Hakone mountains, with their lakes, hot springs, woods, and waterfalls. The number of these parks, which will certainly increase in the future, is a testimonial to the Japanese love of nature. In summer more than 100,000 people climb Fuji. Between July 1 and August 31 its slopes look from the air like those of a huge ant-heap, with two lines of little black dots, one winding slowly upwards and the other winding swiftly and steeply downward, because you come down at speed on the sandy surface. I should really have said white dots, because most of the climbers wear white, the traditional pilgrim's colour.

At the end of the long climb the traveller finds: (a) if there is no cloud, a marvellous view from the Japanese Alps to the Pacific; (b) a small shrine dedicated to the *kami*; (c) an important meteorological station; (d) two cold-water springs, that of Shining Gold (*Kinmei-sui*) and of Shining Silver (*Ginmei-sui*); (e) a small post office from which post-cards may be sent; (f) an enormous number of discarded straw sandals and wooden boxes (which contained *bento,* refreshments) lying about everywhere, and other, less innocent, traces of the passage of this vast flood of humanity.

The crater of the volcano is not very spectacular; unlike Etna, for example, it does not pour forth smoke and acrid vapours, it does not glow or flash at night, no deep rumblings or explosions are to be heard, and the rocks are not encrusted with strange minerals of alchemistic colours. It is, however, a solemn, academic kind of inferno, a deep, cold, bare, and inhospitable pit with straight sides of dark rock.

Here and there around the crater are heaps of small stones deposited by pilgrims which have accumulated over the centuries. According to an ancient myth, the souls of dead children have the grievous task of filling up with stones the *saino kawara,* the Buddhist Styx. Pilgrims therefore have a thought for them, and add their stones to the pile.

Mishima: Local Colour and Local Horror

Before midday we reached the Hakone pass, 'the gate of Kwanto', the point of entry for the traveller coming from Kyoto, of exit for the traveller going east, as we were. This is a famous place in Japanese history. As all travellers along the Tokaido necessarily used the pass, a barrier was inevitably erected and a toll exacted from them. For a long time the right to levy it belonged to one of the big temples of Kamakura, the Engaku-ji. After the unification of Japan in 1600 the Hakone barrier became an integral part of the system set up by the Tokugawa shoguns to protect themselves against possible revolts. Custody of the Hakone barrier was entrusted to the Okubo family, the lords of Odawara, the little town where we left the Tokaido the other day to make for Atami.

The chief of the many tasks entrusted to these faithful vassals of the Tokugawa was expressed in the phrase 'de-onna, irideppo' (watch for women leaving and muskets entering). The Tokugawa had devised a cunning scheme called *sankin kōtai* for keeping the 262 feudal lords in check. For a year, or part of a year, the lord himself had to live at Yedo, the present Tokyo, and when he was not there his family had to be. His loyalty was thus guaranteed by the presence of hostages in this gilded cage. It was assumed that a baron with rebellion in mind would first of all try to get his womenfolk out and then try to get in muskets with which to arm his followers. The examination of caravans at Hakone was therefore extremely strict.

We were now descending from what once was Sagami to what once was Suruga. It should be recalled that in the enthusiasm for change after 1868 the whole face of Japan was altered, including even geographical names. The *kuni* (territories) of the feudal age were transformed into *ken* (prefectures), now reduced in number to forty-six.[1] This had an unexpected literary consequence; the whole country is covered with a network of obsolete names which survive beneath the surface of contemporary names and are capable of being used with powerful evocative effect. There are examples of this in Italy—Trinacria, Etruria, Esperia, etc., but in Japan there is a whole geography of them. We left the Hakone *toge* behind, and drove happily downhill. The ideogram for *toge* (pass) is incidentally one of the most picturesque; it is 'mountain-up-down'; also it is one of the few of native origin, not taken over from the Chinese.

The road, which was asphalt up to the pass, was now concrete. For a time all went well, but then troubles began. An old concrete road neglected becomes a formidable obstacle; the blocks break, bend, flake, and between one and the next chasms, cavities, steps, appear, which no

[1] Some administrative units have special names: Tokyo is a *to* (metropolitan area), Kyoto and Osaka are *fu* (urban prefectures), Hokkaido is a *do* (in this case 'territory').

rain wears away. Every irregularity of surface retains its sharp edges for years; a car bounces over them in an alarming manner. We often had to slow down to walking pace, and even then were badly shaken up.

After an hour of this we reached Mishima, 'the Three Islands'; perhaps 'islands' here stand for 'hills'. The town stands at the foot of three steep hills which rise from the plain like the keels of three upturned boats. It occurs to me that the town of Fukushima in north Japan, 'the isle of felicity', lies at the foot of a rocky height that rises like an island in the middle of a valley.

Mountain

Up

Down

Toge, pass

Nowadays the traffic rushes through Mishima, raising clouds of dust; it is a place like any other. In the old days, before the building of the railway tunnel through the Hakone mountains, travellers ate, drank, rested, and slept here before or after the long climb over the pass. The easy women of Mishima must have been famous; an old muleteers' song said:

> Smoke pours from the top of Fuji;
> Up here nobody knows why
> But down there the girls of Mishima, burning with love,
> Know why. . . .

In those days, and up till 1707, the year of its last eruption, there must have been a constant plume of smoke over Fuji.

Yaji and Kita, the two heroes of the *Hizakurige*, stopped for the night at Mishima, 'where the girls at the inns on both sides of the road began their usual chorus of "Walk in! Walk in!" '[1]

   ' "Don't catch hold of me," said Yagi to one of the girls who caught hold of his sleeve. "Let go and I'll stop here."
   "Well, there then," said the girl, letting go.
   "Wouldn't you like to catch me?" said Yaji.
   But in eluding the girl he bumped into a blind shampooer.

[1] JIPPENSHA IKKU, *Hizakurige*, English translation, Tokyo, 1942, p. 37.

"Oh, oh!" cried the blind man. "Can't you see I'm blind, you fool? . . ."

"Have some spirit," called another man. "Here's the stuff that'll make your eyes go round in your head."

"Now we've got away from there, let's stop here," said Kita.

"Please come in," said the landlady. "San, San, guests have come."

"Welcome, gentlemen," said the landlord. "How many may there be in your company?"

"Six, counting our shadows," said Yaji.'

And so it goes on for pages and pages.

When we reached Mishima it was late, and we were hungry. We stopped, and asked for *care raisu* (curried rice) at one of those monstrous local taverns in which all the styles of history seem to have been distilled into a final residue of hideousness. Sensitive and discriminating as the Japanese are when they move within the orbit of their own civilization, they become barbarians when they renounce their past and mimic foreign ways; that is particularly the case in the first period, before they have digested them. Not that the Japanese are in any way exceptional in this; it is a universal rule. Renouncing a civilization means renouncing civilization. It may perhaps be possible for an individual, by assiduous study and humble use of his intelligence, to penetrate into a world alien to his own and to take part in two or more civilizations, but on a social scale integration takes place extremely slowly. Only after several generations does a new inner harmony arise, with its own equilibrium, its own aesthetics, its own style.

All this would happen with us too, but for the fact that we are in a special situation; the western happens for the time being to be the dominant civilization in the world; wherever we go, we take with us customs, things, ideas, which others take over from us. With us an occasional individual, like Gauguin, seeks escape into another cultural environment, but there are no groups of any consequence who find themselves in such a special situation. Nevertheless I have noticed many times that westerners who adopt Japanese living habits do things just as barbarous as the Japanese do the other way about. Only too often you enter a western house in Japan and find kimonos worn with shoes,

Japanese rice dishes eaten with spoon and fork instead of with chopsticks, *tatami* on which people walk as if they were a floor, beds with
futon instead of mattresses; in other words dissociated elements of one
civilization mixed at random with those of another.

As we ate our *care raisu* on crude white plates (while on a shelf
I noticed some *domburi,* dark plates decorated with marvellously assured
Japanese country taste in simple designs and colours), I looked about
me. What barbaric squalor! In the first place, the bare concrete floor was
covered with congealed mud. When the Japanese abandon *tatami,* the
straw mats on which they walk with bare feet, they are left with a
psychological void. The floor, not being *tatami,* is merely an extension
of the street; the street brought into the house.

Two unprepossessing girls, both oozing sex, dragged their wooden
sandals *(geta)* about noisily and gracelessly. As soon as we entered, the
fatter of the two, who wore trousers of a revolting green colour and
a violet blouse, said to the other: 'They are foreigners, let us put on that
record,' and waddled over into a corner where there was a gramophone.
Once upon a time Mary Ford had sung 'Johnnie is the Boy for Me', but
a lot of things must have happened to poor Johnnie since then. The
record was covered with scratches, dust, grease, and a raucous loudspeaker started producing a bedlam of sound that entered our ears like
ground glass.

The two girls sat down and looked at us. Every now and then the
fat one smiled, displaying a mouthful of gold teeth. Her colleague, who
also wore trousers and blouse, had on an apron which might once have
been white, but now resembled that of a particularly bloodthirsty
surgeon who had been carrying out a large number of particularly
violent operations. The fact that she was eating a piece of melon reassured me, however; the red stains might have been of vegetable origin.
On the wall were price-lists of various drinks *(uiski, remonsoda)* and pictures torn from magazines—some by no means ugly nudes (no doubt
the proprietor's intention was to reflect a certain western refinement)
and landscapes (New England?).

The fat girl came over to serve us, smiling with all her gold teeth.
We ordered a *bifu-katsu,* a steak.

'Where are you going?' the girl said when she came back with the
order. Kyoto, we told her.

She told us that Kyoto was her birthplace, and she had lived there as a little girl. What a lovely place! Then her father had taken a job in a Yokohama factory, and the war had come, and their house had been destroyed in one of the first raids, before the evacuation of civilians had begun, and only her brother and she had survived. *Shikataganai* (it couldn't be helped). Now her brother was studying at the university. . . .

She said no more, but I realized that she must be keeping him. Sisters who keep their brothers at the university by the hardest and most menial work, or by selling their own bodies, are a classic theme in Japanese life.

'She was born at Kyoto too,' the woman went on, referring to her companion, whose misfortunes she set about describing. The other girl stood for a while listening with bent head, her black hair falling untidily over her shoulders. Suddenly she raised her head, her eyes flashed, and she shouted: '*Yoshina-yo!*' (Stop!) The fat girl went on, laughing: 'Yes, you were left pregnant by a Negro. . . .' At that the thin girl flung herself at her, seized her by the hair, shouting: '*Yoshina-yo! yoshina-yo!*' (Stop! stop!) We were just going to separate them when a door opened and a thick-set, middle-aged man, dressed more or less like a chef, appeared. He said nothing, but looked at the girls angrily. Terrified, they slunk back to their seats, like dogs fearing the whip.

Sip of Jewel Dew

We left Mishima much shaken by this incident, and drove on in silence. Then the beauty of the country distracted us.

Our progress was slow, for we had to pass through many villages strung out along the road, examples of the ribbon development which the Germans call *Strassendörfer*. We passed through Shimizu and came to Shizuoka, a provincial capital with nearly 250,000 inhabitants, hideous as nearly all Japanese towns are hideous, but rich in memories of Iyeyasu, the first of the Tokugawa shoguns. Iyeyasu, with Oda Nobunaga and Toyotomi Hideyoshi, is considered one of the three founders of modern Japan; he preferred Shizuoka to all his other residences, and died there in 1616. Shizuoka (then called Sumpu) was famous for the big castle called 'the floating island', but nothing of it remains but the moats and some of the walls.

One reason why Shizuoka is so ugly is that it was almost completely destroyed by fire in 1939 and by air-raids in 1945, and was rebuilt in the most revolting commercial hybrid style. However, the country all round is among the most beautiful in Japan. In general it is true that, while the overall impression created by a Japanese town is a settlement of huts, a fair-ground, a temporary encampment, the impression given by the country is one of beauty, civilization, care.

The geological structure of the archipelago plays its part in all this. The islands, though composed of ancient rock, are of recent (tertiary) emergence and rise sharply, suddenly, and steeply; rounded hills are rare. The constant theme of the Japanese landscape is steep mountains enclosing narrow, winding valleys or small, irregular plains. It is a land of recesses and corners, of circumscribed but ever-changing views; a world of enchanting nooks and crannies, with surprises at every turn.

The work of man has accentuated the mountain-valley contrast. For centuries past every inch of cultivable land has been levelled, divided up, irrigated, often terraced, to grow rice, on which the whole economic and social life of the Japanese people is based. Every valley is an intensely cultivated garden, and in the midst of these gardens men make their homes, generally in villages. The houses vary from region to region, but they are nearly always beautiful, with big, thatched roofs that keep them warm in winter and cool in summer (Photograph 17). Near the houses there are nearly always groups of tall trees, *sugi*, rather like cypresses, but of a more gentle green and less solemn and funereal. Dotted about here and there are small shrines, each with its own little wood, or big Buddhist temples, each with a big roof gently curving like a petrified, silvery wave.

The mountains, on the other hand, really are mountains, always. At the edge of the plain and the rice-fields the forest begins, and climbs either all the way to the summit or up to the rocks. It is rare to see cultivated fields on the slopes, just as it is rare to see a house on the mountain-side; you never find houses on hill-tops, the favourite spots for building castles, villages, and inhabited places throughout the Mediterranean world.

Around Shizuoka the country is particularly well cared for. We were in a rich plain bounded by mountains to the west and the ocean to the south, hence sunny and well protected. The houses are scattered

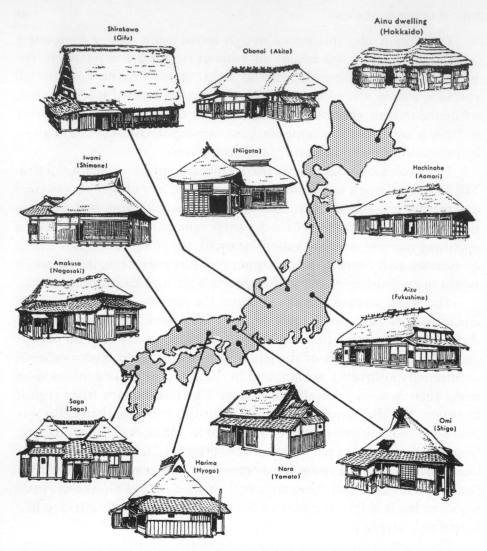

Shirakawa
(Gifu)

Obonai (Akita)

Ainu dwelling
(Hokkaido)

Iwami
(Shimane)

(Niigata)

Hachinohe
(Aomori)

Amakusa
(Nagasaki)

Aizu
(Fukushima)

Saga
(Saga)

Omi
(Shiga)

Harima
(Hyogo)

Nara
(Yamato)

Japanese rural houses

(Drawing by Makino Yone)

about among the rice-fields, and each is in the midst of a small garden surrounded by a high green hedge, trimmed and squared off with the care that English gardeners give to their box-hedges. In Japan these hedges have a poetical name, *ikegaki* ('living walls' or 'living curtains'). Occasionally you see them elsewhere in Japan, but as a typical feature of the landscape I recall them only here near Shizuoka, and at Izumo in the province of Shimane (Photograph 16); both these areas include some of the loveliest countryside in Japan.

As soon as we left the plain for the hills all the cultivable land was occupied by tea gardens. The plants grew in dotted lines up and down the valleys and hillsides. This is, in fact, one of the few examples of hillside cultivation in Japan.

We succumbed to the temptation to stop and call on a family of tea-planters. In these parts the surface of the Tokaido was really abominable; we had left the asphalt far behind, and the macadam was full of potholes. As it had not rained for several days, every vehicle raised an enormous cloud of dust. Our car was white with it, and the fields beside the road were covered in it.

The house was well built; on two sides of it were agricultural implements and baskets. On the *engawa,* the veranda about four feet above ground-level which runs along the whole frontage of a Japanese house, a wrinkled little old woman was squatting, cleaning rice.

As soon as she heard us speak Japanese the slight alarm with which she watched us get out of the car vanished. She smiled, which made her face more wrinkled than ever, and turned her eyes into two almost invisible slits. Then she rose and invited us to enter, apologizing at having to receive honourable guests in such a poor place. She fetched two *zabuton, i.e.,* the flat, square cushions on which you sit; guests must always be offered these. Then she again vanished into the house, to reappear a few moments later with the tea; it was from their own fields, she explained, and she apologized for its poor quality, but the whole crop had recently been sent to market, and this was all that was left.

We talked to the old lady for a long time; she asked us where we were going, why we were travelling, and a whole heap of other questions, and we asked her about the cultivation of the tea that was her wealth and that of her family.

In a sense tea plays a part in Japanese life similar to that of wine in the west. *Saké* might seem a more natural comparison, but it has not the same associations. In classical antiquity wine was associated with the mysteries of Dionysus and Bacchus; Christianity changed the theme, introducing it into the sacraments. Tea has ancient links with Buddhism, though it has not the antiquity of wine, even in China.

The *Tsi Min Yao Shu*, an agricultural treatise dating from the fifth century A.D., does not mention tea, nor does Marco Polo, but that is probably because its use originated in south China and may not have reached the territory of Kublai Khan. In Japan tea has been known for more than a thousand years. For several centuries it made little headway; it was drunk only at court and by a restricted circle of nobles and high Buddhist dignitaries. In the thirteenth century a big impulse was given to tea-drinking by the Abbot Myoe, of the monastery of Toganō, between Nara and Kyoto, who established the Uji tea plantations which are still the headquarters of Japanese tea production. Every year a service is held in a local temple and tea is offered to the spirit of the Abbot Myoe. 'Tea keeps the mind fresh but does not intoxicate,' Suzuki observes. 'It has qualities naturally to be appreciated by scholars and monks.'[1] 'Tea kept the mind wakeful and alert for midnight devotion and was therefore drunk as an accompaniment to Buddhist services.'[2]

Two boys of seven or eight came back from school and looked at us in mute astonishment; the old woman sent them to fetch their father, who, she explained, knew all about tea. The family had come originally from Uji, where tea was really appreciated; here the interest was only commercial. The sound of *geta* behind us announced the arrival of her son, who appeared in shorts, bare-chested and sunburnt, with a lock of grey hair over one eye. His appearance was prepossessing. He bowed low to us, and we responded in accordance with the requirements of etiquette.

When all these had been fulfilled we resumed our seats. He told us that he had spent four years in China, that he had returned home after the war, that his son was studying medicine at the University of Osaka. He said he would like to learn English, but there was no one to teach him in this part of the world. We suggested gramophone records; he seemed sufficiently well off to be able to afford the outlay. His affability

[1] D. T. SUZUKI, *Zen Buddhism and its Influence on Japanese Culture*, Kyoto, 1938.
[2] SIR CHARLES ELIOT, *Japanese Buddhism*, London, 1935.

and his freedom from the usual Japanese inhibitions betrayed the fact that he had spent a considerable time abroad and had lived among people of different nationalities. He was passionate about tea, about which he was exceedingly well informed; seeing that we were interested, he went on talking about it. Every now and then he vanished into the kitchen and reappeared with a book or a trade paper, and he brought us newly gathered leaves to illustrate the methods of working.

Three different products can be obtained from the leaves of the same plant by using different methods. Two of these are rarely seen in Europe. The first is the so-called *usu-cha* ('subtle tea'), a fine powder extracted by immersing the youngest leaves in hot water, which yields a strange, pea-green brew; it has a strong, stimulating effect, and is drunk at the tea ceremony, or on occasions on which it is desired to celebrate in a particularly solemn manner. The second is common green tea obtained by steaming the leaves and then drying them in warmth. In Japan this kind of tea is drunk practically like water; a Japanese will drink dozens of cups of it daily, on every conceivable occasion, on entering an office, paying a visit, at home, even in shops at which he is a regular customer. The third type is the ordinary tea known in Europe, called *ko-cha* (red tea); unlike the other two types, the leaves are made to ferment as soon as they are gathered, which gives them a special colour and aroma.

Our host explained that at Uji things were quite different from what they were here. His grandfather's brothers had remained at Uji, and one of his ancestors had been employed in the special court office that supervised all the ceremonies for the preparation of tea for the imperial household. How things had changed! Now he would offer us a special *gyokuro* ('jewel dew') of the previous year, a thing of no account, but perhaps we might enjoy it. . . .

An hour later we were still sitting on the *engawa*, surrounded by about twenty little cups of various shapes and sizes, while our host with undiminished enthusiasm made us taste more and more varieties of tea, analysing with a connoisseur's discrimination their resemblances and differences, the taste and aroma that remained on the palate and in the nostrils. He went through the whole gamut of the *sen-cha*, and then of the more humble *ban-cha*, and he did not omit the crude country teas, the *hiboshi*, *kamairi*, and *kuroguchi*, which ended by seeming at least as interesting in this enthusiastic atmosphere, and in any case constituted a base from which it was possible to advance to the sublimity of the 'jewel dew'.

The sun was setting when we at last resumed our journey towards Kyoto. Never have I met such discriminating enthusiasm as had been displayed by our host, except for wine in France. The road was bad, stony, dusty, and full of potholes. We met lorries driven in the most outrageous manner. In Japan, as in England and Sweden, you drive on the left, but Japanese lorry-drivers drive on the side that suits them; they know that in an accident the other party will come off worse. This discloses an unpleasant side of the Japanese character, fully conveyed by the Japanese word *ibaru*, which means throwing your weight about.

The fundamental virtue taught by the ethics of the feudal age was loyalty; the Japanese have so consistently shown themselves capable of heroism in observing it as to make it seem almost normal. But—apart from what might be derived from Buddhism and Confucianism—there were few precepts that taught pity for the weak, protection for the defenceless. The samurai was always ready to disembowel himself because of a slight done to his lord, but claimed the right to test the sharpness of his sword on the first beggar he met in the street. Valignani, an Italian Jesuit, wrote in the sixteenth century:

'They are ready to kill those subject to them on the slightest of pretexts, and think no more of cutting a man in half than of doing so to a dog; many of them, chancing to meet some unfortunate, will cut him in half solely to test the edge of their *katana*.'[1]

Many centuries are needed to change deep-seated national characteristics. In Japan today the strong still exploit the weak if there is no intervention from above to stop them; from below nobody lifts a finger, but everybody bows and accepts; it is sufficient for the strong to raise his voice. A Japanese lorry-driver in charge of a huge vehicle loaded with badly secured sacks, bearing down on you like an avalanche on the wrong side of the road to avoid the potholes, is in reality nothing but a poor devil who for a brief hour feels himself to be a *daimyo*, a prince; his behaviour is easy to explain, but hard to forgive.

[1] P. TACCHI-VENTURI, *Il Carattere dei Giapponesi secondo i Missionari del Secolo XVI*, Rome, 1937, p. 50.

We had to make a détour—we hoped that perhaps they were repairing a stretch of the Tokaido—with the result that we found ourselves at Yaizu, a big fishing village on Suruga bay. As we entered it we
had a puncture, and stopped to have it repaired. We approached some
people standing in the middle of the road. A youth answered our questions very frostily. 'Down there, can't you see?' he said. There, sure
enough, was the garage. The proprietor received us coldly too. After
a little he said: '*Amerika-jin kai*' (Are you American?) '*Ie, Itari-jin desu*' (No, we
are Italian), we answered. Normally the reactions to this last piece of
information are varied and curious. A Tokyo taxi-driver, for instance,
stopped, got out, and nearly embraced us, exclaiming: '*Mussorini, Chyano,
sangokudomei*' (Mussolini, Ciano, triple alliance!), not realizing that a lot
of water had flowed under the bridges since his youth in 1939. Others
would say they did not like us, because it was our fault that they had
lost the war, for we had unscrupulously deceived them, pretending to
be strong when we were weak, etc. Others had listened to Communist
propaganda, and believed Italy to be a predominantly Communist
country, and others again sympathized with us, on the ground that we
too had foreign masters in the house. There were also those who congratulated us on having shaken off the past, carried out a rapid reconstruction, and become a pillar of democracy; and those who looked at
us with a blank and sorrowful air, as if to say: What? Another country
of which nobody has ever heard? The fact is that the Japanese, both
educated and otherwise, are normally pretty well informed about
America and Russia, Britain and France, but know exceedingly little
about Italy.

This time the information that we were Italian left the situation
unchanged. The garage proprietor, a big, strong man who had just
emerged flushed from the bath, muttered an '*Ah so ka*' (Oh, yes?) A few
minutes later a small boy arrived with a bundle of newspapers and flung
one into the garage. The man stopped his work to pick it up, avidly
read a few lines, and flung it away. '*Naka naka naoranai, dame da,*' he said.
(There's no hope, he won't get better, it's a bad business!)

Then we understood. We had stopped at the village from which a few
months earlier the fishing-boat *Lucky Dragon* had left for the southern

125

seas. On March 1, 1954, a hydrogen bomb was exploded at the Bikini atoll, and a few hours later a shower of fine white dust fell on the *Lucky Dragon,* which was eighty miles away and well outside the danger area announced by the American authorites. No one on board realized that this was radioactive fall-out. Soon the whole crew fell ill, and the master of the *Lucky Dragon* decided to return to Yaizu. The sick were sent to hospital in Tokyo, where their condition deteriorated. The radioactive dust had got into their hair and clothing, it had lain about the ship and continued to act on their ill-protected organs, they had breathed it in and eaten food contaminated by it.

The gravest case was that of Kuboyama, the wireless operator, and it was with his fate that the village of Yaizu was now concerned. He had recently got worse, and it seemed that only a miracle could save him; it was the latest medical bulletin about him that the garage proprietor read in the newspaper. He finished mending the puncture, and advised us to take the tyre and go on our way; there were hot-headed people in these parts, and you never knew. . . . No doubt he was right; it would have been stupid to irritate these people by our presence. In moments of anger subtle distinctions between westerners of different types might be apt to disappear, for we were all *gai-jin* ('people from outside', foreigners).

A few months later the unfortunate Kuboyama died.

Indestructible Fortress

It was late, and we were tired. The road was dusty, bumpy, and full of potholes, there were innumerable lorries which never dimmed their lights, the villages were long and narrow. We drove on like automata. We came to Iwata, Hamamatsu (which in daylight is so beautiful with its lagoons and pines), Toyohashi, Okazaki, and at last Nagoya. It was very late. It is always best to avoid western-style hotels; they are dear and, with one or two exceptions in Tokyo and Kyoto, pretentious and bad. It is always possible to find a Japanese hotel which is clean and pleasant. A bent old man advised us to go to the Kamome (the 'Seagull'), which did not disappoint us.

Nagoya is one of the five biggest towns in Japan; it has more than a million inhabitants. It was here that the Tokugawa established their

power at the end of the sixteenth century; and until 1945, when it was
destroyed in the air-raids, it was the site of one of the biggest and tallest
castles in Japan, built by order of Tokugawa Iyeyasu in 1610. The huge
stones used are said to have been brought directly from the quarry to
the place where they were to be used without ever touching the ground;
this, according to a belief of the time, guaranteed the indestructibility
of the fortress. Evidently the guarantee applied only to terrestrial
attacks; attacks from air were not foreseen by the seers of those distant
days.

But of Nagoya we shall speak later. It was here that we spent two
years of internment during the war.

4

Wooden Pavilions in the Sacred Wood

Precision Instrument-Making and Mythology

WHILE I was having breakfast this morning, wearing a *yukata* through which the cool air penetrated pleasingly, squatting on the *tatami* in front of a lacquered wooden tray full of little cups and plates with rice, fish, seaweed, soya, eggs, and fruit, the door opened and a distinguished-looking gentleman of about thirty entered and introduced himself, with much bowing and polite words of greeting. He was dressed in European style, and had two cameras slung over his shoulder.

Mr. Tsurugi had heard that I was interested in photography, in which he was greatly interested himself, that was the reason for his visit; in fact he had a small workshop in which he made cameras.

I noticed that he had with him a camera of a most interesting kind, the kind of which I had always dreamt. It had a rotating turret fitted with three lenses, one wide-angle, one ordinary, and one long-distance; you merely rotated the turret to select the lens required. But that was not all; the camera had two rollers, one for black-and-white and the other for colour film. A true portent, the camera of the future!

Mr. Tsurugi explained that it was a rather crude, home-made instrument, but he had taken out the necessary patents, and would soon start production in earnest. His place was near Osaka, between Osaka and Kyoto, a beautiful spot. '*Dozo asobi-ni irasshai*' (Please come there for rest and refreshment), he said (the word *asobu* is strictly untranslatable).

I offered my guest tea. We talked at length about cameras, lenses, and films. I showed him a Pancinor Berthiot, which he examined with the greatest interest. In conclusion he said that he was on a tour taking photographs for publicity purposes; and, as he was here, he proposed to take advantage of the opportunity of visiting the honourable gods before their departure.

'Before their departure?'

'Yes, don't you remember? October, *kami-na-zuki*, the month without gods.'

'Of course I had forgotten, they all go to Izumo for a month's family reunion!'

'Yes, they go there every year. Not till November do they return to their places in the various shrines of Japan.'[1]

In Prehistoric Style

Half an hour later—it might have been about seven o'clock—the early morning sunshine was flooding the street. At that hour all is fresh and smiling in Japan. People are up and about; the women are busy with the housework; the men are washing or walking about with a *tenugui* (small towel) round their neck; boys and girls are playing *ishi-keri*, jumping on one leg from circle to circle chalked on the ground. In Japan everything closely follows the course of the sun; houses are build in such a fashion that it is difficult to find a dark corner when night has gone. The Japanese are great admirers of the dawn; their art and literature are full of its praises. This is a cultural phenomenon, comparable with our admiration of the sunset. We think we admire the sunset because it is beautiful; in reality we admire it because we have been taught to do so. In Japan, except for a few students who have steeped themselves in western romanticism, nobody takes any notice of sunset; in fact it is considered sad, and of bad augury.

At Ise, to which we made our way, there are two places of particular veneration, the Geku and the Naiku, the Outer and the Inner Shrine. The former is dedicated to Toyouke-Omikami, the goddess of rich

---

[1] This is an ancient and very widespread belief. The well-known historian Hirata Atsutane (1776–1843) suggests, however, that *kami-na-zuki* is simply a corruption of *kami-namezuki*, 'month of divine tasting', *i.e.*, of the new rice crop, a suggestion accepted by ASTON, *Shinto*, London, 1905, p. 145. It is often to be remarked that the more modern and better-educated the Japanese are, the less they know about their ancient traditions, which they dismiss as useless and outmoded. This frequently results in an incongruous acceptance of the most absurd old wives' tales side by side with a spaceman's outlook on life. Incidentally the same phenomenon is often to be found in the west.

harvests, and the latter to Amaterasu-Omikami, the goddess shining in the sky, *i.e.,* the sun. The two are a few miles apart, in an area of wooded hills and clear streams that runs glittering along channels of bright stones.

After passing the first of the three gateways *(torii)* normally to be found along the approach to every Shinto shrine, we found ourselves in a wood of marvellous antiquity and stupendous vigour. A gently winding, gravelled avenue was flanked on either side by cryptomerias, which are similar to cypresses, but of a size no cypress ever reaches. There were many people, almost a crowd: mothers with children on their backs, leading by the hand other children, with balls, dolls, bags of sweets; peasants in all sorts of clothing, from pure traditional to impure western style, with every conceivable variation in between (as in Photographs 125, 126, 127); students and school children; old men with young *mekake* ('pendants from the eyes', *i.e.,* mistresses), and geishas with wealthy patrons; serious business men from Osaka, the Japanese Manchester; learned professors and distinguished civil servants, looking a trifle pompous and starched, as was appropriate in such a place; and every now and then a priest passed in his ancient robes of bright, plain colours.

Where were all these people going? Where did all these avenues lead? What should we find hidden in the wood? We were in the east, and should be prepared for the strange, the fantastic, perhaps the monstrous. Would there be a terraced hill covered with sculpture, as at Barabudur? Or a temple in the form of a huge human face smiling enigmatically, as at Angkor-Thom or Bayon? Or a padoga from which two vividly painted eyes look at you, as at Gyantse in Tibet; or two rows of impressive statues of real or fantastic animals, as at the Ming tombs? Or caves carved out of the rock and painted with disturbing pictures, as at Ajanta? Or pinnacles interwoven with marvellous and terrible visions of metamorphoses, couplings, strange, symbolical voluptuousness, as at Tanjore? Should we find a palace, a column, a tower, a monument?

We found none of these things. Instead, the object of supreme veneration to nearly 100 million Japanese at work in the fields, at sea, in the air, in the mountains, in the docks at Yokohama, in the factories of Kawasaki or the laboratories of Osaka; in the big shops along the Ginza, in the universities, the mines, banks, offices, and all the other

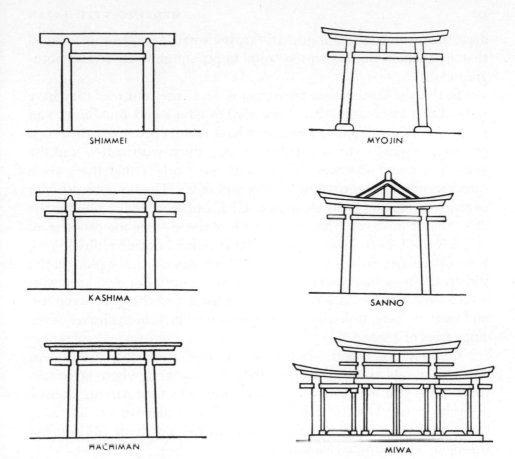

SHIMMEI

MYOJIN

KASHIMA

SANNO

HACHIMAN

MIWA

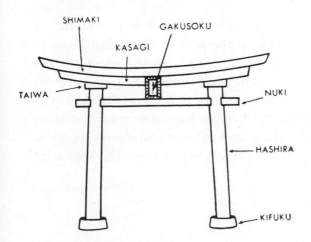

SHIMAKI

GAKUSOKU

KASAGI

TAIWA

NUKI

HASHIRA

KIFUKU

Parts of the *Torii*, and the six
fundamental types

departments of modern industrial life, is a small, bare, and unadorned thatched edifice built of cypress wood in pure prehistoric style (Photograph 81).

In this the Japanese are tremendous. Over the centuries they have resisted first the huge cultural pressure of China and Buddhism, and then that of Europe and the west, and have maintained intact their own primary, original form of worship, linking them with nature and the gods. The gods? The west laughs. But the truth is that there are a hundred ways of approaching the mystery of life. The supreme purpose of every civilization is the creation of God, and every civilization has the deity that it deserves. The logical west, obsessed with the problem of evil, has the Trinity, Jehovah, Allah; Japan, a land not of philosophers, but of poets and artists—artists of the brush, the word, the plough, the slide-rule (ships, machinery, cloth, lenses), a country of men born with a rare sense of the relationship between hand and thing, between eye and matter—hides its happy, human, irrational gods in the leaves of the huge trees of a wood.

Civilizations, beliefs, always look strange from the outside. An Asian once said to me: 'Oh, yes, Italy, the country where at certain times of the year little girls are taken to church by their parents, dressed as brides, to eat God for the first time!' The reader smiles. But nine times out of ten he goes equally astray in talking about phenomena belonging to a remote civilization.

Sacred Gateway

The origin of the *torii,* the triumphal arch built of wood or stone, or sometimes nowadays of concrete (as in the case of the Heian Jingu at Kyoto), is unknown; there is no mention of it in the most ancient Japanese documents, the *Kojiki* (A.D. 712) and *Nihon-Shoki* (A.D. 720).[1] Its shape recalls similar gateways to be found in many parts of Asia; the Indian *torana,* the Chinese *p'ai-lou,* the Korean *hong-sal-mun,* for instance; and similar structures are also to be found in Siam and elsewhere. How and when it reached Japan is still the subject of dispute.[2] The similarity

[1] For the *Kojiki* see English translation by B. H. CHAMBERLAIN, Kobe, 1932; English translation of the *Nihon-shoki* (or *Nihongi*) by W. C. ASTON, Tokyo, 1896 (reprinted London, 1956).
[2] *See* O. KAROW and D. SECHEL, *Der Ursprung des Torii,* Tokyo, 1942.

of the Japanese word *torii* and the Indian *torana* certainly offers food for thought, as Chamberlain remarks. According to an imaginative Japanese theory, the *torii* was in ancient times a perch for sacred birds, the sacred, long-necked, flying cocks (*tori,* cock, hen, bird; *i,* to be, to stand). It is suggested that in the course of time this usage was forgotten and the *torii* was transformed into a gateway. Even more imaginative are attempts to explain it by episodes in the solar myth of Amaterasu and her quarrels with her brother Susanowo, 'the impetuous male'.

Whatever its origin, the *torii* has become an inseparable feature of the Japanese landscape.[1] In the towns it is often an immense and hideous structure of steel and concrete, and its proportions are calculated by slide-rule by well-known engineers, and in the country it may well have been built of tree-trunks by peasants on a holiday afternoon, but, in whatever form, the *torii* is a constant feature of every view, every valley, practically every mountain-top in the archipelago. There are about 100,000 Shinto shrines in Japan. A few dozen are big and important, but the great majority are small, rustic structures. Generally there are three *torii* to a shrine, sometimes there are two, but there is always at least one. The popular belief is that to pass under a *torii* is a first stage in purification. The three *torii* are also associated with cock-crow at dawn.

'As the cock is the announcer of the passing of night and the coming of day, so do the three *torii* prepare the heart of a pious worshipper for his purified appearance before the god. His passing under the god-gate expels the darkness from his heart just as the darkness of night is lifted at dawn.'[2]

Torii, like crucifixes or church towers or steeples in the Christian world, or *chortens* and pagodas in Buddhist countries, are symbols of a civilization. The universal presence of the *torii* in Japan is, I think, comparable to the sound of church bells in the west. I used greatly to miss the sound of church bells here; Buddhist temples have a bell, it is true, but it is rung rarely, and with long pauses between each stroke. But then I realized that it was sufficient to use the eye instead of the ear, for there were the *torii,* particularly the small, bow-legged, country *torii,* covered

[1] *See* Photographs 52, 86, 121.
[2] K. YAMAGUCHI, *We Japanese,* Tokyo, 1952. Note the dawn symbolism again.

with moss and lichen. You catch sudden glimpses of them from the train, see them on promontories on the coast, at the turn of a path on a mountain-top.

Offended Dragon

We completed our visit to the Outer Shrine, that dedicated to the goddess of rich harvests, the guardian of agriculture, horticulture, and sericulture. Near it are some smaller shrines; one of them is dedicated to Kaza-miya, the wind god. Originally he occupied a much more modest position, but after 1293 he was granted the supreme honour of standing next to the major *kami* in recognition of the great service he rendered in raising the storm that in the bay of Hakata destroyed the fleet sent by Kublai Khan to invade Japan.[1]

This recalls a similar Chinese episode to be read in Lin Yutang's life of the poet and philosopher Su Tung-po (1036–1101).[2] Su Tung-po was a magistrate in a certain province. When summer came there was drought; in vain he prayed to the dragon of the Taipo mountain to provide rain for the parched fields. Finally, on referring to ancient documents, he discovered that the divine dragon of the Taipo mountain had been mistakenly described as count instead of duke, the rank to which he was entitled; he must certainly have been offended, and this drought was his way of showing it. Tung-po immediately addressed a memorial to the Emperor, appealing to him to redress the wrong that had been done. 'Then he and the chief magistrate took a ceremonial bath and sent a special messenger to inform the spirit of what had been done in the way of securing a higher rank for him.' Soon afterwards rain came. Su Tung-po, full of gratitude, re-named a temple near his official residence the 'Pavilion of Joyful Rain'. He also composed a short inscription to be placed on it which is a gem in the literature of the period.

Beyond the Cool Curtain

We went back to the car and drove a few miles towards the Naiku, the Inner Shrine. We got out, crossed the river Uji by a handsome bridge,

[1] *See the Shinto Dai-Jiten* ('Shinto Dictionary'), Tokyo, 1941, Vol. I., p. 310.
[2] LIN YUTANG, *The Gay Genius*, New York, 1947, p. 60.

passed under the first *torii*, and soon reached the spot where everyone goes down to the stream to wash his hands and rinse his mouth as a token of purification.

After the second *torii* we came to another avenue flanked by huge cryptomerias. The farther we got from the road, the farther the every-day world, the world of noise and motors, receded, the farther back we seemed to be moving in time, and the more we were seized with the magic of the place. We passed a number of pavilions, including the Kagura-den, the place of the sacred dances, rounded a bend, and came to some crude stone steps. We were now at the edge of the clearing where the sacred buildings stand: the Sho-den, the principle shrine, where the sacred mirror is kept; the two Ho-den, or treasuries; and the Mike-den, where offerings are made morning and evening of rice, water, salt, fish, birds, vegetables, fruit, and seaweed. The architecture with which we were faced was of the most heroic simplicity, the most abso-lute purity; the structural elements are unpainted wooden pillars, and rafters supporting thatched roofs. All the lines are straight, except for the slight curvature of the roofs; the surfaces are completely devoid of decoration and ornament; there has been no secondary treatment of the raw material.[1] A big silk curtain hangs across the entrance; only the Emperor, a few members of his family, and envoys who represent him on certain occasions, are allowed to pass beyond.

In accordance with ancient custom, everyone—including an English-speaking student of Tokyo University who had attached him-self to us ('I am in my third year, I am a student of embryology'), to say nothing of Mr. Tsuguri, with his epoch-making camera round his neck, who saw us in the distance and hurried over to join us—stood to atten-tion for a moment, bowed slightly, and clapped his hands twice. Beyond the wooden curtains (of which there were four, each with its own name: *ita-gaki*, plank curtain, *ara-gaki*, rustic curtain, *tama-gaki*, precious curtain, and *misu-gaki*, cool curtain) there were to be seen the roofs of the small temples in the clearing, with their *chigi*, ornamental cross-beams, which are so reminiscent of the South Seas. The slow and subtle building up of the suggestion of the prodigious and the sacred since we crossed the

---

[1] 'Nature herself must provide noble and beautiful materials for the sacred edifice; all man does is to select and handle them with extreme care, combined with a delicate restraint.'—WERNER BLASER, *Temples et Jardins au Japon*, Paris, 1956, p. 20.

river and passed under the first *torii* could not possibly have had a more impressive climax. A monument or mausoleum would have been a disappointment; these fabulous, archaic temples were not. It was like being transported into remote antiquity, perhaps the evening on which man discovered fire or the morning on which he invented speech. Then you pictured the time centuries ago when the Emperor's daughters lived here like vestal virgins, high priestesses of the temple, and in your mind's eye you saw them in their white silk robes passing like a cool breeze at the head of a procession of dignitaries.

At the conclusion of their brief moment of prayer, people turned and walked cheerfully away. There was not the least sign of strain or tension in the relations between man and the higher powers. For the great majority of Japanese, of course, a visit to a Shinto shrine is less a religious experience in our sense of the word (but of that we shall speak later) than a moment of poetical communion with the past, with the roots of the nation and its civilization. It is difficult, no, impossible, to find any sort of parallel in our own civilization; for that it would have been necessary for Christianity not to have eliminated the ancient pagan cults, for the latter to have survived side by side with the dominant religion; in Italy there would still have to be a Roman national shrine with a cult that had remained unaltered through the centuries; and, on top of that, both cult and place would have to stand in some sort of relationship with a supreme authority handed down through the centuries without interruption, an authority, moreover, that was simultaneously spiritual and temporal. It is obviously impossible to find such a parallel, for it belongs to a different order of things.

Earth Born of the Voluptuousness of the Gods

At this point the reader may be feeling some curiosity about the religions of Japan. What is Shinto and the emperor worship of which he has heard so much? And what is really in the minds of the Japanese, who are equipped with all the apparatus of flourishing industries, company meetings, laboratories, political parties, when they talk of the gods? Let us briefly go back to the beginning.

The original inhabitants of the Japanese archipelago were probably similar to the Ainu, or were their direct ancestors.[1] It seems established that these people reached Japan from northern Asia by way of the natural bridge provided by Sakhalin–Hokkaido–Honshu. A curious fact is that in Ainu the Sea of Okhotsk is called *makun-rep,* which means 'sea left behind, ancient sea'; in other words the sea which the Ainu left behind when they moved south. It is also curious that the ancient Japanese name for Kyushu, the big southernmost island of the archipelago, was Tsukushi; now, in Ainu *chiukushii* means a 'rapid stream, strait, a crossing-place', a description which exactly applies to the arm of the sea between Moji and Shimonoseki, where the currents are swift. Apart from the numerous place-names which the Ainu language can explain better than any other, these people left scattered throughout the archipelago graves and sites at which crude *jōmon-doki* (cord-pattern) pottery is continually being found. Japanese archaeologists are reluctant to identify the makers of these objects with the ancestors of the Ainu, but, until a more satisfactory theory is proposed, the identification can at any rate provisionally be accepted.

A totally different set of archaeological finds testifies to the advance from the south and west of another, more civilized, more warlike, and better-organized, people. From the outset these produced well-made pottery of the Yayoi type, so-called from the place where it was first discovered, and numerous objects characteristic of neolithic culture; this was swiftly followed by bronze, and then iron. As soon as the newcomers had mastered the production and use of metal, the fate of the aborigines was sealed. The first stage of Japanese history consists essentially of a slow and continuous advance northwards and westwards from the south, a perpetual state of warfare between the invaders and the strange, bearded aborigines whom they called either *emishi* or *ebisu* (barbarians).[2]

Where did these colonizing invaders come from? We are confronted with the most varied theories. Plenty of facts are available from the most varied fields, from anthropology and linguistics to archaeology

---

[1] The Ainu are proto-whites; a branch detached from the main trunk in extremely early times and presumably pushed eastwards by events that will probably always remain obscure. Names of Ainu orgin are frequent in the maritime provinces of Siberia. *See* J. BATCHELOR, *Ainu–Japanese–English Dictionary,* Tokyo, 1938.

[2] *See* Photographs 34, 35, a Japanese and an Ainu peasant side by side, now at peace after 2,000 years of warfare. *See also* Photographs 60, 61, two episodes in the Ainu bear festival *(iyomande).*

and history (China), but nobody has yet succeeded in integrating them into a really satisfactory whole. However, links may be presumed with northern Asia, by way of Korea; with central and southern China; and with the South Seas, by way of the Philippines, Formosa, and Ryukyu.

Physically it is hard to distinguish the Japanese from the southern Chinese, except for an occasional marked hairiness on the Japanese part which testifies to the Ainu element now merged in the race. This would seem to suggest that the immigrants came from China, though many of the most ancient and characteristic elements in Japanese culture link them with the cycle of civilizations which some call Oceanic and others Malayo-Polynesian—their mythology, their maritime habits, the position of women in the community, their attitude towards the nude and personal cleanliness, and finally their houses. On the other hand archaeology demonstrates important links with continental Asia, China, and Mongolia (*magatama* jewellery, the long, straight sword, burial of leaders beneath big, artificial mounds). As for the language, it raises more problems than it solves. Its true position in the linguistic picture of the Pacific and the Far East has not yet been established; but broadly it may be said that the grammar and syntax show certain affinities with the Ural-Altai group (Korean, Mongolian, Turkish, and others), while the vocabulary has many points of resemblance with the Malayo-Polynesian group. This suggests that a small nucleus of warriors, better organized but cruder, coming from Asia by way of Korea, amalgamated in the Japanese archipelago with a more numerous, more docile, and perhaps more developed, people who came from the south.

I mentioned the Japanese house; apart from all the other things which make the Ise and Izumo shrines so interesting, there is the fact that they represent the purest possible survival of the Japanese architectural tradition as it existed before the Chinese cultural invasion began in the sixth century A.D. Every twenty years the Ise shrine is taken down and meticulously reconstructed in accordance with the same immutable design, which is followed with the strictness of a religious rite. The last reconstruction took place in 1954 (the next will take place in 1974), and it was the fifty-ninth; the first of which we have documentary evidence was in 685. Before the old shrine is demolished and broken up into amulets and souvenirs, the sacred symbol, the *yata-no-kagami* mirror, is removed and taken to the new shrine, built of timber specially selected from the imperial forests of Kiso, in the depths of the night, so that the *kami* shall feel as perfectly at home in their new dwelling as they did in the old and suffer no disturbance because of the removal.

A striking fact about the appearance both of the Shinto shrine and the characteristic Japanese house is its resemblance to buildings to be found in the Philippines and the East Indies, particularly the Celebes and Sumatra. A. Soper says in the latest history of Japanese architecture: 'The likely inference is not that Japanese culture is rooted in the Indies, but that both island groups received a similar stimulus from a common centre, perhaps on the south Chinese coast.'[1] In all these structures we find features which seem to be variations on a single oriental type. They are of wood; they are on piles, which were formerly tall but in a modern Japanese town house are rudimentary; the roof is of straw or bark, generally with two long gutters, or of the *irimoya* type (*see illustration,* p. 152). Finally the walls do not carry weight, but are merely partitions, just as they are in a modern concrete building.

The Yamato civilization, the first phase of Japanese cultural and political history, fully established itself in the last centuries before the beginning of our era and the centuries that followed.[2] During this period the whole social system already revolved round the Mikado ('Honourable Gate', a title of great honour that names him symbolically, from afar), as is shown by the huge imperial tombs.

The art of this period survives, not only in the architectural monuments of Ise and Izumo, and in the Japanese house in general, but in terracotta carvings called *haniwa,* which were used for burial purposes. *Haniwa* ('clay tubes') were, as their name implies, extremely simple; their subjects are men, women, children, animals, all treated with such modernity of style that the critic exclaims with delight on discovering them. They express all a child's marvel at the miracle of matter coming

---

[1] T. R. PAINE and A. SOPER, *The Art and Architecture of Japan,* London, 1955, p. 163.

[2] The word Yamato has long been used either to indicate the primitive Japanese people or the areas where they lived. In the narrow sense, Yamato is the area round Nara; there is a Yamato prefecture at the present day. In poetry Yamato is often used for the whole of Japan. It is to be noted that in writing the word is represented, eccentrically enough, by two characters which mean 'great peace' and can be read in a variety of ways but not, except by convention, as Yamato. Japan (which the Japanese call Nihon or Nippon) is a Chinese word (*jih-pen*, 'origin, rising, of the sun'). China considered herself to be the centre of the world and named other countries with reference to herself. The oldest examples of the use of *Jih-pen* date back to the sixth or seventh centuries A.D.; Marco Polo speaks of Cipangu or Zipangu.

to life under his hand; and they contain the humour of artists who enjoyed themselves so much making them that after twenty centuries they are still capable of giving us pleasure.

So much for the knowledge of Japanese origins, such as it is, made available by external research. We also, however, possess important documents written by the Japanese themselves as soon as they had mastered the formidable instrument represented by Chinese ideograms and started committing their traditions to paper. I have already referred to the *Kojiki* (A.D. 712) and the *Nihon-shoki* (A.D. 720); to these there must be added the *Kogoshūi*[1] (A.D. 807), besides the ancient Shinto ritual books known as the *Norito*.[2] Prior to that period the depositaries of national history and legend had been the members of the *Katari-be,* a sacred association of singers who on solemn occasions recited in the presence of the emperors the glories of their ancestors and the genealogies of the gods.

According to their own thought and traditions as manifested in these works, the Japanese were of divine descent. Incidentally it should be remembered that these sacred texts are a late re-elaboration of at least three basic mythological cycles, those of Kyushu, Izumo, and Yamato, which often contradict each other; and they were written down when the Yamato dynasty exercised uncontested power over the whole archipelago; thus the final draft is, among other things, like the *Aeneid,* a huge panegyric of the reigning monarchy. At best the light that it can throw on Japanese history before A.D. 400 is, as J. Murdoch remarks in his *History of Japan,* dim.

In the beginning, then, there was the Plain of High Heaven; this latter is the point of departure of the whole highly imaginative story which describes the origin and birth of the gods, of the world, of Emperor and people. It is a jumble of prehistoric traditions and Chinese philosophy, oceanic myths, and continental learning. We meet the sun and the moon, wild love affairs and orgiastic dances, dragons and swords, fabulous journeys to the court of the king of the ocean depths, descents to the next world, to say nothing of transmutations into hideous masses of corruption and playful generations from noses, ears, eyes, mirrors, jewels, and the origin of the cultivation of rice. Things are alive, are transmuted, speak. Miracles are the law of nature, and

[1] English translation by G. KATO and H. HOSHINO, Tokyo, 1924.
[2] English translations by E. M. SATOW, Tokyo, 1879, and K. FLORENZ, Tokyo, 1900.

nature laughs, gets angry, rewards, and threatens. There are delicate poetical episodes and the most extraordinary incongruities; a thing once said does not prejudice the most unexpected subsequent developments; heroes live for hundreds of years or end their brief existence in an hour. All the names are brief descriptions of their holders, such as Clay-Viscid-Prince, Elder-Lady-of-the-Great-Place, Earthly-Water-Drawing-Gourd-Possessor, Great-Mountain-Integrator, Thing-Sign-Master, Thought-Includer, Heavenly-Blowing Male, Youth-of-the-Wind-Breath-Great-Male, etc., etc.[1]

It is impossible to summarize briefly this complicated conglomeration of stories. Let me mention some significant details. After a number of divine generations we meet Izanagi and Izanami ('the Inviting Male' and 'the Inviting Female'), who are probably brother and sister. Their loves, described with magnificently solemn obscenity, result in the birth of a number of deities, and finally of the islands of Japan. The idea of earth and sea, mountains and woods, nature herself, being born of the sacred voluptuousness of the gods throws light on many aspects of the Japanese mind and civilization. But let us proceed. At one point Izanami gives birth to the god of fire; in doing so she burns herself and dies. Izanagi, being desperately in love with his sister-wife, seeks for her in this world and the next. When at last with the aid of magic practices he finds her, she turns out to be a horrible, putrefying thing. Horrified, he returns to the world of the living, and bathes in a stream to purify himself. While he is washing himself numerous gods are born of the clothing which he removes and of the various parts of his body. Among them is Amaterasu, the sun goddess, who is born of his left eye, and the moon god, who is born of his right eye, while from his nose there springs a personage who in subsequent myths acquires great importance, namely Susanowo, 'the Impetuous Male', a personification of storm.

Amaterasu soon ascends to the supreme place among the gods on the Plain of High Heaven. Curious and complicated events follow, and a long struggle between brother and sister; at one stage the offended goddess retires into a cave, leaving the world to darkness. After many attempts by supernatural beings to persuade her to emerge, the 'August Female who Strikes Fear into the Skies' performs an indecent dance which causes the gods to laugh with terrifying loudness. This is too

[1] B. H. CHAMBERLAIN, translation of *Kojiki*, Kobe, 1932.

much for Amaterasu's curiosity, and she appears for a moment, where-upon the gods seize her, and light reappears in the world. Strange and complicated events follow, and other births take place in biologically unorthodox ways, until we meet Ninigi, a grandson of Amaterasu, who descends from the Plain of High Heaven to a mountain in Kyushu to reign among men. With Jimmu, a grandson of Ninigi, we meet the first really human Emperor, traditionally considered the founder of the line of 124 Emperors of Japan.

Jimmu, according to the official chronology, mounted the throne on February 11, 660 B.C.; modern historians consider that the true events of which these traditions are the shadow took place about 400 years later, about 200 B.C. Mythological events still abound in the story of Jimmu, but behind them a flesh-and-blood Emperor can be discerned. His greatest enterprise, which certainly symbolizes the long, warlike, eastward advance of the proto-Japanese, was the conquest, setting out from Kyushu, of all the territory up to the area where Nara later arose.

From the time of Jimmu onwards the contents both of the *Kojiki* and the *Nihon-shoki* gradually assume greater verisimilitude. History increasingly takes the place of fantasy, and chronicle and legend in-creasingly coincide. The joins between the three cycles of myths remain perceptible, however; in all probability they suggest a hard, century-long struggle for predominance on the part of the Yamato, first in their original environment of Kyushu and then in the central provinces, where there were innumerable aborigines who had to be subjected, as well as the rival Izumo dynasty, who were not aborigines, but were probably connected with Korea.[1]

Thus by A.D. 400 Japan had attained political unity, and possessed an interesting civilization, the various elements of which had crystallized into a whole. It was familiar with the use of metals, but had not acquired the art of writing, had a religion of its own, and was, in fact, ready for the gigantic surge forward that it was to make in the next two centuries under the fertilizing influence of China. Soper observes with good reason that the Yamato standard of living, which at the end of the bronze age had been perhaps 1,500 years behind the Chinese, moved forward with a constant acceleration, and that at their final pace the Japanese achieved

[1] *See* Photograph 15 (the great Izumo shrine, Izumo Taisha, after Ise the Shinto religion's most sacred place); and Photograph 46, the high priest of the Izumo shrine.

a forced growth almost unique in world history before the industrial revolution.[1] Fourteen centuries later, in the Meiji period, Japan was to astonish the world by a not dissimilar performance.

It would take us too far afield to expand on the interesting characteristics of Japanese civilization before the first contacts with China, but a feature which I should like to mention is the important place occupied by women. In the mythology goddesses are as powerful as, and more powerful than, the gods. We have already seen that the supreme position in the Japanese Olympus is occupied by Amaterasu, a goddess. But the situation on earth cannot have been very different. Prior to A.D. 769 there were no fewer than seven Empresses, and an Emperor's widow, Jingū (third century A.D.), conquered Korea, 'placing a stone under the belt on her belly to prevent the birth of the son with whom she was pregnant'. Her voyage across the sea was facilitated by fish who kept the ships afloat during a storm; it is not for nothing that in the Chinese annals of the Wei dynasty Japan appears as the almost fabulous land of 'Queen Pimiku'. In ancient Japanese literature there are frequent references to powerful priestesses, and up to the fourteenth century the high priest of the Ise shrine was a daughter of the Emperor. Even in the ordinary life of centuries nearer our own the position of women must have been very different from what it was in a typically patriarchal country such as China. History records several examples of sons who took their mother's surname; in 736, for example, Prince Katsuragi obtained the Emperor's consent to his changing his name to Tachibana in honour of his dead mother. Women took as full a part as men in cultural life, and there were many women poets—Higetabe no Akaiko, Kasa no Iratsune, Ono no Komachi.

From the sixth century onwards Chinese civilization exercised an ever more powerful influence, and the position of women gradually changed; by the thirteenth century women had become perpetual slaves: first of their father, then of their husband, and then, if they were widowed, of their eldest son. Buddhism, and even more the teachings of Confucius, relegated them to total subordination. Nevertheless throughout the ages Japanese women have succeeded in maintaining something of their ancient independence. The most famous work in Japanese literature, the *Tale of Genji,* is the work of a woman, Murasaki Shikibu

[1] T. R. PAINE and A. SOPER, *The Art and Architecture of Japan,* London, 1955.

(978?–1015?). Even today careful observers of Japanese life detect unexpected survivals of an order of things which sixteen centuries have in vain tried completely to obliterate.

What the Kami Really Are

The ancient Japanese had no name for their religion. To distinguish it from *Butsu-do* ('the religion of Buddha'), when the latter was imported from China at the beginning of the fifth century, it was called Shinto, or Kami-no-michi, *i.e.,* 'the way of the gods'.

SHIN-
Kami
god, gods

TO
Michi
way, system
religion

To gain an understanding of Buddhism it is necessary to make clear the fundamental concepts of *samsara, karma, arhat, buddha, nirvana*; and Christianity cannot be understood without full awareness of the meaning of creation, the fall, incarnation, redemption, the last judgment. Similarly, if we desire to make an intelligent approach to Shinto, we must first appreciate the many meanings of the word *kami*.[1]

If we open a Japanese dictionary we shall find a whole multitude. The word originally meant simply 'over, above'. Then its use was extended to objects or beings 'over, above' their surroundings; a mountain-top, for instance, or a leader, or the head of a valley, the hair of the head, the government, authority, a man's wife (often used jokingly), a feudal lord, a supernatural being, the Emperor, a deified hero, etc. Some of these things were indicated by different ideograms, but that does not alter their common origin. Thus the general idea is 'that which is over, above', whether on the physical or the mental plane. Some modern dictionaries include God among the meanings of the word, but that is a crude mistake, a modern extension due to contact with the theocentric religions of the west. Indeed, to avoid continual misunderstandings, the missionaries have had to invent a special term for God, *Tenshu* ('Lord of Heaven'). The *kami,* as Aston rightly says, 'are

Kami
god, god

Kami
above

[1] D. C. HOLTOM, in his well-known *Political Philosophy of Modern Shinto*, Tokyo, 1922, devotes fifty-two pages to explaining the extraordinary wealth of meaning of this word.

superior, swift, brave, bright, rich, etc., but not immortal, omniscient, or possessed of infinite power'.[1]

If anything, the *kami* resemble the gods of Olympus. They are capricious, amusing, frightening, happy or sad, they fall ill, die, are resuscitated; they sometimes get drunk and commit the most appalling mischief; and sometimes they fight like heroes. They are, in other words, essentially human beings who live on the Plains of High Heaven.

But the word is applied to an infinity of other things besides superior human beings. It is as wrong to limit its meaning to 'god' with a small 'g' as it is to translate it by 'God' with a capital 'G'. *Kami* is, in short, a concept round which the Japanese have constructed a most individual mental universe of their own. The great exegetist and historian Motoori Norinaga (1730–1801) writes:

> 'The term *kami* is applied in the first place to the various deities of heaven and earth mentioned in the ancient records, as well as to their spirits (*mi-tama*) which reside in the shrines where they are worshipped. Moreover, not only human beings, but birds, beasts, plants and trees, seas and mountains, and all other things whatsoever which deserve to be dreaded and revered for the extraordinary and pre-eminent powers which they possess, are called *kami*. They need not be eminent for surpassing nobleness, goodness or serviceableness alone. Malignant and uncanny beings are also called *kami* if only they are the objects of general dread. . . . Among *kami* who are not human beings I need hardly mention Naru Kami ("the sounding *kami*", *i.e.*, thunder). There are also the dragon, the echo (in Japanese called *ko-dama*, "the tree spirit") and the fox, who are *kami* by reason of their uncanny and fearful natures. The term *kami* is applied in the *Nihon-shoki* and the *Mannyōshu* to the tiger and the wolf. . . . There are many cases of seas and mountains being called *kami*. It is not their spirits which are meant. The word was applied directly to the seas or mountains themselves as being very awful things.'[2]

Looked at from the outside, the world of *kami* would seem to be incapable of resisting the slightest puff of rationalism. But it is not of

[1] W. G. ASTON, *Shinto*, London, 1922.
[2] MOTOORI NORINAGA, *Kojiki-Den*, Vol. I.

a stuff meant to resist either puffs or storms of rationalism; we are on a different plane, in a world which consists of a poetical attitude towards the divinity in things.[1]

The word *kami* is like a signpost which simply indicates: At this point the invisible, the mysterious, begins. No claim is made to explain or discuss the unity, trinity, or plurality, the omnipotence or omniscience, of the supreme jurisdiction, to possess the keys to truth, to have wrested the final secret from the universe. That is why Shinto has been able to co-exist with the highest level of civilization and to provide a way of communion with the ultimate things of the world for minds which were the very reverse of petty or ignoble.

Divinity of Nature and Orgiastic Dances

Many aspects of Shinto observable in everyday life are essential to an understanding of Japan, both past, present, and perhaps future.

In the first place, there is the absolutely spontaneous and genuine popular aspect, which in all probability constitutes the most ancient nucleus of this religion. It consists, as we have seen, of a sense of deep reverence for the forces of nature, which are always present in a diffuse state but sometimes manifest themselves at a higher potential, with a warmer glow, in places, things, persons, events. Among the forces which would naturally seem most important to a people of peasants and fishermen are those which manifest themselves in the fertility of the fields, woods, and waters; hence the *kami* of the sun and of rich harvests, of the earth (Onamochi), the sea (the three gods of the temple of Sumi-yoshi at Osaka), of the wind (among others Ame no Mihashira, 'the August Pillar of Heaven'), of fire (Homosubi, 'Growth of Flame'), of the trees (Kukumochi, 'Father of the Woods'), of waters and wells, of houses and doors, of the kitchen, and the hearth. Two of the *kami* still most venerated at the present day are Inari,[2] who presides over the sowing, growth, ripening, and gathering of the rice and manifests himself in his messenger, the fox; and Kompira, a divinity of obscure, possibly Indian, origin, who is the protector of sailors, fishermen, and travellers.

[1] '*Kami* should remain for ever mysterious and incomprehensible.' T. HARADA, *The Faith of Japan*, 1914, p. 46.

[2] Photograph 54 shows the interior of the shrine of Inari at Kyoto, during a ceremony attended by Osaka industrialists.

Finally, in the depths of the country you sometimes come across frankly phallic cults, and there are whispers of orgiastic dances and saturnalia, the purpose of which in the past perhaps consisted of magic-ally transmitting human fertility to the soil.[1] Since 1872 all governments have legislated against customs of this kind, which to the bureaucratic mind were uncivilized and offensive to respectable foreigners. But this only shows, if there were any need of it, how deeply rooted and spon-taneous the popular aspects of Shinto are. A phallic symbol about three feet tall is still to be seen beside a pond in Ueno Park in the centre of Tokyo. Near Nagoya there are a number of small shrines dedicated to the *kami* of fertility where Pompeian mementoes of permanent and enthusiastic fullness are distributed. As for occasions on which an ancient and sacred ritual licence is covered by the mantle of darkness, I can say only that I have often heard talk of them. Whether or not they take place it is hard to say; they may be only rumours based on practices which have vanished. A certain veil of mystery surrounds this, as other aspects of Japanese life.

Another aspect of the popular religion is the practice of divination; the oracular pronouncements of men, and particularly women, in a state of hypnosis or catalepsy. Many will remember the scene in the film *Rashomon* in which the *reibai,* the medium, is possessed by the spirit of the dead man and in a terrifying voice tells the story of his murder as seen through his own eyes. This is something which may have been brought to Japan by invaders from Central Asia; it is reminiscent of practices indulged in since antiquity by the shamans of Mongolia.

Apart from some details, perhaps of subsequent importation, like this last, in which an obscure sense of evil is to be detected, and an attitude of fear towards death and the unknown, Shinto in general is a religion of luminous optimism. Schiller described the cult of the gods of ancient Greece as a *Wonnedienst,* a religion of love, joy, and gratitude rather than of fear. Aston remarks that the same applies to the native religion of Japan. Nearly all the chief Shinto gods are benevolent. They do not sit on judgment thrones. The main themes of Shinto prayer and ceremonies are thankfulness or joyous greeting.

[1] G. KATO, *A Study of the Development of Religious Ideas among the Japanese People as Illustrated by Japanese Phallicism,* Tokyo, 1924.

The most important principle of the cult is ritual purity. Given the divinity of the whole of nature, and hence of the human body, there was no necessity to differentiate between sin and dirt; the essential was to carry out certain rites, for which the requirements were scrupulous personal cleanliness (*misogi*, ablutions), concentration and abstinence (*imi*), and contact with certain purifying things (*e.g.*, branches of *sakaki, Cleyera japonica*). For this and other reasons Shinto lays down no system of ethics expressed in commandments and prohibitions. Certain things are prohibited, but they are highly specialized, *e.g.*, connected with the cultivation of rice; more important matters are left entirely vague. Many western students have concluded from this that Shinto is a religion without a morality, but this is incorrect; ideas of good and evil are intuitively derived from the actions and personalities of the *kami*. The emphasis is less on virtuous and honourable action than on a virtuous and honourable mind. Such a 'morality of the heart' is more consonant with the Japanese nature than an abstract, logical, moral code.[1]

It is very doubtful whether even in ancient times Shinto required sacrifices; in all its rites the emphasis is on offerings. A sacrifice implies pain, renunciation, self-punishment; an offering is an expression of pleasure and of a serene mind. The most typical Shinto rite is the *matsuri*, held to celebrate a deification, one's ancestors, a purification, a sowing, a harvest, or a good catch; it invariably ends with processions, games, eating, drinking, merrymaking, song and dance, miming, fires, popular explosions of colour, movement, and gaiety.

Japan is the country of festivals, for which the people have an unbounded enthusiasm. Regimented and burdensome as their every-day life is, on *matsuri* days they fling off every care. Every district in every town, every shrine, every trade, every historical or mythical event, has its own festival, and they are celebrated in an extraordinary variety of ways.[2] There are the famous fire festivals held at night at Kurama (Kyoto) in October and at the Kannokura Jinja (Nagoya) in February; at

---

[1] A. HAUCHECORNE, 'Les Religions du Japon', *Histoire des Religions*, Vol. II, Paris, 1954.

[2] *See* Photographs 9, 10 (procession in the rice-fields at Haramachi); 44, 45 (sacred dance and *gagaku* music at Myajima); 56 (a *kannushi*, Shinto priest, on horseback in a procession); 57 (*kannushi* ready for a procession in Tokyo); 58 (fire festival at Kurama); 59 (horsemen at Haramachi); 62–66 (*Sanja-sai* in Tokyo); 133 (dance to induce the end of the rains, at Shinagawa, at the gates of Tokyo, with gasworks).

Kyoto the solemn *gion* procession takes place in July and the *aoi matsuri* procession in May; gay ceremonial blessings of the sea take place at many places during the summer; there are festivals at which the crowd dances through the streets (the *awa odori*) at Tokushima, in August, and there are strange winter masquerades in the snow at Akita (the so-called *namahage*); in towns some of these festivals, such as the *Kanda myojin* in Tokyo in May or the *sanja-matswei,* again in Tokyo, cause people dressed in ancient costumes to mingle with the trams and the traffic; elsewhere there are cavalcades in ancient costume (the *noma-oi* at Haramachi, in July) or extraordinary tests of skill (the *kantō matsuri* at Akita, in July); there are battles worthy of the *palio* at Siena between supporters of different factions (the *kenka-matsuri* at Himeji, in October). There are also other festivals the central features of which are huge lanterns (the *o-chōchin* at the Suwa Jinja, in August), or sacred cooking pots (the *nabe kammuri matsuri* at Maibara, in May), or huge sandals (at Fukushima, in January), or dragons, fireworks, rowing races, dances, feudal processions, archery on horseback. A booklet which I have at hand[1] lists 447 *matsuri* in the course of the year, ignoring those of purely local or minor interest. One of them is Christian (the *seitai gyoretsu* at Nagasaki, in June), a few are Buddhist (for instance the Dantesque *saidai-ji eyo,* at Okayama, in January), but the vast majority are either predominantly or exclusively of Shinto inspiration.

Ancestors, Emperors, Politics

Primitive Shinto was essentially nature worship. Scholars are not yet agreed whether this included ancestor worship or not. British historians and the Japanese themselves (W. G. Aston, B. H. Chamberlain, G. Kato) generally maintain that it did; French scholars (M. Revon, Father Martin) on the whole argue that it did not. The probability is that Shinto always contained some slight element of it; but it is certain that it was contact with China that caused such emphasis to be laid on it as to make it seem absolutely vital. It is probable that from the earliest times patrons of clans or families were transformed into divine ancestors. The custom of deifying exceptional men has notably enriched the

[1] NIPPON KŌZUKŌSHA, *Nenju Gyōji*, Tokyo, 1953.

Shinto pantheon, and this, gradually filtering down to the popular level, has led to the belief that every dead person is a *kami*.[1]

Here we come to a point of extreme importance in Japanese history. In what circumstances did the Emperor come to be universally recognized as a descendant of the sun goddess? How did he come to combine in himself both supreme religious authority and supreme political power? Perhaps we shall never know for certain. The fact remains that at the time when the *Kojiki* and the *Nihon-shoki* were written, at the beginning of the eighth century, the process was already complete. It is worth noting that the ancient word for 'government', *matsurigoto,* is related to *matsuri,* religious observance; and that to this day the word *miya* means both 'important shrine', 'palace', and 'prince'. Thus from remote times, side by side with the popular Shinto religion, which might have survived side by side with Buddhism (like the Bon religion in Tibet) or disappeared (like paganism in Europe), there was an official, canonical, Shinto embodied in the highest personage in the land.

This variety of Shinto is very different from the first; before 1945 there was actually a legal distinction between the two. The popular religion was officially a denomination like any other, but official Shinto was the state religion, and to make it possible for everyone, even Christians, to take part in its observances, it was declared in theory to be no more and no less than 'a sign of respect towards the civil institutions'. The story of this variety of Shinto is complex and interesting and, for good or evil, is intimately bound up with the fortunes of Japan. Here I shall mention only a few points.

In the first place, there was the encounter with Buddhism. This took place in the sixth and seventh centuries, to the accompaniment of much conflict between opposing factions. A direct comparison between the poetical but primitive native cult and the great religion of Asia, rich in lofty metaphysics and subtle dialectics, must inevitably have

---

[1] To the category of the deified there belong, for instance, Temmangu (the *kami* of learning and calligraphy), *i.e.,* Sugawara Michizane (845–703), a memorable scholar-warrior, who died after being unjustly exiled; a number of emperors or empresses, including Jimmu, the first of the line; Jingū, the fourteenth; Kwammu, the fiftieth, the founder of Kyoto; a number of national heroes; several sporting champions (including Nomi no Sukune, the patron of wrestlers); the poet Hitomaro; the poetess Hime; a great airman of the last war (Kato); and the murderer of a Minister of Education who in 1889 dared lift with his walking-stick a veil which protected from profane eyes the holy of holies of the Ise shrine.

meant the final victory of the latter had Shintoism not been so completely identified with the imperial dynasty and the spirit of the nation.
The Buddhist theologians from the times of Kōbō Daishi (ninth century)
onwards found themselves faced with the problem of what to do about
the native religion, and they had no difficulty in finding a solution. The
kami, they decided, were terrestrial incarnations of the Buddha; Buddhists and Shintoists in reality worshipped the same thing. They identified Amaterasu, for instance, with Dai-Nichi-Nyorai, the 'Great Light',
the Amitabha of the Indians, the Öpame of Tibet. This is the doctrine
known in the history of Japanese philosophy as that of *honji-suijaku*
('manifestations of the primordial essence'). The recent researches of
Professor Z. Tsuji, published in his monumental history of Japanese
Buddhism,[1] have shown that it took definite shape and came to be
generally accepted only in the tenth century.

For many centuries the Japanese, who by nature are inclined more
to the aesthetic appeal of religion than to the logic of an explicit creed,
lived under the domain of what was called *ryobu-shinto,* a Shinto-Budd-
hism 'of two faces'. It was often difficult to tell whether you were in
a Buddhist temple or a Shinto shrine. Except at a few places where
efforts were made to keep the two faiths uncontaminated by each other,
the confusion of statues, rites, liturgy, styles, writings, priestly orders,
became complete. To this day the Japanese popular mind confronts you
with a unique and profoundly rooted eclecticism. The general attitude
is reverence for every manifestation of the divine; we are in the domain
of the emotions, of *kimochi* (mood, state of mind), which is that in which
the Japanese are most at ease.

With the eighteenth century a slow reaction began. At first it was
restricted to a few scholars working on the interpretation of ancient
texts; then it grew more vigorous when certain ideas started spreading
among the public. A demand arose for a return to the pure, original
Shinto, and for a restoration to the Emperor of the power held by the
Tokugawa shoguns. This movement started in the minds of a few great
historians (Kada, 1668–1736, Kamo, 1697–1769, Motoori, 1730–1801, Hirata,
1776–1843); it ended in the hands of plotters and conspirators and, after
the restoration of 1868 (the first year of the reign of the Emperor Meiji),
became state doctrine. Henceforward it was perilously linked with

[1] Z. TSUJI, *Nippon Bukkyo Shi,* six vols., Tokyo, 1944–53.

politics, *bushido*,[1] and *kōdo,* and official Shinto became a diabolical instrument of aggression, tyranny, and obscurantism, which ended in the disaster of 1945.

But of all that we shall speak later. I shall, however, assume that the reader is now better able to understand the Japanese attitude to the Emperor's divinity, which was officially abolished by the decree of September 2, 1945, but might well be revived in a new form tomorrow. No Japanese believes that his Majesty the Emperor Hirohito receives his breakfast by levitation, or that he is able to change the sands of the sea into coal, rice, or gold. The error consists in using western language, and saying that the Emperor is a god instead of saying that he is a *kami*. God is the creator, omnipotent and eternal; a *kami* is a thing or person in whom there is a stronger charge of that divine essence which is concealed everywhere about us. The Japanese are not crazy, incomprehensible, deluded beings, but simply poets.

---

[1] *Bushi-do* ('the way of the warrior') can be described as a body of ideas, rules of conduct, emotional and artistic impulses, which took shape at the beginning of the feudal era (twelfth century); the word, however, and the unifying concept, are recent. *See* p. 273.

5

Buddha and Beauty at Mount Murō

Little Space, Many Places

PERHAPS because the roads, particularly the secondary roads, are narrow and wind their way capriciously up hills and down valleys, past bays, capes, and gulfs, Japan, which is a small country, ends by seeming immense. Moreover, as one is constantly surrounded by woods, and the eye rarely embraces a broad horizon, travel is broken up into a succession of ever-changing glimpses, a continual series of surprises. So much is compressed into a limited space that some days, having with difficulty travelled 150 miles, you feel as if you had travelled a thousand.

This morning we left the sea behind, making towards Nara, crossing valleys and mountain passes, penetrating deeper and deeper into a typically and delightfully Japanese landscape. Valley succeeded valley; everything was small and articulated, and everywhere there were tall, leafy trees. Where the ground was flat rice-fields were laid out with the elegance of ideograms, and ribbons of smoke rose peacefully from the thatched roofs hidden among the foliage.

No Japanese schoolboy can contemplate such a scene without calling to mind the half-mythical, half-historical story of the good, fourth-century Emperor Nintoku ('Benevolent Virtue'). In those days an emperor's death involved his successor in building a new palace and a new capital, often several miles distant from the old. This was a survival of an old and long since vanished Japanese superstition, according to which a death, the consummation of a marriage, and childbirth were impure events. Special pavilions, which were subsequently destroyed, were therefore built for births and the consummation of marriages;[1] the house in which a death occurred had to be abandoned and a new one built elsewhere. The consequence was that until the eighth century the Japanese capital was a kind of big, mobile camp. But in 710 the Empress Gemmyō built the first real city, Nara, where her successors remained for three-quarters of a century and civilization prospered, reaching a level seldom surpassed in Asian history.

The good Emperor Nintoku, then,

'ascending a lofty mountain and looking on the land all round, spoke, saying: "In the whole land there rises no smoke; the land is all poverty-stricken. So I remit all the people's taxes and forced labour from now till three years." Therefore the great palace became dilapidated, and the rain leaked in everywhere; but no repairs were made. The rain that leaked in was caught in troughs, and [the inmates] removed from its reach to places where there was no leakage.'[2]

One day the Emperor noticed that smoke was at last issuing abundantly from the chimneys again. At this he was glad at heart, and gave orders that a palace should be built for himself and the royal household.

Thinking of ancient emperors seems particularly appropriate in these parts. We crossed the Aoyama pass,[3] and passed through the Iga country, where Bashō was born in 1644. Bashō ('Banana') was one of the greatest of Japanese poets, who made famous the brief, epigrammatic poems of barely seventeen syllables called *haikai*. We now found ourselves on the threshold of Yamato, the Japanese Tuscany, the area which for centuries was the scene of Japanese history, where the arts reached their zenith, and every wood and hill and temple has an aura of myth and legend.

The September sun was strong, and we were enjoying the first really fine, bright weather after the endless haze and heat and rains of summer. The miniature valleys became steeper and stranger, and the

---

[1] A survival of this archaic custom was observed by E. Satow in the island of Hachijō, to the south of Tokyo, in 1878. A thorough search of the more remote parts of the country might yield examples at the present day.

[2] *Kojiki*, Vol. III, p. 121.

[3] Aoyama means 'green' or perhaps 'blue' mountain. Only in recent times have the Japanese begun to distinguish the two colours; *aoi* still includes all the cold colours of the spectrum.

road was so narrow that we were continually held up by carts and jolting vehicles marked *basu, i.e.,* bus.

We followed a stream that had worn a deep channel through the quartziferous rock of the extinct volcanoes of Mount Murō, the mountain of the 'living cave'. Trees grew in baroque clusters among the black rocks, and houses grew rarer; suddenly we came upon the huge hollow in the rock wall on the left where thirteenth-century artists carved a dreaming Maitreya, the Buddha of the future,[1] the final saviour of mankind. We were now near the Murō-ji, one of the oldest, remotest, most fascinating, and least-known temples in Japan.

The country grew still wilder; the valley narrowed, the walls on either side with their dark green clumps of vegetation overhung us ominously, the rushing stream turned into a deep ditch, the water glistened among the rocks; and it was easy to see why from the remotest antiquity this has been considered a place of marvels; here it would be natural to expect trees, animals, and rocks to speak, and there would be no difficulty in believing the lord of the place to be a dragon living in a cave.

Brief Digression on Dragons

Dragons are old acquaintances, both in Asia and Europe; they may have a common origin in the Indian *naga,* a serpiform water deity beautifully portrayed among the bas-reliefs of Māmallapuram. Whatever may one day be established by the archaeologists, however, the fact remains that there could not possibly be a greater contrast in personality than that between the European dragon and its Far Eastern counterpart.

In Europe there were Greek and Roman dragons, and the diabolical dragons of the Middle Ages; nowadays they barely survive, except as manufacturer's trade marks, but before they declined to that prosaic level they had a long and proud career. But always and invariably they were associated with evil, like the basilisk, the chimaera, the hydra, the gorgon, and the viper. They started by being guardians of the Golden Fleece, the gardens of the Hesperides, and the Castalian spring, but in a later age they appeared in the visions of the Apocalypse, causing a third of the stars to fall from the heaven with a sweep of their tail,

[1] In Japanese Miroku Bosatsu.

threatening to devour children born of divine women, calling up from
the sea beasts with ten horns and seven heads, vomiting forth hideous,
frog-like monsters; and with the Middle Ages they allied themselves
with, or became manifestations of, the devil, deceiving noble knights
with atrocious cries or sweet song, or intervening between them and the
conquest of virtue, often impersonating beautiful princesses. The
slaying of the dragon by the hero—Perseus, St. George, Siegfried—is
a constant western theme.

Dragons were taken seriously until comparatively recent times.
Ulissi Aldrovandi (1522–1605) devoted 509 folio pages of his *Serpentum et
Draconum* to 'humans of the name of Draco, with sea-serpents, tarantulas,
plants, trees, stars, devils, quicksilver, mountains, traps, fistulae, sirens,
Hydras, anacondas, whales, leviathan, fossils, hieroglyphs and even
with an early form of aircraft called a Dragon'.[1] He added that it was
possible for unscrupulous people to forge a dragon, by plastic surgery,
on the cadaver of a Giant Ray. In 1651 M. A. Sanseverino gave a detailed
description of the dragon and the basilisk in his learned treatise *De vipera
natura, veneno, medicina.* J. Scheuchzer, half-way between myth and science,
was the last serious student of dragons in the Alps in the eighteenth
century.[2]

The eastern dragon is a complex character; he has a fundamental
kinship with water. Now, plants, animals, men, cannot live without
water, on which all life depends. Basically, therefore, water is a friend;
but it can also be an enemy—there is little need to recall the havoc that
can be wrought by storm and flood. The character of the eastern
dragon is a reflection of that of water in all its manifestations; it can be
terrible, capricious, often incomprehensible, sometimes mocking, but
fundamentally it is beneficent, well disposed towards men and, if the
latter treat it right, it will respond by protecting them.

It was chiefly in China that the personality of the oriental dragon
was built up, and the creature displayed a constant and profound
attachment for that country; consequently it is there that it should be
studied in all its magnificent complication. From the remotest antiquity
the dragon has been known in China as the 'father of felicity', the 'king

---

[1] T. H. WHITE, *The Book of Beasts, being a Translation from a Latin Bestiary of the Twelfth Century,* London,
1954, p. 165. *See also* J. BALTRUSAITIS, *Le Moyen Age Fantastique,* Paris, 1955, Chapter V.
[2] J. SCHEUCHZER, *Itinera per Helvetias Alpinas Regiones,* Leyden, 1723.

of animal creation'.[1] Temples and sacred woods were often dedicated to dragons, which were believed to be present everywhere, though generally invisible. They influenced and guided the affairs of men; their home was generally the water, but some lived on mountains (these seem to have been the evil ones). The dragon was considered the chief of the Four Spiritual Animals, of which the other three were the *ling* (in Japanese *kirin*), a kind of horse-giraffe-unicorn; the *feng* (in Japanese *hō*), a fabulous bird related to the phoenix; and the *kuei* (in Japanese *kame*), the tortoise. The dragon was also the tutelary deity of the Five Regions (*i.e.*, north, south, east, west, and centre), and the guardian of the Five Lakes and the Four Oceans (*i.e.*, of all the world's waters).

Chinese authors have repeatedly explained that dragons are not divine beings, but animals possessed of extraordinary power, to be classified with other scaly reptiles. Their appearance is described as minutely as if they were rabbits or cauliflowers. The dragon has the head of a horse, the body and neck of a winged serpent, and four legs. Some dragonologists speak of the so-called Nine Resemblances, *i.e.*, the horns of a stag, the face of a camel, the eyes of a devil, the neck of a serpent, a stomach like a huge shell, the scales of a carp, the claws of an eagle, the pads of a tiger, and the ears of a bull. Some kinds have no ears, and are assumed to hear with their horns. Certain arch-dragons appear to bear on their foreheads the so-called Pearl of Potentiality in which there are combined and united the two Chinese fundamental principles of *yin* and *yang*. *Yin* is the feminine principle, negative, nocturnal, wet, and immobile; *yang* is male, positive, diurnal, dry, and mobile. The experts mention that, if the dragon loses this pearl, it loses its power; some successful dragon-hunters seem to have taken advantage of this peculiarity.

Ryū
dragon

Kirin
horse
giraffe
unicorn

Hō
phoenix

Kame
turtle

The Four Spiritual
Animals

---

[1] F. T. C. WERNER, *A Dictionary of Chinese Mythology*, Shanghai, 1932, p. 285 *et seq.*

Information about the ways of dragons is equally copious. Their home, generally speaking, is in the watery depths. In the spring they rise to the surface. Thunder then galvanizes them into action, so to speak, and like a flash they ascend to the clouds; their great weight resting on these squeezes out the water and causes rain. The kings of the dragons live in the depths of the sea, where they have marvellous palaces guarded by marine animals. There are either four, eight, or ten of these kings; the authorities differ. One authority divides dragons into four categories: celestial dragons who act as guardians of the gods; spiritual dragons who watch beneficently over mankind; earthly dragons who live in the waters and mountains; and, finally, dragons who stand guard over hidden treasure. These last are very dangerous.

Sometimes there is mention of battles between dragons, who then disappear, leaving behind them nothing but a curious kind of fertilizing foam; and of duels between male and female dragons, generally near the confluence of rivers. At this point the water cult is insensibly transmuted into a fertility cult.

Dragons were much sought after as ancestors. The Hsia, the first Chinese dynasty, claimed dragons among its ancestors; a branch of the imperial family enjoyed the privilege of raising and breeding dragons, which it kept in contented domesticity, like cattle. One of the Hsia emperors seems to have lived on a diet of dragon-meat in order to make his realm prosper. Later the dragon became the imperial emblem. The Chinese imperial dragon incidentally had five claws; ordinary dragons have only four. So close were men and dragons in this great and imaginative civilization that the highest praise to which a man could aspire was to be called 'dragon'. According to a rather Baroque simile, good writers use their brushes as a dragon moves its tail. (In the Far East you write with a brush.)

There are enough dragon stories to fill a book. They all illustrate the extreme sensitivity of dragons, their fanciful, capricious behaviour, their fundamental kindness of heart. I have already mentioned the dragon of the Taipo mountain who withheld the rain because he had been called count instead of duke. Another famous dragon in Kiangsu fell in love with a peasant girl. One day she gave birth to a strange, fleshy object which soon changed into a white dragon. It took wing, to the accompaniment of thunder, lightning, and terrifying downpours of rain, and vanished into the sky. It is said that every year, on the eight-eenth day after the third full moon, pilgrims used to flock to the temple dedicated to the white dragon, who used to come down on that day to visit his mother's tomb. Then there is the story of the prince turned into a dragon who caused a famous victory to be won against the Mongols by sending swarms of infuriated bees among them. For this he was promoted to high rank at court and called Golden King Dragon No. 4.

It would take us too far afield to describe the innumerable shapes assumed by dragons in art. According to Williams, the Chinese distin-guish nine types, all with different names:

> '(1) the P'u Lao, carved on top of bells and gongs, in token of its habit of crying out loudly when attacked by its arch-enemy the whale; (2) the Ch'iu niu, carved on the screws of fiddles owing to its taste for music; (3) the Pi hsi, carved on the top of stone tablets, since it was fond of literature; (4) the Pa hsia, carved on the bottom of stone monuments, as it was able to support heavy weights; (5) the Chao feng, carved on the eaves of temples, owing to its liking for danger; (6) the Ch'ih wen, carved on the beams of bridges, because of its fondness for water; (7) the Suan ni, carved on Buddha's throne, on account of its propensity for resting; (8) the Yai tzu, carved on sword hilts in memory of its lust for slaughter; (9) the Pi hai, carved on prison gates, as it was addicted to litigation and quarrelling.'[1]

The Murō-ji

Dragons took to Japan, to which they were first introduced perhaps 2,000 years ago, like a duck to water. The Japanese landscape, with its shady valleys and steep rocks towering above, its streams, its woods, the silence of which was broken only by the song of the *uguisu*, the nightingale, its waterfalls and rivers, the sea, its strange-shaped cloud-capped mountains full of caves, must have struck them like an earthly paradise. They established themselves in the hearts of men as well. If one started following up the traces that dragons have left in Japanese

[1] M. WILLIAMS, *Buddhism*, London, 1890.

folklore, place-names, etc., one would quickly fill volumes. Up to only yesterday, when a Japanese wanted a name for a secret society with aims which appeared good to him, however infamous they were, what did he call it? The Black Dragon Society.

Since times which antedate the first written documents a *kami* has been associated with the springs that rise in the Murō mountains and bring fertility to the Yamato valleys. His home was one—it is not certain which—of three sacred caves still to be seen today, and special prayers are addressed to him in times of drought. When dragons arrived from China he was identified with one of them named Ryuketsu-Jin ('the divine dragon dwelling in the cave'), and he acquired great renown; his aid was sought to procure, not only rain, but every kind of good thing. Between A.D. 770 and 780, for instance, when the Crown Prince (the subsequent Emperor Kwammu, the founder of Kyoto) was gravely ill, five priests prayed at length for him in the solitudes of the Murō mountains. He recovered, and the fame of the dragon ascended to the skies.

Meanwhile the religion of Buddha, with its arts and its civilizing influence, had made a clamorous entry into Japan, and the changes that it wrought spread into the remotest recesses in the mountains. Buddhism has nearly always adopted rather than fought the religions it found in its path; that explains the fantastic variety of forms in which it presents itself, from Ceylon to Lhasa, from Burma to Nara, from Mongolia to China. There are conflicting stories about the origin of the great temple of Murō; according to the most acceptable version, it was built by the Abbot Kenkei, the leader of the five monks who contributed to the cure of the future Emperor Kwammu. Others claim that it was founded by the famous Kōbō-Daishi (774–835), but this seems to be one of the many instances in which a great reputation attracts to itself the work either of predecessors or of pupils.

We left the car under a tree in a quiet old village that hugged the stream, crossed a bridge, and climbed a steep little valley through a dark wood of cryptomerias. At the top of some steep steps we came in sight of the first temples; I was reminded of Vallombrosa before the tourist invasion. With its huge tree-trunks, its silence, and its strange echoes, of the kind that are to be heard only in conifer woods, the place became ever more fabulous. Just beyond the temples there suddenly came into view one of the loveliest things in Japan: an ancient pagoda, small in comparison with other similar pagodas, a perfectly proportioned toy not fifty feet high, which seemed to increase the magic of the huge trees all around.

The total effect that the Murō-ji (*ji* means temple) makes cannot have changed greatly since it was first built at the beginning of the ninth century, during a period of remarkable Buddhist fervour and of great felicity in the arts. True, of the original buildings only the pagoda and part of the Kon-do ('Golden Hall') remain; the rest, as so often happens in Japan, fell victim to fire. But the restorations of the Kamakura period (thirteenth century) merge admirably with it.

A number of sculptures of the highest value survive from the original period. In the Miroku-do ('Hall of Maitreya', the Buddha of the future) there is a wooden statue of Miroku, standing erect, which reminds one of certain Romanesque saints. The magnificent statue of Shaka Nyorai (Sakyamuni, the historical Buddha, the 'Enlightened One'), also in wood, demonstrates a perfect mastery of the material, and the expression combines supreme wisdom with the most gentle compassion. The light and harmonious drapery carries all the way to this remote Pacific island echoes of the Greek art which combined with that of Asia in the Kingdom of Gandhara.

A nervous, skinny, little old man acted as our guide; he repeated a sing-song patter which he had learned by heart. Not even the offer of a tip would halt his inexorable progress. My Japanese friends tried to persuade him that it was only once in a life-time that the poor *gaijin* (foreigner) was able to come from the other end of the world to visit this remote spot in the Murō mountains, but this made no impression; he seemed to think such a pilgrimage the most natural thing in the world. He would not let us take photographs and, if we wanted to look at one statue while he was talking about another, it was just too bad. We had to submit and follow him from Buddha to Buddha like automata. When it was over one of my friends had a brilliant idea. Would he take us round again? Certainly; provided we followed him meekly, without deviating one moment from his intinerary, he would take us round as many times as we liked.

The Kon-do ('Golden Hall') was just beyond. The interior was small and dark. The walls must once have been covered with paintings, but only faded remnants survive; against a partition there stood a row of over-life-size wooden statues of standing figures, all with flame-shaped haloes, as well as a number of paintings of varying merit, but all of the original period, known to the Japanese as the Konin period. Unfortunately the most valuable statue, of Jizo, a Bodhisattva considered to be the protector of travellers, pregnant women, and children, was on loan to a Tokyo museum. There were, however, a number of small statues of *shinsō* (warrior-defenders of the faith) attributed to one of the greatest Japanese sculptors, Unkei (twelfth–thirteenth centuries); these are works of extraordinary vigour.

Everything about us spoke of an esoteric, imaginative Buddhism. The Murō temples, though they originally belonged to the Hossō sect, have for centuries been one of the most important centres of the Shingon ('True Word') sect founded by Kōbō-Daishi. Shingon Buddhism closely resembles that of Tibet or Mongolia, the most sumptuous flower of the Mahayana, the 'Great Vehicle', so rich in mystery and symbolism that in the end it cloys. The few traces left on the walls reminded me of similar murals in Tibet, for instance at the Kum-Bum at Gyantse,[1] with their dozens, nay hundreds, of metaphysical Buddhas, angelic essences, thrones, dominations, principalities, and powers belonging to a universe of gnostic hints, and their interplay of shifting, fleeting harmonies, as in a crystal.

That we were in a temple dedicated to esoteric cults was not in doubt, but what a difference there is between such places in Japan and Tibet! How differently the character of the two peoples expresses itself through the medium of an almost identical religion! In a Tibetan Buddhist temple there is darkness, mystery, magnificence, and filth, the stink of yak butter, a love of death and horror, a strange, twisted mentality, sex mingled with mystical exaltation, barbarous couplings combined with extreme asceticism, magic and gnosticism, a multiplication of arms, heads, and symbols, unbridled audacity and imagination, a continuous metaphysical shudder. Here, however, there is not darkness, but subdued light, cleanliness seems a natural quality of things, the decoration is quiet and discreet, the representations of the gods, though obeying the esoteric dictates of the same Asian doctrine, express a deep respect for the dignity of the human form, a serene pleasure in

G. TUCCI, *Indo-Tibetica*, Rome, 1941, Vol. IV, Part III.

the loftiest impulses of the mind. In Tibet the eleven heads of Avaloki-tesvara become a teratological game, a palaeontology of the jurassic layers of the mind. Here they are a light crown, which you would barely notice if you did not know that they belonged to the icono-graphical pattern. Nowhere else do the two fundamental virtues of the Japanese mind stand out so brilliantly, its love of purity, and its vivid, total feeling for man.

We left the 'Golden Hall' and climbed to the Kancho-do, a graceful building of a somewhat later period (Kamakura, thirteenth century), with its enchanting, slightly curved, bark roof. Inside our attention was immediately attracted by a statue of Nyōirin Kwannon (another form of Avalokitesvara). Here we were really confronted with Tantric fan-tasies. The deity is seated in the *rajalila* ('regal repose') position, has six arms, and in each of his six hands carries symbols, including a rosary, the jewel that grants all desires, a lotus bud, and the wheel of the law. Tibetan artists in such cases seem carried away by the mystic symbolism; but the Japanese sculptor, as Getty rightly observes,[1] concentrated all his efforts into expressing in human terms a calm exterior combined with the most intense introspection. Moreover, the symbols are there because the priests said they were required; the artist's chief aim was to create a harmony in which the six-armed human monstrosity could be resolved elegantly into rhythmical form.

Brief Digression on Pagodas

Beyond the pagoda was a pathway leading into the wood and climbing, first gently and then more steeply, to a temple called Okuno-in Mieido ('Remote Pavilion of the Honourable Shadow'), dedicated to Kōbō Daishi, and containing a statue of him. We were not a thousand feet above sea-level, but the vegetation was almost Alpine; an occasional ray of sunshine, penetrating the foliage like the high windows of a Gothic nave, played on the green carpet of ferns.

When we emerged from the wood on our way back we again found ourselves looking at the elegant tracery of the pagoda. We sat among the ferns and admired it. But what exactly is a pagoda? Why were these

[1] A. GETTY, *The Gods of Northern Buddhism*, Oxford, 1928.

1. The great *stupa* of Sanchi (second–first centuries, B.C.). 2. *Stupa* carved in the rock; cave at Karli (second century, A.D.). 3. *Stupa* inside Cave XIX at Ajanta (fourth–seventh centuries, A.D.). 4. A *stupa* at Nalanda (ninth century, A.D.). 5. *Dagoba (stupa)* in Ceylon, Anuradhapura (first century, B.C.). 6. The biggest *stupa* in the world, Barabudur, Java (eighth century, A.D.). 7. A small pagoda with thatched roofs, Bali (contemporary period). 8. The Mingalazedi *stupa* at Pagan, Burma (fourteenth century). 9. Siamese *prachedi (stupa)*; ruins of Ayudhya (fourteenth–eighteenth centuries). 10. Shwe Dagon pagoda, Rangoon, Burma (sixteenth century). 11. Model of a Gandhara *stupa*, from the excavations at Jaulian (first–third centuries, A.D.). 12. Tibetan *chortens*, Lhasa (fifteenth–nineteenth centuries). 13. The Kumbum at Gyantse, Tibet (fifteenth century). 14. The small Bodnath *stupa*, Katmandu, Nepal (ninth century). 15. Small Nepalese Buddhist temple (Patan). 16. Twelve-cornered pagoda of the Sung-yüeh monastery, Honan, China (sixth century, A.D.). 17. Ta-yen-t'a pagoda, Hsian-fu, Shensi, China (seventh century, A.D.). 18. 'Iron-colour' pagoda, K'ai-feng, Honan, China (eleventh century). 19. Pagoda 'of the Relics', Wu-tai-shan (Shansi, China). 20. Wooden pagoda of the Fo-kung monastery, Ying-hsien, Shansi, China (eleventh century). 21. Pagoda on the Fang mountain (twelfth century). 22. The White Pagoda, Ch'ing-chou, Jehol, China (eleventh–twelfth centuries). 23. Pei-chen pagoda, Chin-hsien, Manchuria (eleventh century). 24. Pagoda at Ch'üan-chou, Fukien, China (thirteenth century). 25. Small pagoda in park at Seoul, Korea (fourteenth century). 26. Pagoda at the Horyu-ji, Nara, Japan (seventh century). 27. Pagoda at the Yakushi-ji, Nara, Japan (eighth century). 28. Yasaka pagoda, Kyoto, Japan (rebuilt in 1618). 29. Small pagoda of the *tahōtō* type at the Ishiyama-dera, Otsu, Japan (eleventh century).

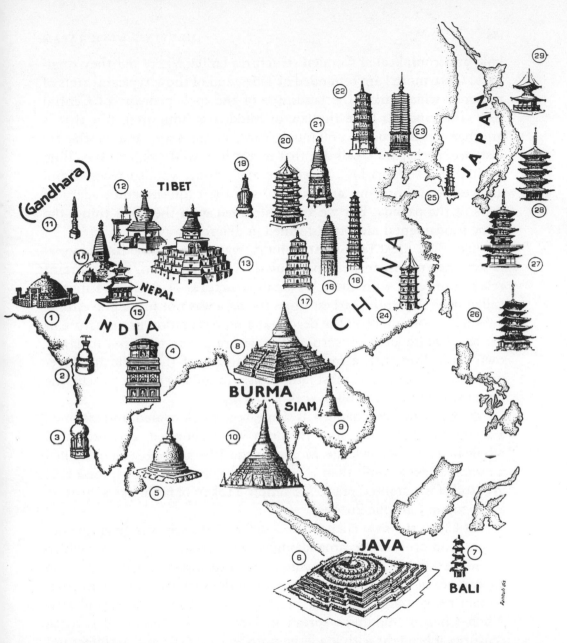

From *stupa* to pagoda. Some of the innumerable buildings scattered about the countries of east Asia all built for the same purpose, namely to preserve sacred relics and honour the religion of the Buddha. The experts are not in agreement on how some of the more striking transformations illustrated above took place.

N.B. The various drawings are not on the same scale
(Drawings by S. Pannuti based on data supplied by the author)

bold and complicated wooden structures built? Where did they origi-
nate? Once more I am reminded of Tibet, and of those typical turrets of
masonry which mark the landscape of the high plateaux of Central
Asia, announcing: Here the law of Buddha is honoured. But that is
another world; rocks, unlimited space, ochre tints, and in the far
distance, perhaps, a small dot that might be a wild yak, or a travelling
monk, or a shepherd. . . . Here we are among wooded recesses and
alcoves, leafy horizons, and before us is the exquisite embroidery of
lines of the pagoda. But we are confronted with the same thing, the
same fundamental idea, transformed in different ways.

Its origin must be sought in India, where since time immemorial
it was the custom to bury particularly venerated men, or important
relics connected with them, in small structures of stone and mortar
called *stupas*. From the earliest times the *stupa* was not just a gravestone,
a tomb, a monument to the dead, but a representation in miniature of
certain definite ideas concerning the nature of the universe. It has its
own symbolism; it is a metaphysical diagram of the world in three-
dimensional stone. The most famous *stupa* in India is that at Sanchi, the
remains of which can still be seen.[1]

In Tibet the *stupa* changed its shape, became elongated, and assumed
a character of its own. Its symbolism was elaborated, and became a
whole branch of knowledge. Moreover the Tibetan *stupa,* which is called
a *chorten,* is less a tomb than a reliquary, a cenotaph, an expression of
gratitude for a granted prayer, or simply a token of faith, like a cross on
a hill-top in Catholic Europe.

In China the *stupa* changed in a different way. It was given greater
height, and probably became identified with ornamental turrets which
already existed in Chinese architecture, and assumed the shape and
appearance of a tower. To the expert eye the various constituent parts
remain recognizable, but their proportions have changed completely.
When Chinese Buddhism spread in Japan in the sixth and seventh
centuries it brought with it a large number of artistic and architectural
motifs, including the pagoda. But while in China the usual building
materials were stone and mortar, in Japan all building was done in
wood. This difference in materials, as so often happens, led to further

[1] Incidentally they are in an enclosure which has four gateways, called *torana*; it is these which
the many authors who attribute an Indian origin to *torii* have in mind.

aesthetic development. The whole outline was marvellously lightened, the tower became a kind of stalk sustaining a fugue of harmoniously curved roofs. I think it can be claimed without much fear of error that the Japanese pagoda is among the most beautiful structures made by man (Photographs 85, 91).

From the esoteric point of view the Japanese pagoda is a reliquary; the sacred relic is said to be placed in a hollowed-out, cup-shaped stone under the central column which supports the whole. Both ritually and aesthetically the metal pinnacle (sorintō) in which the topmost roof mounts towards the sky is most important. Generally there are nine wheels (sorin), then a flame in which angelic essences dance, surmounted by two globes, 'the dragon's car' and the 'precious pearl'. The pinnacle at the Murō-ji is unique in that it ends in a circular canopy and a phial of ambrosia (hobyo); in this it perhaps recalls archaic types of stupa.[1]

Another type of pagoda sometimes found in Japan is smaller, lighter, has two roofs instead of five, is of somewhat later construction (eleventh century), and is called tahōtō ('pagoda of many treasures'). Here too the Chinese model has been profoundly modified. The extreme, almost frivolous, gracefulness of the roof reminds you of a huge butterfly that has settled in the middle of a wood, ready at any moment to resume its capricious flight.

Landscape and Frame

About fifteen miles nearer Nara there is another celebrated temple, that of Hase, which occurs so often in literature and the arts. It is one of the thirty-three temples dedicated to Kwannon, and one of the principal Japanese Buddhist places of pilgrimage.

Here too nature and the work of man are in delightful harmony. The principal temple, reached by a long, covered, ascending approach (Photograph 48), is sited half-way up a mountain, on a great terrace from which there is a memorable view; sacred plays are performed there from time to time. By a strange configuration of the landscape, you seem to be standing in the middle of a crater from which there is no way out; there are steep wooded slopes all round; the timber is never cut, and the forest stands in all its pristine virginity. The horizon

[1] G. TUCCI, *Indo-Tibetica*, Rome, 1941, Vol. I, p. 47.

is limited, for nothing but sky can be seen over the crest of the surrounding hills, but the situation is magnificent. The Japanese do not like vast, unlimited panoramas; the view from the Hase temple is a perfect example of their taste. Its wide sweep is immediately evident, but it is contained in a frame.

The place is undeniably magnificent, though it lacks the subtle, mythological fascination of the Murō-ji. As it is less difficult of access, there are many more pilgrims, and many foreign visitors come; there is actually almost a tourist air about the place, which one tries to forget, thinking of May here, when the famous peonies are in bloom. The temple, though originally founded in the eighth century, dates back barely to 1650; as so often happens in Japan, the various pavilions have several times been destroyed by fire. The pagoda was burned down in 1883; the new one, painted red and lacquered like a piece of furniture, frankly spoils a beautiful corner in the wooded landscape.

Inside the temple there is a statue of Kwannon, thirty-six feet high, made of camphor wood. To see it you enter a narrow corridor at its feet, from where, because of the distorting effect of the perspective, it seems monstrously tall. It is barely lit by vague gleams of light, and is complicated, heavy, and soulless. I noticed that it differed in many respects from the usual representations of Kwannon, and the priest explained that it was a composite representation of Kwannon, Jizō, and Amida—'he thus sums up in his person the present, the past, and the future'. Less celebrated, but much more beautiful, are the thirty-three pictures of Kwannon painted on wooden tablets surrounding the plinth. In the ambulatory behind I noticed many statues of slight interest. One, decadent though it is from the artistic point of view, is a rarity from the point of view of iconography; it is of Inari, the Shinto god of oats and of generation, represented as an aged sage, bent under the weight of two sheafs of rice. Representations of Shinto deities are rare, and it was curious to find one here, in a famous Buddhist temple. But in reality there was no cause for surprise. Up to the reforms of 1872 all temples were also shrines, and some of them still are. Sure enough, here, immediately outside the principal temple, we found a little Shinto shrine, with the typical roof of rafters protruding in the shape of a St. Andrew's Cross (chigi).

For the student of the popular religion the Hase temple offers inexhaustible material. There are, for instance, many of the crude little rustic pictures called *ema* ('painted horses'). The horse is a very common symbol in Japan, signifying success, or the attainment of a desire.[1] But for a very long time indeed the *ema* artists have painted all sorts of other things besides horses. These rough and amusing examples of popular art are sometimes pictorial prayers, sometimes expressions of gratitude for the granting of a prayer.

While my Japanese friends were explaining a typical play on words to me, I noticed an obviously American woman, accompanied by an extremely smartly dressed Japanese; his hair was plastered down, he wore an elegant white suit, and his shoes were as shiny as blackbeetles; the couple were having trouble with a camera, and I went to their assistance. The woman was obviously immensely curious about the temple, the statues, the local customs, everything, and the conversation continued; my Japanese friends assisted in providing information. Meanwhile the smart Japanese looked on with an expression of blank indifference; we must obviously be artists, good-for-nothings, to take so much interest in a lot of old stuff about which he knew and cared nothing.

The woman was on holiday at Nara from her work in an American office in Tokyo; the man was a *ni-sei*, a 'second generation' Japanese-American; he worked in Jane's office, and was acting as her interpreter and guide; his name was John.

It is difficult to imagine any human being from whom a European feels more remote than a *ni-sei*. Europeans and Japanese, if they succeed in reaching below the surface, get on very well indeed; in spite of their profound differences, they are both products of ancient and complex civilizations. Europeans and Americans, superficially separated in a different way, have a thousand ways of establishing links because of their common roots. But between European and *ni-sei* there is not one abyss, but two; it is like trying to establish contact with a man from Mars. The *ni-sei* has generally been taught to despise his Asian roots; on the other hand, all he has taken from the west is a two-dimensional duralumin Christianity, ultra-modernism, the cultivation of jazz as a sacred rite, a Californian veneer.

[1] The same is true in China and Tibet. In the latter flags called *lung-ta*('wind-horses')are flown from houses to bring good fortune. For *ema* see F. STARR, *Ema,* Tokyo, 1920.

Walking back to the entrance to the temple I noticed a huge, luxurious, shiny, green and yellow car which put our ancient, dusty Chevrolet to shame. John got into the driving-seat with Jane beside him, and they said good-bye, not without a look of triumphant commiseration on his part when he compared our respective vehicles. We all set off for Nara, but soon all that was left of Jane and her companion was a cloud of dust disappearing round a corner.

6

Encounters at Nara

Girl Who Died for Love

WE REACHED Nara as night fell. It lies on the side of a gently sloping valley, surrounded by low hills, and spreads out towards the only mountain in the neighbourhood, the Kasuga (1,630 feet), where the sacred forest has grown undisturbed since the beginning of time, concealing whispers of gods and the howling of foxes. Nara is a town of about a hundred thousand inhabitants, and lives on tourists and pilgrims; famous temples, pagodas, and ancient shrines are scattered about a huge park, in which tame deer roam freely.

After the war Nara became an allied rest and recreation centre. We had to pass a whole row of monstrous twentieth-century temples, where in the evening strumpets entertained the honest sons of New England and the Middle West among horrible coloured neon lighting and rasping loudspeakers. All over Japan these places are run up incredibly cheaply, using wood and plaster-board, in a style calculated to delight connoisseurs of the hideous. Strange memories of Chicago mingle with ecclesiastical Baroque, ancient Egypt rubs shoulders with India, 'modernism' is adorned with dragons and pagodas, Hieronymus Bosch looks askance at Le Corbusier, Eiffel shakes hands with Palladio, wooden huts are disguised to look like palaces. I noticed a place called the Furorida (Florida) and another called San Furancisco (San Francisco). At Sapporo at one time there were three places in a row called Binasu (Venus), Benisu (Venice), and Pinatsu (Pea-nuts), an epitome of the glamorous west. The sign 'Beer and Girls' was ubiquitous, and

often the additional information was supplied that 'this place is excep-
tionally clean'. Here and there signs were exhibited saying 'Off Limits'
(American) or 'Out of Bounds' (English).

After passing through this horror zone we were stopped by a crowd
of people in the principal street. What was it? Nothing, only a little
matsuri, a procession. We got out of the car, and mingled with the crowd.
Groups of priests passed, clothed in red and violet silk robes; there were
palanquins, trophies of grass and leaves, and some lovely girls dressed
in ancient fashion, wearing twelve thin kimonos one over the other and
big white veils over their heads; and there was an accompaniment of
melancholy music, as thin as the breath of dawn. People watched in
reverent silence; mothers lifted their children to enable them to see; an
American soldier, accompanied by his powdered and painted *pam-pam,*
mounted a step to take a photograph. What was it all about? On such
occasions Sachiko, my Japanese friend's wife, is extraordinary; she
knows nothing of the shyness *(hazukashisa)* which Japanese normally feel
about approaching strangers or pushing themselves forward. She went
up to the most important of the priests, stopped him, questioned him,
and took down his replies in her note-book, holding up the whole
procession.

'Many centuries ago,' she subsequently explained to me, 'great
Emperor in love with very beautiful *uneme. Uneme* is palace lady. She very
happy, glad, love her master. Everybody love. Then Emperor's heart
change, no longer love *uneme.* She desperate, throw herself in lake. She
hang kimono on branch, walk naked into lake. Poor little *uneme!* Many
years later priest pass, praying. What happen? He see white spirit *uneme,*
ask him to say prayers, read *o-kyō* [sacred texts] to free her from bad
punishment. Understand?'

So every year at the autumn equinox this procession is held to
comfort the spirit of a girl who died for love. Priests in violet robes, girls
in white veils, children covered in flowers, march through the town and
round the lake, stop at the willow-tree, sing hymns, say prayers, and
sound the *shō* on the evening of the September full moon, which the
Japanese hold to be the most beautiful of the year. While Sachiko was
explaining all this to me, the last of the children covered in little red
flowers brought up the rear of the procession. One of them was sulking;
apparently he had no desire to console the unknown *uneme,* or perhaps

he only wanted a sweet. Men and boys got on their bicycles and rode away. The American with his *pam-pam* came over to me and said: 'Hey, what the hell was all that masquerade about?'

Encounters, Old and New

The first Japanese encounter with the west took place about 1540 with the arrival of a party of Portuguese led by Mendes Pinto, and caused the greatest possible satisfaction on both sides. The Japanese learnt the art, first of firing arquebuses, and then of making them, and they called this new weapon *tane-gashima,* after the small island of Tane, where the first fateful disembarkation of *nanban-jin* (southern barbarians), with their fair skins and red beards, took place. The Portuguese were delighted with the Japanese in every way, and unexpected vistas of expansion and trade opened up before them.

A Japanese document of the time says:

'The foreign merchants . . . had one article in their possession which was about two or three *shaku* in length. It was straight, heavy, and hollow. One end, however, was closed, and near it there was a small hole, through which fire was to be lighted. The article was used in this way: some mysterious medicine was put into it with a small round piece of lead, and when one lit the medicine through that hole, the lead piece was discharged and hit everything. When it was discharged, light like lightning was seen and noise like thunder was heard, so that bystanders invariably closed their ears with their hands.'[1]

The author goes on to describe how his father bought two *tane-gashima* from the southern barbarians and spent a long time trying to manufacture them himself. Not till a year later, when the foreigners returned with a blacksmith, did he learn the art of 'closing one end of the tube', which had hitherto been an insuperable technical obstacle. After that the Japanese manufactured about seventy arquebuses on their own in a year.

[1] DAIRYUJI FUMIYUKI, *Nanpo-Bunshiu* (end of the sixteenth or beginning of the seventeenth century), quoted by J. MURDOCH, *A History of Japan,* Vol. II, p. 42.

Meanwhile the Portuguese were enthusiastic about the island 'which has recently been discovered in that part of the north called Japan'. St. Francis Xavier, before leaving Malacca, wrote in 1548 that 'the Japanese are extremely desirous of being instructed, which our gentiles

For two and a half centuries Japan was closed to the outside world. Apart from a few Dutch traders allowed to live in semi-imprisonment on the little island of Deshima (Nagasaki), the only foreigners with whom the Japanese had contact were the aborigines of the northern islands. Here is a Sakhalin fisherman as seen by the explorer Mamiya Rinzō

(From *Kita Ezo Tsusetsu*, Tokyo, 1854)

in India by no means are'. A year later he wrote from Japan itself that these people 'are the best that have so far been discovered, and no better could be found among the infidels'.[1]

Then the Spaniards came, and the rivalry between them and the

[1] P. TACCHI-VENTURI, *Il Carattere dei Giapponesi*, pp. 13, 19, 25.

Portuguese struck the spark which caused the Japanese to decide to expel all Christians and foreigners from their islands. In 1596 the captain of a Spanish galleon had his cargo confiscated by a Japanese baron; to extricate himself from a difficult position he produced a map of the world and started boasting about the vast dominions of his master, Philip II. When the Japanese asked him how a single king had succeeded in dominating so many foreign nations, he replied that he started by sending missionaries to the territories to be conquered; when a large number of converts had been made he landed troops who, with the aid of the converts, forcibly brought about a change of government. When this was reported to the *taikō* Hideyoshi, the man with the iron fist who had recently succeeded in unifying Japan for the first time in centuries, he exploded with wrath against the 'snakes whom he had nurtured to his bosom'; and thus the spark was struck which led to the terrible persecution of Christians and foreigners which lasted for thirty years and ended by almost completely extinguishing the influence of the outside world on Japan. From the beginning of the seventeenth century to the visit of Commodore Perry with his 'black ships' in 1854 Japan remained in a state of isolation.

Throughout this long period, from 1600 to 1854, a single slender thread connected Japan with the outside world, and this was entrusted to the Dutch. The rulers of Japan were extremely suspicious of any western contacts which might involve them with priests; and it was only with the greatest difficulty that Protestant countries ever obtained permission to land. After a period of indecision, the Dutch, who appeared to the Japanese to be the quietest and least dangerous, were granted permission to send one ship a year from China to Kyushu. Their representatives were, however, confined to the small island of Deshima, where they lived at their trading station rather like prisoners. Once a year the head of the mission, the *Operhoofd*, was permitted to travel to Yedo (Tokyo) and pay ceremonial homage to the shogun.[1]

This restricted observation post was, however, used by a number of Europeans of great industry and intelligence (Kaempfer, Thunberg, P. F. von Siebold, and others) to form a complete picture of Japanese life and civilization; and similarly a few adventurous-minded Japanese

[1] *See* C. R. BOXER, *Jan Compagnie in Japan, 1600–1850*, The Hague, 1950; and G. B. SANSOM, *The Western World and Japan*, London, 1950.

(Arai Hakuseki, Honda Toshiaki) used it, particularly from the end of the eighteenth century onwards, to learn something about the mysterious outside world. A new branch of knowledge actually grew up, known as *ran-gaku* (*ran* being *Oranda*, Holland, and *gaku* being the equivalent of our '-ology'—'Hollandology', in other words). But I have mentioned all this history only in order to introduce certain ideas. Let us return to the encounters I have observed in several years of direct experience.

First of all the British. Japan and Britain have many things in common. Both are islands on the edge of huge oceans, both have civilizations with a strong individual imprint resulting from the integration of originally diverse elements (German-Latin, Yamato-Chinese); both have been strongly centralized for centuries, and historically both have had a decidedly aristocratic social structure. The British-Japanese encounter has consequently been characterized by mutual esteem rather than warmth. Each of the two peoples likes form, ceremony, self-control; these characteristics lead to respect for the individuality of the other rather than to close contact. The Anglo-Japanese alliance (1902–21), the longest of modern times, was more than a mere political agreement, though in Japan its influence was restricted to the nobility and the upper bourgeoisie. It is still possible from time to time to meet aristocratic old Japanese gentlemen who were educated at Oxford, dress like country gentlemen, play golf, and tell dry, humorous stories about the hunting field over a whisky-and-soda in front of the fire after dinner.

The Anglo-Japanese encounter yielded lasting results, however, in the field of scholarship. Our deep and thorough knowledge of Japanese is in great part due to the British. The first generation of Japanese scholars, the generation of Satow, Chamberlain, Aston, Murdoch, Eliot, Munro, was succeeded by a second, less numerous perhaps, but equally well, if not better, equipped, that of Ponsonby-Fane, Sansom, Waley. The British compiled the first dictionaries, translated the classics, wrote the most exhaustive histories based on Japanese, Chinese, and western sources.

Thus the Anglo-Japanese encounter has been on a high qualitative level. This, in a sense, is true of the German-Japanese encounter. Here too for many years contact was maintained on a somewhat cold, official level, that of deep bows and high-sounding speeches. In the field of

相觀歌麿考畫
婦女人相十品

33

(34) *Aged peasant, south Japan,* (35) *aged Ainu, north Japan,* (36) *meeting at Tokyo,* (37) *steel worker;* (38-41) *girls, and a mother;* (42, 43) awabi *fisher-girls on the island of Hekura.*

39

0

41

2

43

44

45

Shinto, the native religion of Japan, is essentially nature and ancestor worship. (44) *Sacred music;* (45) *ritual dance;* (46) *a dignitary;* (47) *procession.*

6

47

Buddhism, the great Asian religion, bringer of thought, civilisation, beauty. (48) Monastery; (49) meditation; (50) festival of the dead; (55) at prayer in the temple.

52

Sandal dropped by a pilgrim in front of the torii *of Miyajima (52); stone lantern at night (53); ceremony at a Shinto shrine (54); prayer outside a Buddhist temple (55).*

54

55

Japan, land of festivals. (56) Shinto priest in a procession
at Kyoto; (57) getting ready for a procession in Tokyo;

(58) *purification by torch-light at Kurama, near Kyoto;*
(59) *gathering of Samurai of the north in the Haramachi meadows.*

60

61

In the cold of winter the Ainu of Hokkaido kill the sacred bear (60, 61). In the heat of summer, festivities in Tokyo in honour of the Three Protectors (62-66).

(67) *Narrow street at Kurashiki;* (68) *rain in the Hidaka mountains.*

Clothing and domestic architecture as a single, coherent whole.

(69) *Tea for a guest in a peasant's house;* (70) *farmhouse kitchen;* (71) *Buddhist shrine in a petty bourgeois house;* (72) *Shinto shrine in the house of a small merchant.*

(73) *Lesson in flower arrangement;* (74) *preparations for the tea ceremony;*

(75) *painter of lanterns;* (76) *entrance of an ancient restaurant at Kyoto;* (77) *shop in which the finest teas are sold;* (78) *gathering of peasants.*

79

Twentieth century cathedrals: (79) *Chiba steelworks;* (80) *Osaka stock exchange.*

80

scholarship, contact was exceedingly fertile; it is sufficient to recall the names of K. Florentz and H. Bohner.

There is, however, another, subterranean, level at which Japanese and German hearts easily beat in unison—that at which there is an obscure, imperious need to live in a spirit of heroic self-dedication to something or somebody. At this level one would seek in vain the happy equilibrium which distinguishes the Chinese in so many ways; instead there is a hankering for the terrible which borders on the tragic and sometimes descends to the ridiculous, a state of mind which feels strongly the attractions of the violent and the obscene. The German influence in Japan has been much deeper and more widespread than the British but, except in the field of medicine, less beneficial. The universities, the army, certain public services, have Prussian roots of extraordinary tenacity. The mournful black uniform worn by students comes within this order of influences.

If Anglo-Japanese accord seems possible only at a high social and intellectual level, I should say that German-Japanese accord is easier at all levels; I have the impression that the only mixed marriages that have any chance of success are Japanese-German. In Japan *Doitsu* (Germany) always has a serious connotation. *Igirisu* (England) evokes in the mind of a well-disposed Japanese the picture of a nice, elderly, sporting uncle who climbs the highest mountains in the world, invites you to tea and cakes and raspberries and cream, is not a genius, but is so honest and reliable; *Doitsu,* on the other hand, suggests a cousin whom you do not know whether or not to admire, but with whom you are linked by certain nocturnal adventures and a taste for certain forbidden things. When your German cousin is about, you know that something is going to happen.

The most satisfactory, the happiest, the most natural of these encounters is the Franco-Japanese. Here too contact has always been at a high level, a high intellectual level in particular. The France concerned is not the narrow world of the French provinces, of the petty bourgeoisie, but that of the *littérateurs,* the artists, and the savants. At this level France and Japan are two exquisitely pagan and sophisticated countries, made to understand each other. The Japanese like French taste, its caprice, its fashions, its deep, unpedantic humanism, the tinge of frivolity which serves the better to conceal the flame within. The French like the

3,>

3>3>

 (1>

1

aesthetic sense which pervades the whole of Japanese life; as soon as they set foot in a Japanese house, fall in love with a Japanese woman, read a Japanese poem or piece of good prose, they discover a new, real, and entirely unexpected France among a thousand possible and conceivable Frances. I should say, in fact, that French and Japanese approach each other with the fewest mental reservations, the most open mutual humanity; that is why they achieve understanding.

The French is the only European influence which is not restricted to the world of culture, arts, and letters but has spread into everyday life. It is sufficient to take a stroll along the Ginza in Tokyo and note the signs outside the hundreds of places where one can drink beer, *saké,* or whisky in company with a *jokyu-san* ('honourable waitress')—the modern version of the geisha—to see how strong is the desire to seem in some way Parisian. Often, it is true, the Paris that is the object of emulation never was in heaven or on earth; you have only to look at the places called the Papirion (Le Papillon), the Ramu (l'Amour), the Toaemuá (Toi et Moi), the Kōkkudoru (Le Coq d'Or), the Rameru (La Mer), and other fantastic results of the *nichi-futsu* (Franco-Japanese) axis. A. Smoular, a careful observer of Japanese life, says that he was never able to overcome his surprise at the fashion in which one of these girls of easy virtue who mix up-to-date (and often exceedingly bad) drinks with the gestures of an ancient courtesan 'made sensitive and intelligent comments on Matisse or other French painters'. Perhaps he exaggerates, but at any rate it is not far from the truth.

The Japanese language has adopted not only innumerable English terms, but many French ones too. The disorder and indiscipline of the post-war period, for instance, are referred to as *apuré (après guerre); abeku (avec)* has an endless variety of uses—it can mean lover, mistress, friend, geisha, and is used as noun, adjective, or interjection. The language of artists is full of words such as *atorie (atélier), amachua (amateur), moderu (modèle), ankoru (encore), dessan (dessein),* and others of the kind.

Finally, there is the encounter which from many points of view is the most important of all, the Japanese-American. This is the only one which has taken place on a mass scale. It is estimated that since the end of the war at least a million Americans have spent at any rate some time in Japan. As we have already mentioned, the occupation began under rosy auspices; but relations deteriorated, and ended by being bad. That is a chapter of contemporary history; here I propose to confine myself to a more humble plane.

Apart from the fact that Japanese-American relations were those between victor and vanquished, which always makes understanding difficult, there are many reasons why even in the most favourable circumstances the Japanese-American encounter would tend to be only moderately successful.[1] On the one hand we have America, a country of Puritan traditions, of straightforward, practical men without a true and constant interest in the arts and the things of the mind, always ready to cut the Gordian knot; on the other we have Japan, whose people are as pagan as ancient Mediterranean man, always tending to argue in terms of *kimochi* (states of mind), dominated by what may be called *buai, yōsu, arisama, jōkyō, jijō, moyō, jōtai, jōsei, jitai,* and a hundred other things, but merely mean circumstances; an extremely complicated people, full of ancient fears and new ambitions, extremely sensitive to all forms of beauty, intellectual values, emotional claims, always ready, when confronted with a Gordian knot, not to cut it, but to tie another, bigger one all round it and thus put it out of sight. We are, in fact, confronted with two attitudes to life, two interior universes, which differ so profoundly that it is hard to think that a greater contrast could be possible.

Apart from some rare exceptions, then, the Japanese-American encounter is on the whole unsuccessful. It is sufficient to look at the results; I do not mean in the political field, but in everyday life. Americanized Japanese, with the exceptions of a few examples of intellectual distinction who would shine anywhere, are incredibly crude, vulgar, ignorant, and presumptuous. They have thrown their own civilization overboard, and all they have taken over from the new is a superficial indifference to everything, an arrogance that they mistake for cordiality, a shameless interest in money. The women in particular are unrecognizable. They have not a trace left of the traditional Japanese charm, and yet they are not within a thousand miles of the genuine American camaraderie; they are nothing but little savages taking delight in their own iconoclastic fury, hitting out to right and left, both physically and verbally.

[1] Except the special case of American man and Japanese woman which we have already discussed.

All that most Americans seek in Japan is exotic knick-knacks, embroidered dragons, ivory dolls, painted wooden pagodas. Only rarely do they immerse themselves in Japanese life; they prefer to remain among themselves, thus inevitably encouraging the creation all round them of an area of contamination in which the most atrocious squalor and vulgarity prevail. What is more, all the most strikingly pagan aspects of Japanese life, those that in the natural context of Japanese society have their well-defined place, are changed, displaced, distorted, and, seen through Puritan eyes, turn into irremediable evil. This sense of evil then spreads to the Japanese, who turn into thieves, pimps, rogues, blackmailers; these once existed only in limited numbers in the lowest quarters, but have now in many towns spread and multiplied sufficiently to be a matter of serious concern to the authorities.

It certainly should not be overlooked that, apart from this contact at the mass level, there is contact of another kind, a contact of quality. In America the world of culture is, of course, highly specialized and, though it may frequently exercise an influence on public affairs, it is a long way from the ordinary life of the majority. Entering an American university is like entering a marvellous oasis from which the hustle and greed for gain which prevail outside are permanently excluded; here indeed is the realm of knowledge, of huge libraries, of scholars on whom society lavishes privileges so that they may continue with their work undisturbed. This environment produced what from one point of view is one of the most remarkable books of our time: Ruth Benedict's *The Chrysanthemum and the Sword*.[1] During the war the American leaders decided that it was necessary to know more about the exotic enemy with whom they were at grips; and, because of her distinction as an anthropologist, Ruth Benedict was commissioned to write an interpretation of the Japanese character and attitude to life which would serve as a guide in the formation of American policy. The remarkable feature of all this was that Miss Benedict had never set foot in Japan. Nevertheless, by fitting together bits and pieces, by skilful inference and deduction, she wrote a book which, being the product of the laboratory, so to speak, necessarily fails to give the flavour of the country and the people, but provides one of the best interpretations yet made of a world so different from that of the west. It was largely due to Miss Benedict that the

[1] Boston, 1946.

American Government made the wise decision not to remove the Emperor in the event of victory, realizing that the Japanese would never hold him responsible for defeat, and that he provided the only possible rallying point round whom it would be possible to begin a peaceable reconstruction of the country. The Japanese themselves attach importance to Miss Benedict's work, and some years ago devoted to it a special number of the Japanese *Review of Ethnology*.[1]

The Japanese certainly know little about Italy, and what they know tends to come to them through writers of other countries—at best Goethe, Stendhal, or Aldous Huxley. I recall the celebrated remark of the member of the Japanese Diet who, on seeing the Claudian aqueduct in Rome, said that post-war reconstruction did not seem to have got very far yet.

In conclusion, I should like to mention a recent investigation by Unesco into what young people in Japan think of other countries.[2] The results were interesting, and demonstrated a knowledge that was far from superficial. The United States came first for science and industrial technique, followed by Germany and the Soviet Union; France came first in the category of intellectual values, followed by Britain; Switzerland came first for political development, while Denmark reigned supreme and almost unchallenged for economic development. For spiritual values the palm went to Britain. Italy was mentioned (last but one, after China) only by a few under the heading: Which country would you most like to visit? In other words, the interest was purely touristic.

Youthful Heyday

Nara was the capital of Japan for only seventy-four years, from A.D. 710 to 784, but something of that brief halcyon period still survives in the atmosphere today. Present-day Nara, a town of 100,000 inhabitants, is small in comparison with the capital founded by the Emperor Gemmyō. The Japanese, having decided that it was impossible to continue the system of changing the capital on the death of every emperor, went about things in a big way. Peasants of the villages to the west of the

[1] *Minzokugaku Kenkyū Zasshi*, Vol. XIV (1949), No. 4.
[2] J. STOETZEL, *Jeunesse sans Chrysanthème ni Sabre*, Paris, 1954.

present town still turn up with their ploughs stones which were the foundations of ancient palaces or long-since-vanished temples. A wide and impressive avenue more than three miles long called the Sujaku-oji, the 'Avenue of the Red Peacock', sloped away from the Imperial Palace. At the other end there was a big gate, the Rajomon. Four parallel main roads lay on either side of this main artery, traversed at right-angles by ten other roads; these too were more than three miles long. Such was the design of a city rare in the world at that time; it was built in emulation of the most splendid capital of the age, Ch'ang-an, the residence of the Chinese emperors, the successors of T'ai-tsung (d. A.D. 649), the Charlemagne of the east.

The broad, straight streets of ancient Nara were flanked by houses and temples, monasteries and pagodas, villas and gardens. The reader should not think in terms of the massive town houses of the west, which in the last resort derive from the fortified houses of the Middle Ages. To judge from certain temple districts, which still preserve the ancient order of things, the streets were flanked not by houses, but by low, earth walls (dobei), interrupted at intervals by gateways the impressiveness of which varied with the importance of the owner of the villa to which it provided access. Over the wall the curved roof could be made out among the trees.

In the more popular quarters were the markets, where the going and coming of servants and slaves (who at that time were very numerous) must have created a colourful tumult. There were many artisans at Nara, often of Korean or Chinese origin, producing objects of beauty for the wealthy families and the temples. The embellishment of the capital continued uninterruptedly for several decades.

> Like a splendid corolla
> In flower
> Nara blooms in splendour,
> The capital.

So wrote Ono no Oyu.[1] This was, incidentally, a flourishing age throughout Asia. In comparison Europe lay in the depths of barbarism. Apart from some gleams of civilization in Italy, at the court of the last Merovingians and first Carolingians in France, and in the Irish mon-

[1] Manyōshu, III, 328.

asteries, Europe lay asleep, like a field that has yielded a tremendous harvest and is nursing in its vitals the germs of another, still distant, summer. But in Asia it was full daylight; great empires flourished, and the most populous and civilized of the world's capitals. Baghdad, for instance, was taking over the Greek heritage, and Ch'ang-an was the head and heart of the world's greatest country, China.

Asia was very different from the Asia of the present day, even in the physical respect. The centre of the continent had not yet become a desert. Trade routes connected east and west. Along these there were brought to the west such things as silk, paper, tea, porcelain, playing cards, gunpowder, spinach, sugar, dice, chess-men, the chicken, and perhaps macaroni; and to the east the grape, carrots, glass, and the alphabet. There was also a continual two-way traffic of ideas, religious beliefs, artistic ideas. Nestorian Christianity and Islam penetrated to China along these routes, and, above all, Buddhism, an Indian doctrine which brought with it an art which was to a great extent Greco-Roman. In many of the cities along these routes Indo-European languages were spoken which have since disappeared, Tokharic, for example, and there were flourishing communities of Manichaeans, Christians, and Muslims. Their arts, investigated by Stein, Pelliot, Von le Coq, Hackin, reveal every possible combination and synthesis of elements generally considered remote from one another. Thus we find Buddhas which are in reality somewhat Asianized Apollos, Silenuses who have become *yaksha,* and the features of Pegasus, Jupiter, Hercules, Pallas Athene, variously transformed into Bodhisattvas, genii, Buddhist angels and saints. Greco-Roman and Sassanid motifs combine, and both fuse with other purely Indian motifs of the Gupta style.[1]

In other fields of culture a similar process of *rapprochement,* fusion, superposition, took place. We find Christian frescoes painted in the Persian style, and languages of the Chinese family written in Indian characters; and two Manichaean canonical books—the Manichees professed a doctrine which was in part Christian, our knowledge of which is gained principally through St. Augustine—were included in the Chinese Taoist scriptures, having evidently travelled right across the continent. In what is now Afghanistan money has been found which

[1] R. GROUSSET, *Les Civilisations de l'Orient,* Paris, 1930, particularly Vol. III (*China*). Also his *Bilan de 'Histoire,* Paris, 1946, p. 119.

was coined by the Yüeh-chih, a people probably of Indo-European origin, who were driven out of the Chinese borderlands in the second century B.C.; these coins have engravings in Greek style of Indian gods, as well as portraits of Caesar Augustus and the Buddha. Finally, at the Turfan oasis, there have been discovered Buddhist books with Sanskrit notes, the pages numbered in Chinese, annotated in characters of Syriac origin in a Turkish language, Uigur.[1]

The cosmopolitan character of upper Asia still survived in the time of Marco Polo, the end of the thirteenth century. Carter observes that Kublai Khan's reply to Innocent IV in 1245, 'written in the Persian and Uigur languages, sealed with a Mongol seal of Chinese style that had been cut by a Russian seal cutter and sent by the hand of an Italian monk to the Pope', was typical; as typical as the case of Yahb-allaha III, a Christian of Turkish origin born in north China who was appointed Patriarch of the Nestorian Church, whose seat was in Baghdad (1281–1317). Not till after the final Muslim conquests in Central Asia and the conversion of the Turks to the religion of Allah was the land route between east and west finally cut.

When, after four centuries of wars, divisions, and spiritual travail, China was finally united under Kao-tsu, the founder of the T'ang dynasty (618–907), all the cultural elements that had made their way across Asia from Greece, Persia, and India were fused into a new unity, and a long period of peace and prosperity and splendour began which marked the zenith of the history of the Celestial Empire. There is no doubt that the China of the T'ang dynasty was the most powerful, best administered, most civilized state in the world at that time.

The monks, merchants, and scholars from the Yamato country, who from the sixth century onwards visited China in increasing numbers, must have been left breathless by what they saw. In Japan life still went on timelessly, to the slow rhythm of the natural development of tribal institutions; here they found themselves in a vast metropolis, in the streets of which it was possible to meet Indian Buddhist monks, envoys from the kingdoms of Central Asia, from Samarkand, from Persia; merchants from Tongking, Annam; Siberian nomadic tribal chiefs; strange men with red beards and blue eyes from the territories

[1] T. F. CARTER, *The Invention of Printing in China and its Spread Westwards*, New York, 1925, revised edition, 1952.

of distant Fu-lin or An-tun (Constantinople or Rome; *Roma, Rumi, Hrim, Hu-rim, Fu-lin; An-tun* from the Antonines), to say nothing of students and priests from Korea, Tunguses covered with furs, Tibetans with their yaks, Arabs with their camels.

Ch'ang-an was not only great, but was also learned and beautiful. Buddhist temples stood side by side with Nestorian and Manichaean churches, Zoroaster was worshipped, the doctrine of Mahomet was preached, and the Confucian classics were commented on. In Japan a few old men knew by heart the interminable genealogies of gods and emperors, but here writing and paper (paper was not to reach the west until the end of the tenth century) had been known for centuries, and there were whole libraries full of knowledge. In Japan the *haniwa* (clay tubes) testified to latent artistic ability, but what were they in comparison with the paintings and sculpture to be seen here? Japan did not possess even a properly organized central administration; the supremacy of the Yamato rulers was widely recognized, but in the provinces the heads of big families ruled more or less at their pleasure in a kind of loose, primitive feudalism. Moreover, more than half of the biggest island was still dominated by the *ebisu*, the savage ancestors of the Ainu, who 'gathered like ants to attack, but scattered like birds as soon as you faced them'.

The Japanese, with that extraordinary determination of character and assimilative ability that has distinguished them at other periods of their history, set about the task of wiping out in the shortest possible time their evident inferiority in relation to their great neighbour. Korean scribes are known to have been employed at the Japanese court from the beginning of the fifth century, and many Japanese must have started familiarizing themselves with ideograms from then onwards. In 552 the first Buddhist preachers arrived, and the first Buddhist texts and statues. A few decades later Prince Shōtoku carried out his memorable civilizing work. Finally, in 645, the Emperor Kōtoku reorganized the state on the Chinese model (the Taikwa reform, the so-called 'great change'). Semi-tribal feudalism gave way to a centralized administration embodying the Chinese principle of 'no land under heaven that does not belong to the sovereign'. Provincial governors took the place of the nearly independent local lords; a new system of taxation was introduced, based on a census; and a bureaucracy was established of twenty-

six grades and sub-grades, the members of which were distinguished by
the different buttons and hats they wore.

The culmination of the long process by which the Japanese emerged
from the limbo of prehistory was the foundation, construction, and
embellishment of an ambitious capital. After more than a thousand
years, something of the perfume of that marvellous spring season still
lingers in the air. The whole of Asia now lay open to the inhabitants of
its last remote island outposts in the vast spaces of the Pacific. It was
a cosmopolitan century; the Japanese forgot their narrow world,
looked outside themselves, looked at humanity with the enthusiasm of
adolescents, and wanted to try everything.

Hence Nara testifies to a variety of motifs, styles, schools, influences,
for which there is no parallel in Japanese history until the present age.
So complex was the artistic production that the specialists have not yet
agreed even on a uniform division into periods; they divide 200 years of
artistic history into Asuka, Suiko, Hakuho, Tempyo, primitive Nara,
late Nara periods, in the most hair-raising confusion. Besides the
hieratic groups in bronze showing Buddha and the Bodhisattvas by
Tori and his school, which recall the cave sculptures of Yun-kang in
northern China, there are to be seen the subtly sensuous figures in the
frescoes of the Horyu-ji ('Temple of the Flourishing Law'), containing
echoes of the Central Asian art which fused India and Greece. Besides
the great Buddhas and Bodhisattvas of the Yakushi-ji ('Temple of the
Master of Medicine'), to which the centuries have given a rich dark
patina—they obviously testify to the direct influence of Indian styles as
interpreted by Chinese artists of the T'ang dynasty—there are the first
truly Japanese sculptures, in which there is immediately evident a particular purity of line, surface, and decoration, and a desire to see humanity, flesh, and blood, even in the most abstract of deities. In general a transition can be observed from mysticism and a Byzantine rigidity of form to
a very definite humanism and realism. Nevertheless works contemporary
in date show the simultaneous co-existence of the most varied trends.

Drawing-room Temple

I do not propose to confuse the reader with long lists of names; a guide
to Nara would be out of place here, even apart from the fact that a

number are already in existence. But I do not wish to leave for Kyoto without recalling at least some of the things which have a special place in Japanese history.

Yesterday, for instance, we went to the Horyu-ji ('Temple of the Flourishing Law'), which lies a few miles in the Osaka direction. It is one of the oldest surviving temples in Japan, and probably the oldest wooden building in the world. There are doubts about the exact date of its construction or reconstruction, but it seems that the most important part of it dates back to the end of the seventh century. Chinese ideas and models are evident in the arrangement of its pavilions, which are situated about a square cloister on a nearly flat piece of ground among vegetation and pine-trees. Later the native love of the unexpected and asymmetrical became dominant among Japanese architects and artists, but here a unity with Asia is manifested, and this monument belongs to the history of the continent as much as it does to Japan. It is beautifully situated, not in a romantic valley, like the Murō-ji, or in a secluded recess in the mountains like those in which many of the Kyoto temples are concealed, but in the midst of an open, sunny countryside. The first impression is of peace and serenity; avenues, trees, the play of the curves of the roofs of the Chumon ('Middle Gateway'), the Kairō (cloister), the Kon-do ('Golden Hall'), the Kō-do ('Sermon Hall'), which is repeated up towards the sky in the five-storey pagoda like a musical motif announced and repeated by various groups of instruments in a fugue. Chinese-Japanese architecture is essentially an architecture of roofs, roofs like great heron's wings resting among the trees and on the hillsides.

There are more than a hundred works of the highest value at the Horyu-ji. The big frescoes of the Buddha and the Bodhisattvas, which I have already mentioned, constituted one of the most remarkable works in all Asia; the voice of India, Persia, and Central Asia speaking directly and without any intermediary in this valley in an island at the end of the world. But, after surviving all the perils of the centuries, war, rebellion, earthquake, typhoons, ordinary bombs and atomic bombs, one day in 1949 some workmen engaged in restoration carelessly went away for some minutes leaving a pot boiling in the temple. Half an hour later a furious fire, which miraculously did not spread to the whole building and the whole Horyu-ji, had destroyed these precious relics.

The only consolation is that excellent photographs existed, so that the historical documentation was not completely destroyed. From the artistic point of view, one can only wring one's hands; restoration, recently completed, was carried out with skill and respect, but what had vanished for ever could not be reproduced.

Next to the Horyu-ji is a small convent inhabited by nuns; this is the Chugu-ji ('Temple of the Middle Palace'), which contains the only other work which I wish to mention here; it is one of the greatest treasures of all times and places. While the Horyu-ji is big, majestic, masculine, this little temple and the convent attached to it are small, irregular, exquisitely feminine. We rang the bell at a little door, heard the sound of footsteps on the gravel, and the door was opened by a young nun, with shaved head, but uncommonly good-looking and elegant. When she saw me and my Japanese companions she was taken aback; she blushed, became confused, and left us. She must have been just passing, and must have opened the door by chance. Could she have been a princess who had taken the veil? She was succeeded by an Amazon of

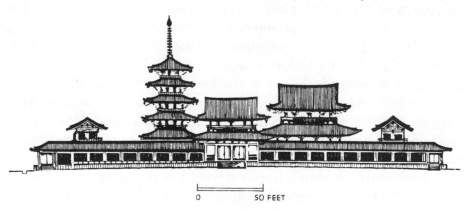

0   50 FEET

View of the Horyu-ji (seventh–eighth century)

(From Ota, Tanabe, Hattori, *Nippon no Kenchiku* ('Japanese Architecture'),
Tokyo, 1953)

about thirty, who unceremoniously told us that it was late, that the place was shut, that we should come back another time. She was about to shut the door when Sachiko, with many bows and smiles, implored her to wait a moment, and explained in rapid Japanese, full of sighs and nervous smiles, that we had come from afar, that we should never be able to come back, that (pointing to me) *kochira-sama* ('Mr. here') set great store before leaving Japan on setting eyes for a brief moment on the famous picture of the merciful Kwannon, etc., etc. She finally succeeded in softening the woman's heart, and she let us in with a grunt.

The inside of the little convent was kept so meticulously, so fabulously clean and tidy that everything, even the gravel in the courtyard, each individual stalk of the moss that always grows round the piles on which Japanese houses are built, seemed to be responding, not just to the external influence of broom, rake, and brush, but to an inner law, like that which regulates the arrangement of molecules in a crystal. The silence was total; our footsteps resounded like a cannonade; instinctively we walked on tip-toe. After passing through a number of rooms and courtyards, we reached an exquisitely elegant little temple in which you could have searched in vain with a microscope for a speck of dust or with rule and compass for the slightest irregularity in the arrangement of things. A gilded ray of the setting sun discreetly penetrated the thin paper of the *shoji*; it gave the room the almost equivocal charm of an alcove.

Indeed, it seemed a drawing-room more than a temple. The Amazon disappeared. We waited in silence, and looked about us. The altar was like a big tabernacle; the lacquered wooden doors opened over a silk veil of tenuous colours, between the folds of which one could guess the presence of a shape—a statue? a motionless person?—weakly illuminated by reflection only. In front of the altar were some miniature golden pagodas, a small table with flowers, candles, incense, a bell laid on a flat cushion, and other liturgical objects. In every detail you could discern the unforgiving eye of a woman of strong character and excellent taste. There were numerous fine fabrics, the colours of which provided a subdued harmony, not without an occasional flame-like note at the right point. The taste for embroidery common to the nuns of all religions was held in check; all that was to be seen was a few herons (the mythical *hōō* bird) over one of the stoles.

To one side was the place reserved for the mother-superior: a small throne of lacquered wood, with a flat cushion. Next to it, I could have sworn, was a whole row of little bottles of perfume and lotions, and jars of cream. A second glance, however, showed that they were liturgical objects—a small bell, a small thunderbolt, volumes of the Buddhist scriptures bound in precious cloths, small cups for holy water, an incense-burner, and other minute, fragile objects of the same kind. Everything seemed set for a small, metaphysical, and slightly frivolous tea-party.

We heard a rustle of robes, and the mother-superior appeared. She was thin, old, minute; her expression lacked the fire that I had expected. We exchanged greetings and apologies, and she listened benevolently to what Sachiko had to say. Then she left us to the pretty young nun who had opened the door and now appeared to have materialized out of nowhere in the silence of the place, which was somehow alive with prodigies.

Armed with her superior's instructions, her self-confidence returned. She led us barefoot towards the altar, lit an electric light discreetly placed inside the canopy, and revealed the masterpiece (plate 82).

What artist in east or west, in ancient times or modern, has ever succeeded in representing divine solicitude in such trenchantly human terms with such purity of means? It is appropriate that the identity of the figure represented is uncertain. Some think that the artist intended to represent Miroku, Maitreya, the final incarnation of the Buddha, the outward form in which he will within three centuries in the fifth *kalpa,* the fifth of the world's great ages, conduct to salvation, not only the whole of humanity, but all living beings, all the *sem-chen,* 'those having minds', as the Tibetans say, from ant to emperor, from whale to cat.[1] Others, however, prefer to identify the figure as Kwannon, the essence of mercy and benevolence, the Bodhisattva who presides over the present *kalpa,* the fourth. There are also those who argue that it is Sakyamuni, the ascetic of the Sakyas, the historical Buddha, caught in the act of renouncing the world, who is represented here.

It does not matter. The distinction between the various Buddhas is in any case purely empirical; ultimately the only final reality is the Buddha, the all, the soul of the universe. Leaving these subtleties aside, what is represented here in such sublime fashion is the key conception of northern Buddhism, that of the Bodhisattva, *i.e.,* he who has seen,

---

[1] 'He whose mind is imbued with compassion for all sentient beings *(sem-chen),* that is (the way of) salvation and divine wisdom.' LU TRUB (Nagarjuna), *She-rab Dong-Bu* ('The Tree of Knowledge'), translated by W. J. CAMPBELL, Calcutta, 1919, p. 64.

has understood, has attained enlightenment, but, not wishing to enjoy it only for himself, turns back his eyes from the invisible threshold to the vortex of becoming in which the living, blinded by desire, are still caught up, and remains with them. Whether we have to do here with Sakyamuni, Maitreya, or Kwannon, the concept is essentially the same.

This, with the western doctrine of redemption, constitutes the highest peak attained by man in the face of the mysteries of life, death, and suffering.

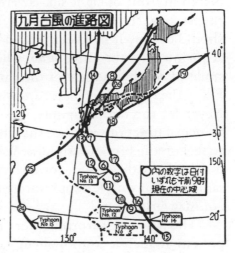

Night of Typhoon

September is the month of typhoons, and tonight a typhoon was in the offing; the wireless kept reporting its progress. It announced an alert in the provinces of Miyazaki and Kagoshima, far away, fortunately, at the southern end of the archipelago. The Americans give girls' names to their hurricanes; no doubt the Chinese would have given them high-sounding dragons' names; the Japanese

Some of the fifteen typhoons of the summer of 1954. Typhoon No. 15, which is mentioned in the text, left more than two thousand dead in its wake. The ringed numerals indicate dates in the month of September

merely give them numbers. That announced today was No. 15, and was said to be a big one. Giorgio descended on us this evening with the suddenness of a typhoon. Half an hour later we were inevitably in an expensive Japanese restaurant.

In a good Japanese restaurant you not only eat and listen to singing, but also bathe. Waitresses brought us *yukata;* we changed, as etiquette requires, facing the wall, with our *yukata* over our shoulders, and went to the honourable bath, men going one way and Sachiko and Jane the other. Only at hot springs *(onsen)* is it the custom for men and women to bathe together. No sooner had we returned and resumed our seats on the *tatami* than an insinuating female voice behind the *shoji,* the paper door, called out: *'Gomen-kudasai'* (May we come in?) *'Hai,'* Giorgio answered, and three attractive *geiko*[1] entered, followed by waitresses with the crockery.

The little procession advanced with a rustling of silk and a fluttering of *tamoto* (the long, wing-like sleeves of the kimono) and innumerable smiles and bows of the head. Eight vessels of lacquered wood were placed in front of eight silk-covered cushions, one of them in front of the *tokonoma*, the place of honour. When the delicate question of who should occupy it had been settled—it went to Jane, our new American acquaintance—the three *geiko*, with their insinuating ways and many smiles, knelt by the side of the three principal guests near the *tokonoma*, filling their little porcelain cups with hot *saké*. The principle followed is: Never let the cup be empty, never let it be full; one of the geisha's principal functions is to see that the guest is put in a good mood, made to feel on the brink of paradise. We at the 'bottom end of the table' had to put up with *jochu-san* (ordinary waitresses), who served us with the same *saké,* but with less sophisticated manners and the shyness of terrified country girls.

This was not surprising, for the poor girls can seldom have been present at such a cosmopolitan gathering; it included, besides Giorgio and my Japanese friends and Jane, a Chinese man of letters and an Italian *marchese*. Nara is often the scene of international gatherings, but foreigners generally stay in places reserved for them. The *marchese* had spent many years in Shanghai, and the conversation turned to that perennial subject of conversation in the Far East, the comparative merits and defects of China and Japan.

The *marchese* appreciated the beauty of the Japanese landscape, the care with which the Japanese preserved the memories of their past, their artistic achievements and their civilization, but it was clear that his heart was in China. Giorgio, who knew China as well as Japan, kept his end up admirably with him. I, alas, could contribute nothing to the discussion; I felt like an ancient Friesian or member of the Marcomanni tribe who had travelled to Rome for intellectual nourishment, and had discerned in the background, distant in time and space, a subtler, richer, more original civilization, that of Greece, only echoes and relics of which would ever be accessible to him.

[1] In Kwansai, the part of Japan that includes Kyoto, Osaka, Kobe, and Nara, geishas are often called *geiko*.

The air was hot, dead; every now and then a rasping voice on the wireless downstairs gave the latest news about the typhoon. It was still far away, but you never could tell, typhoons are capricious things and are liable to sudden changes of route. A typhoon can flatten a house. Someone ran through the streets shouting '*Hi no yōjin*' (Look to your fires!)

Barely had we finished dinner when there were two gusts more violent than the rest. Then the light went out. My Japanese friends and the American woman decided to go home. The announcements about the typhoon grew more and more alarming; there were gusts that seemed about to take the roof off. The departure of the women guests, who always cause geishas a certain amount of embarrassment, led to the circulation of more *tokkuri* of *saké*. What did the typhoon matter? We seemed to be drifting in an ocean of space. The *marchese*, for all his contempt of the Japanese as nothing but a lot of imitative monkeys, obviously found Kogiku ('Little Chrysanthemum') extremely fascinating. One of the other girls, Chiyono ('Eternity'), looked out of the window at the storm-tossed trees and sang the tune of the moment, *Geisha warutsu*, the Geisha Waltz:

Anata no riido de	You guide my footsteps in the dance
Shimada mo yureru	And my hair is loosened; in your
Chiiku dansu no nayamashisa	Embrace I catch a glimpse of a
Midareru susomo	Fleeting love; I am perturbed and
Natsukashi-ureshi. . . .	At the same time happy. . . .

Both words and tunes are Americanized; *riido* is 'lead', *chiiku dansu* is 'cheek dance'. But how Japanese the thing is in spirit, how Buddhist the emphasis on the brevity, the fleeting nature, of all human events; even the brevity of love is discounted in advance. Is not the capacity to deal frivolously with serious things another essentially Japanese characteristic? Surely it is another thing that they have in common with the French.

While the typhoon howled outside 'Little Chrysanthemum', 'Little Slave' and 'Eternity' sang in chorus a comic prayer to Daruma-san, the greatest Buddhist saint: 'Daruma-san, Daruma-san, arrange for a fine day tomorrow, so that Father can go and play golf, Mother can go to a concert, and I, a student, can buy myself a pretty geisha.' Incidentally, this provides a glimpse into Japanese middle-class standards, according to which playing golf sets the seal on success in life.

The light went out again, this time, it seemed, for good. A woman called to take the *geiko* home; everyone was alarmed about the typhoon; outside voices could be heard calling out '*Hi no yōjin*' (Look to your fires!), often accompanied by the sound of two pieces of wood being struck together; a fire fanned by this wind would certainly be a disaster. After the *geiko* had left, the *marchese* asked Giorgio to explain exactly how accessible or inaccessible these girls were.

This launched Giorgio on one of his learned disquisitions about Japanese life. He explained that the world of the geisha was complicated and mysterious, full of traps and pitfalls; you could gain a general impression, but you could never hope to understand it in all its details. It presupposed a stratified, aristocratic society, in which what was granted to some was denied to others; a society of esoteric groups in which privileges were reserved for initiates. Above all, it was a world of men. Women were divided into categories—respectable women, and those of the *shōbai,* the 'profession'.

The *marchese* inquired what was the precise meaning of all the lights and lanterns to be seen in Japanese towns, all the signs and gateways. Where did one go to eat, and where to make love? Was it possible to be given any sort of clue? Giorgio produced a pencil and a piece of paper and started drawing a sketch (*see* opposite). At one extremity, he explained, there were the eating places proper; at the other those whose business was confined to sex. In between lay a vast area in which there was every possible and conceivable variation and combination. The truly pagan element of Japanese life lay in the fact that pleasure, *i.e.*, male pleasure, was thought of as total; in other words it involved bath, meal, song and dance, good company, and finally love-making. But there was nothing crude or coarse about it all; every detail was regulated by customs, prohibitions, restrictions, ceremonies, that had taken shape in the course of centuries. In such a world a foreigner was like a bull in a china shop. The only policy was to decide exactly what one wanted and then formulate a programme, but many places were exceedingly difficult of access without an introduction from a person of consequence. As for the women of this world 'of flowers and willows' (*karyu-kai*), there were innumerable grades and categories, ranging from those who sold

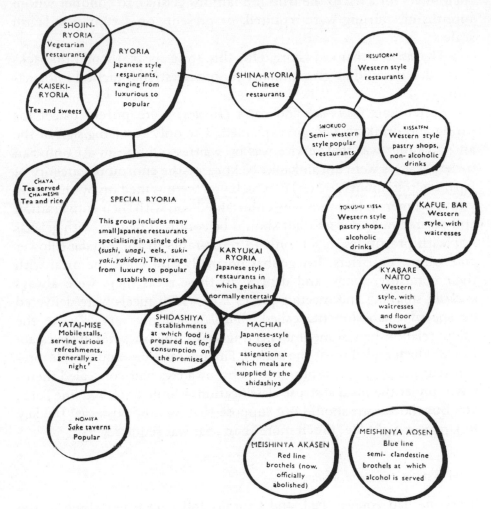

Japanese night life. Cafés, restaurants, and other establishments

themselves for a fee to the true and famous geishas, to conquer whom months of courting were required, or presents on a ruinously lavish scale.

The *marchese* thanked Giorgio for this, so to speak, theoretical background, but could he give him any more terrestrial, practical information?

Restaurants *(shoku-do)* and cafés *(kissaten)* were purely places for eating and drinking, Giorgio explained. The only surviving sign of the ancient order was that service was by waitresses only; in a Confucian society waiters were unthinkable. Next came the enormous category of Japanese restaurants *(ryōriya)* in which you were waited on by charming young women in kimonos who entertained you with their conversation and poured out your *saké,* but should be confused neither with geishas nor with prostitutes. It was only in restaurants in the *karyukai* ('flower and willow') quarters that geishas normally enlivened the meal with their company, songs, and dances. In these areas there were always *machiai* ('stopping and meeting places'), to which meals were delivered by special establishments called *shi-dashiya* ('home service'). At the *ryōriya* relationships, sometimes fleeting and sometimes not, were established which ended up at the *machiai.* Finally, sex pure and simple prevailed at the *joroya,* the brothels, which nowadays half-concealed themselves under the most abstruse classifications—'blue line', 'red line', etc., etc. But the *marchese* should not suppose that he now possessed the key to Japanese night life; much more than that was required.

Storm Without and Storm Within

Everyone had gone to bed, and Giorgio and I were left alone in the streets of Nara. The typhoon still threatened; the light had been cut off because of the danger of short circuits; it was as dark as if an air-raid were expected. Somewhere, beyond the dense layers of cloud, there was a moon; in fact a faint, reddish glow was perceptible in the sky. The wind came in furious, warm, wet, tropical gusts, and the tree-tops danced wildly. The pagoda of the Kōfuku-ji ('Temple of Vast Felicity') stood out darkly,[1] its wooden ribs creaking in the gale. Giorgio suddenly said to me:

[1] *See* Photograph 85.

'You know, I've left Tamako.'

'What? Why . . .?'

'Perhaps because of Enrico. She always knew that I couldn't marry her, but she had grown very attached to me, so it was better to make the break now, before it became too difficult.'

'But why do you think she wouldn't have made a good mother for Enrico?'

'It's not a question of that. There's already Abe-san, who promised my wife on her death-bed to look after the boy. I couldn't marry another Japanese, unless perhaps she were a member of a great family, sufficiently great to intimidate Abe-san. But Tamako, a geisha, just imagine!'

'Have you ever thought of marrying a western woman, Giorgio?'

'I don't know, I don't want to marry again. My only concern is Enrico. It's a terrible responsibility to have brought him into the world between two civilizations; one day he may hate me for it. I'm going to do everything in my power to prevent that from happening.'

'I know, I know, it's a difficult thing to have been born between two worlds.'

'Yes, the Japanese look down on *aino-ko* [half-castes], and foreigners keep away from them.'

'But why not try to exploit the advantages of his position? Most *aino-ko* are held in little account because they haven't had a proper education either on one side of the fence or on the other. As Enrico is so intelligent and wide-awake, why not . . .?'

'That's just what I want to do. Give him the best possible Japanese education and the best possible western education. In a world that's growing smaller and smaller, there's always room for someone capable of acting as a really efficient bridge.'

'Or you could send him home to your parents in Italy; there are no prejudices with us. Having a Japanese mother might actually be an attraction.'

The storm suddenly abated for a moment, as it does sometimes in typhoon weather. Silence fell on the country and the houses. In the distance a voice could be heard, crying: '*Hi no yōjin. Hi no yōjin*' (Look to your fires! Look to your fires!)

It was impossible to leave Nara without going to see the great Buddha of Tōdai-ji ('Great East Temple'), which can no more be omitted from the itinerary than the Leaning Tower of Pisa. A long avenue leads to the Niō-mon, a high gateway at either side of which are the most famous pair of *niō* (celestial guardians) in all Japan, marvellous wooden statues by Unkei and Kaikei (eleventh century). These artists, though obeying the curious conventions of an imaginary anatomy, succeeded with supreme artistry in rendering the effect of monstrous strength yielding to a sudden burst of rage; also the difficulties overcome in dealing with their intractable material should not be overlooked.

We next came to the 'biggest wooden building in the world containing the biggest bronze statue in the world', as the guide-book proclaims with almost American relish. But when you read on, and learn that the Buddha was made in A.D. 749 and that the temple, which was rebuilt in 1708, is much smaller than the original temple, you begin to get really interested.

Both the Buddha and the temple are of slight artistic interest, but they are associated with events which admirably summarize the whole Nara century. In about 735 smallpox appeared in Japan, spread to the capital, and afflicted many important personages. The devout Emperor Shōmu decided to erect a colossal statue of the Buddha to ward off the ravages of the disease.

The huge statue was successfully cast some years later, on the eighth or ninth attempt. This was a great achievement for the period, and Murdoch rightly remarks that in Europe only the Byzantine emperors would have been able to undertake such a task. The statue, which is nearly fifty feet high, was constructed piece by piece and cast on the spot; 500 tons of brass were used, and eight of lead and zinc; these were unheard-of quantities at that time. Consequently for several years the construction of the Great Buddha of the Tōdai-ji constituted a major affair of state.

When the statue had at last been successfully cast, the next task was that of gilding it. This caused the court the gravest concern, for there was not sufficient gold for the purpose in the whole realm. News finally reached the capital, however, that gold in substantial quantities had

been discovered in the forests of Mutsu, among the Ainu, and in gratitude for this good fortune the Emperor, accompanied by the whole of
his court, proceeded in ceremony to the 'Great East Temple' to thank
Buddha Roshana.[1] Thousands of priests took part in the thanksgiving,
to the accompaniment of incense, music, and dancing; and contemporary documents testify to the fact that on this occasion the Emperor
spoke of himself—an unheard-of thing—as a humble *yakko* (slave,
servant) of the Three Treasures (Buddha, Dharma, Samgha; the Buddha,
the Law, the community of monks).

In the same year, 749, the Emperor, in accordance with what was
already a common practice, abdicated in order to retire to the contemplative life; he was succeeded by his daughter Kōken, then aged thirty-
three. The Nara period began to develop in all its complexity; it was
a period in which new worlds were opened up, great enterprises were
undertaken, women held much power, intrigue flourished, and the
power of the Buddhist clergy seemed unbounded. Hence the Emperor
Kwammu, one of the strongest personalities in the history of the
imperial line, decided (A.D. 784) to build a new capital, Heian (Kyoto),
nearly twenty-five miles to the north.

Nara had been founded in the reign of the Empress Gemmyō, who
had been succeeded by her daughter Genshō, the only instance in
Japanese history in which daughter succeeded mother. Genshō had
been succeeded by the devout and pious Emperor Shōmu, who reigned
for twenty-five years. But now there was another Empress, Kōken. It
was she, incidentally, who presided over one of the most magnificent
ceremonies ever seen in Japan, that of the opening of the eyes of the
Great Buddha of the Tōdai-ji. According to an ancient eastern belief,
when the pupils are added to the eyes of a statue or a picture the latter
in some magic fashion comes to life. The Indian ascetic Bodhisena was
responsible for the organization of the magnificent rites, in which,
according to the chroniclers, no fewer than 20,000 monks, dignitaries,
musicians, sacred dancers, and others took part. They concluded with
the serving of vegetarian refreshments for 10,000 persons, both religious
and civil.

The subsequent career of the Empress Kōken was such that after
her death the accession to the throne of another woman was prevented

[1] In Sanskrit Vairocana, 'he who enlightens'.

for many centuries. In 758 she abdicated in favour of her great-nephew Junnin, reserving, however, a number of important rights for herself. Relations between the two had never been good and, when the young Emperor surrounded himself with advisers who were unwelcome in high places, crisis developed. A period of violence ensued, and finally the ex-Empress sent soldiers to seek out her great-nephew, who was abandoned by his followers and pushed out of his palace half-naked into the cold, where a decree was read to him despoiling him of his authority and sending him into exile. He was imprisoned in the island of Awaji, where soon afterwards he was strangled in mysterious circumstances.

In 766 the ex-Empress mounted the throne again, this time under the name of Shōtoku. Meanwhile a handsome and talented monk named Dōkyo had succeeded in gaining her ear; he won an ascendancy over her not unlike that exercised eleven centuries later over the last Tsarina by Rasputin. He was appointed *hoo*, a title hitherto reserved to sovereigns who had abdicated and retired to the cloister, and he lived openly with the Empress at court; and then an unheard-of thing happened, the only incident of its kind in the history of the Japanese dynasty. On the strength of certain alleged oracular pronouncements by the god Hachiman (incidentally a Shinto deity), he demanded the Empress's support for his enthronement as Emperor of Japan. This was too much for her, in spite of her infatuation; she was not prepared to sully the purity of the royal blood after the fourteen centuries that tradition claimed for it. She consulted Hachiman herself, and the reply was negative. Dōkyo tried again, but he had now lost the game. The Empress died, and Dōkyo ended his days obscurely in a monastery.

Eighth-Century Court Relics

Everything at Nara in the century of its glory can be said to have centred on the colossal statue of Buddha Roshana. In the Buddhist cosmology the forty-ninth day after a man's death is especially important, for by that day the future of his spirit is believed to have been determined; either a new Buddha is rising to the level of cosmic awareness, or a re-birth in some form or other is now destined to take place. The forty-ninth day after the death of the Emperor Shōmu, who seven years earlier had abdicated in favour of his daughter Kōken, was celebrated on July 22, 756. As he was a *hoo*, an emperor who had retired to a monastery, the ceremonies were on a particularly lavish scale. After the Nara period religion was never again to play such a big part in Japanese affairs of state.

During the ceremony the Dowager Empress Kōmyō, with a magnanimity common in the period, presented all her dead husband's 'treasures' to the temple, to be dedicated to Buddha Roshana: ceremonial armour, marvellously worked robes, ancient mirrors, musical instruments, gifts from foreign lands; a total of 650 items, carefully and minutely described in a *kenmotsu-cho*, an imperial deed of gift which survives. Thanks to a series of happy chances, as well as to the power of the imperial name, nearly all of them are intact, thus throwing an extraordinary light on an eighth-century oriental court. In India and China only a very few objects, particularly of such a perishable nature, have survived from that remote period; hence the extraordinary value of the collection.

From the outset it was kept in one of those storehouses called *shōsō-in*, which were then to be found near the bigger temples. They were built in an interesting style, entirely different both from that of the temples and of ordinary Japanese houses. They stood on tall piles, the walls consisted of squared beams, and they had no windows; and they are the only type of Japanese building in which the walls carry weight. They are said to be excellent for preservation purposes in a damp climate. When it is wet, the timber swells and is waterproof; when it is dry, it shrinks, and air enters through the cracks.

In the course of time other objects were added to the collection, which now consists of about 3,000 items, 488 of which bear eighth-century dates. Everything—furniture, gilded swords, quivers, incense-burners, robes and vestments, cups made of rhinoceros horn, flutes, lutes, psalteries, mirrors, boxes, pots, cups, vases, plates, chess sets, saddles and harness, jewels and crowns, objects in bronze and precious metals, lacquered wood, and glass (then a rarity)—testifies to a level of elegance and taste which was to be reached in the west only many centuries later.

Many of the objects are of Japanese manufacture; others are clearly reminiscent, not only of China, but also of India, Persia, and even Byzantium. A description of the principal treasures would take too long; I shall mention only a celebrated psaltery with seven strings. It is made of lacquered wood inlaid with gold and silver, is more than a yard long, and is delightfully decorated with human figures, flowers, animals, mythical birds, and butterflies. In a panel three bearded sages are, as it were, inlaid in the flowing drapery of their philosopher's clothing, with fans and cups of intoxicating liquor, listening to the music of a lute played by a girl reclining under a tree; all around are bamboos, strange plants, rocks, insects, dragon-flies, and butterflies, and wizards on phoenixes fly between the clouds in the sky. There is also a Chinese inscription which can be translated thus:

> The music of the psaltery
> Purifies the heart and banishes
> Evil passions.
> It calms us, gives us a tranquil mind:
> Listening to it, something sublime
> Prevails. Every vulgar shadow
> Is dissipated
> And caprice
> Is subdued. Joy, yes, and harmony,
> But not excessive pleasure.

The *shōsō-in* is still opened every year with great ceremony on or about October 21, and the contents are brought out, cleaned, and if necessary repaired; a few people are admitted to examine them; and finally, some weeks later, the doors are closed again with a complicated system of seals, the last and most sacred of which is a piece of paper with the Emperor's signature.

I have said nothing of the Nara museum, which is full of beautiful objects; or of the ancient Shinto shrine called Kasuga ('Of the Spring Day'), the fawns that roam in its park, the broad winding avenue that slopes gently upwards towards the wood and is flanked by hundreds of *ishi-doro,* stone lanterns, of every size and shape, many of them covered in moss, which are lit twice a year, in February and August; and I have also left unmentioned the pagoda of the Yakushi-ji ('Temple of the Master of Medicine'), with the extraordinary rhythm of its roofs, so devised that the Japanese call it *kōreru-ongaku* ('frozen music').

7

Kyoto, in the Month of Maples in Flame

Between the Mount of Wisdom and the Mount of the Cave of Love

WE LEFT Nara in the late afternoon. The road to Kyoto is excellent; it is one of the few concrete highways in Japan. At one point there were obvious traces of a recent flood; embankments, however well made, are of little help in this country when the rain dragons for some obscure heraldic reason feel slighted and unleash the fury of heaven. For several miles the fields were covered with a thick layer of yellow mud, which had cracked in the sun; and over the mud all sorts of flotsam and jetsam—wooden planks, sandals, dolls, articles of clothing —were scattered. Here and there women and old men were searching in the desolation for things which the raging flood-water had carried from their homes. Now the sun was shining cruelly and impassively on their plight.

The typhoon of two days ago was a disaster. After skirting Kyushu and crossing Honshu (the principal island of Japan), roughly between Hiroshima and Izumo, it seemed to be about to head out to sea somewhere in the direction of Korea or Siberia; instead it wheeled eastwards, gathered strength—a most unusual thing—and its full force struck the port of Hakodate, in Hokkaido. Five ships lying at anchor were driven aground and smashed like matchwood, and the Doya Maru, a ferry steamer loaded with passengers about to leave for Aomori, capsized, and more than a thousand people lost their lives.

If ever there was a country in which you would expect to meet sanguinary, ferocious, vindictive gods, it is Japan, with its earthquakes, floods, cyclones, tidal waves, typhoons, landslides, fires, and every

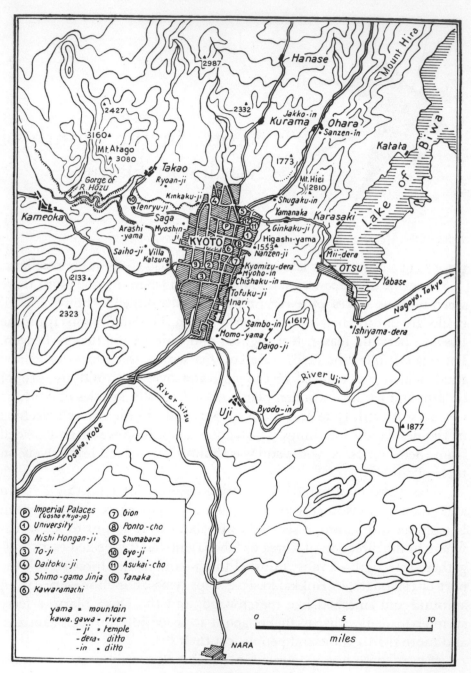

Kyoto and neighbourhood, with principal places mentioned in the text

possible kind of natural disaster. Nevertheless, as we have already seen, the Japanese heaven is populated by deities who are well disposed towards humanity, and the attitude of the Japanese people towards them is one of gratitude and joy rather than of fear and sacrifice.

That is yet another example which shows how cautious one should be in seeing causal connections between men and their environment; ancient influences at work throughout long, formative periods are far more important. In the Lamaism of Tibet, a country of crystalline air and vast horizons, the Indian jungles where Nagarjuna and Vasubandhu meditated centuries ago still survive in spirit; and we Italians, in a Mediterranean environment, insist on behaving like northerners in regard to clothes, housing, and food, and like Palestinian desert dwellers in matters of religion, purely because of historical reasons. The Japanese often live in northern snows with the provisional attitude of southerners forced northwards by events, and so on and so forth. The Japanese religion is probably one more piece of evidence pointing to their origin in southern regions where nature is a kind and benevolent mother.

Meanwhile the shape of the hills surrounding Kyoto, the City of Crystalline Streams, the City of Purple Hills, grew more and more distinct in the calm evening light. Highest of all the mountains round Kyoto is the Hiei, the 'Mount of Wisdom', which rises to about 3,000 feet, a dark mass covered with thick forest which hides a number of temples and monasteries of the powerful Tendai Buddhist sect. Opposite it there rises the Atago-yama, the 'Mount of the Cave of Love',[1] with its Shinto shrines which give protection against fire. Kyoto with its million inhabitants lies between the two, protected on the west by the ancient gods and on the north-east—the most adverse direction, according to geomantic ideas—by the benevolence of the Buddhas.[2]

We finally reached the city at sunset. The humidity, the dust and smoke that had hung over the housetops throughout a fine day, caused a golden haze through which the last light filtered. Huge trams emerged from the purple shadows, were transformed into filigree patterns of light, and were swallowed up in the darkness again. People walked about

---

[1] Japanese place-names of Ainu or unknown origin are transcribed phonetically into ideograms, and a meaning is often subsequently read into these, with the oddest results.

[2] The north-east is called *kimon* ('devil's gate'). The north-eastern corner of the Imperial Palace at Kyoto was carefully cut off in such a way that theoretically 'it has no *kimon*'.

half-blinded by dust and phosphorescent midges; orange sparks were struck under the wheels of vehicles, or flashed from the windows when sun, glass, and eye chanced to meet at the appropriate angles of incidence and reflection. At this season Kyoto has a perpetual holiday air, which at this time of day assumes a dream-like quality. The people, so different from those of Tokyo or Osaka, stroll aimlessly, cheerfully, careless of everything, as if intoxicated by their surroundings. It grew darker, the first lights were lit, neon-illuminated ideograms stood out like huge, electric, living insects against the changing transparencies of the night, and the first stars shimmered. It was quite dark before we remembered the necessity of finding accommodation for the night. I chose, almost by chance, a small hotel nestling at the foot of the eastern hills. It was called 'Silvery Water'; a stream that rose in the forest just above flowed through the garden. The hotel was new; the stairs, the rooms, the bath, all smelled of new, resinous wood. A window opened on to the forest, and the moon rose silently between the trees.

Kyo-
(metropolis)

To
(capital)

Ascetic and Terrestrial Delights

The origin of Chinese-Japanese ideograms as simplified representations of the things for which they stand is still discernible in the shape of many of them; thus, a mountain-top stands for mountain, ears for rice, fingers for hand, scales for fish, legs for horse, horns for goat, roof for house. The original association of ideas is sometimes charming. A woman under a roof signifies peace, tranquillity; a heart at a window signifies anxiety; love is represented by threads of talk surrounding a heart; a dragon by moonlight stands for mystery; water in a wood stands for poetical solitude; talk in combination with work signifies disorder, disorganization; a river of words stands for teaching. Most pleasing of all is a man under a tree, signifying *yasumi* (rest).

This morning I climbed up into the wood behind the Silvery Water. The tree with which I formed my private ideogram was a pine, which cast a slight shadow, like a veil, on the carpet of needles on the ground. Kyoto lay below, in the uncertain sunlight of a morning ready at any moment to dissolve into rain. The flat expanse of roofs lay like a grey fjord between the mountains, broken here and there by the mass of a Buddhist temple or the elegant tower of a pagoda. Kyoto is the only major Japanese city which was not practically wiped out in the 1945 air-raids. The Japanese had the good sense not to have military objectives there, and the Americans, thanks above all to the representations of the noted orientalist Serge Elisséev, spared it. From where I was sitting the view of the city was substantially that which so much struck the sixteenth-century missionaries when they spoke with such enthusiasm of Meaco (*i.e., miyako*, the capital).

Yasumi, rest: man and tree

A comparison between Kyoto and Florence is almost impossible to avoid. Not only do they have similar connotations in their respective civilizations; there is also a physical resemblance. True, the valley of the Arno between San Domenico and San Miniato is narrower than that of the Kamogawa, but Florence seen from the Viale dei Colli and Kyoto from the Higashi-yama are essentially two seas of houses filling flat valleys between mountains and hills; and, just as Florence has Fiesole, the Poggio Imperiale, Settignano, so Kyoto has Higashi-yama, Saga, and Ohara. Moreover, the economic basis of the two places is similar. In both it is agriculture, for the most part in the hands of old families, and in both a class of artisans is gradually being industrialized. However, the view that lay below me was far less beautiful than that of Florence seen, say, from the Piazzale Michelangelo. In this sea of grey roofs you would search in vain for the counterpoint of lines, spaces, and volumes that springs to life from the bridges across the Arno, from the towers, domes, and *campanili*; for the sense of completeness and unity of which the supreme examples are San Gimignano among the cities of the Old World, and New York, the modern San Gimignano, among the cities of the New.

Moreover, going down into Kyoto and walking about the central streets between the Shi-jo and San-jo bridges and the avenues of Imade-gawa, it is easy to feel a great sense of disappointment. In contrast to the cities of Europe, which offer new perspectives at every turn, Kyoto, like every other Japanese town, consists of broad, anonymous streets inter-secting at right-angles and flanked by neat, often attractive-looking, houses, all similar except when they are interrupted by ugly modern buildings of no style at all. True, at Kyoto everything is better cared-for, less brazenly utilitarian, than in other Japanese towns, and near some of the temples (Higashi and Nishi Hongan-ji), in certain streets (Teramachi, Ponto-cho), and in the parks surrounding the Imperial Palaces, there are views which are sometimes impressive, sometimes pleasing and full of fascination, and sometimes truly magnificent; nevertheless a superficial drive through the city rouses no particular enthusiasm.

In spite of that Kyoto has a wealth of beauty which is not surpassed anywhere in the world. Once more we touch on one of the fundamental differences between Europe and the Far East. Florence is western beauty displayed for all to see; Kyoto is eastern; its beauty is concealed, a secret to be wrested from it little by little. True, you can spend a month at Florence, visiting churches, galleries, villas, *palazzi*; but you can also claim to be able to see it in a single afternoon, from the surrounding hills, the tops of its towers, from its streets, squares, bridges. It is characteristic that the Higashi-yama ('Eastern Mount'), the Fiesole of Kyoto, has no street or viewpoint from which the city can be seen as a whole; the point to which I climbed was a woodman's path, full of slippery slopes and covered with pine-needles. The idea of a view is entirely western and entirely un-Japanese. What bad taste, what barbarism, what childishness, to want to see everything all at once! Hence the things that matter at Kyoto are tucked away in little valleys, in green alcoves between the folds of the hills. Its beauties do not present themselves, but have to be sought out.

Kyoto, at the time of its foundation in 794, was called Heian ('Peace and Tranquillity'). The Emperor Kwammu built it as his capital after deciding to abandon Nara, where the power and intrigues of the Buddhist monks had got out of hand. Heian, like Nara, was built to an ambitious chequer-board pattern, about three miles square, modelled on the capital of the Chinese emperors at Ch'ang-an. The court and government buildings, according to the chroniclers, were exceedingly handsome; the most magnificent of them, the Taikyoku-den, contained a great state room nearly two hundred feet long and fifty feet wide and was built on a platform surrounded by a red lacquer balustrade; the whole building was painted scarlet, and the roof was covered with emerald-blue tiles. Not far away was the Pavilion of Sumptuous Pleasures (Hōgaku-den), used for official banquets, the Pavilion of Martial Virtues (Butoku-den), with a courtyard for equestrian games and archery competitions, the Imperial Celestial Pavilion (Shishin-den),[1] used for ceremonial purposes, and the Pavilion of Sweet Coolness (Seiryō-den), which contained the Emperor's quarters. The Empress, the imperial concubines, and the ladies of the palace lived in the 'Prohibited Precinct' in quarters distinguished by the names of the neighbouring trees—the Pear Hall, the Wistaria Hall, the Plum Hall. There were also many houses for noble families, to say nothing of a number of Shinto shrines and a big university with three principal faculties: Chinese letters, mathematics, and law. Heian at the time seems to have had about half a million inhabitants. There is no doubt that it was one of the biggest and most splendid cities in the world.

Nothing, however, could be more alien to the Japanese spirit than the formalism dear to their neighbours of the Celestial Empire. Just as in the case of the Taikwa reform of 645, when they adopted the Chinese bureaucratic system in its outward form only, neglecting its great secret, that of a democratic government of sages and men of letters selected by an extremely severe examination system from every section of the population, so did they now reproduce an impressive, Chinese-style, chequer-board town plan, with wide straight roads which did not lead up to any of the impressive culminating points—arches, gateways, palaces, towers, or monuments—which in the same circumstances other civilizations would certainly have demanded. The outline remains. The roads still cross each other at right angles and convey the atmosphere of a capital of mathematicians and ritualists, but the Japanese love of the devious and unexpected, their aversion to the obvious, to anything that can be grasped at first sight, has ended by concealing the true spiritual centres of the city, its most beautiful and precious things, removing them from the geometrical pattern, hiding them away from the streets behind walls and clumps of trees.

The city falls naturally into two parts. There is the town centre, equipped with every modern urban characteristic—crowded streets, smart women, theatres, restaurants, cinemas, shops; and in addition there are the famous geisha districts. This part of the city can be called that of the terrestrial pleasures. The other, that of the ascetic pleasures, lies outside this, in an area of wooded hills, in which lakes, temples,

---

[1] Literally 'Purple Imperial Pavilion', in reference to the highest of the three heavens recognized by Chinese astronomy.

gardens, hermitages, monasteries are scattered about. There is no hard-and-fast dividing line, of course; there are temples, museums, to say nothing of fourteen universities, in the central area, and in the outskirts there are places dedicated to the pleasures of *samsara* (the vortex of becoming) rather than to the peace of *nirvana*. Nevertheless the distinction is broadly true.

The peculiar spirit of this city is the result of the harmonious co-existence of the most diverse elements: monastic asceticism, the cultivation of the arts, the ephemeral pleasures of *uki-yo*, the 'floating world', devoted scholarship, a patient artisan class, keen tradesmen, and an ancient, impoverished nobility.

But let us return to the domain of ascetic pleasures. The names of the places are a delight in themselves. At the foot of the Mount of Knowledge (Hiei-zan), not far from the imperial villa of the Ascetic Doctrine (Shugaku-in), among the maples which were assuming their autumn red, there is the Temple of the Calm Light, that is to say, of Nirvana (Ohara no Jakkō-in). On the other side of the valley is the Temple of the Absolute (Ohara no Sanzen-in). Nearer the city is a temple dedicated to Manjusri, Enchanting Knowledge, the Buddhist Apollo (Manju-in), as well as the Poet's Pavilion (Shisen-do) and the Silver Pavilion (Ginkaku-ji). In this direction, where the first slopes of the Eastern Mount (Higashi-yama) bring Kyoto to a sudden stop, every little valley, every sylvan recess, every shady thicket along the side of the streams, has been adorned by monkish piety. The Temple of Enlighten-ment (Nanzen-ji) and that of Gratitude (Chion-in) are near the Temple of Pure Fountains (Kiyomizu-dera), that of the Blue Lotus (Shōren-in), that of Serene Quietude (Seikan-ji), and that of the Marvellous Law (Myōhō-in).

To the south the Eastern Mount descends in little hills towards the plain of the Uji river, and the distances are a little greater. Beyond Peach Mount (Momo-yama) and the Palace of Noble Fragrance (Goko-no-Miya) there is the Temple of the Three Treasures, *i.e.*, the Buddha, the Law, and the community of monks (the Sambō-in), near a huge park which conceals the pavilions and pagodas of the big temple dedicated to the Quintessence of Enlightenment (the Daigo-ji).

To the west the mountains are steeper and wilder, the woods darker and more solemn; a big expanse of rice-fields lies between the city and the first slopes. Here too, particularly near the Stormy Mountain (Arashi-yama), where the Hozu river plunges down into the valley, there are some delightful places. As soon as you leave the city there is the Golden Pavilion (Kinkaku-ji), destroyed by fire, alas! in our own lifetime, the Temple of the Dragon's Repose (Ryoan-ji) with its famous abstract garden,[1] the Temple of Benevolent Harmony (Ninna-ji), the Temple .of the Great Science (Daikaku-ji). Finally, hidden in the outskirts of the mountain forest, there is the Temple of the Celestial Dragon (Tenryu-ji), near an enchanting lake, and the Temple of the Western Fragrance (Saihō-ji), where twenty-four different kinds of moss display their humble beauty.

Under the Hill of Wisdom

This morning I went to see the house which was my home for three years before the war, near the University, behind the Chion-ji, the Temple of Gratitude, known also as the Hyakuman-ben, the 'Million Times' temple, because during an epidemic in 1331 the abbot and his monks repeated an extraordinary number of prayers to Amida, 'Infinite Light', the Supreme Buddha, evidently with effect. The temple is not of any great antiquity, having been burnt down and rebuilt a number of times, but it is sober and serene; it stands in the middle of a garden with typical old Japanese pine-trees. The pleasing view from my window of the big temple roof, with its solemn curves among the green foliage of the trees, will always remain in my mind. It is a quiet part of Kyoto, full of low little houses, each with its tiny garden, criss-crossed by gravelled lanes that are hardly more than tracks; it lies at the edge of the city, and not far away there rise the wooded mountains that culminate in the peak of Hiei, the Hill of Wisdom.

The area is called Asukai-cho, the Asuka district; Asuka means 'flying bird'. It is a name which a tradition-loving Japanese would call *miyabiyaka,* old and pleasing. A thousand years ago a certain kind of popular song was called *asuka,* and the name was adopted by a poet and footballer (a champion *kemari* player) well known to the elegant society of the twelfth century; and he handed on the name to his descendants.

I turned the corner and came in sight of the house, which looked

[1] *See* Photograph 104.

yellow and deserted. Two little girls playing in the sand and gravel might have been one of my daughters playing with a friend. A middle-aged woman passed who looked rather like Mitake-san, our *oba-san,* our cook. Who knew what had become of Mitake-san? She was a devout Buddhist, and, though she was willing to cook meat for us, she drew the line at killing a chicken which was once presented to us by a friend in the country. I had to do it myself, and made a terrible mess of it, causing feathers to fly all over the kitchen; in the end I had to cut off its head with a knife. Mitake-san looked at me with horror and disgust; she made me feel like a murderer. That evening she disappeared for at least two hours; she went to the temple to have *o-kyō* read for the soul of the poor chicken.

Kyoto is, I believe, the only Japanese city in which the past survives side by side with the present; in Tokyo everything associated with the past has been changed out of all recognition; here every stone, every tree, every noise, every cat, are reminders of the past. Look! there was a familiar face, that of Hirai-san, who was our chief neighbour, a strong man of few words, whose round face beamed health and self-satisfaction. As in the old days, he called me 'Professor'—because I used to teach Italian at the Imperial University—and I thought I detected in his way of speaking to me the same touch of irony, the irony with which the successful business man regards that useless, if decorative, person, the scholar. As in the old days, he was dressed in Japanese style, but with a soft felt hat. We exchanged greetings, news, good wishes. Then he walked off, his leather brief-case under his arm, to complete yet another of his legendary business deals.

When I first met him Hirai must have been about forty; he was the embodiment of suburban success; a small, self-made business man who, thanks to acumen, a prudent marriage, and the favour of the gods, had built himself his own house and garden, sent his sons to a university, and had acquired vast local esteem (though not a car; in Japan, as I have already indicated, a car is a great luxury). 'He pays 20,000 yen a year in taxes!' Mitake-san used to exclaim with awe; 20,000 yen at that time was a very considerable sum. We were in fact surrounded by Hirai properties; from our windows we could see the Hirai silk factory, a collection of low buildings in which nearly all the workers were Koreans, both men and women.

Some of the Korean women were attractive in a quiet way, in their long white skirts and silk blouses, always of a single colour, either pink or green. The Koreans were immediately distinguishable from the Japanese, the women because they had their own way of dressing and there was something particularly primitive about them, the men because of something wild and barbarous in their expression. For a time we had a Korean maid, who became exceedingly devoted to us. In pre-war Japan there was a secret link of connivance and sympathy between Koreans and Europeans; we had an enemy in common, the Japanese police.

Many Koreans in the neighbourhood were Methodists; on Sundays they used to attend services in the chapel attached to our house, which had originally belonged to a missionary. Their minister, a Japanese, was a good man, and was always busy helping someone in distress. I should have liked to be more friendly with him, but never succeeded. Asian Christians are embarrassing people to meet. As a minority, they live exemplary lives from every point of view, and in their eyes you seem to read a cruel reproach. What! they seem to say. You come from Europe, and do not go regularly to church or seek to convert the heathen? No wonder they feel we are letting them down.

But to return to Hirai. His father-in-law lived in the house next door to ours. He was known as old Hirai. His son-in-law's name in fact came from him; young Hirai was a *yōshi,* having assumed his father-in-law's name on marriage; he had done well with his wife's money, and a few years previously had bought the house opposite his father-in-law's.

Old Hirai never went down into the city. He was a little man of about sixty, very thin, and extremely ceremonious in speech. His sparse white hair was always meticulously combed and he always wore a kimono. He no longer took any interest in business, being *inkyo,* that is to say, having retired, but left it all to his daughter, who let her husband do all the work, but was the guiding intelligence, the *éminence grise,* the true seat of power behind all his activities. It took us several months to discover this elementary fact about our neighbour's life. It is in fact rare in Japan for power and its exercise to be concentrated in the hands of one and the same person, but in practice it is exceedingly difficult for a foreigner to discover this for himself.

Old Hirai's chief interest in life was the house and the flowers, and, above all, the stretch of roadway outside, for which he had an old man's devouring passion; he used to water it, rake it and re-rake it, and when children left paper or rubbish lying about he used to chase them angrily. This road was so typical of Kyoto that I must describe it. It started out as a broad, modern, busy street, complete with pavements, trams, and shops, and after 300 yards ended up among the gardens of the university agricultural institute; here it was narrow, had no pavements, was flanked on either side by low little houses in which middle-class and professional people lived, by the precincts of a temple, and by students' residences. It was gravelled, like a drive leading to a country house, and traffic or passers-by were rare. There was a rural quality about it that made it pleasing, and grass and wild flowers grew in the crannies and along the edges.

Mrs. Hirai senior was said in her youth to have been a geisha; geishas are said to make excellent wives. She was a minute little old lady. At rare intervals she was to be seen at her doorway; neither her age nor her diminutive size restricted her endless flow of compliments and ceremonious phrases and her never-ending and almost monotonous deep bows; she naturally hissed all the time as a sign of profound respect. Her daughter, the true mistress of the house, the silk factory, and all the other property, was much more reserved and circumspect. She too was minute, with delicate though not aristocratic features, but you could tell that she held many reins in her hands and was a woman of exceptional responsibilities. It is extraordinary how a Japanese woman is able to inspire universal respect without needing to appear to exercise any authority whatever.

Next door to old Hirai lived Naruse Kyoko, the young woman who was the black sheep of the neighbourhood. She was neither beautiful nor ugly, neither smart nor slovenly, in fact she was completely ordinary from every point of view. Why did she rouse so much interest? She had been a *jokyu-san* (waitress) in a bar, and a rich industrialist from Osaka had fallen in love with her and set her up in this little house on the outskirts of Kyoto. Twice or three times a month a sleek black car would draw up at the end of the street, and the industrialist got out and disappeared into the house, where he remained for two or three hours. Meanwhile his chauffeur waited at the wheel, impassively reading a newspaper.

One day I caught a glimpse of the famous personage. Uriu-san, that is to say Miki, our nurse, came up to my room in a state of great excitement and told me that the *mekake's*[1] gentleman was just coming along the road, that he was very rich and so kind and, just think, he had six or seven other *mekake,* two at Osaka, one at Kobe, one at Takarazuka, etc., etc. I looked out of the window, and saw a fattish and rather ugly man of about fifty passing by, looking exactly like what good industrialists always look like in bad films, complete with grey spats, gloves, leather brief-case, and felt hat. Naruse-san came out to meet him, and bowed almost to the ground at every nod of his head; the only sign of emotion that she betrayed was a slight, sickly flush that made her pathetically pretty. I smiled to think that all the Mrs. Hirais of the neighbourhood must certainly be eagerly drinking in the spectacle from behind their windows too. As for Uriu-san, I had never seen her so excited and absorbed.

Japanese women are much prone to prying into their neighbours' affairs and prattling about them, but Uriu-san seldom wasted her time over this; she was too busy with the children, taking them to school or fetching them, or taking them for walks, or to see their friends. The children hardly ever spoke anything but Japanese; true, they understood a good deal of Italian and English, but it was practically impossible to get them to speak those exotic languages. They even acquired a Kyoto accent.

Living with one's children in a foreign country is a great help for anyone who wishes to get under the skin of the people surrounding him. Grown-ups, with their minds on literature, philosophy, religion, art, are naturally apt to miss many important little details of ordinary life. Thanks to the children, however, the real Japan was continually entering our house. In March there was the girls' festival (*hina-matsuri*), and we would arrange dolls representing the ancient imperial court at the foot of a gilded screen, together with many other miniature domestic objects, including a *hibachi* (brazier), *tansu* (cupboards), *o-zen* (the honourable lacquered vessels out of which one eats), *cha-wan* (cups for rice and tea), to say nothing of palanquins, musical instruments, models of Japanese shops, inns, boats, all enchanting little things to be touched with the tips of the fingers and looked at through a lens, so minute and perfectly made were they. In August there was the *tanabata,* the festival

[1] *Mekake* means literally 'hanging from the eyes'.

of the tender spouses, the two stars Vega and Altair, who are separated by the Milky Way but meet for one day by crossing the 'Celestial River' on a delicate bridge formed by birds' wings; and there was *o-bon,* when the dead return to their homes, which, though it did not greatly affect us, kept all the neighbours very busy. In November there was the *shichi-go-san,* the festival of girls aged three and seven and of boys aged three and five, an occasion anxiously awaited because of the opportunity of wearing the most brightly coloured kimonos and exciting universal admiration. Finally there was New Year, with presents and visits, rice sweets *(o-mochi),* the special soup called *o-zoni,* chestnuts, seaweed of the kind called *kombu,* lotus roots, cups of *o-toso* (a kind of sweet *saké*), and the game called *hane-tsuki,* which is a kind of very sedate and ceremonious pat-ball.

The girls' games, songs, riddles, dolls, their friends, the news they brought home daily from the kindergarten, all constituted a continual education for us. Some of the songs they sang were unforgettable, for instance that which begins '*Chi-pa-pa, chi-pa-pa, suzume no gakko no sensei wa',* and is all about the sparrows' school teacher, or the invitation to the glow-worms in June:

> *Hotaru koi, hotaru koi*   Come, glow-worm, come, glow-worm,
> *Chichana chochin motte koé.*   And bring your little lantern.

In the evening Miki used to tell fairy stories; that of Momotaro, for instance, the strong, fat boy born of a peach who was brought up by an old couple in the country and ended by conquering the Oni-ga-shima demons and came home with a cart full of treasure, pulled by a dog and a pheasant and pushed by a monkey; or the story of Shita-kiri-suzume, the poor sparrow whose tongue was cut off, or that of Issun-boshi, the thumb-size hero who succeeded in rescuing a princess assailed by demons by taking advantage of his minuteness to scare them, causing them in their ignominious flight to drop the *uchide-no-kozuchi,* the 'hammer that grants all desires', by means of which he was able to become a full-size man and, of course, marry the princess. There were also stories about *kappa,* strange, monstrous beings who are sometimes kind and comic figures, sometimes evil and dangerous; they seem to live in rivers, have shells like tortoises, and frogs' legs; and on their heads they have a kind of receptacle which when full of water makes them dangerous but when empty weak and cowardly. From these it was a short step to stories about *tanuki* (badgers) and *kitsune* (foxes), and the endless acts of wizardry of which they are capable. Then, by way of *tengu* (demons), *o-bake* (honourable ghosts), and cats, the cycle returned to human beings, among whom the most famous figure is that of the great judge Ooka-sama and the subtle wisdom of his memorable judgments.[1] ·

'Little sister' Miki was extremely well informed about all these things, and she was invaluable to us in other ways as well. She helped us to find our way about the labyrinth of Japanese customs and instructed us in the complicated rules of Japanese etiquette. Ignorance of the latter is not held against foreigners, indeed it is taken for granted, but for that reason observance of it gives particular pleasure. There is the whole business of presents, for instance. There seems to be no end to the occasions on which presents are given in Japan. They are *de rigueur* on the occasion of a first visit, and are given on births, marriages, deaths, arrivals, departures, examinations, promotions, successes, the publication of a book, recovery from an illness, etc., etc., to say nothing of New Year and certain other dates in the calendar. Presents are chosen with extreme care, with a view to making the best possible impression without imperilling the giver's solvency; and extreme circumspection must be exercised to avoid *faux pas* such—to quote an extreme case—as giving someone a picture containing horses and stags, because horses are *ba* and stags are *ka,* and *baka* means idiot. One should never be tempted by the marvellous artificial flowers to be seen in some shops, for these are used only for funerals. Tips must always be wrapped in paper or, better still, put in special envelopes *(shugi-bukuro),* on the outside of which there is a piece of dried *awabi* (a highly appreciated marine delicacy) wrapped in red and white paper.

The list of superstitions is also endless. Hot water, for instance, must never be poured into cold, but always the reverse; chopsticks must never be left stuck in the rice; the right side of the kimono must never be worn over the left; no bed must ever be made with the head in the *kimon* (north-east) direction. All these prohibitions derive from

[1] Ooka Tadasuke (1677–1751), lord of Echizen and civil governor of Yedo. His judgments were collected and made into an exceedingly popular book called *Ooka Meiyo-Seidan.*

resemblances with funeral practices, as is the case with the European superstition about leaving one's hat on the bed.

It was Miki who reminded us as soon as we settled in at Kyoto that when you move house it is desirable to send your new neighbours, in strict order of precedence, small gifts of *soba*, appetizing green noodles that are easily to be found everywhere. Puns, whether 'lucky' or 'unlucky', are of immense importance in Japanese. The number four *(shi)* is avoided whenever possible, and is considered as unlucky as thirteen is in the west, because *shi* also means 'death'. You must never offer anyone three slices *(mikire)* of food, because *mikire* also means 'to kill someone'. The nineteenth *(juku)* year is considered dangerous, because *juku* can also mean 'recurring pains'. The kind of seaweed called *kombu* or *kobu* is lucky, because it is reminiscent of *yorokobu* ('to be happy, cheerful'). *Tai,* the four-toothed sparus, is considered the fish *par excellence* for any meal held in celebration of a special occasion, because *medetai* means 'lucky'. Japanese housewives look with special favour on French beans *(mame)*, became *mame* also means 'good health'. One of the reasons for the popularity of the pine-tree is that the poetical name for it is *chitose,* which can also mean 'a thousand years, of great duration'. Funerals must never take place on days which for astrological reasons are called *tomobiki* because *tomobiki* also means 'pull friends', and at least six relatives of the dead man would die too. If, however, a funeral on such a day is unavoidable, it is as well to conceal six terracotta puppets in the bier in the hope of deceiving Emma (Yama in Sanskrit), the king of the underworld. I recall paying a visit many years ago to the rector of Hokkaido University, a professor of pathology, who showed me, among his many other precious possessions, an ancient sword that he intended giving his son on his forthcoming departure for the war in China. The thing to which he drew my particular attention was the hilt, on which there was a tiny golden frog; the word *kaeru* means both 'frog' and 'return', 'and the latter will be the liveliest thought in my mind when I give it him,' the learned professor concluded. To return to the word with which we started, *soba,* it brings to mind both a popular traditional food and the idea of 'neighbour, proximity', and is thus extremely appropriate for indicating the hope of good relations between *tonari, kinjo* and *mukai* (neighbours).

Among the latter we soon discovered a fellow-European, an

exceedingly tall and thin member of the French aristocracy, the Baron de Valsières, a distinguished old gentleman of about sixty who lived next door to Naruse, the *mekake*. His abundant white hair was always brushed with meticulous care over his long, aristocratic-shaped head, and his face was that of a distinguished-looking dreamer, sailing the skies like a balloonist, drifting in the wind with elegant passivity.

He dressed in the most fantastic manner. He must have inherited, or salved from some long-forgotten catastrophe, a complete wardrobe dating from the first half of the nineteenth century. His shirts were of some superb, everlasting material, and he wore a huge white cravat kept in place by a gold tie-pin. He wore a red waistcoat in summer and a fur-lined waistcoat in winter; a black jacket with narrow sleeves made of ancient homespun; long, narrow, tube-shaped trousers of the same material; highly polished brown boots buttoned at the side; and a tiny, round, cyclist's check cap. He might have emerged from an illustration entitled 'Count Landolfo on his return from his journey to the court of the Shah'. All that was needed to complete the picture was a penny-farthing bicycle.

He taught French literature at the University, and led an extremely retired life in a Japanese house with a former geisha aged about fifty, wrote poetry, and translated recondite Japanese ninth-century poets. He was an ardent monarchist, and refused to have anything to do with the authorities *de cette république*. Every now and then I used to meet him in the grounds of the University, returning from a lecture with a book under his arm, and he would reply to my greeting with a nod and a smile and pass on.

Nearly every evening I would see him from my window on his way to the Kitashirakawa public baths, dressed as usual, sometimes without his cap, but always with the white metal bowl in which he used to carry his towels, soap, and shaving materials. The cook and Uriu-san several times mentioned that in the bath he was 'very handsome' and that he was so considered by the whole neighbourhood. *Kirei* in Japanese means both 'beautiful' and 'clean', but in this case I think that what made such a favourable impression was the whiteness of his skin.

I used to go to the Kitashirakawa baths myself when the gas pressure was low, but I never met the baron in the 'honourable hot water'. Perhaps that was because he always went early (*quand l'eau est plus propre*).

Instead I often used to meet the young Nishimura, who greeted me, even if half covered in soap, with a deep bow, and called me *sensei* (professor). The Nishimura lived in a villa just beyond that of 'old' Hirai. As a family they were well off; so were the Hirai, but the Nishimura belonged to a different social category. Only the roof of the Nishimura house was visible among the cypresses and holm-oaks; in Japan no house belonging to anybody of the upper classes is ever easily visible from the street; the idea of a façade, of making a handsome or impressive display, is foreign to the Japanese mentality.

The Nishimura were rarely seen; they had nothing to do with their neighbours, and would never have dreamt of entering into relations with foreigners. Before the war *gaijin* ('people from outside') was a term highly charged with feeling for the Japanese, inspiring on the one hand admiration, envy, curiosity, even servility, and on the other hatred, suspicion, and contempt. Associating with foreigners was always an adventure; it caused an indefinable and often dangerous turmoil in the delicate equilibrium of the small social groups into which the Japanese were, and still are, so rigidly organized. If, on the one hand, we had the fascination of the exotic in Japanese eyes, because we possessed such an extraordinary amount of technical knowledge, were generally fabulously rich, and were surrounded by an infinity of strange and desirable objects, and were skilful and therefore capable of being useful to them, on the other hand we were nearly always immoral and often superstitious; to say nothing of the fact that we stank, had clumsy hands and disgustingly big feet, enormous noses and 'dogs' ' eyes, and were entirely devoid of manners. Moreover, we might well be spies, or emissaries of some occult power, or at any rate the police might decide that we were such, which would be the same thing. In short, those who wished to live irreproachable lives from the point of the view of the local moralists kept away from foreigners. *Gaijin-kusai* ('stink like a foreigner') was a term of great contempt; and *bata-kusai* ('stink of butter') was even worse.

But to return to the Nishimura. The only regular signs of life that reached the neighbours from their villa were that of the young man reading the classics aloud under the guidance of a master, and that of the young woman playing the piano. Reading the classics aloud in the traditional manner amounts almost to a chant. At first I found it monotonous and almost incomprehensible. But the fact that the performance was something to which my ear had not been attuned by my own civilization seemed to me to be no reason to deny its value, and in the end I accustomed myself to it, and saw its charm; the master was excellent, and he unrolled the long phrases with magnificent effect. As for Miss Nishimura's piano-playing, the less said about it the better. She spent months practising the Moonlight Sonata, but always broke down at a point which she must have found either excessively difficult or excessively sublime.

The education of the two young Nishimura was, as far as I could tell, strict and varied. He read engineering at the University, did a great deal of *kendo* (Japanese fencing), played tennis, practised archery, rode horseback, never went out in the evening, read the classics with his master, always wore the black student's uniform, perhaps smoked in secret, but naturally could not dance, and apparently never had anything to do with girls, unless he sometimes went secretly at night to the gay quarter beyond Gion, which, however, I always thought exceedingly doubtful. The girl took lessons in flower arrangement and the tea ceremony, and probably in painting and calligraphy. At home she cooked, certainly secretly read a novel or illustrated newspaper occasionally, and sometimes went shopping with her mother. Did she go to the cinema? I do not know. Perhaps she sometimes did so in the afternoon with her friends. Sometimes her Beethoven, particularly because of the inevitable breakdown always at the same place, seemed so pathetic that you could have wept.

Another thing over which you could have wept, but for entirely different reasons, was the wretched agglomeration of hovels which you came to after crossing the broad, straight street into which our lane ran. After passing a row of gracious, well-kept, sunny, and attractive houses and villas, you suddenly found yourself in a maze of narrow, winding, crowded, poverty-stricken streets and alleys in which it was only too easy to lose your way; even the air had a special, indefinable, strangely unpleasant smell. This was the so-called Tanaka ('among the fields') quarter, inhabited by *eta,* the outcasts and 'untouchables' of Japanese society.

So inconspicuous from the outside was this small, self-contained world that several months passed before we became aware of its existence. Before the war the *eta* were unmentionable as well as untouchable; the government tried to draw a veil of silence over what was rightly regarded as a blot on the country. But there the *eta* were, surrounded by an invisible wall of ancient prejudice, the only Japanese who were dirty, degraded, and utterly without pride. It was not the poverty that was so horrifying in the alleys of Tanaka—much greater poverty existed elsewhere in the big cities, or in the Tohoku ('North-East') countryside; the really horrifying thing was that, while ordinary Japanese held their heads high even in the most desperate circumstances, the *eta* looked and behaved like people degraded, humiliated, and crushed by centuries of universal contempt. I shall never forget the furtive and suspicious way in which they looked at us—like stray dogs shrinking from a friendly pat because they had learnt to expect nothing but blows. One of the contemptuous Japanese terms for *eta* is *kokonotsu* (nine), *i.e.,* not ten, therefore imperfect, incomplete, something less than a man. Another is *yotsu* (four), often accompanied by the gesture of holding up four fingers, *i.e.,* the number of an animal's claws.

The *eta* constitute one of the gravest Japanese social problems; it is calculated that there are still more than two million of them scattered about the country, but with concentrations in the 'old' parts of Japan, Kyushu, the coasts of the Inland Sea, Kobe, Osaka, Kyoto. Their origin is unknown, and has long been the subject of dispute among sociologists. Some—Professor Kita Takeichi, for example—maintain that they started by being butchers, tanners, etc., who fell into disrepute in the sixth century with the advent of Buddhism, the first commandment of which is, of course, 'thou shalt not take life'. Others, with Kikuchi Sanya, maintain that the original nucleus was provided by the aborigines subdued by the Yamato, and the suggestion has even been made (by Oye Taku) that they are one of the lost tribes of Israel. Finally, others, including Brinkley, maintain that the *eta* were originally Koreans (prisoners of war or clandestine immigrants), or continentals of various origin, or even Filipinos. The fact remains that from the dawn of Japanese history there are clear and unmistakable references to a by no means inconsiderable number of people who were considered outside or beneath the law and consequently lived in a state that was more animal than human. Exactly as is the case of their Indian counterparts, all work which in the general estimation bore the stigma of impiety or impurity, or was considered degrading or particularly unpleasant, such as dealing with animal carcasses or removing human excrement, devolved upon the *eta*, who were considered to be entirely without rights.

To write *eta* the Japanese use two ideograms meaning 'much impurity', 'much dirt'. True, in 1871 a law was passed to emancipate these people, among other things re-naming them *shin-heimin* (new citizens), but in practice it remained a dead letter; public opinion in such matters is slow to'change. As recently as 1933 Ninomiya Shigeaki wrote that the *eta* could be said to suffer from discrimination in every field of activity and in all their relations with the rest of society.[1] In fact, during the years we spent at Kyoto before the war the situation substantially deteriorated, and municipal police regulations harshly restricted the liberty of the inhabitants of the so-called special villages (*tokushu buraku*), of which Tanaka was an average example.

In 1922 a vigorous movement, inspired by the most intelligent spirits among the *eta*, was launched with a view to the abolition of discrimination and bringing the problem to the country's notice. This was the so-called *suihei-undo* ('movement to level the waters'), but its links with Communism made it suspect to the militarists, who were powerful from 1925 onwards and from 1936 were in complete control. After the war all the written rules and regulations which put the *eta* in a state of inferiority were abolished; indeed, penalties were laid down for calling them *eta* instead of *shin-heimin*. Nevertheless things have changed but little. The *eta* still marry among themselves, trade among themselves, live in their own 'ghettos'. Occasionally an *eta* manages to escape from his environment and get on in the world, sometimes in state employment. There have actually been generals and university professors of *eta* origin; when they succeed in going up in the world they change their place of residence, try to obliterate their tracks, have their children educated with special care, but live in a state of perpetual terror that their secret will be discovered. The *eta* theme has often been dealt with by novelists; a love affair between an *eta* and an ordinary person has the romantic, heroic quality of a love affair, say, between a healthy person and a leper in a different social context.

The reader may ask how a religion of such high spiritual content as Buddhism was able to tolerate a social injustice of this magnitude.

[1] NINOMIYA SHIGEAKI, *An Inquiry Concerning the Eta*, Tokyo, 1933.

The answer is that the *eta* phenomenon seems to have arisen out of the conflict between a religious belief and human needs, rather as happened in Christian societies in the case of money-lenders and prostitutes. Apart from that, the doctrine of *karma,* that is, of the influence of merit and demerit in one life on a whole succession of future lives, explains a certain passivity in the face of many evils which were faced up to in the warmer glow of Christian love and charity, even in the periods of western history of which there is least to be proud about.

One last memory of my pre-war life in Kyoto. I have mentioned nearly all our *tonari* (neighbours), but I have said nothing about one of them, a well-known master of the *shaku-hachi,* the Japanese bamboo flute. When his pupils played to him, as they did every day, it was a torment, but when he played himself, as happened only too seldom, it was a delight. Sometimes late at night, when the moon flooded the lane and silence descended over the city, the woods and mountains, we would be lulled to sleep by his fluid and silvery notes.

Unruly Monks of Mount Hiei

Buddhism is one of the greatest adventures of the human spirit. It originated at the foot of the Himalayas five centuries before Christ in the meditations of Sakyamuni the Buddha, prince turned ascetic, was enriched by nearly a thousand years of bold and sublime speculation by Indian philosophers, and spread throughout central, south, and east Asia, from Tibet to Japan, from Mongolia to the East Indies. Wherever it went it presented itself in the guise of a fluid, philosophical, moral, poetical attitude towards life and death rather than as a rigid system. It never adopted an intransigent attitude to earlier faiths or other philosophies and when it met with resistance it overcame it by assimilation. Hence the breath-taking complexity of the forms that it assumed. Man's other great adventure, Christianity, has a large number of varieties too, from Roman Catholicism on the one hand to certain Protestant sects on the other which border on an abstract theism or a philosophy of science; there are Copts and Mormons, Maronites and Nestorians, strict followers of Calvin, and orgiastic adherents of Voodoo. But Christianity has been kept within bounds by the restricted canon of the Scriptures, while the Buddha, according to a popular eastern saying, 'preached 84,000 doctrines', and the differentiation that has taken place in the course of centuries has gone to incredible lengths.

An attempt at even the briefest account of the fundamentals of the Buddhist doctrine and its manifold developments would take us too far afield. I shall, however, say something about Buddhism in Japan, which is the country in which it can best be studied, because of the care with which teaching and literature have been handed down from the earliest times.

From its first introduction by Korean monks in 552 until the end of the Nara period in 784, Buddhism in Japan developed around six schools. Perhaps the chief characteristic of this period was a deeply felt piety. testified to by the art which it inspired, but a scanty understanding of its metaphysical assumptions, which were so much more profound than the native Shinto myths as to dazzle rather than convince the islanders' virgin minds. It should also be recalled that during this period Buddhism was primarily a religion of the educated and those in immediate contact with them.

But with the advent of the ninth century, the time of the foundation of Heian, Japanese life underwent a radical transformation. The apprenticeship period was over, and the assimilation of the great continental civilization started to bear fruit; the graft had given a new impulse to the growth of the native tree. Buddhism was itself transformed by two of the greatest figures in Japanese history, Dengyō Daishi (762–822) and Kōbō Daishi (774–835). Both went to China, not as their monkish predecessors had done, as ignorant islanders ready to bow in the face of any kind of wisdom, but as sages enjoying high repute in their own right, desirous of drinking at the purest springs of doctrine. Their different personalities impelled them in almost diametrically opposite directions. Dengyō Daishi introduced into Japan the doctrines and practices of the Tendai sect; Kōbō Daishi introduced those of the Shingon sect.

These two schools of thought, systems, approaches to art and life, dominated Japan for four centuries, left deep traces on its civilization, and are still significant forces even today. Shingon, as I mentioned in connection with the Mount Murō temples, is the form of Japanese Buddhism which is closest to the Lamaism of Tibet; a religion rich in metaphysics and symbolism, magnificent baroque forms and impressive

rites, an esoteric faith for initiates, rejoicing in mystery and subtle intoxication of the senses, combined with extreme intellectual penetration.
Tendai has always presented itself in a more severe and less elaborate
guise; its leaders have always addressed themselves to the foundation
of monasteries and to dealing with the civil powers. For centuries their
ambition was to represent, with the benevolent support of the Emperor,
the moral conscience, the ecclesiastical organization, of the country.

What principally distinguishes these two new schools from the
sects of the Nara period is a different attitude to man. Most of the Nara
sects were aristocratic even in their metaphysics; to them salvation was
the privilege of the predestined few. Both Dengyō Daishi and Kōbō
Daishi rebelled against this; they proclaimed Buddhahood to be the
potential privilege of all; the task of religion was to bring the potentiality to light. Such teachings were considered so revolutionary that
the two masters suffered persecution before their doctrines were
accepted.

In philosophy the Tendai school was eclectic. Their doctrine of
progressive revelation was typical. The Buddha, they taught, realizing
that it was beyond human capacity to attain understanding of his lofty
teaching in a single generation, continued to watch over mankind,
giving ever more subtle and profound metaphysical interpretation in
the course of successive terrestrial lives. This made acceptable the huge
mass of Buddhist literature, the differences of the various schools; they
all represented different phases of the true doctrine. The highest of all
teachings, however, was the famous *Hokke-kyō* ('Lotus of the Good
Law').[1]

The emphasis on the organization of monastic life in the course of
time took on a typically Japanese twist. In periods of insecurity abbots
took to arming their monks, forming what were originally intended to
be monastery guards. The warlike instincts of the Yamato were little
modified by the new religion of love and piety, however, with the result
that warrior-monks (*so-hei*) became powerful and numerous, and
temples were transformed into fortresses.

It became the custom for monasteries to settle their disputes by
force of arms; by the end of the tenth century regular pitched battles
were fought. A time actually came when monks, particularly those of

[1] In Sanskrit *Saddharmapundarika* (*Sacred Books of the East*, Vol. XXI).

Mount Hiei, felt strong enough to challenge the government; a pretext was provided in 989, when the abbot appointed by the Emperor was *persona non grata* to them. A few decades later it had become normal practice for the monasteries, when they considered that their rights had been infringed upon, to send armed bands of monks down to Kyoto with some sacred emblem or venerated relic; this made armed resistance to them sacrilegious, and provided an excellent pretext for reprisals. The unfortunate Emperor Shirakawa (eleventh century), a devout Buddhist, complained that there were three things in relation to which he was powerless: the flooding of the river Kamo, winning at dice, and the monks of Mount Hiei. Using such methods, the worldly prestige and power of the Tendai sect became important elements in the life of the country, 'but moral and intellectual values declined' (Sir Charles Eliot). The monasteries in fact became strongholds of armed adventurers rather than the homes of men dedicated to meditation and good works. A Japanese ruler having sufficient power and authority was bound in the end to uproot and destroy these centres of insubordination which disturbed public order under the pretext of religion; in 1577 this was at last done by Oda Nobunaga.

A visit to Mount Hiei is therefore less interesting than might be expected from the antiquity of its traditions. Dengyō Daishi built the first temple in 788, but the monasteries to be found there today date back barely to the beginning of the seventeenth century. The beauty of Mount Hiei depends chiefly on the harmony between the buildings and their surroundings. Hermitages, pavilions, temples lie among avenues of ancient trees, connected by paths and ancient stone steps between which grasses and moss grow.

The highest peak of Hiei, the Mount of Wisdom, is called Shimedaki ('Of the Four Splendours'), possibly to indicate the marvellous views to be seen in the four directions. Three thousand feet below there lies a great city, Kyoto; a great lake, the Biwa; endless forests and mountains; and finally, in fine weather, there is the distant view of the Pacific. But a clear sky at the summit is not too common; one of the ancient pathways between the temples is called the Moth of Clouds. In fact mist driven by wind into the foliage of the cryptomerias is one of the things that give enchantment to the spot.

The doctrine of original sin conflicts with everything with which the Asian is brought up to believe. Confucianism and Shinto are frankly optimistic about the nature of man and his final destiny. In the west Buddhism is considered to be a pessimistic philosophy, as, indeed, from one point of view it is, as it denies the reality and the importance of the world. But from another point of view it is profoundly optimistic, for it teaches that not just man, but the humblest worm, indeed all living things, are destined ultimately to become Buddha and be merged in nirvana, the absolute. For thousands of years the Chinese and Japanese have been brought up to believe that man is fundamentally good. How, then, shall we convince them of the opposite? How can they hope to understand the doctrine of original sin and salvation until their faith in man's fundamental goodness has been undermined? Man must be sinful, perverse, and damned before there is any point in saving him.

The eternal and absolute distinction between God and the world, between Creator and created, is another thing which sharply conflicts with the eastern conception of divinity as diffused throughout nature and mankind. This is not so much a formal pantheism as a poetical inclination of the mind. But it is ever present, and the alien doctrine of Christianity pitilessly disrupts a whole network of sweet and ancient relationships between man and the world. For the Buddhists most aware of their own traditions this is the point at which the two religions are indeed irreconcilable. On the one hand there is the unreality of the self and the final annihilation of all differences in the absolute, on the other the immortal soul and the permanent dualism of Creator and created.

Moreover, as my friend Jun often used to say, how were they to tell what Christianity really was? There were innumerable versions, and each, according to the missionaries, was the sole true version. We should compose our differences before presenting our faiths to them. Meanwhile the east looked on and smiled. . . .

In Christianity the whole emphasis is on the individual, but in Asia the fundamental social unit has never been the individual; from the earliest times it has been the family. Here again the Christian message is subversive of the deepest attitudes of mind that constitute the essence of a civilization. If the Christian doctrine is so important, so runs the

Asian argument, how did it come about that our ancestors were deprived of it? On the other hand, if our ancestors saw things rightly, can this new teaching really be so important?

Moreover, it should be recalled that the Asian way of thinking, which is intuitive and synthetic, tends to include rather than to exclude, to embrace and sublimate rather than to destroy and substitute. Our universe is solid, objective, compartmentalized, rigorously dualist; it comes naturally to us to divide things into mind and matter, good and evil, past and future, to think in terms of absolute truth and total error, of true beliefs and false. But to the oriental every religion is a way, a path, *tao, michi*. Some paths are better, quicker, more sublime, need greater courage, just as others are quieter and more comfortable, making smaller demands. But all lead to the same goal. The idea of repudiating and casting away a huge and valuable spiritual heritage is a thing profoundly shocking to the eastern mind. But with Christianity there is no alternative. If some Protestant denominations are more broad-minded, with Roman Catholicism there is no escape; you have to take it or leave it. So far they have left it.

Somi often argued that the only way to interest the east in Christianity would be to re-think it entirely, and to present it, not in terms of Greek philosophy, but in terms of Indian and Buddhist philosophy. He was, incidentally, in high spirits today, so there was no getting him to talk philosophy; in any case it was always difficult to get him to talk. When Jun and I reached his house we found him with a young Italian missionary, and all four of us set out together for Ohara. Father Fustelli was about thirty-five, had a frank, open face, and looked much more like a man of action than a thinker. How could he be a friend of Somi's?

Adriano Somigli—known to everybody as Somi—went to the same school as I in Florence, but we did not know each other; chance first brought us together at Kyoto. He was indeed a remarkable man. He started learning Hebrew and Sanskrit at school; he took orders, went through a period of mysticism and severe ascetic practices. At his seminary he distinguished himself by his exceptional intelligence and his extraordinary gift for languages; he was sent to America, where he continued his studies in modern philosophy, scholastic philosophy, Chinese, Tibetan, and Japanese. In Japan, where he went as a missionary, he graduated in Japanese literature in one of the Imperial Universities, and he is still, I believe, the only Italian entitled to call himself *bungaku gakushi,* doctor of Japanese letters.

From the beginning of our friendship I realized that Somi was harassed by a grave problem. In the course of years he had lost his Catholic faith; indeed, having set out to convert the Buddhists, he had been converted by them. Should he remain in a Church to which spiritually he no longer belonged? For a long time we never discussed the subject, but you could tell which way things were going by hints he dropped, by his ways, and above all by the fact that he ceased to wear clerical clothes; instead he wore an ordinary dark suit, and might easily have been taken for a hall porter or a fashionable ladies' hairdresser. Somi, though nurtured on scholastic philosophy, hated discipline, order, and system, and, as I have said, getting him to talk was the hardest thing in the world. It had to happen spontaneously—perhaps when you went round to borrow a book, or to return a cigarette-case he had left at your house, or when you were sitting with him over a glass of beer at a railway station bar, 'just watching the world go by'.

Somi, it appeared, had met Father Fustelli at a seminary in America, where they had spent three years together. It was hard to imagine a greater contrast. In every word and gesture (I could see him in the driving mirror) Father Fustelli was a man of decision and action; clearly, I said to myself, he stood for the hope of converting the heathen by works—schools, consulting-rooms, printing presses, orphanages. A dangerous path; the heathen would take what they wanted and then kick you out, as had already been demonstrated. Should we not do the same with Buddhists who established charitable institutions in our midst? However, Father Fustelli obviously had a great liking for Somi; friendship is capable of overcoming all barriers. This miracle, I felt prepared to swear, was primarily due to Somi's essential saintliness—*anima naturaliter buddhica, anima naturaliter christiana.*

The road to Ohara followed a valley lying between Mount Hiei and the hills above Kurama. Now it broadened out into terraced rice-fields, now it closed in again, and the tree-covered slopes in their autumn tints descended steeply towards a rushing stram. We passed through several villages; the thatched roofs were of an unmistakable local style; such a vigorous style, indeed, that there were actually specimens of it in metal sheeting—thatch, after all, has to be renewed every twenty or thirty years. Once more the valley closed in, and then, about seven miles from Kyoto, we came to the 'big field', the plain of Ohara.

It has been the private property of the Imperial House since ancient times. Wooded mountains rise on either side, and it is dotted about with villages, temples, hermitages. The peasant women still wear a special costume, which is sometimes exploited for the benefit of tourists, but is pleasing all the same because of its cut and its colour; they carry bundles of wood on their head, just as women carry water in southern Italy.

Jun remarked that there were few places in Japan where loads were carried in this manner. There were many legends about the origins of the people of Ohara.

What a strange company was ours! A Catholic priest, a missionary who had been converted to Buddhism, a Japanese of Christian upbringing who had reacted against it because of the claims of his traditional civilization, and . . . myself. We were, however, united by admiration of our surroundings, and the complicated spiritual bridges and abysses that united and divided us were tacitly ignored. We left the car, and followed a row of maples (momiji); the leaves filtered the light like a Gothic glazed window (Photograph 13). Some steps, completely covered in red leaves, led to the gateway of a temple with a gently curving roof. A gaku, a carefully worked wooden board, bore the words 'Sanzen-in', the Three Thousand Temple. Before entering we stopped for a moment at a chaya, tea-hut, opened for the season when the momiji were 'in bloom'.

'Why "three thousand"?' I asked Somi while the girl poured our tea.

'Oh, how much you want to know today!' Somi replied. 'I expect they just started counting, and by the time they got to three thousand they were bored to death and stopped. Why don't you look at the girl instead of worrying your head about such things? Haven't you noticed how pretty she is?'

There was no point in trying to draw Somi when he was not in the mood, and the girl was certainly worth looking at—eyes worthy of a heterodox Aphrodite by Phidias, peach-blossom complexion, and mouth that the French would call troublante. According to Jun, however, hers was seiyo-rashii no bi da, beauty of the western type, not in accordance with Japanese taste. Western or not, Somi and I were delighted with her. Father Fustelli, toying with his tea-cup, returned to the subject of the

Temple of the Three Thousand, and Somi was forced to open the store-house of his knowledge.

The name indicated that we were in Tendai territory, he explained; the temple was called after one of their doctrines. So subtly and intricately was the universe composed that the whole of it could be deduced from the smallest of its parts; the Buddha could be deduced from a grain of dust. The Tendai philosophers said that the Three Thousand were implicit in every thought. By Three Thousand they meant the universe; complicated calculations had shown that that was the number of the essential elements and their combinations.

'In other words, a huge Mendeleeff's table, for metaphysics instead of for chemistry,' remarked Jun, who was not very interested. He was all for science; only the pursuit of reality by scientific methods could result in a picture of the world that was not entirely fantastic. He did not say so now, but I had heard him often enough.

'But Somi,' Father Fustelli said, still toying with his tea-cup, 'don't you think your Tendai Buddhists make a terrible confusion between subject and object, mind and matter?'

As soon as he had said this he looked at me, embarrassed, as though he had thrown a stone. I realized that, though he was used to argument with Somi ever since their time in the seminary together, he now felt embarrassed as a priest discussing serious things lightly in front of a stranger.

'But that is just where the depth of the Buddhist metaphysics lies!' exlaimed Somi, who was now well away. 'Everything is mind. With us Hegel and the idealists made a lot of noise in the world with a few wretched little notions with which the Indians Nagarjuna, Asangha, Vasubandhu had preceded them by twelve centuries. If they had realized it, they might have been a little more modest, don't you think? Would you like a characteristic illustration of the Tendai school? That of the mirror. Its brightness belongs to the first form of being, *ku*, the void, nothing; the things reflected in it belong to the second form of being, *ka*, that of contingent things; only the mirror itself is *chu*, literally 'the thing in the middle', *i.e., substantia, dharmakaya*. Independently none of the three has any existence; even the mirror, without light and the things reflected in it, is no longer a mirror. In other words *ku, ka* and *chu* have no existence except in relation to one another. Nothing can exist apart from the whole, nor can the whole exist apart from the infinite complexities of nothings and contingent things. *Isshin sandai,* one thought, three truths. . . .'

When Somi started talking like this his eyes flashed, he became as handsome as Dionysus, or Monju, 'Enchanting Knowledge'. But when he noticed that we were watching him, fascinated, he pulled a face, laughed, and started talking about *ka,* contingent trifles.

The girl reappeared with the tea-pot. He asked her name.

'Mika,' she replied; the word means 'So Much Beauty'.

'Look how well named she is!' he exclaimed, turning to us. Then he spoke to her again.

'*Koibito wa nai ka?*' he asked. (Have you a young man?)

'Yes,' she answered, with a laugh—Enchanting Innocence facing Enchanting Knowledge. '*Sochira-sama o-ari ja arimasenka?*' (Has the honourable gentleman here perhaps not a young lady?)

Somi's brow darkened, for a moment he was at a loss for a reply, and when it came it was late, and was rather forced.

'I?' he said. 'I'm an old Buddha; I've reached an age when I think only about flowers, or the *momiji* in bloom.'

Many true things are said in jest. There had been something strange about Somi lately, I could not say what; he seemed tired, disillusioned, on edge; at one time nobody ever succeeded in catching him off his guard. Was a new crisis looming in his life? Or another love affair? Who could tell?

I believe that there has been only one woman in his life, and that was many years ago, when we were neighbours in Kyoto. For a long time it was no more than a suspicion. Somi was a night bird, surrounding himself with mystery, like a Tantric deity. But once I detected in his study the trace of a perfume of unmistakably feminine origin; another day I found among his books a lace glove, of the kind worn by smart Japanese women; and one night, when I was just about to drop in on him unexpectedly, a feminine shadow slipped past me, leaving in its wake a perfume exactly like that which had lingered in his study.

Months later he dropped her photograph from between the pages of a book on Indian art. This left him with his back to the wall, and I discovered that she was a poet. In Japan the arts are much less specialized than they are with us; an artist tends to express himself in several ways; a poet is likely to be also a painter, a calligrapher also a sculptor or master potter. She was also a dancer, and had an enormous passion for everything Indian.

More months passed, and at last one evening we met. Somi, ritualist and master of symbolism, would not have liked the encounter to have been left to chance; and my wife and I were invited, a mask of apparent indifference concealing the immense importance of the occasion, to a little dinner in a hermitage-restaurant in the woods of the Eastern Mount. Somi was extremely nervous. None of his friends had any inkling of the affair, and we were the first to be let into the secret. I realized that all sorts of things were at stake which Somi had never had put to the test in real life: his pride as a man, to say nothing of all the aspects of his taste. We were slightly saddened to discover that he seemed to be in love, not so much with the woman as with the situation. With what care he had prepared every slightest detail! Perhaps he had come in the afternoon to arrange the *tokonoma,* the flowers, the poem, the picture. The perfection of the whole was breath-taking. Or perhaps it had been her work. But all that was a secret which we should never penetrate.

At last she arrived. There was a rustle of skirts on the stairs, and a melting, caressing voice said: '*Gomen-kudasai*? (May I come in?) She was small, thin, elegant, and moved like a stalk bearing a big flower in a breeze. The flower was her smile; a luminous, mobile smile that was not so much an expression of a state of mind as an acquired virtuosity, a total dance of all her muscles, and hence of her face. She was not in her first youth; she was perhaps thirty, or more. In Asia it is difficult to tell. She obviously accept Somi's love with regal dignity, and her liveliest, but not deepest, feelings seemed to be engaged.

This occult, symbolic, ritualistic love affair went on for a long time, betrayed only by trails of perfume, looks and sighs, withered petals, and long absences. Then—and not without considerable relief to his friends —the woman disappeared from Somi's life, and he became absorbed once more in work and ascetic practices. He rose early, retired late, lived on rice, herbs, and a little fruit, drank nothing but milk, and there were no more trails of perfume in his room; instead there were trails of incense left by the robes of Buddhist monks who came to read him great tomes of Tantric philosophy.

It was during this period that Somi told me one evening that, if I wanted to see something which would interest me, I should go next day to the Tōji, which is the chief temple of the Shingon sect, and one of the biggest in Kyoto.

Shingon Buddhism has characteristics that mark it off from all other Japanese sects. We are still in the realm of the most uncompromising monism; only mind exists, all else is illusion. But this, like all the other tenets of this bold and complicated system, are presented, not in the abstract, but in an empyrean populated with gods, demigods, spirits, furies and superhuman beings: 'the inexhaustible beauties, potentialities, activities, and mysteries of the world'[1] transformed into celestial person-ages. Hence a deep and fundamental link with the arts. The universe itself is the body of the supreme Buddha Vairocana, 'He who Enlightens', and, as he is the all, his ritual gesture (mudra) is he. This provides the connection with liturgical practice; hence, by way of music, incense, song, we return to art, closing the circle, as it were.

Shingon and Somi seemed made for one another; its doctrines might have been waiting for him since the beginning of time; the fact that he came from the other end of the world seemed only to underline the remarkable workings of fate. Somi scorns the obvious, and is natur-ally attracted by the difficult, the intricate, the devious, and the obscure. Shingon offered him ten steps to knowledge, nine of manifest doctrine (kengyō) transmitted by books and writing, while the tenth, the abstruse and recondite mikkyō, is handed on only by word of mouth, from master to initiate. He who has attained this summit is said to form part of himitsu-shogon-shin, the Ornate Heart of Mystery. Such was Somi's realm. He was never content with pure, abstract thought; he had to combine it with satisfaction of the eye and the ear, i.e., music and art; and, in addition to this, Shingon provided a wealth of symbolism and sacred gesture, and the indestructible diamond of ultimate truth.

A young monk admitted me to the Tōji; he led me through halls and corridors, courtyards and gardens, until we reached a hall where a service was in progress. The place must have been dark at all times, but on that rainy day it was particularly dark. The altars were covered with coloured cloth; gold surfaces gleamed, as did the eyes of Buddhas, bodhisattvas, dharmarajas, protectors of the law, in aspects ranging from

[1] M. ANESAKI, Buddhist Art in its Relation to Buddhist Ideals, London, 1916.

that of serene enlightenment to that of ferocious combat with the forces of ignorance and evil.

In the deep silence I was offered a *zabuton,* cushion, in a corner behind a wooden pillar where total darkness prevailed. I became aware that other people were near me, most of them elderly women, I thought, though I could not see them. But I could see well enough what was happening in the feebly lit centre of the hall. Monks were reading in chorus from the sacred writings in that fascinating baritone chant of theirs, to the accompaniment of an irregular drum-beat. Occasionally, when there was a pause, you could hear rain dripping from the eaves.

After I do not know how long a patter of bare feet on the mats and a rustle of robes announced the arrival of more monks, important dignitaries among them. The abbot took his place on a lacquered chair; an attendant monk spent what seemed a long time arranging his robes so that the folds fell correctly. It seemed a highly complicated service; monks came and went, burnt incense, made offerings, always accompanied by the chanting of sacred texts, the beating of drums, and the ringing of bells.

At one point a number of persons advanced humbly into the centre of the halls; at first sight they looked like monks, but then I noticed that, though they were in monks' clothing, their heads were not shaven. Then I saw that one of them was Somi. He looked pale, transfigured, extremely serious. I realized that this was the ceremony called *kanjō,* 'supreme purification'. The term is often mistranslated 'baptism'. True, it includes aspersion with water, but the resemblance is superficial. Only a few Buddhist sects (in Japan Shingon, Tendai, Kegon) practise it, and its sole purpose is to mark entry into the most recondite and esoteric mysteries.

When the climax approached, Somi and his four or five companions were blindfolded with pieces of red cloth, and a picture *(mandala)* was laid on the ground in the centre of the hall. *Mandala* are popularly called magic pictures, but are in reality mystical representations of the universe divided and organized into its manifest forms. The chanting of sacred texts faded to a murmur, and each acolyte in turn rose to his feet and dropped on the *mandala* a flower that had previously been handed to him by a monk; the spot where it fell was immediately examined by eight scrutineer-monks, to see what Buddha or bodhisattva it lay nearest to or touched. This established a link between the Buddha or bodhisattva and the acolyte, who henceforth took his name.

Somi was the last to go through this ceremony. He was preceded by a big man, who looked more like a grocer than a mystic and committed any number of *faux pas*, treading where he should not have trodden and accidentally propelling a monk among the spectators. His crowning feat was to drop his flower outside the universe altogether, with the result that one of the eight scrutineers, unseen by the others, I think, had to move the picture slightly, so that the flower was left touching its edge. After this performance the ease and grace with which Somi played his part seemed marvellous. His flower, a gardenia of the kind which bloom in the rainy month in Japan, dropped right on Vairocana, 'the Great Light', whose body is the substance of the universe. Nothing could have been more felicitous, and everyone congratulated him, the only foreigner to take part in the ceremony, who nevertheless brought it to such a highly satisfactory conclusion.

8

Aesthetes and Soldiers

The Exquisite Centuries

FOUR centuries of Japanese history are connected with the name of Heian, from the foundation of the new capital in 794 until the establishment of a new militarist government at Kamakura in 1185. First the city was known as Heian ('Peace and Calmness'), but later simply as Kyoto ('metropolis'). This was a colourful and fascinating period.

Apart from warfare against the Ainu on the distant north-east frontiers towards the beginning, and a less clear but more turbulent period of internal troubles towards the end, it was on the whole an age of peace and tranquillity, of isolation, and hence of assimilation. For various reasons—above all the decadence of the T'ang Empire in China —contacts with that country, which had been so close and fruitful, diminished both in quantity and in importance, and in 894 the regular embassies exchanged between the two countries ceased. Japan was thrown back on her own resources.

A large number of important consequences of this were felt down the centuries, and to an extent are perceptible to the present day. With the Taikwa reform of 645 the Japanese, as they were again to do twelve centuries later, adopted wholesale a grandiose system of government of foreign origin. A centralized bureaucracy took the place of primitive feudalism, codes and laws took the place of custom and precedent, a permanent imperial militia replaced the feudal rallies, provincial governors took the place of feudal lords, roads were built, private property was recognized, censuses were taken to provide a basis for

238

taxation; in short, the foundation was laid for a system of government such as the west had known under the Roman Empire. But the Japanese never understood the Chinese political philosophy behind this system, according to which the Emperor enjoyed the support of the people so long as he was considered worthy of the celestial mandate, while the bureaucracy was recruited, by means of an exceedingly stiff examination system, from the whole nation. China, a country of rationalists and philosophers, has always had profoundly democratic propensities. Its true aristocracy was for thousands of years the society of educated men (*ju,* men of letters); while Japan, a country of artists, men of feeling rather than of intellect, always instinctively tended to yield to the claims of the hierarchical pyramid, the aristocratic order.

As for the imperial line, its destiny was marked out from the beginning. Its members, in the general estimation, were *kami,* men and women qualitatively distinct from the general run of mortals. 'Those who dwell at court are called Dwellers above the Clouds' (*The Tale of Genji*). Only once in the course of centuries was the principle endangered —the incident of the monk Dōkyo will be recalled—and the Empress involved ended by rising to the occasion. There was also the case of the Emperor Yōzei, who went mad and took to killing his courtiers for his entertainment, but he was deposed and a successor installed. The nameless dynasty continued to reign uninterruptedly through all vicissitudes. Succession was not necessarily from father to son; there were frequent complicated leaps between collateral branches, and events are made still harder to follow by the typically Japanese principle of abdication, a reigning emperor's withdrawal to the religious life. In the year 988, for instance, the Emperor Ichijo occupied the throne (or rather was in possession of the three sacred symbols, the mirror, the sword, and the jewel), but there were simultaneously living in retirement—and not without exercising a powerful influence in certain court circles—his cousin and immediate predecessor Kazan, who reigned from 985 to 986; his father Enyu, who reigned from 970 to 984, and his uncle Reizei, who reigned from 968 to 969. Many of these sovereigns lived their hour of glory as children; Ichijo, for instance, in the year 988, was not yet ten. It is easy to imagine the intrigue that must have prevailed at court behind the backs and generally at the expense of the nominal ruler.

Only the first emperors of the Heian period exercised any measure of personal power. After the abdication of Junna in 833 the *de facto* rulers of Japan were the Fujiwara family (the name means 'Wistaria Field'). So great was the influence and power that they accumulated that historians call the second half of the Heian age the Fujiwara period. The Fujiwara avoided violence, were consummate masters of intrigue, and consolidated their power both by the internal cohesion of the clan and by their system of marrying into the imperial family. During this period the reigning emperor's father-in-law was nearly always a Fujiwara, and thus in the course of time there were more and more Fujiwara relatives of the imperial line. Needless to say, the family supplied all the principal officers of state, the Minister of the Right, the Minister of the Left, and the Regent during a boy-emperor's childhood (*sesshō*), who later developed into Regent during his maturity (*kampaku*). In other words, there slowly grew up a typical example of the oblique system of government familiar in Asian history, in which power is delegated to an omnipotent, hereditary figure. It was this monopolization of power which differentiated Japan from China. The Middle Ages in Europe were distinguished from classical times by the predominance of the Teutonic family and dynastic principle over the elective principle of the Roman *imperium*, and Japanese history is distinguished from Chinese by the predominance of the same principle. The Fujiwara were of course the most conspicuous example, but there were many other similar minor galaxies all the way down to the petty provincial lords. At all levels the lamentable principle prevailed that a man's status was irrevocably fixed at birth; and to the present day Japanese life is governed by the subtle ubiquity of the concept of *mibun* (personal position); a person's *mibun*, which depends on his sex, age, birth, education, rank, and occupation, governs his behaviour at all stages. This means that the same conduct can be praiseworthy, indifferent, or actually reprehensible, depending on a person's *mibun*. The merchant's duty is to enrich himself, but a samurai who concerns himself with money is unworthy of the name; a second son is permitted amorous adventures; indeed, they earn him applause and respect; his elder brother, however, is expected to behave irreproachably; and so on and so forth.

Let us return to the Heian period. The predominance of hereditary privilege over merit not only led to a distortion of the political institutions so hopefully imported from China, but soon rendered inoperative the Taikwa economic reforms. The possession of land, originally communal and tribal, had been theoretically arrogated to the Emperor, who had then distributed it according to a national land register. In the atmosphere of privilege, which no one thought of abolishing, the first tax exemptions on landed property were soon made, and these were extended in a constant and alarming manner. Many of these privileged holdings (shōen) belonged to the big temples or to Buddhist orders, many were obtained for services rendered, but many were simply the result of intrigue and business acumen. Thus the first fiefs were established, and the agricultural population had to support on their shoulders an ever-growing number of leisured masters.

With the decay of the land tenure system as envisaged by the reform, the tax system decayed too, and a collapse took place of all the institutions from which a great state extraordinarily modern in character might have emerged. Other organs of state were created as necessity arose, but in haphazard fashion, and the result was deplorable confusion where previously order and clarity had prevailed. Thus the ordinary archivists' office (kurando-dokoro) ended by actually acquiring legislative powers as a result of its direct contact with the central administration; and the same happened with the police commission (kebiishi-cho) and other obscure organs called into existence to fill a gap. In the field of justice summary rules and precedents once more took the place of codes and a juridical doctrine.

No attempt was made to find serious remedies. Sansom has an excellent passage on the 'government by exhortation' that prevailed; rivers of decrees poured forth in the purest literary Chinese, and nobody troubled whether they were carried out or not; a wit coined the phrase chōrei bokai ('decreeing in the morning and amending in the afternoon'); in other words, 'never obey an order, always wait for the counter-order'. Decrees laid down in the most minute detail what was correct in matters of ceremonial, clothing, etiquette, emblems of rank, and such things. According to a decree of 810, ministers of state of the second class were allowed to wear light but not ordinary purple; princes and officials of high rank were allowed to wear ordinary but not light purple. The official records of the time note such things as that 'the Emperor gave a winding water banquet and caused scholars to compose verses', or 'a great wind broke down two trees in the Southern Park. They turned

into pheasants', or 'red sparrows collected on the roof of a palace building and did not leave for ten days'.

Similar situations have occurred in innumerable civilizations; at
the centre an elegant, exquisite aristocracy staving off dull care with
entertainments, pleasures, ceremonies, music, while all round them
an old order slowly declines and decays and in the provinces crude,
strong, new men lay the foundations for a new order. If that had been
the whole of the story, it would scarcely be worth speaking of it at
length. But the Heian period was distinguished from others, was indeed
rendered almost unique, by the fact that the small, privileged court
circle was motivated less by the vulgar myth of pleasure than by art;
indeed, vulgarity is the one thing of which the Heian period cannot be
accused; if anything, it erred in the opposite direction. It was a period
of rarefied search for perfection, both in poetry and in doctrine, of
storms, not in tea-cups, because tea was not yet known, but in small
cups of *saké*. Everything was turned into aesthetics; even Buddhism, the
paradises of which seemed more like the alcoves of repentant princesses
than the empyreans of enlightened philosophers.

With the eleventh century the two trends of the period increasingly
diverged. On the one hand the nobles crossed the shadowy line of
demarcation that had separated them from effeminacy; and the court,
impoverished and impotent, became the retreat of gilded dilettantes
devoted to the game of versification in learned languages, the art of
calligraphy, and the technique of ceremonial and precedence. On the
other hand, in the general disorder outside certain nuclei began to
form which started by being independent of and ended by being
opposed to the constituted authority. For many years now it had been
taken for granted, whenever the imperial guard noisily demanded its
arrears of pay or riotous monks occupied the palace to secure further
tax exemptions—to quote two typical examples—that recourse should
be had for aid to the heads of the great military families, such as the
Taira and the Minamoto, which were junior branches of the imperial
line. The strength, and the rivalry, of these families grew, and finally
they engaged in a death struggle, taking no notice of the impotent
government, and they ended by plunging the whole country into civil
war. At first success went to the Taira, but the tide turned, and after
a generation the Minamoto were victorious. The epic events of this

period correspond to the deeds of Charlemagne and his paladins in the west. They mean to the Japanese what the Trojan War meant to classical Greece, or what the struggle among the Bharatas meant to India.

'The important provincial families had to be armed for the protection of their lands. This led to the creation of local armies, and finally the samurai system.'[1] The age of feudalism had begun. Minamoto Yoritomo, the final victor in the struggle, established his tents at Kamakura, far from the intrigues of the court. His government was called *bakufu* ('camp administration'), a name retained by the *de facto* government until 1868. The star of Heian, with its aestheticism and the poetical melancholy of its princesses, had set for ever.

The Heian period was marked by a long, slow recovery in every field of the native, Yamato, spirit as against the elements imported from China and India in the luminous centuries of Asuka and Nara. Warriors ended by prevailing over courtiers or bureaucrats, and the sword took the place of the brush. The Japanese always prefer a man to an abstract principle, and under the new order society came to consist of a rigid pattern of personal loyalties, from warrior to vassal, from vassal to lord, from lord to shogun, the supreme commander. There could be no conflict between loyalty to your superior and loyalty to your principles, because the two were identical. Your superior's word made and unmade good and evil.

In religion a somewhat similar development took place. The aristocratic and ritualistic schools of Nara were followed by the two great metaphysical schools of Tendai and Shingon. Now, with the eleventh century, two new schools of thought made their appearance, that of Amida and that of Zen. The latter became an effective spiritual force only with the passage of time; the cult of Amida spread immediately and, with the numerous sub-sects and sub-divisions that developed out of it, still has the largest number of adherents in the country. It must therefore be in peculiar harmony with the Japanese attitude to life.

What was the reason for this? In the cult of Buddha Amida ('Unlimited Light')—perhaps an ancient Persian sun-god adopted by Buddhism in its peregrinations through Asia—Buddhism has undergone a profound transformation. In contrast to its predecessors, its metaphysics are simple and remain in the background; the whole emphasis is on faith

[1] T. TSUCHIYA, *An Economic History of Japan*, Tokyo, 1937, p. 60.

and love. There is no more mention of empyreans, manifestations, adamantine heavens, womb-heavens, illusory heavens; all the emphasis is on Amida's charity towards his children and on loving-kindness among all living things. Ceremonies, rites, services, are reduced to a minimum. Salvation resides in Amida; to be reborn in *jodo,* the Pure Earth paradise, it is sufficient sincerely to call on his name.

Thus a genuine theism addressed to the person, not to the concept, of Amida took the place of a philosophical monism; nirvana was transformed into a paradise; and dissolution of personal identity into the all yielded to the survival of the self in the vast warmth of a paternal solicitude. It is a religion of warmth and tenderness, of self-abandonment to the divine kindness. Hōnen (1133–1212), one of the patriarchs of the Amida cult, says: 'A heavy stone put in a ship crosses the ocean without sinking; similarly we, in spite of our sins as heavy as stones, if we are carried in the ship of prayers to Amida, can complete the voyage of eternal beatitude without sinking in the sea of births and deaths.'[1] The metaphysical profundities of Tendai and Shingon were for the edification of the elect; in the cult of Amida the Japanese found something nearer their ancient Shinto traditions, their traditional, kind, and solicitous gods, living in flowers, trees, or the waves of the sea by moonlight.

The same process by which originally foreign motifs are assimilated and then given a new, native colouring is to be observed in art. Practically throughout the Heian period, but particularly during the Fujiwara phase, there is a progressive transition in sculpture and painting from the severe purity inspired by Tendai, from the tormented passion inspired by Shingon, to elegance, sometimes to splendour, but above all to gentleness and grace. The trend was encouraged both by the new Amida doctrines, which humanized religion, made it lovable, affectionate, sometimes even cosy, and by the tastes of the court and the nobility. It was, generally speaking, a time of small, precious, delicate things: little boxes and cupboards, statues, which it is easy to imagine exercising the admiration of delicate princesses with names like Oborozuki ('Veiled Moon'), or Akikonomu '(Beloved Autumn'), of screens made for the concealment of nocturnal intrigues, of fans, of sacred writings, illuminated or covered in rare bindings and decorated with

[1] R. GROUSSET, *Les Civilisations de l'Orient,* Paris, 1930, Vol. IV ('*Le Japon*'), p. 102.

gold and jewels, paintings that illustrated paradises or court scenes which, were it not for iconographical conventions, might easily be interchangeable (Photograph 84).

Little of this period survives. Its single important monument is the Byōdō-in, the Temple of Identity, that is to say of Immutability, of the Absolute, between Kyoto and Nara. It was built as a villa in about the year 1000, when the Fujiwara period reached its climax in the person of the Regent Michinaga, father-in-law of three emperors and grandfather of four. Fortunately the Byōdō-in does not reflect the character of its

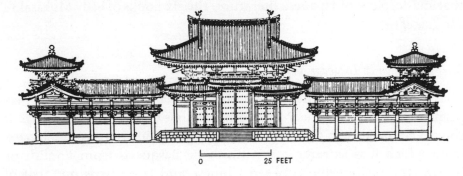

View of the Byōdō-in, near Kyoto, a wonderful example, in a perfect state of preservation, of the architecture of the Fujiwara period (eleventh century)

(From OTA, TANABE, HATTORI, *Nippon no Kenchiku*, 'Japanese Architecture', Tokyo, 1953)

powerful, extravagant, magnificent founder so much as the aesthetic ideals of his time. It is an enchanting retreat, all porches and viewpoints, resting among gardens and lakes like a phoenix that has just gently alighted; its reflection in the water is like a vision of the Amida paradise. Michinaga's son Yorimichi (932–1074) transformed the villa into a temple, and added a chapel for which the sculptor Jōchō made a big statue of Amida the Merciful (*see* Photograph 83). After governing for forty years, Yorimichi retired here to live the life of a monk.

As for literature, a language capable of expressing thought and feeling with a wealth of elegance and allusive power was evolved out of the complicated mixture (using the word in its chemical sense) of the Yamato and Chinese tongues. In prose Chinese predominated, and might perhaps have crushed the native genius, for the conventions of the age required men to write Chinese, rather as they were required to write Latin in the age of humanism. Salvation, however, came from the poets—and from women. It was above all the latter, of whom too much learning was not required, who were free to express themselves in the vulgar tongue, and did so with marvellous skill and intelligence. Among the works of the period two stand out in particular: the first is *The Pillow-Book* of Sei Shonagon, that is to say the malicious and profound, amusing and astringent, frivolous and passionate observations of a court lady, whose follies, according to ancient traditions, reduced her to ending her days as a beggar, picking up rags and bones. The second is that masterpiece of Japanese literature, the six books of Lady Murasaki's *The Tale of Genji*.

Brief Digression on Language and Ideograms

I have several times mentioned the Japanese language; the reader may perhaps be curious to hear a little more about it. In the first place, it should be made clear that basically it is entirely different from Chinese, from which it is as remote as Finnish or Basque is from English or Italian; the relationship between Chinese and Japanese is not that of cousins or brothers, as between Latin and German or Spanish and French, but that of complete strangers. The position of Japanese in the linguistic picture of Asia is an unsettled question; in general it can be said that its grammar and syntax seem to associate it with the Ural-Altai group (Manchu, Mongolian, Turkish, Samoyed, Finnish, Hungarian, and, some say, Korean), while its vocabulary includes elements that encourage one to look southward. To form an idea of the language as a whole reference should be made to the chapter contributed by Serge Elisséev to Meillet's monumental *Les Langues du Monde* which, however, dates back to 1924.

From the point of view of pronunciation Japanese is simple. The vowel sounds are generally open, as in Italian, and some of the consonants are lacking. 'R' and 'l' are not distinguished, though a sound similar to 'r' prevails. What happens in regard to the latter is the exact opposite of what happens in Chinese. A Chinese pronounces 'Lorelei' *Lolelei*; a Japanese pronounces it *Rorerei*. A characteristic feature of Japanese is the lack of accent; in reading Japanese equal stress is laid on each syllable unless there is a specific indication to the contrary.

As for grammar and syntax, applying the patterns characteristic of the Indo-European family to a language that developed in a totally different environment is like trying to fit a square peg in a round hole. Japanese philologists accordingly classify the parts of speech in a manner very different from that familiar to us. Miyazaki,[1] for instance, distinguishes four basic parts of speech: substantives, conjugatives (and this is where the interesting part begins, for reasons which we shall see in a moment), modifiers (*i.e.*, attributive adjectives and adverbs), and particles (prepositions, postpositions, and conjunctions). The conjugatives are of interest because they include not only verbs, but certain adjectives as well. In Japanese you can very neatly and conveniently say 'yesterday colded' (*kinō samukatta*) for 'yesterday it was cold' or 'if tomorrow hots' (*ashita atsukereba*) instead of 'if it is hot tomorrow'; in other words, adjectives are conjugated. This is one of many examples which show that we are confronted with an entirely different kind of organism.

Moreover, the very conception 'word' has a different connotation with the Japanese. A Japanese text proceeds continuously, itisasifwe wrotelikethiswithoutanybreaksorinterruptions. One of the most striking difficulties which confront a Japanese who tries to write his own language in Latin characters is that of dividing it up into words. Probably we too, if we lacked the aid of philological custom and tradition, would have the same difficulty. For instance, if we look at the phrase we strung together just now, is 'interruptions' one word, or two, or three? The nucleus *rupt* ('break') is accompanied by a prefix and by a suffix which are variously employed in innumerable other cases, and we could, if we wished, regard them as separate, independent elements. In a system of writing such as that used by Japanese, the basic thought, the word in the etymological sense, is represented by the ideogram (or logogram, as some prefer to call it), and everything else is termination, flexion, etc., etc., and belongs to the category of modifiers.

Bearing this in mind, then, and remembering that our own terminology is only very approximately applicable, let me mention some interesting features of this language. At the outset it appears extremely easy; there is no article, gender, or number. Relations between words are indicated simply by particles, generally suffixes. You do not say 'in

[1] S. MIYAZAKI, *The Japanese Dictionary Explained in English*, Tokyo, 1953.

the garden', but 'garden in' *(niwa ni)*; instead of 'to my son' you say 'I-son-of-to' *(watashi no musuko ni)*.

The verbs too seem easy at the outset, as they lack both person and number. But their almost inexhaustible wealth of forms soon imposes a severe lesson in modesty. In Japanese tenses have little importance. More important than past, present, or future is whether the action in question is certain or doubtful, has definitely ended or has only probably ended. *Mairimasu,* for instance, means 'I shall certainly go', either today, tomorrow, or when the context requires; *mairimashō* means 'perhaps I shall go', whether today or tomorrow or the next day, though it is generally used as the translation of our future. *Mairimashita* means 'I went'; the act has been completed, and is therefore past. Japanese tends much more to represent a human situation than to refer to the co-ordinates of the four-dimensional space-time continuum; it is less important to define when the act of going took place, or is to take place, than to translate it into subjective, emotional terms. Hence Japanese verbs, poor in tenses, are rich in moods; potential, optative, prohibitive, and frequentative; and they all have both active and passive, affirmative and negative, conjugations. This sometimes results in tongue-twisters, such as *koshiraesasetakunai* ('I should not wish to have built'), or *irassharanakattarō* ('he honourably probably did not come').

As for the honorifics, these are characteristic of many oriental languages. Something of the kind exists in Europe too; the French distinguish between *tu* and *vous,* the Germans between *Du* and *Sie,* the Italians between *tu, voi,* and *lei.* It is a matter of changing the tone of the conversation, registering a change of key. In Japanese the relationship between the speakers permeates the whole conversation in a far deeper and more subtle way, which it is exceedingly difficult to analyse. In the case of certain basic ideas entirely different words are used, depending on whether you are addressing a superior, an equal, or an inferior. For instance, 'to go (humbly)' is *mairu,* 'to go (as an equal)' is *iku,* 'to go (respectfully)' is *irassharu.* This explains the lack of persons in the verb. The humble *mairu* can refer only to the first person, myself or ourselves, *iku* to a person or persons with whom you are on terms of equality or familiarity, *irassharu* to a person or persons to whom you wish to indicate deference. It is interesting to note that the principal verbs which have these special honorific forms, these ceremonial conjugations, refer

almost exclusively to states or actions of great human and social significance, involving persons and contacts between them—to go, drink,
give, ask, be, do, look, meet, eat, show, receive, know, come, visit.
Nouns and other parts of speech are also modified according to honorific requirements, generally by means of the prepositions *o, go, mi*.
O-uchi ('honourable house'), for instance, is always 'your house'; *uchi*,
just 'house', is my own wretched and unworthy dwelling.

Japanese is, in short, an exquisitely subjective language, in which
the outside, objective world remains a vague and shadowy background
for dramas, comedies, human vicissitudes, in all their infinite variety.
It does not tend to clarity, to accurate definition of when and where and
exactly how many people and of what sex are doing this, that, or the
other. Instead, it prefers to suggest, leaving the details vague, surrounding
the subject with approximations rather than revealing or disclosing it.
Hence the great wealth of elliptical forms *(areba yō gozaimasu ga . . .* 'it
would be beautiful if it were so, but . . .'), double negatives *(naku wa nai*
. . . 'it is not that it is not so . . .'), the extraordinary wealth of personal
pronouns (for the first person singular alone there are at least half a
dozen), the use of periphrasis *(kochira sama,* 'the gentleman here'; *Mikado*,
'honourable gate'), etc., etc. What matters above all are the relations
between *mibun* (personal position) and the infinite shades of *kimochi*
(states of mind). In this domain Japanese attains incredible and utterly
untranslatable heights of subtlety of nuance. Hence it is a magnificent
language for love, as it is for the ceremonies of social life; a language
made for poetry and allusion, as well as for invective, panegyric, solemn
discourse, for expressing feelings, and for underlining individual or
social circumstances. Where it fails is as an instrument of abstract
thought; when it comes to the world of ideas and their logical exposition all the defects of its qualities are brought harshly to light. Its allusive
vagueness, so valuable in literature of the imagination, makes it incapable of constructing sentences of unequivocal meaning; the habit of
oblique speech often introduces an element of personal interpretation
which, if it is helpful to art, is certainly detrimental to scientific or
philosophical discussion.

Typical of this state of affairs is the lack of the relative pronoun or
any substitute for it. Until I set about learning Japanese, I had never
stopped to consider how useful are those little words 'who' and 'which'.

To get round the lack of them in Japanese you have in the simplest instances to construct what are in reality enormous substantives. 'The pine that stands on the top of the hill' becomes 'hill-of top-on stand pine-the' (*oka-no chojo-ni aru matsu-wa*). In more complicated cases you have to go through the most formidable manœuvres, helping yourself out with gerunds.

Finally, a characteristic of Japanese that always strikes foreigners is that things are rarely counted in the abstract; different suffixes for different categories (there are about fifty of them) are added to numbers and modify their pronunciation. The system is rather like our 'three pairs of shoes' or 'six head of cattle', but far more complicated. One vehicle, for instance, is *ichidai*, one boat *isso*, one animal *ippiki*, one book *issatsu*, one bird *ichiwa*; one long cylindrical object is *ippon*, one flat, broad object *ichimai*, etc., etc.; that is to say, the classifier *-dai* (vehicles), *-so* (boats), *-hiki* (animals), etc., is added to the root *ichi* (one), with varying modifications resulting from the fusion of consonants and vowels. All this at first seems exceedingly difficult and complicated, but it is much less formidable than the intricacies and subtleties of honorifics. In any case, the foreigner can always use the single series *hitotsu, futatsu, mitsu* (one, two, three) without the classifiers; he will be understood, and probably forgiven.

Another characteristic is that the answer to a negative question is in the affirmative where we should use the negative. If, for instance, your host says to you: 'Wouldn't you like some more?' the answer, assuming that you do not wish for any more, is *hai* ('yes'); in other words you reply in the affirmative to the affirmation contained in the question, *i.e.*, 'yes, I should not like any more'. A polite Japanese always puts his questions in such a manner that the answer can be in the affirmative; nothing is considered ruder than an openly negative reply. In Japan harmony always takes precedence over logic.

I have mentioned that Japanese is entirely different from Chinese. This applies only to the primary Yamato nucleus. In this connection it can be said with Sansom[1] that Chinese and Japanese are two organisms with basically opposite characteristics. Japanese is polysyllabic and diffuse; Chinese is monosyllabic and concise. In Japanese the relations between words are indicated by particles, in Chinese by their position

[1] G. B. SANSOM, *Historical Grammar of Japanese*, Oxford, 1928, p. 62.

in the sentence; Japanese has few homonyms (words of same form but different sense), while Chinese has myriads; the Japanese word order is the opposite of the Chinese, etc., etc. The language of poetry is still full of Yamato words, and Yamato words prevail in the language of women. Typical Yamato words, polysyllabic and with open vowels, are *yama* (mountain), *samurai* (warrior), *kokoro* (heart), *otonashii* (good, quiet), *ikusa* (battle), *miyabiyaka-na* (ancient and charming), *imamekashi* (fashionable, up to date).

But at an early stage the Japanese came into contact with the Chinese, who spoke a highly evolved language, into the texture of which centuries of thought and experience were already woven. This language was and is still written by a complicated system which is not alphabetic, but has a sign for every idea. Ideographic writing is certainly clumsy and unmanageable, but being tied to the content rather than to the sound of words has its advantages. To quote an example, 312 is to a Frenchman *trois cent douze,* to a German *dreihundertzwölf,* to an Englishman 'three hundred and twelve'. Chinese ideograms, like Arabic numerals, could be adapted to any language. English or Italian could perfectly well be written in ideograms if we were willing to make the by no means inconsiderable effort.

The Japanese, called on to read any particular sign—for example the broken line standing for a bow (*see* page 253)—had two alternatives: they could use the Chinese word (which in this case they pronounced *kyū*), or they could use their own word for bow, *yumi*. If Japanese had been an evolved language at the time when ideograms were introduced, there would have been no hesitation about following the second course, and no difficulty would have arisen. But, in view of the huge cultural prestige of China at that time (fifth–seventh centuries) and the enormous wealth of terms that still had to be invented in the land of the Yamato, not only ideograms were imported, but words as well. Thus the native Yamato, enriched by Chinese, yielded the composite language which is Japanese, just as Anglo-Saxon, enriched by Latin, resulted in English. Hence its vast vocabulary and its terrifying complexity. It can be said without fear of contradiction that for the last fifteen centuries the history of the Japanese language has been a long and painful process of compromises.

Every ideogram can be read in at least two different ways. The first, called *on*, more or less resembles the Chinese original (*i.e.*, in the case of the bow, *kyū*). The second, called *kun*, is the Yamato way (*i.e.*, in the case of the bow, *yumi*). Often there are several *on* and several *kun*; sometimes there are more than a dozen possible readings. Let me quote an example from the names of three Italian towns. Civitavecchia, Viterbo, and Orvieto (*civitas vetula, vetus urbs,* and *urbs vetus*) express the same idea in different sounds. If Italian were written in ideograms the same signs (for 'old' and 'city') would be used in each case, but they would be read differently. In Japanese this is continually happening; you are confronted at every step by the Civitavecchia-Viterbo-Orvieto problem; it is one of the most infernal of the difficulties presented by this infernal language. In practice you have to know the individual answer in each case, as you do with the pronunciation of English, *e.g.*, with such words as comb, tomb, bomb, or shoe, poem, toe; or though, through, plough, cough, enough. Imagine an infinitely vaster labyrinth of this kind and you have written Japanese.

As a rule the Yamato reading is used in poetical, traditional, familiar, or unpedantic contexts; for more solemn, formal purposes the Chinese reading is used. English behaves in somewhat similar fashion in regard to Latin or Greek roots; *e.g.*, amnesia for loss of memory, encephalitis lethargica for sleeping sickness. Modern Japanese is full of originally Chinese forms corresponding to our demo-, hydro-, litho-, neo-, psycho-, necro-, proto-, archaeo-,[1] etc., etc., and these are freely used to provide the new terminology constantly required by modern science and technology. It has several times been remarked that the impact of modern industry and techniques of the west has resulted in Japanese being more thoroughly impregnated with Chinese than it was when Japan depended for her intellectual sustenance on China alone.

Another difficulty that confronted the Japanese in adopting Chinese ideograms arose from the fact that, while Chinese is monosyllabic, Japanese is rich in inflections. As early as the seventh century (the idea is traditionally attributed to Kōbō Daishi), ways were found of indicating the latter, secondary parts of the language by true and real alphabets: the two *kana*, the capital *(katakana)* and the lower case or cursive *(hiragana)*. Nowadays a page of Japanese confronts us with a complex of *(a)* ideograms (some read as Chinese, others as Japanese, depending on the most

[1] These are in order: *min, sui, gan, shin, shin, shi, shi, ko.*

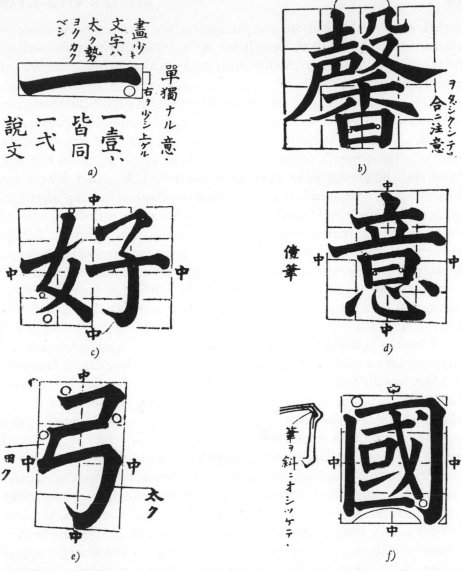

Ideograms as abstract art. Some of the many formal patterns in the architecture of the language of signs:

(a) The simplest stroke: *ichi*, one.
(b) An ideogram of notable complexity: *KEI, kobashii*, fragrant.
(c) Harmony of apparently irregular movements: *KO, su(ku)* to love.
(d) A light, elegant, precise ideogram that borders on the symmetrical: *I, kokoro*, mind, idea, will.
(e) A nervous, dynamic, unsymmetrical ideogram: *KYU, yumi*, bow.
(f) An unsymmetrical but extraordinary strong and decisive ideogram: *KOKU, kuni*, country, province, state.

(From R. MURATA, *Sho-hō Sei-kai*, 'Correct Interpretation of Calligraphy', Tokyo, 1909)

varied rules and traditions), representing the fundamental subject-matter; and (b) alphabetic or syllabic signs, indicating particles, inflections, recently imported neologisms, and various other elements of minor importance.

The result of the long symbiosis between two such fundamentally different languages is that there is not one Japanese language, but several, all differing substantially from one another. The two extremes are the almost pure Chinese of some official documents on the one hand and the almost pure Yamato of poetry on the other. There are innumerable varieties in between. There is the classical literary language, there are the male and female epistolary styles, there is the language of the newspapers, that of ordinary conversation, that of men, that of women, etc., etc. The list is endless. Efforts are now being made as far as possible to devise a single, unified language which would be universally acceptable, but it is sufficient to scratch the surface of Japanese life to realize that for a long time to come that can be no more than a beautiful dream.

Thus the Japanese language, viewed as a whole, is an instrument of extraordinary wealth, but of the most infernal complexity. A Japanese child spends the first six years at school learning to read and write more than a thousand basic signs. It is true that learning an ideogram means learning an idea at the same time, and that the process is therefore not so time-wasting as it might seem. Nevertheless the strain on eyes and memory is great. Anyone brought up in a civilization in which ideas are communicated phonetically naturally asks: Why not change the system? This has been suggested many times, both by individuals and important groups, but nothing has ever come of it. It should not be overlooked that for a very long time (nearly 2,000 years in the case of the Indian syllabic alphabets, and five centuries in the case of the European languages) the Far East has been in contact with much simpler systems, but has failed to be influenced by them; there must be important reasons to explain the vigorous survival of the ideographic system. The tendency today is to reduce and simplify the signs rather than to do away with them. Moreover, in this important respect China and Japan are tied to each other. The intention of adopting an alphabet has been announced in China, and if she succeeded Japan would ultimately have to follow suit.

It would certainly be a step of extreme gravity. According to Sansom it would involve 'a complete revolution in the style and content of the written language, since the latter has ended by assuming its present form under the influence of ideographic transcription'. The Japanese, confronted with a page of their language transcribed into the Latin alphabet, say *pinto-ga awanai* ('it is out of focus'). The fact is that ideographic writing—leaving aside the immense labour involved in learning it—presents things, ideas, feelings, to the eye, to the mind, to the emotions, with an immediacy and a vividness with which an ordinary phonetic system cannot compete, particularly in the case of a language in which homonyms are numerous. Moreover, abolition of the traditional system would involve a long, painful period of transition, apart from the fact that the country's whole literary heritage would at a stroke become 'foreign', accessible only to a few specialists, a source from which it would be necessary to 'translate'.

Finally—and perhaps this is the fundamental reason for the perennial vitality of the ideographic system—the place that it occupies in Far Eastern civilization is only to a most superficial extent analogous to that occupied by the alphabet in our own or other 'phonetic' civilizations, for example those of India or Islam. In our written language we are principally concerned with meaning and pronunciation. The quintessence of language is poetry, which approaches song, music; western poetry is composed essentially to be recited. But a language written ideographically is concerned with three things: meaning, sound, and appearance. When it ascends to poetry it tends to become rather the sister of painting or of architecture, the latter being understood as the art of spatial relations. Chinese poetry is written essentially to be seen; it penetrates to the mind by way of the eyes.

Thus in the Far East calligraphy is the mother of the arts. Writer and artist use the same instrument, the brush; and the same aesthetic principles govern the activities of both. Far Eastern civilization could be well represented as a spiral on which nature, gardening, calligraphy, painting, style of life, architecture, formed, as it were, so many stops. Photographs 105 (ideograms in the grass style), 106 (a tree), 107 (pine-tree on a wild coast), 108 (pine-tree in a famous garden), and the illustration on page 188 (architecture), touch some points on this imaginary projection. When a civilization has reached a high degree of perfection, every part implies the whole; here every artist, from gardener to calligrapher, from painter to architect, vibrates in harmony, as if all handled tools designed to capture the same series of invisible harmonics. The classical, Gothic, Baroque worlds, to quote a few well-known examples, approached this ideal, which is always implicit in every civilization, but becomes explicit only in those which have had time and opportunity to reach maturity.

I shall not linger to discuss the origin of ideograms, or to describe how in many cases their present shape resulted from the transformation into abstract form of the original, primitive picture as a result of constant usage and the consequent trend to simplification. I shall mention only that there are at least three different styles in which they can be written: the lapidary, solemn style called *kai-sho,* which is square and regular (*see* page 253); the intermediary, cursive style called *gyo-sho*; and the sinuous, personal, rapid, light style called *so-sho* (Photograph 105); to say nothing of the two 'seal' styles, the great and the small.

Ideograms, with their ancient history, are marvellous examples of abstract beauty, organisms of lines, of spaces filled and unfilled, of visible and invisible relations the sum-total of whose equilibrium is the result of the work of generations of artists. Every stroke of the brush has attained a perfect aesthetic functionalism within the whole. From this merely static point of view, its beauty is that of bones. A bone is function which has assumed form, form which has been turned into matter, limestone modelled by the ages.

But it would be the worst of errors to regard ideograms as static, as living mechanisms which have died on paper. The Chinese and Japanese masters never cease insisting that the fully successful ideogram must vibrate with life, must 'be an adventure of movement'.[1] The first point to note is that every ideogram occupies, animates, an imaginary quadrilateral. The strokes are rarely symmetrical; in asymmetry, which is essentially dynamic, there is already a germ of life. Most important of all, it should be noted that in writing an ideogram, a sentence, a whole page, no correction, no change of mind, no second thoughts, are in any circumstances permitted; the brush must never go back over its work. This is not an arbitrarily imposed, external rule; the simple reason for it is that the writing is conceived dynamically, as representing the continuous trace of a dance; a dance of hand, arm, and fingers; a symbolic,

[1] CHIANG YEE, *Chinese Calligraphy,* Harvard, 1936, p. 126.

miniature dance which fully engages both body and mind, involving participating in a vital flow in which there can be no stopping.

Finally, this dance, with its qualities of elegance, strength, and sensitivity, is not only addressed to the emotions; it is also a precise language addressed to the mind. The ideogram is the only abstract art in which form and content complete each other; every ideogram has a well-defined meaning, a history. In comparison with this, its Asian grown-up sister, abstract art as known and practised in the west stands condemned to the inferiority of the vague and merely pleasing.

The relations between shape and meaning rarely depends on pictorial realism; instead the meaning emerges as a secret subtly conveyed by line and rhythm. If the reader glances at the ideogram for Man (page 106), he will note the strength and virility with which the bold, strong oblong and the two agile and decisive strokes of the brush underneath it lie on the page. The sense of Man is conveyed without any recourse to external resemblance, for etymologically the ideogram consists of a field (the square) combined with strength (the divergent lines). The same can be said of the ideogram that means 'country, province, state' (page 253), a citadel of lines, a harmony of centripetal and asymmetrical relations; or of the pattern that stands for a bow—tension of muscles ready to be released.

Years of work and effort are required before true freedom can be attained in this art, before it becomes an intimate and personal means of expression. The results, however, are to be included among the great aesthetic attainments of mankind. I believe it possible to argue that the failure of Asia to develop an art of music comparable to that of the west was due to the fact that in the east the need for abstract beauty found full satisfaction in writing; the same satisfaction that Europe discovered in the harmony and orchestration of sound.

Japanese Wife

Professor Nishikata is an art historian and teaches in one of the Kyoto universities; he is also a writer, a critic, and an organizer of art exhibitions, He is aged about sixty, that is, the age at which people either improve like good wine or deteriorate like meat left in the refrigerator. I unhesitatingly put Nishikata in the former category. He looks at things with

Buddhist detachment and serenity, though he participates with elegance and good humour in the vortex of becoming by which he is surrounded. Tonight he invited me to dine with him at one of the little restaurants along the Kamo river. Like all self-respecting Japanese, he reserved a table in advance; the Japanese do not like disappearing into public anonymity; the whole of their lives is conducted on a basis of relationships, personal ties, introductions. In this, incidentally, they are exactly like Sicilians. In a society of fundamentally aristocratic texture, what counts is not so much the man himself as his *mibun,* the place he has occupied in the system since the beginning of time.

Preceded and followed by charming young women solicitous for our wellbeing, we went and squatted on two silk cushions on the *tatami.* The big, low table was lit by a paper lantern of elegant simplicity. The assimilation of elements imported from abroad into Japanese culture (using the word in its broadest, anthropological sense, including everything from religion to slippers, from funeral rites to economic structure) is a slow process, but I have full confidence in Japanese taste. Twenty years ago, for instance, electric light, which had taken the place of the tremulous, poetic flame of the ancient *andon,* shone crudely and violently from a lamp suspended in the centre of the room; in such circumstances no architecture or furnishing could survive and everything was reduced to the level of a railway station waiting-room. But since then a great step forward has been taken; the Japanese have realized that electric light, properly shaded and protected, can be used, not only to produce the charming effects of former times, but an infinity of new and unexpected effects, merely with the aid of two typically Japanese materials, paper and bamboo.

The warm bubble of light that enclosed us at our table, as if suspended over a lake of liquid black lacquer, made it barely possible to see the houses, windows, roofs, on the other bank of the river, or the sharp outline of the Eastern Hills, over which the moon was rising. Autumn in Japan ripens more slowly and serenely than with us; it is associated, not with rain and bad weather, but with clear skies and bright sunshine. Near us, on other little terraces, were other parties of diners, and we could hear their gusts of laughter. Girls (geishas?) sang and played the *samisen.* Some terraces were occupied by silent couples; one of them was evidently a business man, and his companion one of the innumerable members of the Japanese half-world, met by chance one night heaven knows how, in a bar, a *kafué,* an *onsen.*

Why had Nishikata invited me to dinner? True, we had known each other for some time and got on well enough, but that was not a sufficient reason. One's true friends in Japan are few and last a lifetime; they constitute a small and restricted circle, outside which, in my experience, you rarely entertain, except for business reasons or with some other definite purpose in mind. If I represented something it would be different, and the invitation would be easy to explain. In Japan invitations are directed to one's position, rank, office, rather than to oneself. Any connection with a university, an embassy, a church, industry, the press, with any duly constituted and recognized organization, will procure you any amount of invitations, but as an individual . . . What is an individual in Japan? He can almost be said not to exist. If he attempts to do so, he can hardly move a finger without generating a slight aura of suspicion. If he does not appear to be connected with anything, it can only be because he is connected with something clandestine, so he had better be kept at a distance. The individual enjoys no true citizenship in these longitudes.

I soon tumbled to the explanation of Nishikata's invitation; he wanted to talk to me about Giorgio; Giorgio had in fact at one time been one of his students, and this had established between them the mystic relationship of master and pupil which remains sacred for the lifetime of both. Just as the pupil has certain duties towards his master, so has the master certain duties, of a paternal nature, towards his pupil; and Nishikata-sensei, Professor Nishikata, had from the outset conceived a great liking for Giorgio, whose talents and character he admired.

He told me that Giorgio was wasting his brilliant gifts in business, doing work which others could do equally well, that he was greatly worried about this, and that it kept him awake at night. I, as Giorgio's old and close friend, should help him to bring him back to the right track.

At bottom I agreed, but a certain taste for argument and a sense of youthful solidarity with Giorgio made me stick up for him.

The professor wondered whether it was true that Giorgio was as first-class a business man as I maintained. Every time he saw him, he looked more strained and nervous. He was doing well, but not so extraordinarily well as all that. He had his fingers in a hundred pies and was walking a razor's edge. What would happen if things went wrong? With Giorgio's gifts . . .

Snatches of conversation came floating over from the next terrace, where four or five men were dining with as many women. I kept hearing the phrase *tayo-zoku* ('race of the sun'), a name taken from a recent novel which enjoyed a *succès de scandale,* referring to the wild, post-war generation which had grown up without filial piety or a god-emperor. The men must have said some pretty strong things, because the young women laughed nervously, covering their faces with their fan or *tamoto,* the sleeve of their kimono, exclaiming '*Iya da wa*' (I don't like that! How horrid!) It is infuriating when two conversations in which you are equally interested are simultaneously in progress.

The professor went on to say that the trouble with Giorgio had begun with his disastrous marriage. I became ashamed of putting my friend's life on the same level as that of society in general, and shut off the *tayo-zoku* channel to devote myself entirely to what Nishikata-sensei was saying. He said he had known Mineko from childhood, and she had always been spoilt, the most spoilt girl in all Tokyo. Her mother, a woman of aristocratic family, had married, out of caprice, a small industrialist, who worked himself to death to keep her in kimonos and French perfume and enable her to travel and go to the theatre. Mineko had grown up under her mother's guidance, and had learnt with her mother's milk that the sole purpose of men, husbands, fathers, brothers, was to be milked. . . . Oh, yes, in novels, and generally in films too, Japanese women were all submission, sweetness, solicitude, affection. But in real life what claws there were in those tiny hands! What schemes of conquest lay concealed in those little heads that looked like innocent rose-buds!

The professor sipped his *saké* and slipped on his jacket; a damp breeze was bringing cool air down from the mountains. Mineko, he went on, could not have married anyone but a foreigner. If she had married a Japanese, it would have broken down immediately. But we westerners made a cult of women, and Giorgio might have been made to measure for her selfish and elegant tastes. She was certainly elegant in her tastes, and she had gifts sufficient to charm anybody; she was intelligent, witty, beautifully dressed, and showed admirable taste in the things with which she surrounded herself. Giorgio had found in her everything that he found most delightful in Japan. If they had remained lovers, well and good. But marriage? When Giorgio had come to him and told him they were going to get married, he had remained silent. But Giorgio had understood. Certainly he had understood. When he married her he had put himself completely in her power.

The professor clapped his hands, as is the custom in Japan to call the waitress, who brought the bowl of steaming white rice which always ends a meal of any importance.

As had been easy to foresee, the professor continued after a pause, Giorgio was quickly reduced to the position of a slave. If she had a head-ache, who had to look after the house? Giorgio. If she wanted to go to the *kabuki* theatre, who had to accompany her, even if he had had an exhausting day at the office? Giorgio. If she needed this or that, a fur, a holiday in the country, a studio, a jewel, a collection of expensive books, Giorgio had to find the money. That was why he had abandoned his work which, if it had been published, might not have brought him in much money, but would have given him deep and lasting satisfaction, and assured him of a brilliant academic career. He had gone in for busi-ness as a post-war expedient but, once involved in it, it was hard to extricate oneself; it had turned into a chain. Then Mineko had fallen ill. That had been a terrible time for everybody. Giorgio had behaved like an angel. He had been like a man possessed. He had spared nothing in efforts to save her, but it had all been in vain. Perhaps it had been for the best.

Nishikata-sensei paused, slowly and thoughtfully eating his rice. Behind us the gusts of laughter, the shrieks of the geisha, went on. I had lost interest in piecing together other people's conversation. I had never met Mineko. In the eyes of Abe-san, Giorgio's housekeeper and his son's nurse, she had been a saint; for Giorgio, she had been the embodiment of an entrancing civilization, the soul of Japan. Was Nishikata's pitilessly objective picture inconsistent with this? No, at bottom it was not. The shadowy picture of Mineko took on flesh and blood.

I recalled a little episode I had heard about. Some years previously Giorgio had taken Mineko on a short visit to Europe. From every point of view it had turned out a disaster. She had taken a violent dislike to Italy; at Naples, where Giorgio's parents lived, she hardly ever went out of the house; she was disgusted by the dirt, the sentimental exhibitionism, the butcher's shops. She felt as if she had married a Basuto or a Yemeni tribesman, and said so. One day Giorgio's mother invited some friends to the house to meet her exotic daughter-in-law. Wishing it to be a surprise, she merely asked Mineko to wear a kimono at such-and-such a time. When Mineko appeared in the drawing-room in her kimono, with an *obi* (sash) round her waist which she had chosen with the most painstaking care in some shop in the Nishi Ginza, she took one look round her, walked straight out of the room without speaking to anyone, and locked herself in her bedroom, from which she did not emerge till next day. She gave no explanation whatever of her behaviour, and merely sulked; for once even Giorgio, the great orientalist, the subtle psychologist, the acrobat of the twenty-six civilizations, was unable to pour oil on the ruffled waters. Mineko shut up like an oyster; all she wanted was to go back to Japan. '*Napori wa iya*' (Naples doesn't suit me), she repeated with childlike obstinacy.

Years later, in Tokyo, I heard the other side of the story. I was talking to Abe-san, trying to find out what sort of picture she had formed in her mind of Italy through her mistress's eyes, and as a result of daily contact with Giorgio and his friends. The picture was not very flattering. Its three principal features were the dirt (were there really people who bathed only once a week?); the laziness ('she said there were people who actually didn't get up till nine o'clock and then had a *hiru-ne*, a snooze, in the afternoon!'); and finally the selfishness (everyone thought in the first place of himself and no one cared two hoots for his *kuni-no-koto*, his country). Then the kimono story came out. 'When she suddenly found herself in a drawing-room full of people, she felt she was being put on show, like a rare animal in a circus, and she was mortally offended.'

'But, after all, Abe-san, your mistress was a little difficult, don't you think?' I remarked.

'She had the right to be. Don't you know that she was a great poet? Haven't you seen how many books she wrote? Well, then, her feelings deserved to be respected!'

So much for Abe-san and her mistress.

Nishikata-sensei went on to say that he had two important things to put to Giorgio, and he wanted my help in preparing the ground. The first was the offer of an academic post, not very rewarding financially, to be sure, but that would improve with time.

And the second?

The professor drew nearer to me, lowered his voice, then fell silent. A shadow crossed his wrinkled brow; conflicting thoughts obviously flashed through his mind. Perhaps I as a foreigner would not understand.

Yes, the second thing, he at last went on. Well, a close friend of his at Kobe, a man of substance and of very great culture, who had spent many years abroad, had a daughter, aged about twenty-five, who would be just the thing for Giorgio. It was time he married again, dropped all the chimeras he had in his head, and thought about making a career in the field for which he was cut out. . . . There was still time if he acted quickly and liquidated his business affairs. In a year it would be too late.

Nishikata looked at me. I noted with satisfaction that he was reassured by the calm with which I listened to him. In Japan it is natural for anyone in a senior position to concern himself with all aspects of the life of anyone who is or has been entrusted to his care, particularly in the matter of matrimony. Nowadays *ren-ai kekkon* (love matches) are numerous, but *miai kekkon* (arranged marriages) are still perhaps just as numerous. Many of the latter are the work of *nakodo,* professional marriage brokers—readers will recall the *nakodo* in *Madame Butterfly*—but many others are the work of employers or heads of offices concerned for the welfare of their subordinates, or of professors, magistrates, colonels, heads of hospitals, elderly nobles, admirals, ambassadors, prefects, who on the appropriate occasion drop the few words necessary to arrange a future which, incidentally, often turns out to be very happy.

I assured the professor that I should do all in my power to second his efforts to bring about Giorgio's return to the academic world, to which I too believed that he really belonged. As for the young lady, I suggested that a meeting be arranged without telling him anything in advance. If a spark were to strike, it would have to be spontaneous. I knew Giorgio too well to believe that he would take to a girl proposed, not to say imposed, on him. In many ways Giorgio was more oriental than the orientals, but in others, for instance his ferocious cult of personal independence, he was more western than the whole of the west combined.

.   .   .   .   .

Next day Giorgio turned up in Kyoto in his characteristic, unexpected fashion. He telephoned me from the Miyako, 'the Grand Hotel of the Capital'. There was no trace of strain or nervousness about him; on the contrary he was bursting with cheerfulness and vitality, the very epitome of confidence and self-assurance. He was accompanied by Enrico and Abe-san, who was all bows and smiles. During lunch I tried to elicit some information about Tamako, but found myself up against a brick wall. Instead I was given some spontaneous information of another kind.

'Do you know who wishes to be remembered to you? You'll never guess—Jane!'

Jane was the American girl whom I had met at Nara.

'How is she? Do you see her occasionally? She's charming. What a pity she's so plain!'

'Yes, but beauty's very dangerous; it goes to the head. Plain women are full of surprises!'

A *jochu-san* brought the fruit. Kyoto lay at our feet, and beyond lay the Eastern Hills and the temples of Yoshida-yama ('Mount Happy Field'). It was a serene and delightful spectacle. I remembered how the night before, on the little terrace over the river, I thought I had made up my mind to talk to Giorgio. Now it was totally out of the question.

The Transformation of Little-South

This morning I called on the professor who teaches Italian language and literature at the University. Some lectures must just have ended; students in their mournful black uniforms came streaming out, talking and laughing. Many wore glasses; bad light at home and too small ideograms in their books impose a strain on their eyes from childhood. In passing many of them greeted the professor with a deep bow and a nervous smile.

How different Japanese students are from our own! Their docility is extraordinary; the problem of discipline does not exist, or at any rate did not in my time. Now one reads occasionally of students' strikes, and even of violence towards their teachers, but these things are exceptions, due to the general confusion of the post-war years. In the east a teacher possesses an authority of a nature entirely different to that to which we

are accustomed. The western professor is in the last resort descended
from the Greek rhetor, transformed by Renaissance humanism; he
is a specialist in a single branch of knowledge. The sharp division between sacred and profane which is characteristic of our civilization is
reflected in this sphere too. Moral and spiritual authority was for centuries the monopoly of the Church, and the moral and spiritual guidance of the young still tends to a large extent to be entrusted to priests,
pastors, or archimandrites rather than to schoolmasters and professors.
In the east, whether in the Confucian sphere of influence, where the *ju,*
the man of letters, prevailed, or in the Indian and Buddhist sphere, where
the master has always been the *guru,* the guide to enlightenment and
transcendental knowledge, the teacher has been surrounded by an aura
which is closer to mystic transcendentalism than to the mere respect
due to one who possesses greater knowledge or skill. 'Your father and
mother are like the sky and the earth, your master is like the sun,'
a maxim says.

When a Japanese student says *'sensei-ga osshaemashita'* (the master said
so), it is as if he were quoting an oracle; the matter is settled, and that is
that. As against this, teachers and professors generally try to live as far
as possible as if they were following a vocation; the best of them at any
rate take very seriously their task of the total guidance of youth. In
Japanese *sensei* means literally 'born before', *i.e.,* senior, presbyter, priest;
thus words sometimes complete the circle and bring us back to the
starting-point.

Another important fact is that in Japan, as in many other eastern
countries, society is based on the implicit assumption that the ideal
season of life is not youth, but age. Westerners, having but one short
life to burn up, with a divine judgment looming at the end of it,
and for other complex reasons as well, have almost continually laid
emphasis on youth; the extreme example is America, where old men
and women pathetically ape the ways and manners of the young. In
Japan there is nothing of all this; the old have no need to imitate, to
pretend, to justify themselves; they leave their affairs to their eldest son
or son-in-law and set about enjoying the autumnal pleasures of art or
thought, of good living, with the calm assurance of being thoroughly
entitled to do so. And if any old gentleman wants to have a fling, people
smile, and say: 'Look how sprightly the old chap is!' In Japan the gay

quarters are in fact much more frequented by old gentlemen on the spree than by young men.

Thus the young grow up in the unquestionably burdensome shadow of their fathers and grandfathers. For this reason, among others, they seem much more childish, much less mature in some respects, than their counterparts in Europe or America. Perhaps they obscurely feel that there is plenty of time, that they are living through a mere passing phase in a great cycle, and that one day their personality will be able to expand and fulfil itself, even if only in the failing light of sunset. On the other hand, because of the repression to which they are subjected, their deprivations, humiliations, poverty, they reveal to those who succeed in gaining their confidence interior riches, particularly emotional riches, rarely to be found in young westerners who have grown up in a freer atmosphere. Two significant facts are that many Japanese university students are virgins,[1] *i.e.,* their sex life is either repressed or distorted, and that suicides are numerous,[2] which implies excessive emotional difficulties.

This introverted life, all obstacles and difficulties, is made the harder to bear by the low public esteem in which students are held. The word *gakusei* (student) has derogatory implications; a student is a person who owes everything to society and his parents, and to whom nobody owes anything; the hideous black uniform tends still further to identify and isolate them. A Japanese does not fully become a man until he has put his studies behind, has married, and occupies a position of at least a minimum of responsibility; to become a man really worthy of respect he generally has to wait until he is about forty. A son's dependence on his father, a pupil's dependence on his teacher, is such that situations arise which to our way of thinking seem totally absurd. Thus I heard recently of a learned professor who could not publish his theories, though he had most interesting things to say, because they conflicted with what had been said twenty years earlier by his master, aged eighty, who was still alive.

Though the student stands so low in the general estimation, the prestige of the academic world, from the humblest lecturer to the supreme luminary of any branch of knowledge, is high. This is in part

---

[1] *See,* for example, T. TAKAHASHI, *Reports of Sexual Experiences,* Tokyo, 1953.
[2] *See,* for example, *Asahi Evening News,* Tokyo, various articles in 1956.

due to the influence of Buddhism, with its emphasis on right knowledge, but it is above all due to Confucianism, according to which a good
man of letters makes a good governor, and *vice versa*. Apart from the
closed caste of the nobility, only the army and navy used to enjoy
higher prestige. The place of the soldier in Japanese life was (and, let
there be no mistake about it, might again become) entirely different
from that which it is in our own. Let me remind the reader of what
I have said above about the different boundaries of the sacred and profane in east and west. Every member of the armed forces, the humblest
naval rating, aircraftman, or private soldier, was a representative of the
Emperor, that is to say, of the supreme peak to which the whole life of
the nation, both sacred and profane, converged. A recruit was not just
a citizen in arms; like the knights-members of certain mediaeval orders,
he was entitled to consider himself a member of a church. 'It is the duty
of the warrior to resemble a monk who lives in obedience to a rule'
(Sasaki Sadatsuna, twelfth century).

I shall never forget Ko-minami-san, or 'Little-South' as his name
means and as we used playfully to call him. Little-South was, however,
a big and robust youth, much stronger and sturdier than most of his
pale, often rickety, and nearly always bespectacled companions. He was
a medical student, and therefore not my pupil; I met him, I think, at
a concert at the Franco-Japanese House of Culture. Knowing that I was
fond of ski-ing, he offered to accompany me on expeditions into the
mountains round Kyoto; we went to Hanase, the Makino, and the top
of Ibuki, with its steep and exciting slopes. He was devoted to music, and
had a really exceptional knowledge of the eighteenth-century masters;
it was the period when Vivaldi was being rediscovered, and when we
managed to get a new record his enthusiasm knew no bounds. In contrast to the conformism which prevailed at the time, Little-South
showed great independence in his tastes, his reading, and his sympathies.
He wanted to win scholarships to enable him to travel, and he hoped to
go to Europe. 'I am in the first place a citizen of the world, and only in
the second place a citizen of Japan,' he used to say. He read Gide and
Huxley in the original; that may not seem very daring now, but at that
time, when the general reading was expurgated translations from the
German, it was evidence of a decidedly independent and liberal attitude.

Regional differences in Japan are far less marked than they are with us; the homogeneity of the country reflects the whole unifying trend of their history. Apart from the two poles, Kwanto (Tokyo–Yokohama) and Kwansai (Kyoto–Osaka–Kobe), there is little differentiation. The people of the north, Tohoku, are poor, rural, tenacious, and of the south, Kyushu, rich, industrious, prone to enthusiasms or violence, and have *jo-netsu-teki* (passionate, inflammable minds). Ko-minami came from Kyushu, and all the explosive energy of his island of volcanoes and steel-works and rice-fields that yield two crops a year was evident in his black eyes, which were capable of looking at you with almost trance-like fury.

One day he disappeared; I was told that he had been called up. About six months later he came to see me in officer's uniform, which he wore with rare elegance; a *katana,* the samurai's sword, hung from his side. Seeing him transformed in this fashion, I thought that he must be protesting in the only way he could. I should explain that Japanese officers used to display the utmost contempt for their personal appearance; anything else would have been effeminate. Your true samurai never brushes his hair; alternately he shaves it off like a Buddhist hermit; as he is ready to die at any moment, what is the point of personal adornment? However, I realized from Little-South's first words that he had undergone a complete inner transformation, even if his outward appearance belied it. There was the same frank, delightful smile, the same enthusiasm, but they were now directed elsewhere, in the direction which in our many talks we had always despised. 'The hour of our destiny has come,' he said, saluting me. 'England, France, America, are rotten, and are ready to fall. If his Majesty the Emperor called on us, we should all be ready to die to bring about the *hakko-ichiu*' (the 'Eight Directions of Space under a Single Roof').[1] Years later I learnt that Little-South died in the southern seas from which his ancestors had come centuries ago. I have no doubt that he died bravely.

The Myth of the Sword

What were the deep forces that brought about the change in Little-South? It is time to talk about a side of Japanese civilization with which everyone is familiar, a side that is sometimes so predominant and spec-

[1] In other words, 'the whole world under the guidance of the Emperor of Japan'.

tacular as to persuade many that it springs from the quintessential
character of a people who, as we have seen, are rich in other gifts; I mean
the cult of martial heroism.

The history of Japan, taken as a whole, is like a symphonic poem.
So far, apart from the overture for gods, nature, and man, we have had
Asuka, Nara, and Heian; Asuka, the window on to the world; Nara, the
serene and Greek; Heian, the recluse, the exquisite, languid with perfection. With 1185 and Kamakura everything suddenly changes; voices,
instruments, timbre, and key; even the players no longer seem the same.
Gilded wood and silk give way to horses and iron, delicate harmonies
and nocturnal intrigue to strength, decision, and death. The warriors
had shaken off the courtiers' yoke, and the whole of Japanese life, from
the system of government to habits of everyday life, from art to love,
from religion to economics, was profoundly modified in accordance
with the tastes of the new men. 'We shall have no such dramatic transition again in Japanese history as the shift from twelfth-century delicacy
and aestheticism to the virile, boisterous period of Kamakura from the
end of the twelfth through the fourteenth century.[1]

The question arises whether the true, the real, Japan was that of the
Nara and Heian centuries, or that of the period we are to deal with now.
There is no doubt of the contrast between them; they were opposites in
everything. It is also true that since the fatal year 1185, apart from a few
brief periods, the ultimate, supreme power in the state has been in the
hands of soldiers; it was only yesterday that they plunged half the world
in war. On the other hand, if Japanese history is looked at more carefully, it will be seen that it does not consist of the exclusive predominance of one aspect over the other, but of a predominance of co-existent
elements in ever-changing relationship. The conclusion is that both
aspects, the fundamentally pacific aspect, that of refinement in the art
of living and enthusiasm for knowledge and beauty, and the fundamentally warlike aspect, an extreme refinement in barbarism and a
terrifying enthusiasm for an ideal absorbed to the point of complete
identification with it, form part of the complex Japanese personality
revealed to us through the centuries.

A brief digression. Do peoples change? It would seem that they do
not. The more one reads ancient accounts and descriptions, the more

---

[1] L. WARNER, *The Enduring Art of Japan*, Harvard, 1952, p. 38.

one is struck by the permanence of certain characteristics. The Germans of Tacitus, the Milanese of Bonvesin da Riva, the Russians of Custine, the Americans of Tocqueville, the Indians of Hsüan-tsang, the Japanese of St. Francis Xavier, might, apart from such minor details as dress, etc., have been observed by their authors at the present day. The explanation is exceedingly simple; it is the extraordinary antiquity of man, which we are only now beginning to realize. History as we know it throws light only on the protruding pinnacles of huge icebergs, the vast mass of which remains invisible beneath the surface of time. Prehistorians now believe that the remarkable palaeolithic paintings found in Europe date back to a period between 28,000 and 30,000 years ago; and what a long, slow evolution may not have preceded those extraordinary examples of artistic ability. So far as most of the important things in our life are concerned, we are governed by attitudes, preferences, internal reconstructions of reality, the roots of which are lost in inconceivable abysses of time. History goes back two, three, five thousand years, but we, ten, twenty, thirty thousand years ago, and perhaps even earlier still, had our gods and our wars, made love, fashioned things, made agreements, undertook complicated courses of action. What we are, our interior world, was determined over a huge period of time, and real changes take place so slowly as to be almost imperceptible in the short course of written history.

But to return to Kamakura. It is unnecessary here even briefly to follow its complicated story.[1] It was the period of the Japanese high Middle Ages, which has always been the delight of the Japanese heroic chroniclers. It was a time of war and bloodshed, picturesque customs, heroism and cruelty. Only in such an age could there flourish men—to take but one example—such as Yoshitsune (1159–1189), the story of whose legendary deeds and loves, and sad end due to the jealousy of his brother Yoritomo, have moved the Japanese for centuries; or women like Masako, Yoritomo's wife (1157–1225), who grew up among battles, flights, conspiracies, and by her astuteness, charm, and decisive character became such a power behind the scenes that after her retirement to a convent she came to be known as Ama-Shogun ('Abbess Military Governor'); or warriors such as Taira no Tadanori (1144–1184), in whose

[1] The most important event was the failure of the attempted invasions by Kublai Khan in 1274 and 1281.

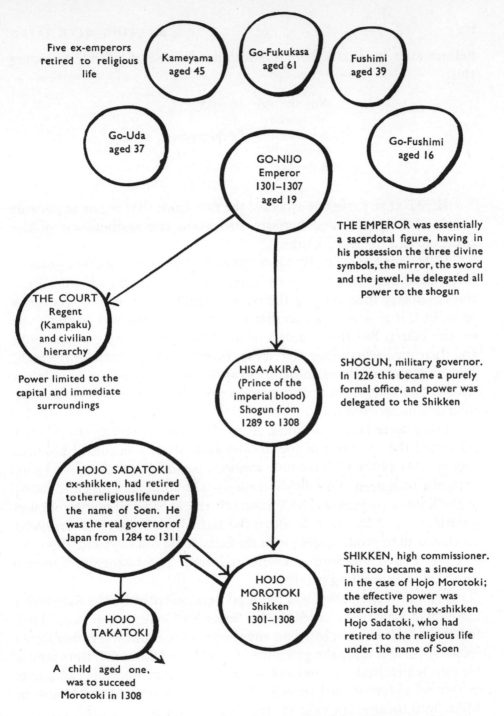

Five ex-emperors retired to religious life

Kameyama aged 45

Go-Fukukasa aged 61

Fushimi aged 39

Go-Uda aged 37

GO-NIJO Emperor 1301–1307 aged 19

Go-Fushimi aged 16

THE EMPEROR was essentially a sacerdotal figure, having in his possession the three divine symbols, the mirror, the sword and the jewel. He delegated all power to the shogun

THE COURT Regent (Kampaku) and civilian hierarchy

Power limited to the capital and immediate surroundings

HISA-AKIRA (Prince of the imperial blood) Shogun from 1289 to 1308

SHOGUN, military governor. In 1226 this became a purely formal office, and power was delegated to the Shikken

HOJO SADATOKI ex-shikken, had retired to the religious life under the name of Soen. He was the real governor of Japan from 1284 to 1311

HOJO MOROTOKI Shikken 1301–1308

SHIKKEN, high commissioner. This too became a sinecure in the case of Hojo Morotoki; the effective power was exercised by the ex-shikken Hojo Sadatoki, who had retired to the religious life under the name of Soen

HOJO TAKATOKI

A child aged one, was to succeed Morotoki in 1308

How Japan was governed in 1304, when the principle of the delegation of powers had reached its peak of complexity

helmet after his death there was found a bundle of poems, including this:

> Now the night descends;
> My hostelry
> Is the shadow of a cherry-tree;
> My host
> A flower.

Here is at any rate one aspect of the new spirit that began to prevail; a cult of simplicity and heroism succeeded the aestheticism of the courtiers and nobles of Kyoto.

Historians are generally agreed in regarding the Kamakura government as an improvement on the direct administration of Kyoto. True, the hereditary incapacity of the nobles had in the course of centuries brought things to such a pass that almost any change was bound to be for the better. But the founders of the *bakufu*, the 'camp government', and their successors administered the country with a paternalism which, if it was sometimes hard, sometimes capriciously easy-going, was always swift-acting and practical, as was to be expected of soldiers in their more tolerable incarnations.

These were empirical times. After the Taikwa reform of 645 Japan presented the spectacle of the decline and fall of a beautiful political theory, that of the Chinese philosophers, partially and therefore badly applied to a nation of totally different social traditions. This culminated in the Kamakura period. The Taikwa reform, as Sansom points out, was an attempt to adapt facts to ideas; the Kamakura military government tried instead to produce ideas to fit the facts. It did not start with theories, but improvised solutions as events required. The history of England provides an interesting parallel.

Typical of the period was the legal code adopted by the Kamakura Council of State of 1232 called the *Joei Shikimoku* ('Collection of Laws of the Joei Period'). It was not based on any theory of law, but was rather a collection of maxims for the guidance of judges and administrators which for purely practical reasons came to be more and more widely adopted; in fact what had started by being the family charter of the House of Minamoto became law valid for the whole of Japan.

The result of this military empiricism, combined with the innate

8

Ise, the shrine of the sun goddess; architecture in its purest traditional form.

83

Art inspired by the greatest religion of Asia. (82) The meditating Buddha of Chugu-ji, at Nara, seventh century; (83) Amida, the merciful, in the Byodo-in at Uji, eleventh century; (84) Amida Buddha and other celestial personages, at Hiraizumi in north Japan, twelfth century.

8

Two favourite Japanese symbols are the pagoda and the torii. The first is essentially a reliquary, a diagram of the universe, the second a gate of honour. (85) The pagoda of Kofuku-ji, at Nara, by night; (86) a torii of Tosho-gu, at Nikko, on a wet afternoon.

Cities, towers, pagodas, and gardens. (87) Tokyo; (88) Osaka; (89) Kyoto; (90) Himeji, (91) wood at Nara; (92) Tenryu-ji garden at Kyoto.

91

92

99

100

102

103

Autumn at Kyoto. (102) *Two* maiko *at the Temple of the Pure Waters* (*Kiyomizu-dera*); (103) *formal visit to the Villa of the Doctrine* (*Shugaku-in*); (104) *solitude and silence in the abstract garden of Ryoan-ji* (*fifteenth century*), *stones, white sand, and lichen.*

Subtle unity of things. (105) *Ideograms of Buddhist wisdom;* (106) *tree in a painting;* (107) *tree on a deserted shore;* (108) *tree in a garden.*

Sense of the theatre. (109) *The popular lion dance;* (110) *masked actor in a No play;* (111) *Kabuki, the popular theatre.*

Traditional link between house and garden.

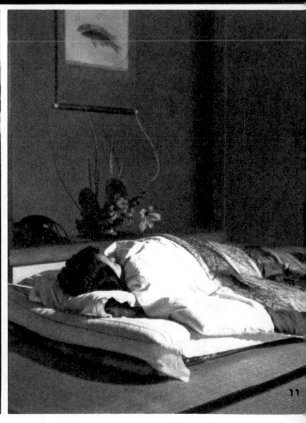

The elegance of simplicity.

Japanese respect for tradition, was a system of government so complicated that it is one of the curiosities of history. The frequent abdications
of those in prominent positions, the delegation of power, the interplay
of individuals, in a short space of time produced an astonishing state of
affairs which can be made clear only with the aid of a diagram (*see*
page 271). The emperors delegated their power to the shoguns but, after
the death of Yorimoto's sons and as a result of the intrigues of Masako,
these too became purely ornamental figures. The exercise of power
passed to a third dynasty, that of the *shikken* (high commissioners) drawn
from Masako's family, the Hōjō.

The delegation of power, which was carried to such absurd extremes
towards the end of the Kamakura period, is still to be found everywhere
in Japanese politics, business, and family life, and is frequently a serious
cause of incomprehension by foreigners of many of the facts of Japanese
life. Similarly the formulation of the Japanese concept of law dates back
in essence to these centuries. Fundamentally only the Emperor had any
rights; all others enjoyed them only as a concession granted from above.
Under the influence of these beliefs, the feudal administration promulgated laws which not only remained practically unknown to the people
but in some cases were actually considered secrets of state.

However, the chief heritage of the iron centuries was what was once
called *kyuba no michi* ('the way of the bow and the horse'), and was later
re-christened *bushi-do* ('the way of the warrior'). In the narrow sense of
a codified body of teaching and a particular outlook on life, there is no
doubt that *bushido* forms part of the great movement quietly initiated by
a group of eighteenth-century scholars and men of letters, of whom
Kamo Mabuchi (1697–1769), Motoori Norinaga (1730–1801), and Hirata
Atsutane (1776–1843) were the chief. It reached its apogee with the 1868
revolution and the reign of the Emperor Meiji, and was finally broken
by the violent follies and tragedies of the third and fourth decades of this
century. The name *bushido* seems to be very modern. According to
Sansom[1] it was known in the eighteenth century, but its use was very
limited, and Chamberlain[2] says that 'the very word appears in no
dictionary, native or foreign, before the year 1900'.

But, if the use of the term is very modern, the nucleus of ideas on

[1] G. B. SANSOM, *Japan, a Short Cultural History*, London, 1931, p. 487.
[2] B. H. CHAMBERLAIN, *Things Japanese*, London and Kobe, 1939, p. 86.

which it is based is very ancient. Not only do the Japanese appear to have been warlike from the earliest times of which there is historical or archaeological evidence but, as Sansom says, there is reason to believe that the relationship of total mystic dedication between vassal and lord, between the samurai and his chief, dates back to the patriarchal system of pre-feudal and even prehistoric times.

The spiritual content of the 'way' is indicated by the concept of *giri* (moral obligation), the duty that ties man to the Emperor, his superiors, equals, and inferiors; its nature is indicated by the concept of *chugi* (loyalty). *Giri* and *chugi* are the pillars on which the whole structure of *bushido* rests. Soldiers, men of action, do not favour complicated philosophies; a few simple, profoundly felt, ideas are always preferred to subtle or complicated theories. In literature and the theatre, both of which are a reflection of life, the plot is nearly always based on a conflict between *giri* (duty) and *ninjō* (human feeling). The same conflict often appears in the Japanese cinema. I was recently told by an acquaintance that before the war it was always *giri* that triumphed. Now the boot was on the other foot, and *ninjō* had started to get the upper hand. The terms of the emotional dialectics remain the same.[1]

In the course of time a whole mystique, a whole philosophy of life, gathered round the original nucleus. The links with recognized philosophies, particularly with Confucianism, became clearer. However, while in China, as has many times been observed, more importance was attached to filial piety *(ko)* than to loyalty towards leaders and kings *(chu)*, in Japan the reverse was the case. Loyalty to one's lord was always an absolute imperative, about which there could be no discussion.

The ideal samurai was also guided by wisdom *(chi)*, benevolence *(jin)*, and valour *(yū)*.

Wisdom did not mean knowledge; the aim was the intense living of what were considered to be supreme and eternal ethical principles. It is here that there lies the bridge between the samurai and Zen Buddhism. We shall discuss Zen Buddhism later; here we shall mention only that this variety of Buddhism, which differs notably from the others, almost completely repudiates all the work of the intellect and all teaching

---

[1] A Japanese friend points out that a change has taken place in the meaning of *ninjō*. Before the war its primary meaning was mercifulness, magnanimity, love of one's neighbour; now it has acquired another, more western meaning, that of respect for the human personality.

contained in books; the ultimate truth is not to be attained by the mind working in isolation, but is something which you have to live with your whole being.

Benevolence implied pity for the conquered and the weak. The ideal samurai had to be magnanimous as well as strong and courageous. In later centuries he was expected to cultivate the tea ceremony, one of the few occasions on which he laid aside his sword. He was, of course, devoted to music and poetry. Nitobe observes, with some exaggeration: 'What Christianity has done in Europe towards rousing compassion in the midst of belligerent horrors love of music and letters has done in Japan.'[1] Beauty consisted essentially of purity of line, colour, feelings, sounds, actions, a principle that has left lasting and profoundly favourable effects on Japanese taste. Luxury, display, softness, were reprehensible in all their forms.

Finally, the supreme measure of personality was courage, valour, but this must be combined with serenity and composure. Flinging oneself headlong into danger was not considered worthy of a *bushi* (warrior). 'True courage is to live when it is right to live, and to die only when it is right to die.' The samurai was expected always to maintain perfect calm, even when others were losing their heads, or rather, particularly when others were losing their heads. Most admired were those able calmly to read or recite a poem shortly before drawing their last breath; and every samurai was expected to be always ready to take his own life if circumstances required it. Every detail of the rite of *seppuku*[2] was meticulously laid down.

You were born a samurai; you could not, except in the most exceptional circumstances, become one. A samurai's education was hard. He had to learn to betray not the slightest emotion, whether of joy, of fear; and learning the necessary degree of self-control took years. His word—*bushi-no ichi gon*, 'the single word of the warrior'—was sacred, and lying

[1] I. NITOBE, *Bushido*, Tokyo, 1900; many subsequent editions and translations.

[2] Commonly known as *hara-kiri*, disembowelling oneself. The classic account of a *seppuku* is of that of Taki Zenzaburo, written by an eye-witness (Lord Redesdale). In 1868, when Japanese public opinion was deeply divided about the desirability of the many innovations being introduced by the new government of the Emperor Meiji, Taki Zenzaburo, a vassal of the Prince of Bizen, gave orders to open fire on a party of foreigners in the port of Kobe (then Hyogo). By desire of the Emperor himself, Taki, as the individual responsible, was ordered to commit suicide. Seven foreign representatives were invited to the self-execution ceremony. *See* LORD REDESDALE, *Tales of Old Japan*, London, 1871; many subsequent editions.

or deception (*ni-gon*) meant death. The long training included fencing, archery, wrestling, riding, throwing the javelin, some idea of tactics, calligraphy, the study of ethics, literature, and history. At fifteen the samurai received his sword, one of those incomparable instruments made by famous craftsmen to the accompaniment of prayers to the gods. There was only one thing which the samurai must not understand, and that was the use of money. The sign of a really good education was inability to recognize the various coins in current circulation. A samurai would often work in his fields with the peasants, but he was rigorously forbidden to take any part in trade.

Chi
Wisdom

This severe, if limited, ideal was not without a certain magnificent, primitive beauty, and it inspired innumerable deeds of extraordinary, if sometimes revolting, valour. The classic example is the story of the forty-seven *ronin*, the 'forty-seven wave men', that is to say samurai, left without a lawful lord.[1] When they simultaneously committed *seppuku* in 1703 they concluded a tragic story full of all the elements dearest to the Japanese heart: summary justice, plotting, unshakable resolution, dissimulation long persisted in, revenge, final self-sacrifice. In 1748 a play, the *Chushingura,* was made of their story. It is in eleven acts and takes all day to perform, and since it was first produced it has remained the *pièce de résistance* of the Japanese theatre, whether in its complete, original form or in one of the innumerable shorter versions. Theatrical managers say that when you are doing badly you must put on the *Chushinguru* and you will fill the house again.

Jin
Benevolence

Yū
Courage
Valour

Another notable suicide, nearer to our own day, carried out with all the ceremonial required by protocol, was that of General Nogi, the conqueror of the Russians in the war of 1904, and of his wife—he was

---

[1] The Japanese prefer to call them the forty-seven *gishi* ('just men'), because of the consistency of their conduct.

sixty-four and she ten years his junior—after the death of the Emperor Meiji in 1912, just at the time when the funeral procession was leaving the Imperial Palace. Next to the two corpses, dressed in the white kimonos which are *de rigueur* on such occasions, a brief poem, written in ancient Japanese, was found. It said: 'My sovereign, abandoning this fleeting life, has ascended among the gods; with my heart full of gratitude, I desire to follow him.' The general and the Emperor had lived and fought together, and transformed Japan from an Asian state isolated and shut off from the world into a modern great power. If the general's self-immolation upon his master's death is moving, what are we to say of his wife? In the last analysis he acted on his own free will, but she did not. How did they come to agree on their last act, maintaining complete secrecy? Did the old general, perhaps somewhat shamefacedly, simply say to her: 'I have decided to follow my master, would you like to come with me?' Or had there been a long-standing agreement between the two? Or—and this is the most plausible suggestion—was there no need to say anything at all? Perhaps things—so full of symbolism to the oriental mind—spoke their own terrible, silent message: a *ko-gatana*, the short dagger, the last weapon of self-defence when all else has gone, placed on the empty mat; a crystalline imperative surrounded by *mu* (infinite nothing.)

It is intelligible that this sort of thing should exercise a strong fascination for certain types of generous, sensitive, and at the same time virile mind. Following an ethic of this kind means maintaining a constant and difficult equilibrium. One false step and you relapse into barbarism, gratuitous violence, theatricality, flagrant injustice, or pathological masochism. After looking at the ideal, after admitting that in the course of centuries the elect were many, it must be admitted that there were more who made the system infamous. I shall return to this theme in a later chapter. For the time being it is sufficient to have attempted an explanation of how it was possible for such a change to have come about in the mind of my friend Little-South, a change that was so total as at first sight to seem incomprehensible.

9

Wisdom in a Grain of Sand

Zen Monastery

WHEN I first visited Kyoto many years ago I noticed that the fascination of the temples of the Shingon sect lay in a certain air of mystery, intensified by the half-light of the chapels, which suggested the sensations of fear and voluptuousness roused by the *lha-kang* ('dwellings of the gods') in Tibet; that the feature of the Tendai temples was their severe solemnity; and that that of those of the later Amida cult was a magnificence that was nearly always free of vulgarity. But the temples by the beauty of which I was most impressed either belonged to the Zen cult or had undergone its influence.

They were generally huge. I should really speak of monasteries rather than of temples. The word 'temple' *(tera, ji),* as the reader will have noticed, implies in Japanese a whole complex of buildings, which in the case of Zen include the great gateway at the entrance *(sammon);* the chapel of the Buddha, or temple proper *(butsuden);* the sermon hall *(hattō);* the hall of meditation *(zendō);* the abbot's residence, the refectory, and the bath. In the case of the older sects there were generally one or more pagodas, a low bell-tower, a treasury, a library, as well as chapels and pavilions dedicated to various celestial personages. Gardens, roads, and park, which gave an organic unity to the various elements, aesthetic as well as administrative and ecclesiastical, also belonged to the temple.

In Zen monasteries this fusion of nature and the work of man continually reaches the heights of perfection. In the Kyoto area alone it is sufficient to mention the Nanzen-ji or the Tofuku-ji, hidden in the pines at the foot of the Eastern Mount, or the Shokoku-ji, the Daitoku-ji, and the Myoshin-ji on the north-western outskirts of the ancient capital, each one of which is like a little town in which you could easily lose your way among winding lanes bordered by walls covered with grass, moss, and wild flowers; every now and then you come to a door, hear the sound of a bell, or an invisible voice rhythmically reading aloud from a sacred text. In these miniature townships are hidden works of art, which you approach barefoot, after walking long distances down corridors or along verandas, discovering unsuspected gardens, sometimes bowers of stones and flowers, sometimes big parks. If it is spring, cherry and wistaria will be in bloom, if autumn the *momiji* will be red; at other seasons the scene is dominated by the evergreen pines, gnarled even in their youth, juicy with adolescent vigour even in age.

Today we went to the Tenryu-ji, the Temple of the Celestial Dragon, some miles from the centre of the city at the foot of the Western Mountains, near the Arashi-yama. Later the sky cleared and the sun shone brightly, but when we reached the temple the sky had the mother-of-pearl quality that a high veil of cloud sometimes gives it in autumn; you notice, if you pay it a moment's attention, that the diffused light brings out the colours of the landscape in an extraordinary fashion. At the ancient, solemn gateway that marks the entrance to the park we exclaimed with delight at the sight of the *momiji*, their leaves aflame with every shade of red, mingled with the green needles of the pines. On the right was a long row of minor temples, each with its garden and dwelling. An elderly woman, wearing a large conical straw hat, was sweeping up the fallen leaves; otherwise there was no one to be seen. Silence would have dominated the valley but for the sound of some horrible Japanese jazz-style songs from a loudspeaker somewhere in the distance. In front of us lay the central buildings of the monastery, built in the style characteristic of the Muromachi period, their white walls broken by the timber skeleton of the structure. The effect was curiously like the English half-timbered style, or what the Germans call *Fachwerk*.

We mounted some steps, and came to the entrance proper. Every detail, the gravel in the park, the wood of the walls, the whitewash, the way the trees were kept pruned, even the moss growing in places where the shade favoured it, betrayed the constant care lavished on the place,

guided by the most scrupulous taste. Enemy number one was superfluous decoration, display, vulgarity; most favoured were things like
spades and bill-hooks, everything that suggested useful work connected
with the soil, closeness to nature and to the essence of things. One of the
distinguishing features of Zen Buddhism, as we shall see later, is the
integration of spiritual and everyday life. There is therefore nothing
strange in finding an abbot or famous theologian (if I may be pardoned
that inappropriate expression) hoeing, painting, pruning, cutting wood
for the fire, or repairing tiles on the roof. 'No work, no food' has been
the monastic rule ever since the times of the Chinese patriarch Pai-
chang (in Japanese Hyakujō, 720–814).

This morning, however, we found no theologians engaged in
housework or abbots busy with a hoe; instead we were kept waiting
a long time at the gate, calling out *'Gomen kudasai! Gomen kudasai!'* (May we
come in? May we come in?) Eventually a tall, thin monk appeared, and
looked at us crossly over his spectacles; he evidently considered
foreigners incapable of appreciating the subtleties of oriental beauty.
We silently removed our shoes, put on slippers, and entered the temple
proper, which looks out on to the garden. Meanwhile the sun had come
out, and we started filming, trying to capture some of the magic of the
place. At first the tall monk followed us, grumbling, but then, seeing
that we chose points of view that fitted in with his esoteric tastes, he
took us under his wing, and we were given the freedom of the place.

This, like many other Kyoto temples, for instance the Silver Pavilion
(Ginkaku-ji), the Golden Pavilion (Kinkaku-ji), the Nanzen-ji, and the
Daikaku-ji, was originally built as a villa, in this case apparently by the
Emperor Saga in the ninth century. Ashikaga Takauji, who established
a new dynasty of shoguns early in the fourteenth century, then transformed it into a place of meditation, employing for this purpose a
famous personage of the time, Musō Kokushi,[1] who was prelate, philosopher and artist, gardener, poet and calligrapher, as well as skilful
statesman behind the scenes in the oriental manner. The shogun's aims
in founding this monastery were political as well as religious; he wished

[1] Born 1275, died 1351. During his lifetime he was called Chikaku and subsequently, after a dream
which affected his whole career, Soseki. Musō, meaning 'Window-Dream', *i.e.*, 'Window on to the
Dream', was the name given him posthumously. *Kokushi* is a title of great honour given to only a
few exceptional men; it might be translated 'Master of the Nation'.

to strengthen Zen Buddhism to counter the excessive power of the Tendai monks barricaded on Mount Hiei who, like the monks of Nara, were a continual source of embarrassment to the government.

Ashikaga Takauji's intention was that the Temple of the Celestial Dragon should eventually become the parent institution of a whole network of interconnected monasteries throughout Japan, but this ambitious plan remained on paper. Indeed, the inauguration of the new temple was vigorously opposed by the monks of Mount Hiei. The Emperor was to have attended the ceremony in person but, in view of the threats of violence by both sides, prudently decided to send a representative. The monks of Mount Hiei descended in force with their sacred palanquins, resistance to which was equivalent to sacrilege, and demanded that Musō should be sent into exile and the new temple dismantled. Fortunately the shogun succeeded in persuading them to return to their wooded fastness, with the result that Musō's work survived for the pleasure of posterity. The temple itself was several times destroyed by fire, and the present building was erected in 1900, but the garden is one of the most exquisite in Japan and in the world (Photograph 92).

Originally the garden was built on the Chinese, T'ang dynasty, model; *i.e.*, the centre-piece was a lake, with islets, bridges, pavilions on the bank. The Japanese of the Heian period (ninth to twelfth centuries) enthusiastically developed all the possibilities of this. To them a garden was primarily a background for the brilliant spectacle of court life; barges sailed on the lake, while on the banks courtiers and their ladies beguiled the fleeting hour with poetry and song.

During the Kamakura period (twelfth to fourteenth centuries) the impact of the Zen philosophy brought about profound changes in Japanese life, and the new influence can be discerned in every sphere of art. Japanese gardens had been 'gay and refined, open and full of sun';[1] they were now invaded by ever more serious and important philosophical meanings. Carefree times of peace had been followed by years of bloodshed, retirement meant meditation, searching for a reason for life, and this meant searching inside oneself. A garden was no longer a place for pagan pleasures, but a means of entering into communion with the secrets of life and death.

[1] L. E. KUCK, *One Hundred Kyoto Gardens*, London, 1936.

Zen shares with most schools of Buddhism, and a large body of oriental philosophy, the belief that the key to understanding of the universe lies in the overcoming of all illusory dualisms—self and non-self, life and death, good and evil, matter and spirit. What does death matter if the universe survives? What differentiates Zen from the others is its rejection of all reliance on the intellect. Enlightenment, it holds, is to be reached in a flash of intuition. One of the best aids to the merging, the sublimation, of the self into the all is held to be a garden, which is far more important than treatises, syllogisms, or sacred books. Hence some of the best minds of Asia devoted themselves to garden design. During the Heian period gardens were conceived as places in which things were intended to happen, but those of the Kamakura and Muromachi centuries were designed to have symbolic value. Their size was reduced, the lake became a pool, or its place was taken by white sand as a symbol of water. The whole was arranged to be looked at from a few vantage points at which you stood and meditated.

The garden of the Celestial Dragon can be said to be half-way between the innocent, sunny gardens of the most ancient times and the sometimes excessively tormented gardens of later times. It consists essentially of a pool at the foot of a thickly wooded hill over which the clouds sail. There are few flowers; an eastern garden is not nature dominated and tamed by man, but nature absorbing and sublimating man. Flowers are therefore too few to draw excessive attention to themselves; there are only those that might be found there if the place were not a garden, but an uninhabited valley. The fundamental elements are rocks, trees, and water. The supreme aim is, while shunning anything trite or insipid, to permit no casual association of one thing with any other, and at the same time to ensure that the hand of man shall nowhere be perceptible. Thus a garden is a place of privilege for things, where they can expand, supplementing and setting each other off in the play of light and reflection, living with the rhythm of the seasons and the hours. It is a place of things invited to communion with man. There is no human pride; a Zen garden is not a place where man displays his virtuosity as the lord of creation, but a place where rock invites to ecstasy, water to tenderness, tree to thoughtfulness. All limits are abolished; the ultimate wisdom, Buddha, is to be found in a grain of sand.

I walked round the little pool, stopped, walked on, bent down, touched the stones, breathed rock, thought rock, was rock; rock as a fragment of the world, or the flesh of heaven. One of many Zen sayings, speaking of the sage, who is naturally also a poet, is:

> Walking in the forest he does not disturb a blade of grass;
> Entering the water he does not cause the slightest ripple.

In the oriental garden this supreme respect for nature has become a symphony. Every rock or stone has a meaning, in itself and in relation to everything else; in itself as shape, grain, surface; in relation to everything else by reason of its association with neighbouring objects, the angle at which it lies, its state of concealment or display. The stones are not chosen for their intrinsic value or rarity; the most beautiful things lie all about us without our noticing them. It is sufficient to examine the bed of the nearest stream, stroll along the nearest beach, climb the nearest hillside, to find treasures scattered everywhere: rocks, stones, trees, leaves, moss. These humble things are then arranged in the garden so that we shall see them in a new light, revealing themselves in their true essence to the observer for the first time in his life.

A young monk was carefully sweeping the sand round the temple. Every now and then we caught each other's eye. Once he passed near us, stopped, smiled, and said:

'Maraini-san, you will never understand the whole secret of the Celestial Dragon. But you do well to try!'

'Eh?' I stopped and looked at him. 'Yes, that is true,' I said. 'But how do you know my name?'

He laughed.

'Don't you remember Takeoka?' he said. 'Well, here I am! You would not have expected it, would you? Now my name is Tokō. New life, new name! I am pleased to see you. Come and see us. I do not live here; it is by chance that we met. I am at the Shokoku-ji, down in the city. . . . And you? Have you been in Japan the whole time, or have been "there" and come back?'

We sat down and talked; after fifteen years there were many threads to pick up. Takeoka-san had for a short time been a student of mine, but I had difficulty in recognizing him. In his student days twelve years before he had been a strange and not very attractive type, untidy, dirty, unkempt, and with a week's growth of beard, as was common with students obsessed with some idea, who aspired, if not to martyrdom, at any rate to a hairshirt. Now he seemed taller and stronger, and he was immaculate. His head was shaved, he wore a working kimono of pleasing blue country cloth, and straw sandals. His whole appearance suggested inner peace and self-assurance, and an inordinate desire to laugh. Everything about him except his voice was so changed that I could hardly believe that he was the same man.

In the old days his whole outlook had been coloured by a supreme contempt for everything Japanese. The first time I met him he told me that he came from the province of Nagano, at the foot of the Japanese Alps, an area of great beauty and ancient customs. I remarked that I should very much like to see his village and meet his family, but he insisted that that would be impossible, for I should have to eat Japanese fashion and sleep Japanese fashion, and he was convinced that I should find both disgusting. If I praised anything Japanese in his hearing, he insisted that I did so only to give him pleasure, for the Japanese in his opinion were dirty, poverty-stricken, thievish, stupid, and presumptuous. The impossibility of making any dent in this fixed idea sometimes infuriated me; it was the equal and opposite of the idea held firmly by other Japanese that everything 'that stinks of butter', *i.e.,* is foreign, is inferior, contemptible, ugly, and depraved. Perhaps the fact of being islanders encourages these heated emotional attitudes towards foreigners. Continental man knows that there are many different kinds of people, and contact with them leads to an easier and calmer evaluation of their differences and resemblances and their relative merits and defects. But for an islander, or member of an isolated society, every meeting with a foreigner is an adventure, and that is a bad foundation for sober judgment. Besides, the Japanese, who are artists, a people of intuition and instinct, have a limited critical sense; they tend to love or hate, accept or reject things, including their own civilization, *en bloc.*

Takeoka-san's mental journey must have been exactly the opposite of that of so many of his compatriots, for whom the war meant a painful plunge from the heights of an enormous self-complacency to the depths of an enormous disillusionment. The Italians went through a similar experience, but in the case of the Japanese the plunge was far deeper. Takeoka-san, however. seemed to have gone through the reverse process; he had climbed to self-confidence from the depths of the abyss. When I knew him he had been studying agriculture, which seemed to hold out the prospect of a tranquil future among rice-fields and lotus roots. A certain intellectual curiosity had led him to learn Latin in order to be able to understand the botanical names of plants (and hence, by way of *O sole mio,* to my courses in Italian). After graduating he had been sent to some university in the southern seas. When war broke out he had been called up, had fought, and had been taken prisoner. All his companions committed suicide, as was expected of them; he did not, because he was wounded and unconscious. When he came round he found himself in the care of an American sergeant, and renounced the idea of suicide. Gradually he started feeling an enormous sense of gratitude towards these strange people who took such care of their wounded enemies, and he became a convert to Christianity. After the war he was sent to the United States for a course of religious studies, but the result was another spiritual crisis. So this was how the Christians lived! he said to himself. These people, whom he had worshipped like gods since boyhood, were of the same clay as the Japanese. At this point the influence of a master, a family acquaintance who was a monk in the Shokoku monastery, seems to have become the decisive influence in his life. The Japanese always tend to succumb to the fascination of a human personality rather to any system of ideas; in resolutely submitting to the guidance of a master they are able with marvellous ease to still the whirlpools of emotion that arise from the paradoxes of the intellect. There is a Japanese word *makaseru,* almost untranslatable in all its implications, meaning to give one's confidence to somebody, implying submission, complete self-dedication to him; it is frequently used to describe the age-old relationship between man and his leader, between sage and acolyte. '*Sensei-ni o-makase shimashita*' (I have left it to my master to decide), said Takeoka-san.

'Come and see us,' he said, saying good-bye to me. 'I should like you to meet my master, he is a truly exceptional man. *Honto-ni asobi-ni irasshai. . . . Sayonara, sayonara.*'

He resumed his sweeping. Then he bent down and picked up a pine-needle. I recalled another Zen saying:

> Picking up a blade of grass,
> He makes of it a tall, golden Buddha.

But what is Zen? The question brings me to the hardest part of the book. In the first place it is open to doubt whether it is a branch of Buddhism at all; it is so unorthodox in many respects that it could well be described as a separate religion. The roots of all the Buddhist sects lie in India; even the Sino-Japanese Amida cult and the Tibetan Rnyin-ma-pa, in which the original doctrines have undergone profound transformation, have obvious links with the great original tree, if only because of their reverence for the Indian sacred books, the Sutras. But, though it is claimed that the essence of its teaching is contained in the Lankavatara Sutra (in Japanese *Ryoga-kyō*), the most notable exponents of Zen have always maintained the uselessness of sacred books and writings and proclaimed that enlightenment *(satori)* is to be achieved, not by the strivings of the intellect, but directly from the experience of life itself; and in any case that the doctrine is transmitted, not by the written word, but by word of mouth from master to pupil.

Tradition has it that this school, or faith, or way (Chinese *tao*, Japanese *michi, do*), was founded by the Indian patriarch Bodhidarma, who went to China at the beginning of the sixth century A.D. The Indian roots of his doctrines, at any rate as they were understood by his successors, are by no means evident; Sir Charles Eliot suggests that his teachings were essentially Hindu (Vedantic) rather than Buddhist. In China, at all events, they underwent a remarkable transformation, with the result that, if their Indian origins are still a matter of learned discussion, their Chinese roots are plain, and constitute an obvious link with Taoism.

This brings us to Lao-tsu who, with Confucius, laid down the fundamental tramlines which the Far Eastern philosophical debate was to follow for centuries, rather as Plato and Aristotle did for western philosophy at the other end of the world. Confucius stands for reason, the world of human relations, life as discipline, conduct, manners; Lao-tsu for the world of relations between man and the universe, life as intoxication with the divine, and *docta ignorantia*. Confucius is the spokesman of north China, a land of cereals, poverty, prose, mass-man; Lao-tsu for south China, a land of rice and abundance, lyricism, individualism. In Lao-tsu the word *tao* originally meant 'the way', but subsequently assumed the meaning of law, nature, the ultimate truth, the absolute. Just as in the west the wind *(anemos)* became progressively charged with loftier and more subtle meanings, becoming the breath of life *(anima,* the soul), and was frequently identified with God (by Giordano Bruno, for instance), so in the east the ordinary path across the fields or footway between the houses was enriched with concepts which became the pillars of a whole cycle of civilizations. The *tao,* 'the womb, principle, and reason of all the things that it contains, that develop out of it, and return to it in an alternating process which has no end', works through the opposing principles of *yin* (the female, negative principle, the moon and water) and *yang* (the male, positive principle, sun and earth).[1] 'Into this universal flux the human reason enters like a jarring note which, departing from the naturalness and spontaneity of the cosmic process of becoming, sets up an arbitrary world of its own which it would like to substitute for the balanced, predestined course of the *tao.*'[2]

Thus the Taoist, in direct contrast to the Confucian, is at perpetual loggerheads with reason and society. His ideal is the Real Man, the benign and serene sage who has understood the law of life according to which 'for whosoever hath, to him shall be given, but whosoever hath not, from him shall be taken away even that he hath'. The sage delights in simple, ordinary, everyday things, and thinks and speaks like a child. 'They spoke in paradoxes, for they were afraid of uttering half-truths. They began by talking like fools and ended by making their hearers wise.'[3] The sage contentedly withdraws, a leaf with the leaves, a grain of sand with the sand, a cloud with the clouds; he is *hsien* (in Japanese *sennin*), a word written with the roots for 'man' and 'mountain'; in other words he might be called a hermit, but incorrectly, for he does not flee from the world, but towards it; in fact the world, the real world, is what he is searching for. Clouds, dew, trees are more real to him than man and his empires. His motto is *wu-wei* (in Japanese *mu-gyo*), which is commonly translated 'non-acting, non-action', though its true meaning is rather that 'man must adopt simplicity as his rule of life'. 'When knowledge and intelligence appeared, the Great Artifice began.'[4] The more the

---

[1] In Japanese *in* and *yō.*
[2] G. TUCCI, *Asia Religiosa,* Rome, 1946, p. 231.
[3] K. OKAKURA, *The Book of Tea,* New York, 1906.
[4] FUNG YU-LAN, *A History of Chinese Philosophy,* London, 1952.

Great Artifice interposes itself between man and the *tao*, the harder becomes the identification with the universe which is the ultimate and supreme wisdom.

Zen—the word derives from the Sanskrit *dhyana*, meditation, by way of the Chinese *ch'an*—is in reality the offspring of Tao, because of the ideas it shares with it and the attitude which it inculcates towards society, art, knowledge, conduct. Its teaching is summed up in four well-known lines, which Sir Charles Eliot quotes as follows:

> A special tradition outside the scriptures;
> Not to depend on books or letters;
> To point direct to the heart of man;
> To see [one's own] nature and become Buddha.

We now come up against an insuperable obstacle. How are we to write about what is not communicable in words? The nature of enlightenment, according to Zen, is inherently incommunicable. 'He who has not experienced it knows nothing about it, he who has experienced it cannot describe it.'

Under the early Chinese patriarchs the school seems to have lived for a long time in tranquillity, both physical and metaphysical. Then Hui-neng (in Japanese Enō, 636–717), who can be described as the second founder of Zen, made his appearance. Tradition has it that he was illiterate, and worked in a monastery kitchen. The great patriarch Hung-jen, feeling that his end was approaching, decided to hold a poetry competition to decide who was to be his successor. A favourite pupil of the patriarch's composed the following, which excited universal admiration:

> The body is the Bodhi tree;
> The mind is like the bright mirror's stand.
> Clean your mirror continually
> Lest the dust make it dim.

Hui-neng, being unable to read or write, could not enter the competition, but he asked a monk to write this on the monastery wall:

Bodhi is not a tree;
The mirror has no stand.
From the beginning nothing exists;
How could dust cover it?[1]

Loud disputation followed, but the succession went to Hui-neng. It was he who gave Zen its peculiar character; on the one hand extreme nihilism, the most intransigent intellectual monism; on the other an exceedingly severe discipline of mind and body. There were no scriptures, no sacred formulas, no divine saviour; the individual was left confronting the universe alone, striving to attain communion with it in a flash of enlightenment.

Hui-neng and his immediate successors established the pattern of the ideal Zen master, a strange, paradoxical individual, cheerful, bad-tempered, capricious, unpredictable in his actions and his repartees. His aim was to free the mind of the tyranny of reason, with its pernicious distinctions between the self and the non-self, between mind and matter, between gods and the world, in order to guide it towards *prajna* (in Japanese *hannya*), the mystic knowledge that transcends all dualisms. To this end the mind must be purified of *karma* (in Japanese *go*), of the burden of ignorance and evil accumulated during this and previous lives because of attachment to vain and fleeting things.

There are two schools of thought about how *satori* is to be achieved. The first, the more rational and orthodox Sōtō school, says that it is attainable by meditation, good works, immaculate living; and that by this means enlightenment follows upon enlightenment until life is raised to the level of sanctity. The other, the nihilist, lyrical school, represented by the Rinzai sect, says that there is not one, but an infinite number of ways; sometimes morality, a holy life, good works, can actually be an obstacle; some find enlightenment where others find destruction. The only essential is to strive for it with the whole of one's being. It is here that the characteristic anecdotes come in which form such a large part of Zen literature. The teaching of this sect is done in short, paradoxical conversations (*mondō*), or by confronting the acolyte with strange themes for meditation (*koan*).

[1] SIR CHARLES ELIOT, *Japanese Buddhism*, London, 1935, p. 166. (The author quotes the Chinese text of the two verses.)

In *mondō* dialogues like this take place. A monk asked Gensha:

> What is the One?
> G: The Many.
> M: What is the Many?
> G: The One!
> M: What is the Buddha-mind?
> G: The mind of sentient beings.
> M: What is the mind of sentient beings?
> G: The Buddha-mind.
> M: What is my Self?
> G: What do you want to do with Self?
> M: Am I not just facing you?
> G: I have never seen you.
> M: Who is the right master of this Gensha Monastery?
> G: You are he, and I am the guest.
> M: Why so?
> G: What do you ask?[1]

More frequently, perhaps, the *mondō* ends in blows, laughter, or totally meaningless replies. There is a celebrated story of a monk who was so roughly handled by his master that he fell and broke a leg; the sudden pain brought him enlightenment. The aim is to free man of all intellectual presumption, to shake him inwardly by paradoxes and outwardly by sudden blows or practical jokes, and so open the way for the subconscious to lay the bridge between the self and the non-self which reason is unable to provide.

In the twelfth century this mystical system, only some of the least disconcerting aspects of which we have described here, was introduced into Japan, where a number of interesting developments took place. Most surprising of all was the way in which the warriors took to it. Buddhism, the doctrine of love, peace, and *karuna* (universal benevolence), entered into a close alliance with the military. One of the wonders of life is how it puts up with such inconsistencies, of which there are many examples in the western world as well. The Zen monks' complete devotion to an idea appealed to the Kamakura warriors, as did their 'pointing directly to the heart of man' without the encumbrance of sacred books or subtleties of exegesis, and their courage in

[1] D. T. Suzuki, *Living by Zen*, Tokyo, 1949, p. 47.

defying ridicule, paradox, the intellect. The severity of their discipline also appealed to the military mind. The Japanese warrior regarded himself, not as a bully who took advantage of brute force, but as a hero who defied it.

To this spontaneous and lasting alliance the Zen philosophy owed its practical success in Japan. After the sublimities and casuistry of Shingon, the rationalist, hierarchical pride of Tendai, the good works, the softness of Amidism, the reign of pure instinct began, the reign of man as flame and sword. The Zen masters, in spite of their contempt for reason and reasoning, were adroit politicians; they never resorted to the violence of their Tendai colleagues or relaxed the discipline of their order. They thus gained the unlimited confidence of the rulers of Japan and, among other things, acquired the funds with which to build the most beautiful monasteries in Japan.

The second development on Japanese soil was the alliance between Zen and the arts. It is impossible to over-estimate the importance that the life and doctrines of the monks who lived by the principles of Zen had for the development of every field of Japanese art, from painting to ceramics, from gardening to poetry, from the theatre to printing, from dancing to the cinema. Of typical Zen inspiration, for instance, is the universally accepted principle that there are no such things as major and minor arts; any activity can be art, for art takes place in man, from which everything radiates and to which everything returns. A point of tremendous importance is that for the Zen masters art is never decoration, embellishment; instead it is work of enlightenment, illumination, salvation, not in a narrow, pietistic sense, but in the sense of a flash of sudden, profound significance. Art, in other words, is a technique for acquiring liberty. The intellect having been dethroned, the artist's intuition becomes the connecting link between the self and the all.

Here Zen sublimated immemorial trends of the Japanese mind. The Japanese now approached nature, the realm of the *kami,* with eyes infinitely more mature and sophisticated than in their first poetic *élan,* but, if the spiral now mounted infinitely higher, it led back again to the same familiar earth. In Japan there has always been an intimacy, unknown in the west, between man and rock, man and grass, or fire, or sea-shell. Similarly, with its emphasis on the personal transmission of wisdom, its finger pointed to the heart of man, Zen fitted in with the native educational tradition, in which personality counted for more than ideas, the concrete was preferred to the abstract, and communication took precedence over independent thinking. Zen can therefore be said to have taken the best and most real elements of the Japanese spirit and moulded them into a new pattern, which in turn profoundly influenced the life of the whole nation.

Historically the work of mediation and ferment between Zen and the arts took place in connection with the humble tea-leaf. But here I do not propose to discuss in the abstract things which are essentially concrete. We shall return to Zen and tea when we visit the Ginkaku-ji, the Silver Pavilion.

Kurama Fire Festival

This evening we went to Kurama, prepared to remain there till dawn, as tradition requires. The *hi-matsuri,* the annual fire festival, starts at dusk and continues till first light. With us was Jane, who had appeared in Kyoto for a short holiday.

Kurama is a long, narrow village at the bottom of a narrow valley. At night it is even darker than usual; the wooded mountain-sides hide the stars and make it seem the entrance to a subterranean world of elves and toadstools. Perhaps it was that which prompted the inhabitants to honour their gods with a festival of light and fire; for fire serves as a protection from evil. 'Water and fire are things of extreme importance in Shinto as purificatory elements.'[1]

We joined the throng making for Kurama from Kyoto and the surrounding countryside, and we could see from a distance flames blazing among the trees, as if a house were on fire, or the place were full of open furnaces. When we reached the village we found huge bonfires of lopped tree-trunks blazing opposite every house for half a mile or more; I say tree-trunks advisedly; the blazing timber was of a kind that with us would have been set aside for making furniture. But Japan is so rich in timber that it is never a problem.

One of the Japanese in our party took us to the house of some friends where, after elaborate greetings and bows and cups of tea, we sat by a window looking out on to the street. The first parties of small

[1] J. P. HAUCHECORNE, *Le Japon,* Paris, 1954, p. 56.

boys were already marching by, carrying on their shoulders big torches (*tai-matsu*) made of twigs wrapped in bark, shouting *sai-rei sai-ryo! sai-rei sai-ryo!* The first part of the festival, which lasts from nine or ten o'clock until about midnight, consists of boys and young men marching through the village, carrying the biggest and heaviest torches that they can handle. First come boys, then youths, then men, but none are older than twenty-four or twenty-five. The festival obviously originated in an initiation ceremony. The torch-bearers gathered round the Shinto shrine of Yuki, dedicated to the gods who cure all evil.

The village was packed. Heads were peering from every window, and the throng in the streets was dense; it parted to make way for the torch-bearers, and closed again behind them. As youths succeeded boys and young men succeeded youths, the torches grew bigger and heavier and burnt more fiercely, and it grew so hot at our window that we took off our jackets. The bonfires outside the houses blazed furiously, the torches multiplied, and the whole village seemed alight.

'Why on earth don't the houses catch fire?' I asked the old *obe-san* of the family whose guests we were.

'The *kami* watch over us,' she replied. More literally what she said was: *kami-sama no o-gake de* ('it is thanks to the honourable shadow of the honourable gods').

The torch-bearers did not seem to take the least notice of the crowd. They climbed the slope shouldering their flaming burden, wearing fantastic clothing which would certainly have pleased the great leader of the *Tengu,* with his weakness for adolescents.[1] They were nearly naked, save for a short coloured coat (*haori*) and silk belt, from which there hung a kind of white string skirt (*sagari*). The belts were tied in a big, black, shiny bow immediately over their bare buttocks. No Paris choreographer ever devised a more diabolically striking costume.

Jane wanted an explanation of all this incendiary enthusiasm, but nobody seemed to have anything to suggest; all the local people had to say was that it was the custom; their grandfathers had done it, so they did it too. It did not, however, seem to me to require much anthro-

---

[1] In a famous *Nō* play the boy Yoshitsune, banished to Kurama by Taira Kiyomori, the slayer of his father, is taught swordmanship by the great leader of the *Kurama-tengu*, the Kurama demons in order to enable him one day to avenge his father. The great leader of the *Kurama-tengu*, when he first appears to the boy, makes him a declaration of love in terms of the loftiest poetry. Thus homosexuality has been idealized in Japan as well as in Greece.

pological acumen to see that it was a virility test, such as occurs in many societies, from the most primitive, such as that of the Piaroas in Venezuela, to the most advanced (*e.g.,* the student duels in Germany), to which the young are subjected before being accepted as grown up.

Notice how everyone claps when a particularly heavy torch is carried by,' I said to Jane. 'Look at the weight that that one's carrying!'

The torch-bearer in question rotated the cornucopia of fire on his shoulders, and wind scattered sparks in all directions. People shouted, girls clapped. Now the biggest torches of all were arriving, some of them so huge that two or three grown men were required to carry them, sweating and covered with sparks and ashes.

'How Giorgio would love to see all this!' Jane exclaimed. 'What a pity he isn't here! How much he would enjoy all this colour! He says you learn more about Japan on an occasion like this than from a hundred books. He's right, isn't he?'

We talked about the festival, we talked about Japan, we talked about Giorgio. It suddenly dawned on me that Jane had fallen in love with him, though perhaps she was not yet aware of it; she kept bringing the conversation back to him. She said that he was such a good man, had such a wonderful brain, was such a loving father. They had seen a lot of each other in Tokyo; he had taken her to museums, private art collections, popular festivals, gardens, temples, and to some of the most curious restaurants, the Momonji, for instance, where you could eat fox, badger, bear, and even giraffe or elephant, it appeared, if a zoo happened to be short of cash.

This discovery about Jane gave me great pleasure; it might be a way of extricating Giorgio from the complications of his present situation, trapped as he was between the tyranny of his housekeeper Abe-san and the despair of Tama-chan. But now it was midnight, and our conversation was interrupted; it was time to go up to the temple.

Walking along the fiery street with its throng of gay and happy people, every now and then we met men carrying *kemboko,* poles more than twenty feet long with swords shining at the top; I was told that they were gathering for the procession of palanquins a little later. Many houses were half-open, displaying the family treasures to passers-by; old samurai armour, swords, flowers artfully displayed, paintings,

specimens of calligraphy. Whenever we stopped to look the people of
the house invited us inside and offered us *saké*.

But here were the temple steps, mounting broad and steep up to
the entrance gate and the mountain beyond. Here the whole forest
seemed to be alight. The festival was at its height. Grown-ups had
started passing round bottles of *saké* 'to keep their strength up', and the
result was a glorious bacchanalia. People were shouting, singing, quarrel-
ling; bare shoulders, bare chests, bare buttocks, ecstatic faces, intoxicated
faces, faces in pain, faces of fawns and satyrs, seethed and swirled like
a sea in torment beneath showers of sparks that vanished in acrid smoke
floating away into the black tree-tops.

About one o'clock, in that unexpected manner so characteristic of
the Japanese, the dozens, nay hundreds, of torch-bearers who a moment
before had seemed a disorganized, shrieking mass of drunken pyro-
maniacs, formed up in two orderly rows on either side of the steps, and
at the gateway at the top there appeared the first of the two *mikoshi,*
gilded, lacquered, palanquins decorated with silken fabrics and golden
bells: they are enormously heavy, and are carried by about forty youths
—youths are always the most important feature of any Shinto religious
procession. The palanquins certainly contained the *shintai,* 'the divine
body', no doubt represented as usual by an ancient, shiny, metal mirror.
To keep time the youths shouted in unison *wasshoi! wasshoi! wasshoi!*

Our friend Harima-san succeeded in joining us in the mêlée, and
he explained to us many details of what was going on. In the distant
past what we were witnessing must have been a spectacular ceremony
of initiation of young men to full membership of the tribe. Girls and
young wives from Kurama and the neighbouring villages held long
ropes attached to the heavy palanquins, thus helping to keep them
balanced, by this useful service assuring themselves of happy childbirth
when the occasion arose. Youths of a certain age, however, were picked
up bodily by their companions, tilted backward and carried with their
legs apart to the bottom of the steps, where they took first place in the
procession that accompanied each palanquin. This rite was known as
choppen, a word of unknown origin. 'The reason for this curious custom
is not understood,' Harima said. I replied that it seemed pretty obvious
to me. Nowadays everyone wore *fundoshi,* a strip of white material
gathered round the lower part of the body and sides like a big bikini,

but in the old days they would all have been naked. The *choppen* rite was a public demonstration of sexual maturity. Harima seemed rather shocked by this suggestion, though it seemed natural enough to Jane. An old man with whom we struck up an acquaintance added some corroborative details; he said that a boy who had not been subjected to the *choppen* ceremony was, as it were, not a man. At one time he might not have been able to marry.

The *mikoshi* passed through the sea of yelling people, and we went down the steps again, which were suddenly almost deserted; the crowd had left behind a trail of smoke and smouldering embers; here and there a branch of a tree was still alight. The old man—with his magnificent head he looked just like a wise man of the woods—accompanied us and told us many things. It seemed that those responsible for organizing the festival (the *yakutsuki*) were the four leaders of the *uji*—clans, groups of related families—under the guidance of a *dairyō*. The ceremonies lasted for several days; the fire festival was only a climax; the preparations and the concluding rites were just as important, though less spectacular. Finally, all the participants took home a little *tai-matsu*. If things went wrong during the course of the year, they burnt them to exorcize the evil.

When we got back to the village we found that the family who had been our hosts had prepared *futon* for us in two rooms. It was late, they said, and we could do with some sleep; in fact the first light was appearing in the sky.

One of the great advantages of Japanese domestic arrangements is that it is always possible to put up a large number of people at short notice without inconvenience. There being no beds, and rooms being always bare of furniture and other encumbrances, all that is necessary is to produce the required number of *futon* from the capacious wall cupboards. It should be added that the great personal cleanliness of the Japanese, and their slight glandular secretions (a characteristic common to the whole of the Mongol family), mean that there is nothing disagreeable about using bedclothes which have been used by others.

We men were put in a room where we could hear the rushing waters of the stream. Some hold that the sound of water keeps you awake, others that it sends you to sleep. The latter must be right, because it was midday before we awoke.

Hanase: Kitchen Temple

Instead of returning to Kyoto we decided to go on to Hanase, a tiny mountain village on the other side of a pass nearly 2,500 feet high, to take the opportunity of filming some scenes of Japanese country life; the gathering of the rice, for instance, which down in the plain was nearly over.

The immediate surroundings of Kyoto are wild and uninhabited, and of a primordial beauty, and this impression is increased towards sunset. We climbed a long, narrow, wooded valley, full of *sugi* (cypresses), along a road that ended by degenerating into a narrow track, winding its way between rocks, along streams, past the sites of landslides. When we met a lorry loaded with stones, long and complicated manœuvres were required to pass. The ascent grew steeper, the scenery more Alpine; the car developed strange noises, and the water in the radiator boiled. At last we reached the top of the pass and began the descent. Forests stretched as far as the eye could see; the luminous evergreen of the pines, and the autumn tints of the deciduous trees.

After two or three miles the valley broadened, the forest opened out, the landscape grew gentler, and we reached the first houses of Hanase, with their ancient roofs of grass and straw. We were barely an hour from Kyoto, but we might have been in a valley in another world; it was hardly possible to imagine a more perfect retreat.

During the afternoon I was able to shoot some of the scenes I wanted, particularly the gathering of the rice. Making a documentary in Japan is always a pleasure; it is sufficient to have some knowledge of the language and to be able to explain what you want, and everyone responds willingly, quickly, and intelligently. Only twice in Japan have I met with refusals, and both, though firm, were polite. The first occasion was at Nagasaki, where an old woman, taking her grandson to present him to the local Shinto shrine,[1] declined to be filmed; the second was a fisherman at Akase, near Kobe. I had serious difficulties only with women pearl gatherers and with some *pam-pam* near allied military camps, but these were special cases.

We had intended to return to Kyoto the same evening, but were so enchanted by the local inn and the peasants' hospitality that we decided to stay overnight. 'Inn' is scarcely the right word; the place was

[1] After childbearing the mother is regarded as impure, and therefore cannot do this.

an old country cottage with a big thatched roof, perhaps slightly bigger than its neighbours; the owner, who cultivated his own little plot, had a few extra rooms which were at the disposal of travellers.

There was a magnificent, huge, irregular-shaped kitchen, in the dark, mysterious recesses of which there gleamed enormous cupboards, the wood darkened by many generations of smoke and scrubbed clean by many generations of housewives; the battery of black, polished, spotlessly clean *kama* (pots for cooking rice) stretched across a good part of the room like the side of a battleship; they cast blue reflections of the light that came in through the doors and little windows, and were decorated with fresh branches of *sakagi* in honour of the *kami* protector of the hearth, known locally as Sambō-san ('Mr. Three Directions' *i.e.*, 'Mr. Looking in Three Directions'), who is popularly represented with three heads. Here the kitchen was really the centre of life. The more spacious area where the work was done, the fire was lit, water was carried, and the washing-up was done, was of carefully beaten earth, and it was permissible to walk there in *geta* (wooden sandals), as if it were outside, but in the raised part, with its *tatami* and shining wooden tables, your shoes must be removed; here you squatted round a small, open fire (*irori, see* drawing on page 278), used to boil the water for tea, or to warm yourself. High overhead, rafters, encrusted with soot—they were tree-trunks taken from the forest centuries ago and squared with the axe—formed an irregular pattern. A thin ribbon of smoke vanished into the dark (Photographs 69, 70).

When we returned at sunset the kitchen was humming with women and girls preparing the dinner, among clouds of steam from the *kama* in which the rice was cooking. There were a number of guests besides ourselves—men helping with the rice harvest, as well as thatchers who had come to mend the village roofs; the latter, as usual, came from the distant island of Shikoku ('Of the Four Provinces'). I was reminded of the Fratta kitchen described by Ippolito Nievo at the beginning of his *Confessions*. But one big difference was that we had had a hot bath, which I think must have been a rare event in the eighteenth-century Venetian countryside. Finally, feeling rested and relaxed, our appetites pleasingly stimulated, our bodies wrapped in the soft warmth of *tanzon,* a kind of padded kimono-dressing-gown, we responded with enthusiasm to the information that dinner was ready.

Our host wanted us to dine in our rooms, as is the custom in Japan, but Jane and I insisted on eating in the kitchen. 'It's like dining in hall at Christchurch, Oxford,' Jane insisted. We succeeded eventually in overcoming the landlady's resistance, sat down by the *irori*, and voraciously attacked our rice, seaweed, and fish straight from the mountain stream.

Afterwards we remained for a long time talking round the fire. Peasants from neighbouring houses, helpers who had come to give a hand, women who had finished their work, came in and joined the circle, partly drawn by curiosity to see the foreigners, who are rare in these parts. Meanwhile night descended over the valley, and during pauses in the talk you could hear the wind in the rafters, and outside the occasional cry of a distant bird.

Fujii, our host, a broad-shouldered man of about fifty with greying temples and good, strong hands, which were continually engaged in refilling his tiny pipe, told us that there were bears in the mountains, particularly in the Kamikuroda direction. Occasionally they killed a few chickens, but they spent most of their time climbing trees and eating *kaki*; they were very greedy.

His son, a student at the Buddhist Otani University at Kyoto, who had come home to help with the rice harvest, said that there were also many badgers and foxes, and even stags.

His father said that this was the stags' mating season. Hadn't we heard them? They kept calling '*Kaero, kaero*' (We're coming back! we're coming back!) They called out once for each branch of their horns; the oldest had three branches on their horns.

A peasant known as Chubé (nearly all of them were known by nicknames, as there were only two surnames, Fujii and Monobe, in the village) said he had heard that if the stags increased the boars diminished, and *vice versa*.

'Where I live,' my friend Uriu remarked, 'they say that if money increases honest women diminish, and *vice versa*.'

Some laughed, but others thought the remark excessively daring. The *hyotan* was passed round again, and everyone took a sip of *saké*.

A man known by the name of Oke-ya remarked, *à propos* of money, that thirty years before a golden statuette had been found on the site of a former temple, the Amida-ji, on a neighbouring mountain. Perhaps more might be found if the place were searched thoroughly.

Fujii, speaking with special emphasis, as if his words had some special reference to somebody present, said that at the time someone had proposed selling the golden statuette, but it had been decided instead to present it to the local temple, where it was now put on view three times a year: on the first day of the tiger in January, on May 20, the anniversary of the day when it was found, and at the time of the summer festivals.

An old man who had been silently watching us for a long time said, *à propos* of temples, that when he was a boy heads of families had used to gather round a table on which a straw snake was put; each one of them, armed with a new wooden stick, then 'killed the snake' in turn. Positions round the table were fixed by immemorial tradition. Nobody remembered these things any longer. Who knew why they had done them?

The conversation moved further and further away from the earth and became more fantastic. It turned, among other things, to *o-bake* (honourable ghosts), who played with foxes and badgers which possessed supernatural powers and turned into beautiful women, with whom men fell desperately in love. It was late indeed when, having got rather cold and very sleepy, and with slight shivers going up and down our spines, we went up to our rooms.

We were just creeping under our *futon*—Uriu and I in one room, Jane in another—when the silence of the night was broken by the sound of a car drawing up outside. It was Giorgio. We hurried down to greet him. He had gone to Kyoto on business, and had called at our hotel and found out where we had gone.

Jane made her appearance. 'Oh, Giorgio, what a wonderful surprise!'

Giorgio was in better form than I had seen him for a long time. He wanted us all to go for a walk in the moonlight. Uriu and I looked at each other; we were much too tired. Giorgio's insistence on our coming too grew weaker and weaker, and we went back to bed, while the moonlight flooded the mountains, and the stags in the distance called '*kaero, kaero*', and the badgers meditated strange transformations, and ancient golden statues gleamed mysteriously in the forest.

The Kamakura period (1185–1333) ended with one of the ferocious, blood-thirsty, and heroic episodes so characteristic of Japanese history. I shall not relate here the numerous economic, social, and political causes which led to the decline and fall of the government of the *shikken* of the Hōjō family, which lasted for more than a century. But, when the Emperor Go-Daigo, a man of great ambition and personal courage, mounted the throne and decided to do away with the delegation of powers and restore direct imperial rule, he did not find it excessively difficult to gather forces sufficient to destroy Kamakura. The city fell on July 5, 1333, after a desperate struggle; Takatoki, the last of the Hōjō *shikken*, and 800 followers and members of his household committed *seppuku* in the cemetery of a temple after drinking the three farewell cups of *saké* required by etiquette.

The adventures and misadventures of this bold Emperor, who had dreamt of governing the countries as in the old days, through the *kuge* (court nobles), and of seeing it administered by the decrees of the *buke* (military nobles) were most romantic. Before he overthrew Kamakura he had been defeated, deposed, and exiled to the island of Oki, from which he escaped in the best film style; he completed part of his journey in a palanquin reserved for ladies of the court, and another part hidden under a load of seaweed in a fishing-boat. After two years during which he tried to re-establish an imperial government centred on Kyoto, he was defeated in 1335 by the treachery, strength, and the wiles of Ashikaga Takauji, the commander who had defeated the Hōjō of Kamakura on his behalf.

Between then and the beginning of the Tokugawa ascendancy in the seventeenth century war and disorder prevailed. The Ashikaga shoguns took the place of the Hōjō *shikken* as the *de facto* rulers of Japan, but, except for short periods, disorder prevailed and their power was limited or violently opposed. From 1336 to 1392 two rival branches of the imperial family, the northern, with its capital at Kyoto, and the southern, established in the Yoshino mountains, contested the succession; victory finally went to the southern branch.[1] Battles were fought round the capital and in the capital itself. In the disastrous Onin war (1467–1477)

[1] This period is known as the Namboku-chō.

Kyoto was reduced to a heap of smoking ruins. The Imperial House was reduced to incredible straits; one emperor was reduced to selling his autograph on the public highway. Brigandage prevailed in the interior and piracy along the coast. The only law was that of the jungle, and the only justice that of the sword.

Nevertheless these were centuries of great, if disorderly, vitality and, while everything seemed to be collapsing into chaos, new heights were reached in the arts and the refinements of civilized living. Moreover, the confusion of events concealed the consolidation of a true feudal system. The small, tax-free holdings *(shoen)*, which had constituted the economic foundation of the warrior class, were gradually consolidated into larger groupings, and there started to emerge the figure of the *daimyo* (literally 'big name'), who was a true feudal lord. The population increased steadily. In the eleventh century it was between four to five millions; in the late sixteenth century it was between fifteen to twenty millions.[1] In every branch of technique important progress was made. In a sheltered bay not far from Kyoto a flourishing centre of trade, manufacture, and finance arose, first at Sakai, then at Osaka, a true free city outside the feudal domains, similar in many respects to a western mediaeval commune. 'Japan entered the feudal period in the twelfth century, a small, weak, economically backward land on the fringes of the civilized world. It emerged in the sixteenth century from a prolonged period of feudal anarchy, an economically advanced nation, able, in many ways, to compete on terms of equality with the newly encountered peoples of Europe and even with the Chinese.'[2]

The second half of the sixteenth century, the period in which three great men, Oda Nobunaga (1534–1582), Toyotomi Hideyoshi (1536–1598), and Tokugawa Iyeyasu (1542–1616), reunited Japan and laid the foundations of the modern state, had many interesting characteristics, with which we shall deal later. Here I shall mention two individuals, Yoshimitsu (1358–1408) and Yoshimasa (1435–1490), the third and fourth shoguns of the Ashikaga dynasty, in whom both the lights and shadows of those agitated times are admirably summed up.

As enlightened patrons of the arts the Ashikaga have several times been compared to the Medici, but the comparison is undoubtedly to

[1] *See* M. REQUIEN, *Le Problème de la Population au Japan*, Tokyo, 1934.
[2] E. O. REISCHAUER, *Japan Past and Present*, New York, 1953, p. 76.

the advantage of the latter. The Medici made Tuscany almost out of nothing and turned it into one of the great centres of European civilization; the Ashikaga did little to pacify Japan; they found it devastated, and that is how they left it. They were, however, great patrons of the arts, and much is owed to them.

With Yoshimitsu the age of samurai austerity ended. For too long the warriors, who felt themselves to be superior in everything, had lived in a state of uncomfortable inferiority in relation to the court nobles, whom they regarded as soft and effeminate, but envied for their capacity to distinguish a T'ang vase from a Sung, a good poem from an imitation, genuine good manners from false. Yoshimitsu became hereditary shogun when he was barely nine years old. Before retiring at the age of forty he surrounded himself with unheard-of splendour while his country was torn by war, and he retired to a delightful pavilion, half-sacred and half-profane, in which he lived a life half-sacred and half-profane. The Golden Pavilion (Kinkaku) survived as one of the most precious architectural relics of the period until 1950, when it was destroyed in a few moments by the inevitable Japanese fire.

Yoshimasa, his grandson, more or less repeated his grandfather's career. As so happens in such cases, the greater the ruin and devastation in the outer world, the more subtle and imaginative became the aesthetic refinements of the elect. He, too, became shogun in boyhood and retired in his forties; and for another sixteen years lived the life of a supreme connoisseur of the arts in a villa he built at the foot of the Eastern Mount, called the Silver Pavilion (Ginkaku).

Today I visited the Ginkaku-ji with Midori, a westernized young relative of a friend of mine; she appeared punctually at eight o'clock at the Silver Water on a bicycle, in white tennis shoes, light blue jeans, and an open-necked red blouse. A little later she was joined by a boy of about the same age, also on a bicycle and wearing jeans and a white baseball-player's cap.

'This is Nishimura-san,' Midori said, introducing her companion with a slight blush. 'I hope you don't mind if he comes with us. He wants to learn how to use a film camera. He speaks English, don't you, Nicky-chan? Let Maraini-san hear how well you speak English!'

Nicky's English was an incomprehensible pseudo-American jargon. He tried to laugh as Americans laugh, and to slap people on the back with American heartiness. The trouble with these Japanese boys is that they do not realize that the things which they believe to be western and non-traditional are in fact highly traditional. An American really is cordial, but the Nickies, the Johnnies, the Sammies succeed only in being barbarous.

The weather had changed suddenly, as it so often does in Japan. A ceiling of high haze obscured the sun, which was perceptible only as a shapeless blaze of light. We climbed to the temple along a lane flanked by houses and gardens. I went on ahead with my two assistants, and the revolutionary young couple followed us, chattering. I was not too pleased at their company; at the temple they would certainly be looked at askance. I heard Nicky calling the girl 'Middy' (short for Midori?). They did not say *hai* (yes) to each other, but *okay*. Did they know how often in the course of the centuries their ancestors had done the same sort of thing? At Asuka in the sixth century they had aped the Koreans, at Nara in the eighth century they had aped the Chinese, at Nagasaki in the sixteenth century they had aped the Portuguese. Documents, screens, paintings, bear witness to their faithfulness to the *dernier cri* from Lisbon, the latest in lace collars or silk breeches. At Yedo in the nineteenth century it was the thing to be a *boulevardier*, a dandy. Now it is the turn of the United States. Fifty years ago Japanese students sang a song the refrain of which was '*dekansho, dekansho*' ('Descartes, Kant, Schopenhauer'); now they prefer *chiiku dansu* ('dancing cheek to cheek'). Perhaps it should not be taken too seriously. The *mobo* (modern boy) and *moga* (modern girl) of the Ginza of twenty years ago have utterly vanished, and no doubt the *tayo-zoku* ('race of the sun') will go the same way.

The Silver Pavilion was near the house where we lived before the war. We often used to visit it, and had made friends with the family that looked after the temple and the garden, which consisted of three brothers and a sister. The eldest brother was what is known as a *namagusu bozu*, a priest who has a weakness for the pleasures of *samsara*, wine and women; the second was a famous master of archery; the third, the most intelligent and best educated member of the family, spoke excellent English and was the first friend we made at Kyoto; alas, he died a few years ago. Who knew whether the family was still there, or would remember us? I suddenly felt very old—like Urashima Taro, the fisherman who followed the daughter of the sea king down into his realm of

seaweed. One day he had an irresistible desire to see his family and his
native village again, but when he got there nobody recognized him, all
his relatives and friends were dead, and in the temple he saw his own
memorial tablet saying that he had been lost at sea. He thought he had
been away for three years; he had been away for three centuries.

'*Ará! Fuosko-san desu-ka?*' They spotted me even before I reached the
doorstep. Unlike Urashima Taro, I thought I had been away for fifteen
years, but I might have been away for only fifteen minutes. Even Nicky
and Middy, who had probably never before set foot in such traditionally
Japanese surroundings, were drawn into the warmth of the welcome.

Meanwhile the sky had darkened; the mother-of-pearl haze had
turned to grey, and it seemed advisable to go and look at the garden
now, before it started to rain. Animated conversation was in progress;
the men were talking about cameras (the priest had a magnificent
Nikon, with the latest in wide-aperture lenses), and the women were
chattering gaily, with gusts of loud laughter. Middy was telling the
priest's wife her whole family history, going back to the fifth generation.

I took advantage of the opportunity to slip away into the garden.
It was a wonderful moment. The sky was threatening; there was not
a breath of wind. The light came at surface level from the edges of the
sky and left no shadow; the colours were unusually vivid. In the deep
silence a frog jumped crazily in the irregular little lake, subtly emphasizing all sorts of things. I thought of the lines of Bashō:

> *Furu-ike ya*   ⎫   The ancient pond! A frog plunged . . .
> *Kawazu tobikomu*   ⎬   The sound of the water!
> *Mizu no oto*   ⎭

The pond is small, even tiny, but it offers such a variety of views
that it ends by seeming huge. It is cut up into arms, bays, recesses
between pine-covered rocks; some table-sized islands are joined to the
bank by bridges of rough, flat pieces of rock. These rocks were presented
to Yoshimasa by the leading *daimyo* of his day; in each case the name of
the giver appears on a small wooden board. This detracts somewhat
from the naturalness of the scene but, apart from this trifling detail, the
supreme artistry with which the garden was conceived and executed,
and is still maintained, lies in the fact that the artistry is altogether

concealed.[1] You might, while on a mountain excursion, have suddenly come upon an enchanted valley in which rocks, stones, and trees had been gathered together in an arrangement of intense significance. No single connecting thread runs through it all; each stone and tree-trunk has its own meaning; mosses, ferns, pine-needles do not just fill space, they infuse it with life. Water, the most homogeneous of the elements employed, is used to frame the masses; its subtle fingers playfully insinuate transparencies and reflections between stone and grass.

We are at the opposite pole from the geometrical Italian-style garden. The basis of the latter is the pattern, the intellectual rhythm of lines, surfaces, relationships—homage to Euclid, in fact; matter, however skilfully it may be employed to create pleasing effects of colour, light, shape, contrast, is essentially a space-filling material. Flowers are allowed only in beds, gravel only on paths, trees and shrubs only in the space allotted to them. All this is artifice of the first degree, man imposing his law on matter, which at bottom he despises, in honour of what he values most—that is to say, his own thought. In the eastern garden, on the other hand, though it is true that artifice is pushed much further, it is artifice of the second degree. By it nature is twice subdued, first by the imposition of man's will, and then by its total concealment. This twofold process closes the cycle; the homage is not to Euclid, but to life. No external, abstract pattern is imposed on the plot and the things that are destined to fill it; instead the latter are dynamic nuclei which determine and modify the space around them—exactly as the heavenly bodies do, according to modern physics. The western garden is the child of the intellect, the eastern garden is the child of love. The former is hierarchical—man, animals, statues, plants, earth, and water, each in its place. The eastern garden is man-leaf, sun-joy, water-thought.

Walking along the path that winds its way irregularly and inconspicuously about the place, as if it desired to hide itself for fear of spoiling the magic, is like unwinding one of those scrolls (emakimono) of the Ashikaga period on which there are drawn rocks, views of rivers and lakes, trees battered by storms, mountain-tops lost in the clouds; every now and then a tiny human figure is to be made out, a fisherman drawing in his nets, a pilgrim, a slightly crazy old poet who has detected the

[1] According to some it is the work of Sōami (1472–1523); others hold it to be that of Zeami (or Senami). See J. HARADA, The Gardens of Japan, London, 1928.

infinite in a blade of grass; or sometimes a temple or place of meditation, or a hut almost hidden in the forest.

But here is a real pavilion beside a real pond; it reveals itself gradually as you make your way along the little path. This is the famous Silver Pavilion (Ginkaku) built by Yoshimasu in 1483, when he handed over the cares of government to his son Yoshihisa and determined to create for himself an environment of the most perfect beauty in accordance with Zen teachings. The pavilion was to have been covered in silver (for the moon), but this was not done, and the building has remained unadorned throughout the centuries, its bare timbers gnarled by time and the weather. There is no doubt that Yoshimasa desired to emulate his grandfather Yoshimitsu, who built the Golden Pavilion in 1397, but everything here is smaller, more subtle, more perfect. It is easy to detect that it was a century of philosophical depth, of search and inquiry in every field of aesthetics which had become an ingrained habit of mind. The pavilion is a small, two-storey structure of Franciscan simplicity, built of wood and paper. Its beauty lies in its perfect proportions, its lightness, the rhythm of the vertical lines which provide a subtle counterpoint to the gentle curve of the roofs. The ground floor is in Japanese style, and the first floor contains many Chinese elements. But the whole is the work of such a sure eye that the different elements are not evident; in order to discern them stylistic analysis is required.

It was in this garden and temple, and its other pavilions—all of them exceedingly modest and simple—where the priest and his family now live with some acolytes—that Yoshimasa spent the second part of his life in company with the great artists of his time, pursuing its austere aesthetic ideals. The influence of the ideas which then came to fruition survived through the centuries and still permeate Japanese life; moreover, there are signs that they may now be going to enjoy a new lease of life on a wider scale outside Japan, in Europe and America. Many of the most acclaimed novelties in architecture, furnishing, style of life, in the last analysis date back to Yoshimasa and his household, and the nights they spent in meditation in their wooden temples, surrounded by objects made of straw, lacquer, paper, and porcelain, in the metaphysical intoxication of tea-drinking.

The role of grand master of aesthetics at the court of Yoshimasa was played by the three Ami, grandfather, father, and son: Nōami

(1397–1494), Geiami (1431–1485), and Sōami (1472–1523). With the aid of these brilliant masters of the Zen philosophy, who brought to aesthetic maturity what was implicit in the teachings of the patriarchs, Yoshimasa collected paintings of the Sung dynasty in black and white, porcelain, earthenware, masterpieces of calligraphy, objects of all sorts of the highest value to be found in the east. Nōami and his descendants acted as arbiters in this supreme court of aesthetic judgment. Everything was rejected that smacked, not just of vulgarity, but of a too obvious display even of deep and genuine feeling. The aim was only to suggest, to strike a spark which would cause the mind to take a leap into the infinite.

Today there were few visitors to the place; I came across an old couple reverently admiring the garden, holding a silent child by the hand, walking round the strange heap of white gravel, shaped like a little Mount Fuji, near the entrance. The background to the garden is provided by the Eastern Hills, the densely wooded flanks of which mount abruptly behind it. I remember coming here many years ago on the occasion of the September full moon; our friends at the temple had invited us, together with some Japanese and foreign acquaintances. The pavilion was open for the occasion, as perhaps happened in the time of Yoshimasa himself; the sliding partitions (amado, fusuma, and shōji) had been removed, and the moonlight flooded the tatami, the mats, on which we squatted at what was no doubt the very spot where Yoshimasa and his friends gathered to compose poetry and listen to the flute. The conversation, however, turned to a topic very different from what tradition would have required in such a place on such an occasion.

A Protestant missionary whose name I forget remarked that for him the whole thing was spoilt by the thought that Yoshimasa spent his time enjoying himself here while people were being killed by bandits in the streets of Kyoto or dying of hunger or disease.

This led to a lively argument, in I do not know how many languages. The poor Japanese, who had come here to enjoy the moon and the garden, must have said to themselves: Just listen to these foreigners, at it again as usual! It was easy enough to make a strong case against Yoshimasa; he was shogun during one of the most disastrous periods of Japanese history. Not only was the whole country in disorder, but in the so-called Onin civil war (1467–1477) fighting extended to the capital itself. 'When at length, in 1477, the rival forces were withdrawn, the city presented a picture of almost complete desolation';[1] the population had been reduced from more than half a million to about forty thousand, and everyone, from the Emperor downwards, camped as best he could among the ruins. The chronicles of the time speak of nothing but of want, pestilence, and revolt. Destitute samurai borrowed from money-lenders and subsequently had the debt cancelled by complacent edicts of the shogun called *tokusei-ryo*. Yoshimasa at one time issued nine of these in a month,[2] thus creating more discontent and new causes of disorder. Meanwhile he held expensive receptions to admire the cherry-blossom or watch open-air dancing, and built sumptuous villas for his mother and for his wife, Tomi, who made or unmade laws at her pleasure. It was only too easy to make out a devastating case against Yoshimasa, and we all felt slightly guilty that evening, as if we in some way had contributed to neglecting the sufferings of the unfortunate inhabitants of Kyoto of four centuries ago.

But good and evil are so inextricably mixed in human affairs that I doubt whether I should be so hard on Yoshimasa today. There is no denying that he was an appallingly bad shogun, but he did not indulge in the wild and useless extravagances of which there are so many instances among the rulers of every country. Thanks to his passion for beauty, incomparable treasures of the Chinese Sung period (tenth to thirteenth centuries) have come down to us, and much of what is most delightful in Japanese life at the present day can be traced back to him. It was thus with a feeling of gratitude that I slowly retraced my steps to the Tokyu-do, the principal temple.

I was, however, distracted from this, and from all other possible thought, by the strident tones of a loudspeaker giving in hoarse, official-style Japanese a long, detailed description of the beauties and history of the place; a swarm of school children came noisily pouring in and raising the dust. The guardians of the temple had evidently grown tired of conducted tours; recording tape and loudspeakers were obviously ideal for the job, so why not make use of them?

On the *engawa* (veranda) I found Middy sitting with Nicky. They looked bored.

[1] R. A. B. PONSONBY-FANE, *Kyoto*, Hongkong, 1931, p. 149.
[2] N. KONRAD, *Breve Storia del Giappone Politico-Sociale*, Bari, 1936, p. 60.

'*Iya da wa!*' Middy exclaimed. She had decided that the guardians of the temple were an insufferable lot of boring old chatterboxes. Everybody was alike at Kyoto. What an intolerable place! When was I going to start shooting the film? She liked Kobe, where everything was *modan,* there were plenty of cinemas, and you could buy nylons from the Americans; sometimes they even gave them away. She hated Kyoto, which was a cheesy old place. Why did I waste so much of my time here?

One of the temple brothers appeared and summoned me with a smile, and I left Middy and Nicky to their nervous irritation. I asked the priest to switch off the loudspeaker, but he did not seem to see why. If I really disliked it, he would certainly switch it off, but it was the latest invention, it enabled everyone to hear distinctly, and was better than a guide, because it never made mistakes. When the blessed silence returned I was led into the famous tea-room, the prototype of all such places throughout Japan. I saw that everything was ready for a short and simple tea ceremony. The peace and tranquillity here seemed a thousand miles from the din which had descended on the garden outside. We took our places, kneeling and motionless, while the master with ritual gestures prepared the simple things that serve to boil the water and mix the fine green powder in the small, plain, carefully selected earthenware cups.

Tea Ceremony

Since the earliest times tea has been used by Buddhist monks to keep their minds alert during the long hours of meditation. Gradually the way of preparing and sipping it became a ritualized sequence of movements, a formal dance of significant gestures, designed to purge the mind of irrelevancies or mere petty or personal concerns and establish a state of tranquil, alert receptivity, free of all contingent things. It is a state of mind closely akin to that aimed at by monastic discipline, the discipline of meditative yoga, and the ancients considered it the proper state of mind in which to examine a painting, an old vase, a rare object brought back by a friend from a long journey. Thus, in the framework of the Zen philosophy, there was born the fascinating figure of the *cha-jin* (teamaster), who was monk, thinker, artist, critic, craftsman, judge or creator or missionary of beauty. The Japanese in fact speak of the *cha-do,* 'the way of tea', thus returning to the fundamental concept of path, way, *tao, michi,* and investing tea-drinking with a high philosophic dignity.

In the general striving for aesthetic perfection everything connected with the rite was the object of extreme care. The room, for example, had to be small, of cell-like simplicity and rustic serenity, so that on entering it an immediate sense of purification should be felt, as was the case in the room in which I was then sitting. I looked round; nothing was to be seen but wood, straw, the dry earth of the wall, irregular and pleasing to the touch. I reflected that in this room Yoshimasa, Nōami, Sōami, Shūkō, Shūbun, and many other explorers of virgin aesthetic territory used to meet.

This room was the starting-point of a branch of architecture, that of the tea pavilion, the canons of which spread to Japanese domestic architecture and today exercise a subtle influence on the whole world through Frank Lloyd Wright and other leading architects. This room was of the archaic type, and formed part of the house, the temple-villa; later, in the sixteenth century, particularly under the influence of Sen no Rikyu (1518–1591), that great master of the tea ceremony and all that went with it, separate huts were built with their own tiny garden. These rustic refuges, the purpose of which was the elevation of the mind by the contemplation of beauty, were called *sukiya;* they were approached by a narrow garden path, scattered with big stones eroded by time, which served to mark it off from the outside world (Photograph 93). In its classic form this modest building includes a small waiting-room *(machiai);* another small room, which might be called the pantry *(mizuya);* and finally the tea-room proper—or would it be better to call it tea-chapel? Words, as usual, fail when you try to apply them to the things of another civilization; in the face of oriental phenomena western words are like inch and yard rules set to measure metres and centimetres; eastern words are of course just as inadequate to describe western phenomena.

Sukiya, as Okakura explains in his colourful manner, was originally written with two characters which can be translated Abode of Fantasy. This implies that it is a highly personal thing, subtly expressing the personality of its designer. Another important thing to note is that it is not intended to be permanent; it is not made for posterity. Just as the body, according to Buddhist teaching, is a mere clothing, a shell, a temporary dwelling, so is the hut a fleeting, transitory thing, a resting-place for a night or a brief morning. The perishability of all things is suggested by the thatched roof; the fragility of life by the slender pillars; lightness by the bamboo support; and the use of commonplace materials testifies to non-involvement, non-attachment.[1]

Chajin, the tea masters of later generations, also used other combinations of ideograms to write *sukiya,* for instance Abode of the Void, or Abode of the Asymmetrical. 'Abode of the Void', besides the obvious reference to Buddhist metaphysics, implies an important aesthetic principle: that the pavilion must be only itself. When guests are not expected it must remain pure form, rigorously bare, scrupulously clean. The few things required to adorn it are arranged by the owner *ad hoc,* according to the occasion and the pattern that he will have in his mind to draw attention to some event, to suggest a state of mind or to evoke a person's memory, or to establish a relationship. The hut is, so to speak, a musical instrument; the manner in which it is furnished on any particular occasion is the music. This may be in honour of friendship, love, reverence, joy, even hatred or contempt. These things can be expressed in words, notes, rhythm, and tones; they can also be expressed in pictures, flowers, things, odours. The principle at work here is totally different, not only from that of the west, but I imagine from that of all other civilizations, under whose aesthetic dictates 'an interior permanently filled with a vast array of pictures, statuary and bric-à-brac gives the impression of mere vulgar display of riches.'[2]

One of the results of this was that until very recent times the idea of a museum or art gallery was completely alien to the Japanese mentality. The idea of a collection of works of art accessible to one or a thousand visitors is—like that of a panorama—typically western. In the east the communion between work of art and connoisseur is profoundly individual, an art in itself. The owner likes to keep his precious things hidden in his *kura* (store-room), and to produce them for the delectation of his friends one at a time, as one might a special bottle of old wine. Nowadays there are good museums at Tokyo, Nara, and Kyoto, but it is still difficult to gain an adequate idea of certain periods in the history of

[1] To paraphrase K. Okakura, *The Book of Tea,* New York, 1906.
[2] K. Okakura.

Japanese art because many important works are in inaccessible private collections.

Incidentally, it should be noted that the very idea of a history of art, with its objective, rigid, hierarchical evaluations, its kings, barons, and plebs among artists, is an entirely western phenomenon, typical of our dualist universe, which is as full of pigeon-holes and filing cabinets as a big business office. Orientals approach a work of art much more instinctually, much less with their intellect and their culture behind them, and open their whole personality to it. What counts with them is the subjective impact, the spark that is struck at the moment of integration, which is always new, always different, always unpredictable. They know that they are perhaps less endowed with culture, but they feel that they are subtly closer to life. From this point of view museums and galleries and histories of art have no more than a practical value, similar to that of a railway time-table.

But to return to the *sukiya*. 'Abode of the Asymmetrical' brings us back to the heart of Zen. Symmetry suggests completeness, the aping of an abstract and artificial perfection, an outward, unreal pattern, and Zen refuses to have anything to do with it; it desires to plunge directly into the world of becoming, into the palpitating, living world, into the life-blood which animates stars, plants, and men. It therefore prefers the asymmetrical, which it equates with the dynamic. Symmetry is repetitive, mechanical; asymmetry may sometimes yield a flash of intuition of the truth. Symmetry imposes an abstract pattern on things; in asymmetry things impose their own life on patterns. An important corollary of this is that in the decoration of the *sukiya* the artistic representation of the human form is excluded. Man is already in the room, whether as host or guest, and for him to be represented there in painting or sculpture would be repetitive, 'symmetrical', unnecessary, and therefore excessive. In this respect Zen teaching had a profound effect on nearly the whole of the art of eastern Asia. Greek art, and European art which is derived from it, see the universe in man; here man is seen in the universe.

The tea masters paid the same meticulous care to the painting, the arrangement of the flowers, the burning of incense, the choice of utensils, teapot, cups, bamboo mixers, the stylization of every gesture in the accompanying rites, as they paid to the place where the ceremony took place. The clothing worn, the style of speech used, and even the poetry that might be composed or recited, all claimed their attention. Once the great principles of Zen were accepted, its influence extended to most aspects of everyday life. Here I shall briefly refer to three spheres in which Zen influence was particularly profound, namely, painting, flowers, and poetry.

In painting Zen had inspired the great Chinese masters of the Sung period (960–1279), leading to a technique of extreme simplicity, that of black ink on white paper (*sumi-e*) and a rigorous purity of line; the aim was to surprise the essence of the world with the simplest means. Had it not served to interpret an elegiac and romantic vision of life, this would have been a hard path indeed. The object was to seize the ultimate essence of rock, water, tree, and flower. But it is not analytic passion, but a spirit of warm brotherhood, that guides the artist's hands; there is nearly always a little temple, a distant fisherman, a meditating sage, to tell us how the vast white voids pregnant with space are to be understood. When Zen was introduced into Japan this kind of painting came with it, and it was taken up, developed, perfected by an extraordinary series of artists, many of whom formed part of Yoshimasa's circle. Grousset says:

> 'The true heirs of the Chinese Sung masters, those who continued, developed, surpassed their work and their formulas, are not the landscapists of the Chinese Ming dynasty (1368–1644), who were pedestrian artists without originality, but the Japanese landscapists of the temper of Jasoku, Sesshu, Sōami.'[1]

This applies above all to Sesshu (1420–1506), whom Grousset calls one of the most vigorous landscapists of all time. The trees howling in the storm born of the imperious and disdainful strokes of his brush are not just seen with the eye, but felt with the fingers, with the cold of winter in the blood, with the anguish of one who has been a tree through successive incarnations and knows all that is to be known about trees. The sea, the oldest thing in the world, strikes the rocks which bar its way with a fury that can have been felt only by one who has been a wave; his mountains writhe like giants in torment, his boats have

[1] R. GROUSSET, *Les Civilisations de l'Orient*, Vol. IV, *Le Japon*, Paris, 1930, p. 178.

a heart-rending fragility; and he does all this with a brush dipped in ink, with no recourse to formulas, decoration, embellishments, compromises. Grousset says of Sesshu: 'Chinese art, even among the great, was a school art, a collective religion. Japanese art, even in the joint work of a whole school, impatiently betrays the artist's irreducible personality.' In Sesshu you feel the personality of a *kamikaze* directed, not to the madness of destruction, but to the penetration of the ultimate secret of things.

This impassioned discipline caused eastern artists many centuries ago to try things which in the west have been tried only in the last century; namely, to penetrate to the essence of personality (human, animal, vegetable, mineral), striving, not to capture its outer resemblance, but to reveal aspects of it unknown until the artist revealed them, aspects truer than any mere resemblance; and then, choosing the simplest and purest of these possibly infinite aspects, stripping them, denuding them, laying them bare, until finally the soul, the ultimate 'wind' of life, lay exposed.

After pictures come flowers. From the earliest times Buddhist altars have been decorated with flowers arranged according to certain principles. With the Zen masters and the tea cult flower arrangement developed into a fine art. It subsequently spread, and many different schools arose; it became independent, grew more and more specialized, and in the modern age reached crazy extremes which are nearer Surrealism or abstraction than to the spirit of Zen. Common to them all is the fundamental principle that the flower has the dignity of individual personality. With us there prevail the sad standards of abundance, riches, symmetry, repetition. What is the use of one flower? You need at least fifty. Flowers are used as splashes of colour, as a source of pleasing scents, a luxurious embellishment—that is to say, when the chief interest is not their human background, who sent them, or how many of them there are as a measure of the homage intended. The Japanese, however, believe that quantity hopelessly submerges the beauty of the individual flower, and have an infinite number of ways of bringing out and emphasizing it by contrast and association. Just as silence emphasizes speech, so is a single flower, or a handful of flowers, able to express a whole gamut of emotions in the hands of a master. The Japanese apply the same principle of seeking out the beauty in ordinary, simple, everyday objects to many things besides flowers.

It was only natural that the intransigent attitude of Zen, which takes life by the throat and shakes it—surely it must be one of the most original philosophies that any civilization has produced—should have a profound effect on poetry. Here I shall overlook the long formative period in Japanese literary history, and come straight to Basho (1644–1694), in whom Zen attained a poetical pinnacle. Poetry went through the same process as painting; the superfluous was ruthlessly cut away, leaving everything to be concentrated in the *haikai* or *haiku* of seventeen syllables. Poetry is not an explosion, but an implosion; there is no point of arrival, only a point of departure. The reader does not follow, but takes part in the creative act. A *haiku* is an invitation to the reader's imagination to take wing. Parallel with the heroic formal discipline of the *haiku* went an enlargement of theme until every aspect of life was included, but particularly the ordinary, humble, trivial details which by the law of contrast and compensation reflect more vividly the eternal and infinite.

> *Ochi-zama ni*   Behold! A camelia flower
> *Mizu koboshi-keri*   Spilt water when it fell!
> *Hanatsubaki*

The influence of Zen philosophy on Japanese life and of the tea masters in particular was so vast, subtle, and profound that, though there are other forces that conflict with it, it is still to be met with at every step. Serenity and purity are the two nuclei round which it revolves. Serenity implies engaging in life, not withdrawing from it, though clearly aware that only the relative is absolute, that nothing is permanent except change, that only death is life. Purity implies insistence on essentials, aesthetic cleanliness, intolerance of ornamentation and display. Hence in the moral sphere it implies self-commitment and loyalty, and undeviating pursuit of a course once decided on.

Two words often to be heard in Japan in connection with these things are *wabi* and *sabi*. As so often happens in the case of words charged with subtle intellectual and emotional overtones that go to the heart of a civilization, their full meaning is hard to render. *Wabi* in the narrow sense indicates 'a life of poverty and avoidance of luxury, remote from falsity and intrigue'. He who lives according to *wabi* is content with simple things, has understood the wisdom of rocks and grasshoppers, serenely accepts poverty as an enrichment of the spirit, as a state in which it is easier to gain an understanding of the secret flux of the universe. Here we reach the level of that total philosophy of life which is so typical of the Far East. *Sabi* has a not dissimilar meaning, but refers rather to things and places; it brings to mind a certain 'unpretentious rusticity, an archaic imperfection' (D. T. Suzuki), which puts men and matter into a relationship of loving intimacy. This implies somewhere in the background a solitary, a hermit, actively putting all this into practice.

Another term that belongs to the same order of ideas and is also frequently to be met with is *shibui ;* its literal meaning is 'astringent', but in the domain of aesthetics and conduct it is used in the sense of 'good taste'. There is no need to add that this kind of good taste implies sobriety, and excludes richness, display, and ostentation.

Finally, the term *fūga* (or *fūryū*) indicates a way of life fully inspired by Zen principles. It is 'the chaste enjoyment of life . . . identification of the self with the creative spirit, the spirit of the beauty of nature. A man of *fuga* finds his friends among flowers and animals, in rocks and water, in showers and the moon.' (D. T. Suzuki.)

Needless to say, everything has its obverse side. In the hands of foolish persons the tea ceremony degenerates into a meaningless formality, a lifeless fossil, an absurd form of aesthetic snobbery. Similarly, the cult of simplicity has often led to aridity in painting, triteness in poetry, coldness in interior decoration. All in all, however, the aesthetic vigilance of the Japanese has enabled them to avoid these rocks with surprising consistency.

I found Middy still sitting on the veranda. She said that she was fed up, and was going home. I had kept them hanging about all day without showing them anything. Nicky had not been able to stand the stink of incense any longer, and had gone. Had I a cigarette for her? What? Not even a cigarette?

By now it really was time to go; the garden was closed to the public. I had one more walk round; I enjoyed the feeling of belonging to the place, of not having to share it with the crowd. Middy followed me. We sat on the grass and talked; or rather my contribution was an occasional monosyllable, while she unburdened herself.

She had been so happy at Kobe, she said, producing some more chewing-gum from her pocket and starting to unwrap it. Her father was going to Tokyo, on business, or so he said, but what about her? She had to stay with her sisters, the boring Kimi and the provoking Rei-ko. And at Kyoto too, *iyana tokoro da-wa,* that disagreeable place where everyone was so stuck up, though they didn't have a penny. Who did they think they were? They were still in the Middle Ages, they had no spirit of enterprise. Did I know what she would like to do? Go to Tokyo! She had had enough of school and all that nonsense; she wanted to go into films. But her family wouldn't let her.

I asked her whether she had ever been to Tokyo.

Yes, she said, they had lived there during the war. She remembered as if it had been only yesterday the Emperor's speech in which he had said he was no longer a god. What a shock! She had really believed him to be a god, just as surely as that tree over there was a pine. It had been a shock from which she had never recovered. But what did it matter? They had all been very stupid in the old days. It was just as well that they had lost the war, and that the Americans had come. Now they were free, and could do what they liked. We did what we liked at home, didn't we?

Middy picked up a pebble, and threw it into the ancient pond; it made the same splash as the frog had made earlier, but this time it sounded like an angry frog, a frog on the war-path. She picked up another pebble, and threw it farther. The third pebble she threw ended up in the Silver Pavilion, where it tore a piece of paper of the *shoji,* making a sinister, rasping sound.

'Midori, stop it! What's the matter with you?'

She got up, laughing bitterly, and ran away. I ran after her, caught her up, and stopped her.

'Don't be silly!' she exclaimed, still laughing. 'Why do you make so much fuss about that stupid old wooden pavilion? One day it'll be rebuilt in concrete, as tall as a skyscraper!'

IO

Kyoto, Golden Skies

Momoyama, Peach-Tree Hill

A GLANCE at the history of almost any field of activity in Japan is
sufficient to show the importance of the dynastic principle; the
imperial pattern is reproduced practically everywhere. A notable and
famous example is provided, for instance, by the tea masters. These,
descended from Nōami (1397–1494), multiplied, formed a genealogical
tree of extreme complexity, and transmitted the consecrated oil to the
present day (schools of Ura-senke, Omote-senke, etc.). Other famous
dynasties are those of the great actors—the Danjuro, for instance, of
whom the first lived from 1660 to 1704 and the ninth from 1838 to 1903;
the sword-makers, of whom the greatest were the Goto family; and the
great financiers, such as the Mitsui, who are active in fields as diverse as
banking and heavy industry, retail trade and chemical manufacture.
There are similar dynasties of calligraphers, musicians, masters of flower
arrangement, wizards, woodworkers, and Prime Ministers. The pattern
is endlessly repeated in every department and at every level of Japanese
life. Anyone who has seen the film *Akasen Chitai* ('Street of Shame')[1] will
recall the brothel-keeper's boast that his family 'has honourably kept
this place for four generations'.

The dynastic principle rests on two foundations: the pyramidal
order of society and the family. The former is inherent in the Japanese
attitude to life. In the case of the latter, the link is mental rather than
biological; what counts is not so much consanguinity as breathing the
same air for many years. Every dynasty, from that of the Emperor to

---

[1] Literally 'Red Line Quarter'.

that of the humblest artisan, is, when possible, carried on directly from father to son, but, if the male line fails, or a son shows no aptitude to follow in his father's footsteps, resort is had to adoption. Sometimes a favourite pupil or son-in-law steps into the son's place,[1] sometimes a total stranger is sought out. All this reflects a fundamental axiom of the oriental mind, that knowledge, skill, an art, can be transmitted only by direct and constant contact with the master, involving all the faculties of the mind; books, or the intellect alone, are capable only of grazing the surface.

Two of the most famous dynasties in the history of Japanese civilization, which have left indelible traces on the Japanese artistic tradition, are those of the Tosa and Kano schools of painting. The Tosa dynasty was founded in the thirteenth century by Fujiwara Tsunetaka, the lord of Tosa—hence the name taken by his descendants—and continues nominally to the present day. The Kano school originated with the painter Kano Masanobu (1434–1530), who was also connected with the Fujiwara family and was a member of the Higashi-yama group whose patron was Ashikaga Yoshimasa; his descendants, divided into half a dozen schools and sub-schools, were active until recent times and some are still active today.

The Tosa school specialized in a genre called *yamato-e*, which developed exclusively out of native traditions and owed hardly anything to Chinese influence. Its principal application was the illustration in miniature books and on scrolls of classical literary subjects, such as the *Tale of Genji*. The Kano school, on the other hand, stood for Chinese ideals, modified by the highly personal Japanese sensibility. Tsuda illustrates the mentality of the two schools by contrasting the way in which they would paint the same object, a pine-tree.

'The gorgeousness of feeling and naïveté in those pine pictures are due much to the influence of the military atmosphere of the age in which the Kano school developed. Quite in contrast to the vigorous style of the Kano school, the Tosa school, which originated in the court of the Fujiwara period, produced an art both delicate and feminine.'[2]

[1] A classic example is that of the painter Kano Sanraku (1561–1635), the son-in-law and successor of the great Eitoku (1543–1590).

[2] N. TSUDA, *Ideals of Japanese Painting,* Tokyo, 1940.

Incidentally, this author's choice of a pine-tree with which to make his point provides a luminous and unexpected glimpse of the difference of attitudes between east and west. A western critic would in all probability have chosen the human figure for his purpose, no doubt the female nude; he would no doubt have pointed out that some painters —Van Eyck, for instance—painted undressed women rather than true nudes, while others, such as Michelangelo and the Venetians, revealed an almost pagan attitude. Examples such as these illustrate the differences in the attitude to nature of east and west.

At the end of the fifteenth century an event took place which had important repercussions on the subsequent history of Japanese art; the son of Kano Masanobu, the young Kano Motonobu (1476–1559), married the daughter of Tosa Mitsunobu, thus merging the two traditions. The result was a dynasty—still that of the Kano—which for three centuries held a supreme position in the Japanese pictorial arts. Among the countless artists of this school—Mitsunobu, Sadanobu, Noriboru, Tansen, Tanrin, Tangen, Einō, Eikei, Eigaku, all members of the Kano clan—three great names stand out: those of Kano Eitoku (1543–1590), Kano Sanraku (1561–1635), and Kano Tanyū (1602–1674). It should not be forgotten, of course, that other notable schools were also active at this period, notably those founded by Kaiho Yushō (1533–1615), Hasegawa Tōhaku (1539–1610), and Unkoku Tōgan (1547–1618).

Let us leave these great masters for a moment and consider the Japan in which they lived; their art is difficult to understand without reference to their environment. The line of Ashikaga shoguns which, it will be recalled, started in 1338 with Ashikaga Takauji, theoretically continued until the deposition of Ashikaga Yoshiaki in 1573. Distinguished though this dynasty was for its patronage of the arts in the persons of Yoshimitsu and Yoshimasa, as governors its members were generally weak and incompetent. From the end of the Onin war (1477) onwards Japan was in a continual state of anarchy; Japanese historians call this period, which lasted for about a century, *sengoku jidai* ('the period of the country at war'). Clearly, if Japan had not been isolated from the Asian land-mass and had had hostile neighbours on her borders, she would have fallen an easy victim to invasion, with a profound effect on her subsequent history. But her privileged position postponed disaster for another four or five centuries, perhaps making it the more terrible when it came.

Half-way through the sixteenth century things were ripe for change, and the next fifty years constituted an extremely important phase in Japanese history. On the one hand, feudal consolidation had reached a point at which individual domains were big and powerful enough for the more energetic among the barons to be tempted to think of uniting Japan under their sway. To give some idea of these violent and tempestuous times, it is sufficient to note that Sansom records that, of the approximately 260 great feudal lords known before the Onin war (1467–1477), barely a dozen survived at the end of the sixteenth century; an entirely new aristocracy superseded the old.[1] On the other hand, from 1542 onwards strangers of a type never seen before made their appearance in Japan, that is to say *namban-jin* (southern barbarians), *i.e.*, Europeans. First the Portuguese arrived, and then the Spaniards, bringing with them new things which profoundly affected the traditional play of forces; fire-arms and Christianity. The second half of the sixteenth century was a period in which great forces were at work and great new influences made themselves felt; it seemed a prelude to a period totally different from that which in fact followed under the influence of Iyeyasu and his descendants.

'Thus at the opening of the sixteenth century [Grousset writes], Japan resembled fifteenth-century Italy. The moral authority of the Emperors descended from the sun had disappeared just as that of the Roman pontiffs had done. The military power of the Ashikaga shoguns, like that of the Germanic Caesars, had vanished. In Kyoto, the imperial city, the Emperor and the shogun were held in check by the local clans just as the Pope had been in Rome. In place of these two great traditional authorities some ten principalities, as restless and ambitious as the houses of Rimini or Borgia, Visconti, or Medici had been in Italy, divided up the archipelago among them, exercising a supremacy as sovereign as theirs. These great *daimyos* of the sixteenth century should, indeed, be regarded something in the light of the princes of the Italian Renaissance, each pursuing a dynastic policy by force or cunning, and keeping up a regular system of mutual embassies, elegant social relations, and artistic intercourse—not to speak of espionage and treachery—and

[1] G. B. SANSOM, *loc. cit.*, p. 395.

all swayed solely by reasons of state. But in addition to this they
were splendid Maecenases and great lovers of art and poetry,
attaching the same importance to the acquisition of a *kakemono* or
the composition of a *haiku* as to winning of a battle.'[1]

Fortune had it that at this period three great men arose who for
a substantial part of their lives collaborated to the same end, the reuni-
fication of the country. The first to emerge was Oda Nobunaga
(1534–1582); the son of a minor baron, he displayed brilliant military gifts
from his youth, and in a succession of victories subdued the majority of
his rival *daimyo,* the Takeda, the Uesugi, the Asakura, the Asai, the
Miyoshi; destroyed with terrible completeness the turbulent monks of
Mount Hiei (1571) and of the Ikkō sect (1576); and deposed the last Ashikaga shogun (1573). After reuniting the central and most important part
of Japan, he was killed by a rebel general at the age of forty-eight. He
was courageous and persevering, though violent and quarrelsome, and
showed a political wisdom in advance of his time. He was well disposed
towards foreigners, favoured trade with the rest of Asia, and aimed at
overcoming Japan's natural isolation. He also favoured Christianity,
perhaps for more than just political reasons, and the new religion made
great headway, particularly in Kyushu and the Kyoto area.

After his death his place was taken by Hideyoshi, who until modern
times was the only Japanese of truly popular origin who ever exercised
supreme power in Japan. He was a peasant's son, and his exceptional
qualities of intelligence and courage gained him a high position in
Nobunaga's forces. He seems to have been small and ugly, but to have
possessed unlimited ambition and self-assurance. His career was a succession of battles, alliances, intrigues, victories, which resulted in his
ending up on terms of familiarity with the Emperor and brought him
the highest titles in the land, those of *kampaku* and *taikō*.[2] More interesting
is the strong influence that his personality had on his times; he had in
over-abundant measure the characteristics which so many observers
have found lacking in Japanese civilization as a whole, that is to say

[1] R. GROUSSET, *loc. cit.,* p. 168.
[2] 'He has been compared to Napoleon and to Alexander the Great, and if the room in which
he fought and schemed had not been a little one, remote from the great continental impulses, the
character of the man might well have changed history in Asia and in Europe.' L. WARNER, *The
Enduring Art of Japan,* Harvard, 1952, p. 63.

a desire for greatness, space, grandeur. Everything about him breathed
a robust, peasant paganism, and everything he did had to be on the
grand scale. Not satisfied with shocking the bourgeois and the plebs, he
took special delight in shocking the court, the tremulous nobles of
Kyoto. Had a huge statue of the Buddha been erected in the Nara period,
and another in the Kamakura epoch? Well then, a bigger one must be
built in Kyoto. Had it taken twenty-seven years to complete the Nara
statue? This time the work must be done in five. When it was pointed
out to him that in all the forests of Japan there were no trees big enough
for the purpose except at the foot of Mount Fufi, he sent 50,000 men to
cut them down and bring them back.

As no residence worthy of him was available after his appointment
as regent, he built himself a villa-palace-hermitage-park which he called
Juraku-tei ('Dwelling of Pleasure'), where he gathered all the splendid
things that the Empire could supply. The greatest artists of the time were
summoned to decorate halls, verandas, galleries with an unpre-
cedented magnificence. Contemporary chronicles (*Taikō-ki*, 'The Annals
of the Taiko') speak of gates guarded by iron pillars and copper doors;
of high towers which shone like stars in the sky; of roof-tiles which
roared in the wind, and of golden dragons which sang songs among the
clouds.'[1] When the building was complete Hideyoshi sent an invitation
to the Emperor in person; and the latter and his court were entertained
at celebrations that lasted for five whole days. On such occasions
Hideyoshi used to distribute gifts on a fabulous scale among the nobles
and ladies of the court; not even the esoteric tea ceremony held him in
awe. On November 1, 1587, he gave a party on the Plain of Pines, outside
Kyoto, to which he invited literally the whole of Japan; public notices
announcing the fact were put up a month in advance in all the chief
cities, and on the appointed day connoisseurs arrived from all over the
country to sip green tea and admire the works of art displayed for the
occasion. Other favourite pastimes of his were the public distribution of
gold coins to members of his household and his vassals. At Osaka he
built the biggest and most formidable castle known in Japanese history
(it was destroyed by partisans of the Tokugawa in 1868). At Momoyama
('Peach-Tree Hill'), near Kyoto, the magnificent palace that he built
gave its name to this whole period.

[1] F. BRINKLEY, *A History of the Japanese People*, New York, 1915, pp. 506–7.

Under Hideyoshi's leadership the Japanese attempted their first big oversea venture, the invasion of Korea and an attack on China. Two expeditions were sent, in 1592–3 and 1597–8, but the results were dubious and did not lead to the establishment of a real empire. The first serious persecutions of Christians took place at this time; Hideyoshi suspected them of aiming at the political and military conquest of the country. The first twenty-six martyrs were crucified at Nagasaki in 1597. When Hideyoshi died in 1598 the work of national unification was well on the way to completion, and he did all in his power to ensure that it would be completed by his descendants.

It was completed, however, not by them, but by Tokugawa Iyeyasu (1542–1616), a member of a great family ultimately descended, like nearly all the great families of Japan, from the Minamoto. Iyeyasu had fought under Nobunaga and Hideyoshi; now his moment had come. Both his predecessors had been violent, impulsive men; Iyeyasu, however, was a Machiavellian. Nobunaga and Hideyoshi passed across the skies like meteors, leaving only glory behind, but Iyeyasu made his way like a fox or, perhaps better, a spider, craftily enclosing his enemies in a net from which there was no escape. He had himself appointed shogun by the Emperor in 1603, and fourteen members of his family succeeded him and held Japan in their grip until 1868. In the battle of Sekigahara on October 21, 1600, he defeated an alliance of *daimyo* who rejected his overlordship, and 40,000 enemy heads were the trophy of the day. Henceforward Japan was at his feet. In 1615 he destroyed the descendants of Hideyoshi, who represented the last force hostile to him.

With Iyeyasu a new age begins; a heroic, luminous age, rich in infinite possibilities, had ended; its successor was meaner and pettier, dominated by fear and suspicion, spying and bureaucracy. Once Iyeyasu had gathered power completely into his own hands, his only thought was how to preserve it for his descendants. Was it necessary to shut Japan off from contact with the outside world? Well, he shut it off. Was it necessary to exterminate Christianity, or any germ of new thought which might open new horizons to his subjects? Without hesitation he did so. Was it necessary to force political, social, artistic life into patterns intended to be immutable? Let the means be found for attaining such absurd aims.

The characters of the great men of the sixteenth century have been

neatly summed up in some epigrammatic couplets. Nobunaga, faced
with a reluctant cuckoo, said:

> *Nakaneba korosu*   I shall kill the cuckoo if it will
>   *Hototogisu*   not sing.

Hideyoshi, was cleverer; he said: '*Nakashite miyō*' (I shall invite it to
sing). Iyeyasu, the cleverest of the three, said: '*Naku made matō*' (I shall wait
for it to sing). There is also a print, probably dating from a later period,
which shows Nobunaga, aided by some faithful friends, pounding rice
in a mortar, Hideyoshi kneading it, as Japanese peasants do, and
Iyeyasu calmly eating the cake made by the work of others.[1]

To an extent, and making the due allowances, the resemblance
noted by Grousset between Japan and Italy can be carried further forward in time. In both countries the sixteenth century was a period of
disorderly splendour, followed by a long period of peace and repression,
imposed in Italy by French, Spaniards, Austrians, in Japan by a dominant
family oligarchy. In the second half of the nineteenth century both
countries reawakened to find that the modern world had passed them
by. Both tried desperately to overtake the arrears, and in both an
anachronistic experiment ended in defeat.

But let us return to the field of art. As the reader will have realized,
conditions in the second half of the sixteenth century were profoundly
different from those of the immediately preceding period. Previously
all creative effort had been drawn off into the ethereal atmosphere in
which a few recluses lived remote from the world, but now there was
a glorious song of life, a desire for space, abundance, and splendour. The
masters of the Kano school, notably Eitoku (1543–1590) and Sanraku
(1561–1635). to say nothing of those of the lesser schools, such as Yushō
(1533–1615), Tōhaku (1539–1610), or Tōgan (1547–1618), responded admirably
to the new spirit without sacrificing anything to vulgarity, exhibitionism,
crudeness. Starting with Nobunaga, the great *condottieri* built themselves
castles the like of which had not previously been seen in Japan. Hideyoshi and his vassals built impressive palaces and magnificent villas, in
which important personages gathered to deal with matters of state; and
the builders of these edifices left vast surfaces which required decoration.

[1] Reproduced in E. PAPINOT, *Historical and Geographical Dictionary of Japan*, Yokohama, 1909, p. 666.

Hitherto colour had been confined to the illustration of books or miniature scrolls Now, applied with the consummate Chinese brush stroke, it flourished across the entire walls of council chambers, throne-rooms, banqueting halls, and reception-rooms. Gold was used royally to serve as sky, cloud, light, distant background. The period which Warner calls that of the Great Decorators began; the age of Rubenses, not of buxom queens and Muses or Venuses with breasts swollen with Flemish milk, but of pines, the moon, wild duck, plum, and cherry, Chinese hermits and sages.

Homage to the Great Decorators

This morning Giorgio, Jane, and I decided to make a brief tour of homage to the Great Decorators. I drove to Giorgio's hotel, hidden among the pines of the Eastern Hills just above the Yasaka pagoda, where he likes staying in Kyoto when he is not in too much of a hurry. Like so many of the best things in Japan it is a place you hardly ever hear mentioned; it never advertises, and I believe it is not mentioned in any list of Kyoto hotels published for travellers, either Japanese or foreign. But it has existed for many years, and it has its loyal habitués; admission is by introduction only. It is a place of concealed luxury. When you enter the little garden by which you approach it, it is like entering a hermitage, but the sophisticated eye notes the fine quality of every detail, the rare woods (which look like ordinary woods), the sober-coloured lacquer, a meticulous cleanliness that betrays the constant attention of a big staff which keeps the place with the care due to a precision instrument. At the door I noted a magnificent *tsui-tate,* the small screen across the passage-way which incidentally serves to ward off evil spirits. In front of it was a magnificent example of the art of flower arrangement; an almost breath-taking arrangement of pines and chrysanthemums.

Before I had time to say *gomen kudasai,* a young waitress appeared, wearing a white dust-coat over her kimono such as Japanese women wear for housework, and asked me what I wanted, her eyelids fluttering in a manner clearly intended to convey to the honourable gentleman present that he had made an enormous mistake in being so bold as to desire to cross the threshold. Then an old lady appeared, of severe distinction in dress, manner, and appearance, followed by two small, strongly built, bald, old men dressed in blue, looking like two gnomes who spent their lives engaged in extremely delicate but strenuous work. I had some difficulty in making myself understood; Japanese are sometimes so firmly convinced that they are unable to understand foreigners that they listen to you without hearing. However, the miracle-working name of *Jyorujiyo-sama* (Mr. Giorgio) eventually did the trick; the girl dissolved in smiles, the old lady bent like a reed in the wind, the gnomes beamed at each other with enormous satisfaction. '*Ah sayo de gozaimasu-ka, kochira-e irasshaimase*' (So that's what you want, please come in!) After walking down a number of irregular corridors opening on to tiny courtyards where bamboos and twisted pine-trees grew and you kept coming across unexpected views of gardens, I reached the room, or rather the small pavilion, occupied by our luxurious hermit.

'Greetings, Giorgio Pasha,' I said. 'Have you eaten your morning lotuses? Have you addressed your prayers to the sun? Have the fairies been reading poems to you about the vanity of human affairs?'

Actually Giorgio was sitting on a pile of cushions and glancing through a newspaper. He was wearing a Savile Row suit (no doubt for an important business engagement later in the day) and, while looking at the paper, was dictating a letter in English to his secretary—who was old and plain, a *nisei* (Japanese-American), I think, but of formidable efficiency—and at the same time sipping a cup of *miso,* a soup made of fermented beans of which we all got fond during our war-time internment. Giorgio did not condescend to answer me. After a few moments he made some reference to the latest political news, and then said we must hurry, because Jane was waiting for us. We left, saying good-bye to the secretary, who said, 'Okay, okay' in reply to everything.

How depressing in comparison was the entrance to the big, western-style hotel in which Jane was staying. Gone was the hush, the sense of mystery and secrecy, the subtle connivance of looks, silences, quiet noises full of subtle implications. Here everything was public, commercialized, symmetrical. Giorgio's hotel was the essence of Kyoto, but here we were in Osaka, or New York.

On the way to Hideyoshi's mausoleum, beyond the Hoko-ji, we stopped at the Chishaku-in at the edge of the city. The architecture was not particularly interesting, and on a grey day like today temples which are not surrounded by a great deal of green take on a funereal colour which verges on the disagreeable. Inside, however, a feast awaited us—the huge murals attributed to Kano Sanraku in the hall of honour (*dai-shoin*), which seems once to have formed part of the Momoyama castle. Pines, cherry-trees in blossom, *momiji* in their autumn sunset blaze, stood out against a background of golden skies; they seemed to possess a truth, a reality, exceeding that of any real forest. Berenson would talk of tactile values; one might also talk of olfactory values, values of the taste papillae. A kind of biological alchemy is at work; you become pine, cherry, *momiji*; feel the joys of the wind, the dew, the moon after a storm, the birds, the righteous sleep of the ancient stone.

Giorgio, polishing his spectacles, talked with his usual learning about the artistic history of the period. All these attributions were terribly uncertain, he told us. For centuries the artist had been said to be Sanraku, but now the tendency was to connect these works with the name of Hasegawa Tōhaku, a contemporary of his, who was influenced rather by the Sesshu school. Fortunately these details did not matter very much; they were of interest only to a small number of scholars. The fact was that the whole of the Momoyama period was marvellous—intoxication with life expressed in symbols.

Our next halt was at the Daitoku-ji, the Temple of the Great Virtue, a huge Zen monastery, one of the smaller pavilions of which contains some famous paintings by Kano Eitoku; pines, rocks, cranes with enormously long legs, some flowers. We should really have come here first, Giorgio explained, for here we could see the beginnings of the Momoyama style. The sobriety was still that of the preceding period; colours were barely indicated by a fine dusting of gold. The beauty lay all in the nervous, wakeful line.

As we were in these parts, we also visited the tiny garden of the Daisen-in, a famous example of Sōami's art. For centuries it was regarded as the supreme example of the style inspired by the principles of the tea masters. It contains nothing but stones and a few plants; water is represented by white sand. With its rocks, waterfalls, and wild vegetation it is a Sung painting. But the predominance of symbolism and learned references makes it, at any rate to the freer taste of our time, seem painfully restricted and forced.

Next we went to the Myoshin-ji ('Temple of the Sacred Heart'), another huge Zen monastery, with I do not know how many chapels and cloisters. It, too, is rich in paintings by the great masters of the period, Kano Sanraku, Kaiho Yushō, Kano Motonobu. As usual, the traditional attributions have been revolutionized recently; the very uncertainty illustrates how uniformly high was the level of the period. After removing our shoes, we were led by a benevolent, talkative monk down some ancient corridors of shining dark wood, and suddenly found ourselves surrounded by strange, imaginary tigers in a bamboo wood under a golden sky. These paintings, traditionally attributed to Kano Sanraku, strike you by their violence held in leash. This is something characteristically Japanese, which one keeps coming across in the most varied forms—in the dance, for instance, the theatre, and of course the cinema. It is a vibrant, explosive quality lurking behind the smooth, highly polished, perfectly controlled surface; the ecstatic sensuality of a snake in love betrayed only by symbols and echoes. Heavens, the green of those bamboos, and that golden sky! You feel that these artists are giving you new eyes with which to look at the world, that no bamboo will ever seem the same after you have seen theirs. For a moment you are admitted to a marvellous, mystic relationship between man and things, between man and the rest of the universe.

In the neighbouring rooms—there are many of them in a row in the cloister called the Tenkyū-in, and all are of the highest importance— flowers bring spring to life, snowy winter sleeps between trees and stones, not sufficiently, however, to stifle the perpetual youth of a gnarled old trunk which is putting forth shoots. A tiny bird, ready to take wing, is like the sound of a flute against a bass accompaniment (Photograph 106).

In the last rooms of the Tenkyū-in there are several series of pictures in the Chinese manner; human figures, architecture, landscape. There are three philosophers, a group of sages, the four noble arts of music, chess, calligraphy, and painting; and so on and so forth. The drawing, rhythm, and colour are first-rate but there is a flavour of erudition and neo-classicism about these works; they represent skill pursuing a shadow, not genius opening a way.

Last of all we visited the Nishi Hongan-ji, back in the city. But there are innumerable places at which homage should be paid; those of the Nanzen-ji, for instance, where Eitoku left many traces of his creative brilliance, and the Kennin-ji among others. There is no end to the things which must be seen at Kyoto.

The Katsura villa and garden date from the last years of the sixteenth century and the first of the seventeenth. Together they represent, not only 'the supreme example of Japanese civil architecture',[1] but, in view of the great Japanese influence on the ideas of modern architects, it is one of the key points in the artistic history of the world. Here there converge and fuse the ancient Yamato building tradition as preserved in the Ise temples and a few other places; the Chinese Sung influence as developed and transformed under the more specifically Japanese impulse of Zen; and, finally, the spirit of the tea masters at the time of its fullest flower. The Katsura villa was the starting-point of influences which profoundly affected the subsequent development of Japanese architecture, and laid the foundations for the taste which excites so much admiration at the present day among the architects and interior decorators of the world. It is a work of superb purity and a subtle, allusive beauty. There is no yielding to the temptations of pomposity, grandeur, superficiality; instead there is a heroic self-discipline, a rejection of all superfluities; man stands purified in front of nature purified, so that both may merge and participate in ultimate being, the great secret.

It is interesting to note that the Katsura villa dates from the Momoyama period, or at any rate the years immediately after it; it thus shows how rich and varied the Japanese artistic panorama can be at any given moment. Nothing is falser than the idea of oriental fixity and monotony, which still survives with us, and is due simply to the fixity and monotony of western ignorance.

The villa was built by order of Hideyoshi for Prince Toshihito, a nephew of the Emperor Ogimachi. Hideyoshi had adopted the prince in order to associate his family with the royal blood, with all which that implied. But then he had a son of his own, and Toshihito was relegated 'to peaceful obscurity remote from politics'. The prince was one of the most cultivated men of his time; as a pupil of the critic and poet Yusai there were entrusted to his care literary manuscripts of the first importance, those of the *Kokinshu,* for example, as well as the original of the *Tale of Genji.* When he started busying himself with this villa on the bank

[1] T. Yoshida, *The Japanese House and Garden,* London, 1955.

of the river Katsura, not far from Arashi-yama, at the gates of Kyoto, he wished it to be a repository of all that Japanese civilization had to offer. 'The *Tale of Genji* is particularly rich in descriptions of country mansions, palaces and gardens, and it appears that the Prince drew up his instructions to his gardeners and architects with these instructions in mind.'[1]

It seems established that he entrusted the work to a celebrated tea master of the period, Kobori Enshu (1579–1647). Legend has it that Kobori undertook it on three conditions: that there should be no limit to what he was to be allowed to spend, or to the man-power that he was to be allowed to use; that in no circumstances whatever was he to be hurried; and that, in order not to disturb the plan in his mind by any untoward suggestions, nobody was to be allowed to see the work until it was complete. In other words, he is said to have been granted all the conditions which all artists since the beginning of time have always dreamt of and always will.

I had arranged to meet my friend Ernesto Lanzetti on the bridge not far from the entrance. It was a magnificent day; the wealth of blue that is so typical of Japan, because of the great humidity, was in the air. The tops of the mountains stood out sharp and clear against the sky; their bases were lost in a horizontal curtain of haze, which shone like *tsurugi,* ancient Japanese straight swords. The trees, seen against the light, looked like strange, untidy shadows caught in the middle of a dance.

In this part of the world it is the custom for weavers to send their workers, who are mostly Koreans, to wash their fabrics in the river; it seems that the combined action of water and sun helps to fix the colours. On some days the scene resembles some fantastic carnival. Long lengths of cotton, silk, and other materials are stretched out on the gravel to dry (Photograph 11), while others dance in the wind, hanging from lines held aloft by tall bamboo poles. Today some men were washing a load of violet and pink fabrics immediately under the bridge, and the whole river was stained violet and pink, as if an ink factory had over-flowed. When they saw me the men called out: '*Tabako ippon kudasaranai-ka?*' (Had I any cigarettes for them?) Alas! I am a non-smoker. However, I went down to the stream-bed and took photographs, promising to

---

[1] A. DREXLER, *The Architecture of Japan*, New York, 1955, p. 157.

send copies to those who gave me their name and address; they seemed well content with this bargain.

Meanwhile Lanzetti's car drew up on the bridge. I went up and greeted him. He told me he had a surprise for me. The surprise was sitting in the car; I could make out some shiny black hair and a thin neck. It was Tamako. She greeted me with her enchanting smile, and held out her hand to be shaken in the western manner. She wore a dark blue kimono with a light brown pattern, and a plain, straw-coloured *obi* of some rough material; the whole effect was very *shibui* (astringent), as was appropriate for a morning visit to the villa-hermitage of an ancient prince-poet.

'How is Tamako?' I asked. 'Better now?'

'*O-kage sama de, genki de orimasu*', she replied (Thanks to your honourable shadow, I am very well). She spoke as if she had made up her mind that every day and in every way she was getting better and better. She had evidently decided to turn over a new leaf, and forget about Giorgio. But how did she manage to get on with Ernesto, who spoke no Japanese? He explained that their conversation was conducted in English of the type: *You not like, we not go,* or *if you tired, here can rest.*

Ernesto was missing a great deal by not understanding Japanese, for Tama was a delight to listen to—voice, intonation, the way she expressed herself, everything. The Japanese spoken by men and women differs greatly, of course. Men use brief verbal forms, rather like military commands—*itta, yutta, aru, minai, kuré*: in the mouths of women this phraseology is modified, softened, turned into silvery cascades—*ikimashita, iimashita, arimasu, mimasen, kudasai*. Apart from this, women to a large extent use a vocabulary which is exclusively their own; they use interjections that a man would use only in special cases; and they express themselves in an allusive and elliptical fashion, employing frequent interrogatives and making great use of euphonious pleonasms. It is rather as if Englishmen used predominantly Anglo-Saxon words while women chiefly used words of Latin origin, with their elaborate cadences and academic associations.

We went on to the villa, showed our passes, and entered. In the old days ceremonial dress, or at any rate a dark suit, was *de rigueur* for visits to villas or palaces belonging to the Imperial House, but nowadays things are simpler. Ernesto remarked that this was an echo of MacArthur's famous reception of the Emperor in his shirt-sleeves. In a sense this was true; shoguns always dictated fashion for a short time after achieving power; and for some years MacArthur was *aoi-me no shogun* (the blue-eyed shogun), the direct heir of Iyeyasu.

I asked Ernesto whether we should see the house or the garden first; his reply was to denounce me as an impenitent dualist. They were one and the same thing, and it was impossible to differentiate between them. Had I not yet learnt the lesson of total fusion of house and garden?

We both laughed. Tama's curiosity about what we were talking about made her eyes nearly pop out of her head. Thus my work as interpreter began. Ernesto took advantage of the occasion to tell her a lot of things about his ideas and artistic tastes, putting to a hard test my knowledge of one of the most difficult languages in the world—difficult, not because of its accidence, but because of its syntax and the phenomenal wealth of its vocabulary.

Tamako led the way towards the house, and we followed, taking off our shoes at the entrance, as is the custom. The villa should not be thought of as a little Versailles, or Villa d'Este, or even one of the Medicean country houses; we are in another world. The simplicity here is no mere return to the primitive, but the distilled essence achieved by one who has run through the whole gamut of richness, complication, magnificence, and has now found his way to the core of things and rejected the rest.

The villa is a single-storey wooden building, raised from the ground on piles a good three feet high, and with a roof of tiny wooden shingles, arranged with great care to form a rough, slightly curved surface. The floors are covered with *tatami,* the doors are of thin wood and paper.[1] Fortunately the guide left us to our own devices, for which we were grateful; generally parties are taken round like sheep, totally unable to breathe the spirit of the place; and this is one of the places in which there is, perhaps, very little to see, but a great deal to breathe in. My impression is that it is only by staying there for a considerable time, perhaps by sleeping there, that you begin to have the feel of the place. It is like the high mountains; unless you have slept among them you know them only as a tourist.

[1] The villa as a whole 'creates the effect of a piece of furniture, made with great taste and care, placed in the middle of a garden'. W. BLASER, *loc. cit.,* p. 75.

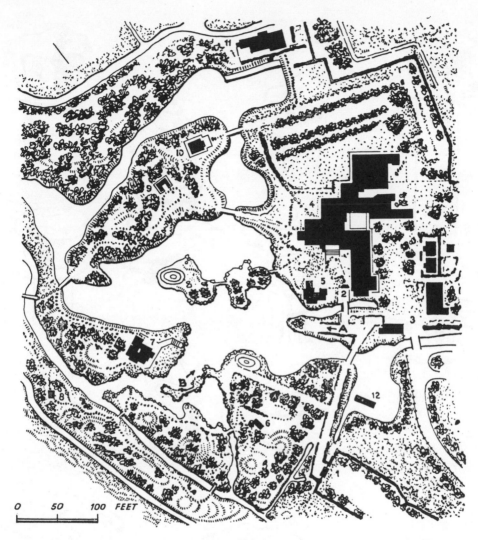

Plan of the Katsura villa, Kyoto

(1) Imperial gate; (2) inner gate (Photograph 115); (3) ordinary entrance; (4) main building;
(5) Gepparō ('Waves by Moonlight') pavilion; (6) bench for guests waiting to be admitted to the
tea ceremony; (7) Shōkin-tei ('Murmur of the Pines') pavilion. (Photograph 112 shows view from
the interior); (8) Manji-tei ('Swastika') pavilion (the swastika is a Buddhist symbol); (9) Shōka-tei
('Flower Delight') pavilion; (10) Enrin-do ('Buried in the Wood') temple; (11) Shōi-ken ('Cheerful
Heart') pavilion; (12) place where small boats are kept
(A) Point from which Photograph 108 was taken
(B) Point from which photograph on back of dust-cover was taken

(Drawing by S. Pannuti based on data given by various Japanese authors)

Stone lanterns in the garden of the Katsura villa (Kyoto)

(Drawn by Makino Yone)

Now, as there was no one to hurry us, we could squat on the *tatami* where we pleased; this was most important, because Japanese architecture is designed to be seen and appreciated by a man squatting on the floor in the position of meditation. From this level, views and the perspectives which otherwise seem small, cold, out of balance, become warm and welcoming, and made to the measure of man. As soon as we squatted we saw 'the garden entering the house'; the fusion between interior and exterior was perfect. Every tree, every stone, every ripple on the pond, was thought of in terms of how it would look from inside the house; similarly, the house was designed so that it appeared in perspective from wherever it was looked at. You are immediately struck by the totally irregular plan of the building; the effect is as if it had happened by chance. But then you see that it is an elegant avoidance of symmetry, that it respects every slight undulation of the soil, that it models itself on nature. Three hundred years later these things seemed extraordinarily important to a great western architect for whom a visit to Japan was of decisive importance: Frank Lloyd Wright.

Another matter in which the Japanese preceded by several centuries trends which we regard as being the height of modernity is the fact that their building is essentially modular. Their special unit is the *tatami*, which at Kyoto and in the Kwansai measures 77½ by 37 inches and elsewhere in Japan 71½ by 37 inches. A *tatami* represents the smallest area in which a grown man can sit, work, rest, and sleep. The area of a room is calculated in multiples of *tatami*; the smallest occupy the space of two or three *tatami*, the average six, eight, or ten; in big temples or palaces the *tatami* are counted in hundreds. The whole building is conceived in multiples or sub-multiples of this fundamental unit; the height and width of the *fusuma* (sliding doors) are calculated by it, as are the height of the room, the breadth of the columns, the width of the verandas, and so on. At least four centuries before Le Corbusier worked out his 'modulor', his minimum human space, these poets of simple things at the other end of the earth had preceded him.

While Ernesto and I sat on the floor, talking or thinking, Tama walked up and down, humming a tune. She leant on a pillar and looked at the garden, or the tea pavilions that could be made out among the trees on the bank of the irregular-shaped pond. Then she turned, and asked us with a smile:

'*Nani-wo kangaete irassharu no?*' (What are you thinking about?)

'I was thinking how delightful you are!' I answered. 'If I were an ancient prince who had retired here, I should insist on your walking up and down like that every day!'

'Well, in that case I should need hormone cream for my face in bad weather.'

'What is she saying?' asked Ernesto.

'Oh, nothing, she says that she's quite happy.'

While Ernesto talked I looked at Tama sitting on the little veranda made for listening to music by moonlight. She was delightful, exquisite, fascinating, perfect, but somehow I could not manage to think of her as a real person; Middy, for all her wildness, seemed infinitely more real; a totally unformed human being, but still, a human being. But did Tama have a soul? If there had been a Japanese equivalent for 'soul', if I could have made a joke about it, I should have asked her. But *tamashii* would be rather like saying 'spiritual essence', a much too metaphysical conception; that left the word *kokoro,* heart, which would have been much too cruel. It is only with difficulty that a joke survives transplantation to a different civilization.

We resumed our tour of the villa, enjoying every view of the garden, examining the now faded paintings to be seen here and there in the rooms, nearly all of them in the sober *sumi-e* style, black on white, carried out with light, casual strokes of the brush: a landscape of rocks and waterfalls surviving as in the memory of a dream; an old sage riding a donkey; all suggestions that led back to Tao, the Way, to a lightly borne, anti-pedantic, slightly crazy wisdom; though always absolutely engaged.

Apart from these pictures, which have now almost completely faded with the years, there is practically no decoration; unless you regard the structure itself as decoration, because of the perfect balance of its parts, and the beauty of the bare surfaces, wood, paper, straw, bamboo. The only use of metal, so minimal that it might easily escape the eye of one who did not know where to look, is for small fittings called *kugi-kakushi* (cover-nails) at the top of the columns, and for *hikite,* in which you put a finger to open or shut a sliding door; the *hikite* are shaped like baskets decorated with wistaria or chrysanthemums. In accordance with the usual principle of surrounding things with *mu*—absence, silence, nothing—the slightest of them acquire an extraordinary significance.

Ernesto remarked that another extraordinary modern feature was the sense of surface. The Japanese, with wood, paper, and dried earth, had, unlike the west, discovered materials which aged well. How depressing those concrete boxes were, even in maturity, to say nothing of age! They were fine on the architect's drawing-board, and tolerable when new. But they peeled, flaked, got stained and dirty, and after a few years they were monstrous.

À propos of monstrosities, while we were sitting in a corner enjoying the view of the pond framed by the veranda where Tamako was squatting and powdering her nose, a party of foreigners approached, led by a guide who was saying his piece at the top of his voice in appalling English. While we waited for the storm to pass a corpulent gentleman detached himself from the party and came over towards us. 'Oh, Lanzetti, how delightful to see you!' he said. We rose, and introductions followed. He was Dr. Macchia, the representative of some commercial company, in Japan on business. For a few minutes we found his company enjoyable, but then we discovered that we had nothing in common; moreover, he refused to go away. He remarked how delightful it was to meet two friends in this remote place lost in the depths of Japan (actually we were only twenty minutes from Kyoto). He had heard such a lot about this villa, but what was it, after all, but a wooden hut? What did we think? To him it was obvious that these Japanese hadn't got very much; after all, they had emerged from the woods only the day before yesterday, so to speak. Didn't Lanzetti think they would be well advised to go to Italy for a little instruction? After all, Italy was the mother of the arts. When you considered what Italy had given the world, this stuff only made you smile. You couldn't compare it, could you, to the Boboli Gardens, or Hadrian's Villa, or the Villa d'Este, or the Brenta villas! These trifles had a certain charm, of course, but in reality they were nothing but toys. All you needed was some stones, a lantern, a little imagination in digging the pond. . . .

The storm showed no sign of abating. Very selfishly, on the pretext of talking to Tamako in Japanese, I left Ernesto to cope with it alone. Tamako and I went down into the garden, past the Gepparō (the 'Waves by Moonlight' pavilion), discovering marvels at every step:

stones, moss, maples, water, pines of innumerable different species, ages, shapes, lanterns which were amusing, sad, severe, pathetic, proud, charming, as absurd as a drunken old man; there was a whole population of lanterns.

I managed to get Tamako to walk in front of me; then, on the pretext of taking photographs, I stopped. The girl walked with incredible grace; both in movement and repose she seemed instinctively to hold herself perfectly, and she also seemed to be in silent and instinctive communion with everything about her. Her kimono was in perfect harmony with every petal of this supreme flower of a civilization; villa, garden, water, sounds, scents, colours, the ancient savour of earth and time. If Japanese women only realized how much better they look in *wafuku* (Japanese dress), they would never wear *yōfuku* (western dress). The kimono is made for them, was born on them (Photographs 99, 100), but *yōfuku* brings out all their defects; their short, often bow, legs, broad waist and tube-shaped body, small breasts and round shoulders. During all the years I have spent in the east I have never, I repeat never, had my breath taken away at the sight of a Japanese woman dressed in western style. When Japanese girls, and still more Japanese women, abandon their own style of clothing, they look like housemaids. The kimono brings out all that is best in them. True, the breasts disappear, but another delightful element, the neck, is brought out—the plasticity of its surfaces, and the continual play of its movement and the light upon it. Western women have other weapons; their neck is merely a supporting column to carry the head; in the case of Japanese women the neck has the expressiveness, the elegance of movement, the lightness, the intelligence, all the qualities of a hand with thin, nervous fingers.

At the 'Murmur of the Pines' pavilion we stopped to wait for the others. The pond, the island, the comic little lantern, seen from here (Photograph 112) are really the quintessence of Japanese perfection. I prayed that Tama would not speak, fearing that if she opened her mouth she would spoil everything. Meanwhile Dr. Macchia's torrent of words came floating towards us on the breeze. I hoped that Ernesto had not set out on the uphill task of trying to convert him.

The torrent of words faded; perhaps the two had gone round a corner. Tamako, without speaking, approached and took my hand. Male vanity is such that for a moment I thought . . . I had always liked

Tamato. Who would not? When I first met her she had been with one friend of mine, and now she was with another. But could I have made a mistake? Her hand clutched me tightly, desperately.

'*Né, Maraini-san,*' she burst out suddenly, with an expression I had never seen on her face before, looking at me with eyes in which there were two large, shining tears. '*Né, Maraini-san,* you, who know Giorgio well, is it true?'

'Is what true, Tama-chan? What is the matter with you?'

'*Né, Maraini-san,* they've told me! Everybody knows it now!'

'Knows what, Tama-chan? I don't know what you are talking about!'

'That Giorgio's in love with a *gai-jin,* a foreigner. . . . It's no good denying it, there's no more hope. . . . *Né, Maraini-san,* will you tell me it isn't true!'

She raised her *tamoto,* the wing-like sleeve of her kimono, and quickly wiped away the tears on her cheeks; Ernesto and Dr. Macchia were coming, you could hear their voices quite close. A moment later Tama looked at me, smiling again, looking incredibly cheerful and different. She drew her *obi-dome* about her with a gesture characteristic of Japanese women, and murmured:

'Let us forget about it, shall we? *Shikata ga arimasen,* it can't be helped, there's nothing that can be done about it.'

Abstract Garden

One of the most delightful experiences in Japan is wandering from place to place, with no prearranged plan, but taking the hint when an old man says: 'What? Haven't you seen the hermitage over the hills?' or a child claims that the local *ayu,* a kind of river fish, are particularly good, and that his grandmother, who lives in that house over there hidden among the bamboo-trees, is particularly good at cooking them. Sometimes even a puncture can be a piece of luck, as it was in the mountains behind Hiroshima, for instance. While we waited for it to be repaired, the local schoolmaster, who was also the local priest, took us to see some most interesting wooden statues of the Fujiwara period, hidden in a little Shinto shrine, which looked like a barn in which agricultural implements were kept.

Yesterday we visited the garden of Ryoan-ji (Photograph 104), which is one of the boldest and strangest in Kyoto. It consists of a stretch of white sand, carefully raked into broad parallel lines, and fifteen rocks, both big and small. The only vegetation consists of some humble coloured lichens on the stone, and a border of moss round the bigger rocks. It is thus an abstract garden; its interest lies in the harmony of its spatial relations and the significance of its tactile values. It makes no facile appeal to the senses, and ornament is totally excluded. It is a direct journey into the void from which the all is born, an absurd, chaste embrace of the mathematics of the heavenly spheres.

The author of this Zen poem in minerals and light seems to have been Sōami, the tea master who also made the Silver Pavilion garden, as well as the tiny Daisen-in gardens; he was responsible for the three Kyoto masterpieces, in fact. The Ryoan-ji garden was probably made in 1499, in other words four centuries before our own artists discovered the same language by a different route. Thus it is not surprising that the Japanese should be so very much at home in modern art. Their tradition is our present, perhaps our future. True, the ignorant read childish symbolical meanings, pleasing fairy tales, into this garden-ideogram— see in it things like a mother-tiger with her cubs in a stream of sand-water, or the tops of mountains over a sea of cloud such as might be seen from a high peak, or merely little islands in a calm river. Little reflection, however, is required to divine its true message; its stark simplicity, its asymmetrical equilibrium, stand for the meaning of ultimate things; they are not a pictorial representation of them. In Asia the artist's work is nearly always religious, because the life of the mind is not compartmentalized; life is itself religion. 'Picking up a blade of grass you make of it a lofty, golden Buddha.'

There was a continuous flow of visitors to the Ryoan-ji—students, honeymoon couples, old women, professors dressed with studied carelessness and wearing flabby hats, mothers with their adorable, chubby-cheeked, Japanese children, peasants on silent pilgrimage, ready to bow in reverence to every important thing, young men in shirt-sleeves with elaborate photographic apparatus, soldiers, an occasional foreigner. Thanks to the *kami* here, there is no appalling loudspeaker as there was in the Silver Pavilion; there is, in fact, nothing to explain. The pilgrims are rightly left in silence to look, feel, think.

We had a few hours to spare, so we drove away towards the slope of the Arashi-yama. This neighbourhood is extraordinarily reminiscent of the surroundings of Florence, the roads leading towards Scandicci, Santa Margherita a Montici, Settignano; there are the same gravelly, winding lanes, the same dry walls. Every now and then you come to the entrance to a villa, two or three houses, a temple among the trees, and you meet few people, an occasional peasant leading a cow, children playing *ishikeri,* a priest, or a pair of lovers.

We reached the foot of the wooded mountains. The sun played in the foliage, and made the tree-covered summits look like green fire. We were wondering whether to go back or not when we saw a sign saying 'Giō-ji' and decided to see what it might be. We followed a path that climbed steeply into the forest, and when we stopped we heard the wind whistling through the sun-kissed branches of the trees at the top. A boy in the distance heard us and came running up. '*Tabako okureyasu*' (Give me a cigarette!), he said. Sachiko told him he ought to be ashamed of himself at his age, but we ended by making friends with him, and he showed us the way. We came to a small straw archway leading to a tiny wooden building with a newly thatched roof hidden among the tall trees. This was the Giō-ji. The boy called out '*Anju-san! Anju-san!*' and an aged Buddhist nun appeared, who greeted us with great courtesy and led us into her domain. She had none of the unctuousness sometimes to be found among her eastern and western sisters, and looked us straight in the eye with a regal detachment. She looked like a woman who had lived a great deal and then one day decided that she had had enough; her face suggested a past life of prosperity rather than of renunciation. She told us about the history of the place with cultured eloquence.

It seemed that the temple had been founded in the eleventh century by Giō, a courtesan with whom Taira Kiyomori was in love; she retired here after the death of her lord and the destruction of the Taira by the Minamoto. The *anju-san* disappeared for a moment to make us tea; she brought it to us a few moments later in exquisite little rustic cups on a simple lacquered tray. Then, after we had removed our shoes, of course, she took us into the little chapel. Everything was so small that we might have been in a cupboard rather than in a room. On the altar, which occupied the whole of one wall, there were some statues. In the centre there was a small and very fine Dai Nichi Nyorai (metaphysical Buddha of light, *see* page 151), a copy of the famous original in the Chuson-ji at Hiraizumi in north Japan, one of the greatest works of the Fujiwara or late Heian period (tenth to twelfth centuries). Beside it were idealized portraits in the style of the Kamakura period of Giō, her mother, and her sister; and finally there was a portrait of Hotoke Gozen, Giō's great rival for the heart of Kiyomori. Giō herself, we were told, had wished to have her portrait there to show that she forgave her, for had not the lord Buddha bade us love our enemies?

My friend Hiroshi Bamba vanished into the garden to make some drawings, and I followed him to take photographs, leaving Sachiko Bamba to talk to the *anju-san*; the animated buzz of their conversation was audible some distance away. When at last we left the wood, which faced eastwards, it was dark; the evening sun gilded the trees on the highest hilltops opposite. Sachiko told me about her fascinating conversation.

The *anju-san,* now aged nearly seventy, was named Chisho-ni, Mother Shining Knowledge. In her youth she had been a famous geisha, and her name had been Teruha, Shining Leaf. She had been famous, very famous indeed, Sachiko remembered having read her name in the newspapers as a child, and there had been some scandals about her. Then she had become the mistress of a famous personage, and had gone round the world with him—London, Paris, Rome, New York. No, she had not been willing to mention his name. She had said that she could speak English, but was no longer willing to.

Instinctively I looked back. Shining Knowledge was standing by the gateway of her tiny realm, and she bade farewell to us, not as a Japanese nun would have done, by bowing, but by shyly waving her hand like a western tourist.

Night Life of Kyoto

At Kyoto there are about ten districts entirely devoted to night life. Each of these has its own character, its own style, its own recognized grade; but it is a complicated, mysterious world, difficult for a foreigner to understand. At the top are the two geisha quarters of Ponto-cho and Gion Kobu, as well as the Shimabara quarter, with its *oiran*;[1] at the lower

[1] Courtesan, ancient style.

levels there is no more talk of gesihas, but of *joro*, prostitutes. There are innumerable intermediary grades. As so often happens, a term originally applied to an aristocracy is vulgarized and depreciates, and the term geisha is used by an ever wider circle of women who have very little indeed in common with the 'cultivated persons of former days;[1] this has been particularly the case since the American military invasion; for the American troops *geisha* came to mean simply 'Japanese girl', brutally eliminating all the ancient distinctions and differences.

But what exactly is a geisha, and why does she play such an important part in Japanese life? Many strange ideas are current on the subject. With Mount Fuji, paper lanterns, hara-kiri, and the Child of the Sun seated on the imperial throne, it is one of the few ideas about Japan that everybody has in mind. But how many misunderstandings there are about her, and how many slanders.[2]

In the first place it should be noted that the geisha is not an exclusively Japanese phenomenon. Nearly everywhere in Asia a man admits to his home only his relatives and his closest friends, and his wife does not take part in ordinary social gatherings. But, as men are generally not satisfied with the company exclusively of their own sex, there has existed from the earliest times a class of women, often recruited from among the wives and daughters of the vanquished in war,[3] whose principal function is to entertain, particularly at dinners and banquets, by their beauty, charm, wit, and skill in dancing, music, and song. In India of the classical period there were the *naikin, ganika,* etc., in China the *chi,* in Tibet the *gyen-sang-ma,* in Korea the *kisaeng.* The westerner, born and bred in a society in which by immemorial tradition (respect for the human personality, the influence of Christianity) it is not just the right, but also the duty, of wives, sisters, mothers, and daughters to assist in the entertainment of relatives, friends, and guests, jumps to the conclusion that these women must be prostitutes. Now, in the lower levels of the profession this is certainly true, for payment for carnal pleasure,

---

[1] *Geisha* is written with two ideograms meaning 'culture', *gei,* and 'person', *sha.*

[2] 'Most foreigners and many Japanese think of the geisha as a pretty but pathetic young girl who has been sold into a life of shame and longs for some young knight-errant to rescue her from it with an honest marriage.'—F. D. PERKINS and F. HAAR, *Geisha of Pontocho,* Tokyo, 1954, p. 13.

[3] This was the fate, for instance, of the women of the house of Taira after the victory of the Minamoto in the battle of Dannoura (1185). This is a classical theme in Japanese art, literature, and the theatre.

whether more or less concealed, inevitably creeps into such a system, as it does at the fringes of the entertainment industry in the west, but at the upper levels, among the Japanese geishas of real class, for instance, the two things are separate and distinct. It is interesting to note that in the American matriarchy, which in so many respects is the antipodes of the Asian world, an institution by no means dissimilar to that of the geisha is arising; that of the hostess in all her innumerable and varied forms, who 'sells' her charm, her smile, her company, without in any way committing her private life.

Giorgio left suddenly yesterday, and Jane, Somi, and I dined to-gether at a charming little restaurant along the river, typical of the Japanese taste for nature and country things; it is furnished like the inside of a forest hut, and the most delicious roast quail is served. The menu, hand-written on carefully chosen rough paper, looked like poetry written by a hermit, and when the bill was presented it looked liked a *billet doux* from a court lady of the Heian period.

After dinner Somi left us. Jane insisted that she wanted to see Kyoto night life. I tried to explain the difficulties. I told her that there was nothing to prevent her from going wherever she liked, but did she want to embarrass everybody, freeze the whole atmosphere by her presence? I felt sure that was not what she wanted. I explained that the great difference was that in the west night life was public; you put down your money, and in you went; money was the only criterion. But here night life was semi-private. The places where entry was open to all were hardly worth going to; they were either utterly revolting, or were parodies of the Place Pigalle, or Basin Street, or Soho. But here the primary requisite was a good introduction, and you had to keep on going to the same place and keep on seeing the same people before you were properly accepted; and at bottom you always remained a foreigner, with clumsy great hands and feet, who moved like a bear straight from the primeval forest, and was in any case incapable of taking a proper part in conversa-tion made up of subtle, piquant, and witty allusions.

Jane was so crestfallen at this speech that I agreed to take her for a short stroll through Gion and Ponto-cho. It did not take us long to get to Ponto-cho, which was not far from the restaurant. As soon as we left the main road with its roar of traffic and went down the short slope towards the river we found ourselves two centuries back in feudal Japan (Photograph 138).

It is a narrow street, which first curves and then runs straight, flanked by doll's houses built of dark brown wood and paper, looking like toy houses for toy love affairs.

'But sometimes there's a ping! and a toy heart is broken,' I remarked. 'And next day you read in the paper that a geisha has committed suicide.'

'How romantic!' Jane exclaimed. 'It's wonderful to be here. I never thought there was anything so romantic in the whole world. Oh, it's cruel that Giorgio had to leave us!'

Outside the local theatre, the Kaburenjo, red lanterns were hanging in honour of the dances that take place there in spring and autumn. There had been a shower some time previously, and the colours were reflected in the puddles; the whole effect was like fairyland. Through the *shōji*, the paper windows, there came the sound of a *kouta* being sung, or gusts of high-pitched laughter, or the notes of a *samisen*. Sometimes we caught sight of a fleeting shadow, or heard the characteristic sound of a sliding door being opened and saw one, two, or several *maiko* (pupil geishas) emerging in their magnificent costume, or a geisha, or a *samisen* player with his instrument and its cat's-skin-covered box. The girls laughed, or talked their delicious dialect, all accents and little exclamations, saying *ōkini* instead of *arigatō* for 'thank you', and *kitsu-kitsu kannin dossé* instead of *domo sumimasen* for 'excuse me, please'. They sound like children; they say *bebe* for 'kimono' and *bubu* for 'tea'. The sound their wooden sandals make as they walk away is enchanting; *kara-koro, kara-koro*, the Japanese call it.

There are some Japanese sounds that you never forget. You may wake in the middle of a moonlit night, for instance, and hear through the frail wood-and-paper walls that separate you from the street the sound of a passer-by wearing *geta*; you hear them from a distance, with their musical *kara-koro, kara-koro, kara-koro*, coming nearer, passing under the window, and then fading away. You can tell at once whether it is a man or a woman, and often you can tell a lot of other things as well. You can distinguish, for instance, the glide of the contented female cat, the proud footsteps of the beauty, the listless footsteps of the disappointed. Then there is the sound of the distant pipe of the *sobaya*, the seller of *soba* for hungry noctambulists, or of the man on his way home who takes his flute from the folds of his kimono and plays.

Haru no yo wo	A spring night;
Shakuhachi fuite	Sounding the flute,
Tōri keri[1]	A man passed by.[1]

Meanwhile there was nothing about geishas that Jane did not want to know. 'How does one become a geisha?' she asked. 'What do they do? What are all these little houses?'

I explained that most of them were *o-chaya* (honourable tea-houses), which was the name given here to what elsewhere in Japan were known as *machiai* (waiting and meeting) places. You could not gain entry to them without an introduction, and the better the place, the more important must your sponsor be. Once inside, however, the place became your second home; you were looked after like a nabob. The hospitality, though fundamentally venal, never appeared to be. Naturally it was very expensive and, if you showed any signs of stinginess, the *o-kami-san,* the mistress of the establishment, showed you her claws, with the greatest politeness, of course, but in a fashion which permitted of no reply.

Jane said she wanted to hear about geishas, not about their clients.

I told her not to be impatient, and to let me tell her things in their proper order. Many people thought that clients visited geishas in their houses, but nothing could be more mistaken. The centre of the whole system was the honourable tea-house, the mistresses of which sent for the geishas, who lived elsewhere. At Kyoto, for instance, they lived in houses called *yakata,* sometimes together, sometimes alone. Before going to the honourable tea-house they called at the *kemban,* the local office where all services were registered; only then did they appear before their client, who would normally have invited some friends for an agreeable evening. Our normally accepted ideas on the subject required complete revision; in the vast majority of cases geishas were sent for purely and simply to entertain, to dance, play, and sing. Moreover, their services were exceedingly expensive and, though a geisha party

[1] Shiki (1866–1902).

enhanced the host's prestige, the cost was ruinous. An elaborate *enkai* could easily run away with fifty, a hundred, two hundred dollars; many were given on expense accounts.

'You've gone back to the clients again, and I want to hear about the geishas. How do you become a geisha?'

'Why? Do you want to leave the service of your honourable government and become the first oversea geisha?'

'Well, that might be an idea.'

I told her there were various ways of becoming a geisha. First of all, there was the system by which a girl was sold by her parents for a sum of money which she had to recoup by her work. This system was, of course, rightly inveighed against by all the reformers; legislation existed against it, but it still went on, in ways which in practice it was impossible to check. It prevailed chiefly in the lowest branches of this ancient profession. At Ponto-cho, it appeared, most of the girls were geishas because their mothers had been geishas; it was hereditary. It was a closed world, with its own professional pride. When girls were from five to seven years old they first appeared in the spring and autumn dances at the Kaburenjo theatre, then they went to an ordinary school, then to a special school, a kind of academy attached to the theatre, where for two years they were taught singing, dancing, music, poetry, the tea ceremony, elocution, recitation, even sociology (who on earth taught them that?), to say nothing of arithmetic and, nowadays, elementary English.

'So there's at any rate one thing I should be good at,' Jane remarked.

'Wait a bit!' I answered. 'I haven't yet told you the best part. Do you realize that you would have to blacken your teeth? After the *shikomu* (little pupil) stage there comes the *maiko* (pupil geisha) stage, which generally lasts for twenty-three months. Then comes the *début* as a fully fledged geisha. In the old days this was a highly important ceremony; the girl still has to lacquer her teeth black a month in advance. It is a curious custom, which was all the rage among the nobles of the Fujiwara period in the tenth century and gradually filtered down among the people. Nowadays it is still possible in the remote countryside to come across an old peasant woman with this sociological fossil in her mouth. I remember seeing one in the Shirakawa valley, north of Gifu,

where many archaic customs still survive. Anyway, geishas still revive
this ancient custom for a month.'

'What do they look like?'

'Wonderful! The face becomes a kind of living mask; the mouth is
like a window from which you look into nothing. It makes you feel as
if you yourself were part of an inanimate world that had suddenly come
alive and could speak. I remember an evening many years ago at the
Ichi-riki, in Gion, on the other side of the river. It's probably the most
exclusive restaurant in the world; they let me in only because I was with
some diplomatists. It's entirely unchanged since feudal times, and every
breath you draw in it costs a fortune. Anyway, at one point a *débutante*
geisha came in silently, and sat with us. She was extraordinarily beautiful.
Her face was covered with the thick wax make-up which in daylight
looks like plaster and is revolting, but by artificial light, particularly if
it is subdued to resemble that of the flickering lamps of the old days,
looks like porcelain. She kept her mouth half-open; her teeth were
black, lacquered like dark metal. She smiled, and said something in the
delightful Kyoto dialect, bending her head, with its mass of black, shiny,
lacquered hair. Then she sang. Heavens, I could have gone crazy about
her!'

'And did you? Confess it, even if it isn't true!'

'What do you expect, on the pay of a poor university lecturer?'

'Was it hard to forget her?'

'Yes, I admit it.'

'But supposing she had liked you?'

'Jane, how can you be so absurdly romantic? Don't you know that
high-class geishas are surrounded by invisible walls that are stronger
than steel? They're like racehorses, worth thousands. To become the
patron of one of them captains of industry, cabinet ministers, great
aristocrats, the cream of Japanese society, go through the most extraordinary hoops.'

'What do you mean by patron?'

'A geisha's patron finances her, enables her to outdo her rivals in
extravagances, clothes, luxuries. Her kimonos, jewels, hairdresser's bills,
and beauty treatment are all wildly expensive. That the arrangement is
profitable to her is obvious. That it should be profitable to him too—
over and above the pleasure of female society, which he could certainly

find with much less trouble and expense—is one of the peculiarities of Japanese society. There is not the slightest doubt that when the name of a distinguished man is associated with that of a famous geisha it helps him enormously; it establishes him as a man of the world, a man who has arrived. The geisha's relations with him may be merely a matter of convenience, or may be based on love. Incidentally, the most famous geishas are by no means the youngest and most attractive; instead it is much more a matter of somehow succeeding in attracting prestige and glamour. The geisha's supreme aim, of course, is marriage, and such marriages are pretty frequent and cause no more surprise than when a peer marries a film-star. If marriage eludes her, she will endeavour to become a kept mistress, a member of the invisible harem which so many Japanese men acquire as soon as they can afford it.'

'And then a young student turns up, doesn't he? That's the part I like!'

'Yes, the eternal triangle. Cabinet minister, beautiful geisha, brilliant, penniless, young student. Secret meetings, weeping willows, moonlight, tears, suspicion, detection, rage, revolvers, confrontation, money handed back, elopement—all the ingredients of a popular novel!'

Farewell to Kyoto

All my friends left Kyoto, and the time came for me to go too. The last of them to leave was Uriu-san, who did so with a characteristic gesture. His relatives had decided for some reason to close their Kyoto house, and he spent the last few nights at my hotel; I explained to the landlady that he was an old friend, and told her to look after him, and let him have whatever he wanted. When I was brought the bill, it included some mysterious ideograms for one very expensive item, which I could not understand at all. When I demanded an explanation the landlady looked at me with an absolutely neutral expression on her face. 'It's for your friend's geisha,' she said. 'Didn't you tell me to let him have whatever he wanted?'

The old man had also left me a note. 'Maraini-sama, *au revoir*,' it said. 'Thank you for this autumn which ended in such a marvellous spring. Her name is Junko, she's DELIGHTFUL. Talk about me sometimes!...'

But it was not spring, it was winter. A telegram had come for me that morning, and I had to leave for Tokyo on urgent business.[1]

[1] The reader will, I hope, forgive my pedantry, but I cannot conclude this lengthy account of Kyoto without mentioning at any rate some of the things to which we have not had occasion to refer in the course of our wanderings in and about the City of Crystal Streams. Here they are:

(1) The Imperial Palace (Gosho, 'Honourable Place'), a broad expanse not far from the centre of the city, where pavilions and gardens form a serene and exquisite pattern of earth and water, architecture and foliage. The names of the various buildings are still those of the Heian period (ninth to eleventh centuries). There is a Shishin-den ('Purple Imperial Pavilion') and a Seiryō-den ('Pavilion of Sweet Coolness'), both of which are open for ceremonies from time to time, but they have repeatedly been destroyed in the course of centuries by fires, the last of which, in 1854, was exceedingly violent.

Nevertheless the various buildings have been reconstructed in a style of noble simplicity worthy of the best Japanese traditions, and they are among the most notable things in Kyoto. The only decoration in the immaculate expanse of gravel in some courtyards consists of two small trees, bamboo, cherry, or orange, which, as W. Blaser rightly observes, acquire the spatial and suggestive values of sculpture; the roofs have the slight curves peculiar to Japanese architecture at the happy moments when it has integrated continental experience with its own pure native traditions; the fittings are of bare wood, unpainted, but polished until it shines like a mirror. The views on which the Emperor's eyes must have rested, both in his hours of repose and when he was attending to affairs of state, consisted of a dark rectangular architectonic background (beams) and light surfaces (walls); in other words, an abstract, asymmetrical harmony of extraordinary serenity and purity, in striking contrast to the throne-rooms and audience chambers in other eastern countries, or, for that matter, in the west.

(2) Palace of the Shogun (Nijo-jo). In regard to preservation this has been much more fortunate than the Imperial Palace. Here, too, pavilions, trees, space, gardens, water, rough stone from the mountains, and fragile paper doors form a magnificent organic whole. The taste displayed is still exquisite but, in comparison with the marvellous simplicity of the Imperial Palace, could be called sumptuous. Even the modular unit of construction is bigger than usual; the whole has a grandiose solemnity which is rare in Japan. The decorated gateways, the walls, the corner towers, are a reminder that the building was a fortress (jo) as well as a palace. Inside there are fine murals in the style of the Great Decorators by Kano Tanyū (1602–1674), Kano Naonobu (1607–1650), and others of their school. Some of the panels seem to have been brought here from the Fushimi palace, built by Hideyoshi. A thing to note is the particular care in the carvings and in the painting of the dividing panels between the rooms, and in the decoration of the ceilings. We are at the beginning of the Tokugawa period (seventeenth century), but the bold and generous spirit of the Momoyama period still survives here.

(3) Shugaku-in ('Villa of the Doctrine'), at the foot of Mount Hiei. Architecture, gardens, and paintings; the ensemble lacks the exquisite completeness of the Katsura villa, but is more varied and spacious. Beginning of the seventeenth century.

(4) Kiyomizu-dera ('Temple of the Pure Fountains'), half-way up a spur of the Eastern Mount (Higashi-yama); it is one of the rare temples built at an altitude and having a view. Its terrace, suspended over a shady, densely wooded valley, filled with the sound of rushing waters, is famous throughout Japan. It was founded in 805 B.C., but suffered the usual fires, and the present buildings date back to the first half of the seventeenth century. It is dedicated to the Bodhisattva Kwannon ('Benevolent Enlightened One'), whose eleven-headed image is very ancient, of mediocre artistic value, and greatly venerated. This temple (like that of Hase, see page 167) is one of the group of thirty-three dedicated to Kwannon and belongs to the Shingon sect); it is a famous and venerated sanctuary. It is an interesting place to visit because of the opportunity of observing the popular

manifestations of a great faith: pilgrims at prayer, priests saying *kuyō* for the dead, sacred talismans and statuettes being sold, and meditation being practised in the depth of winter by motionless, half-naked devotees in the spray of the Otowa waterfall.

(5) Sanjusangen-do, in the city, near the Municipal Museum. The temple dates back to 1251, but is not particularly beautiful or interesting. However, its long, dark nave contains more than a thousand similar, erect statues, all shining with gold, of the Bodhisattva Kwannon. The central statue, and some of its neighbours, are said to be by Tankei (thirteenth century), one of the greatest Japanese sculptors. The total effect is tremendous, perhaps bordering on the terrifying, unreal; the idea of the creators of this hieratic forest of golden heads, arms, eyes, was a pious, literal, ritual glorification of Kwannon's infinite benevolence; but the effect on the twentieth-century mind is as disturbing as that of an infinite number of light-years in infinite space, or the eyes of an insect seen through a microscope. In the long corridors behind the thousand bodhisattvas are powerful wooden sculptures of the Kamakura period, including Fu-jin and Rai-jin, the gods of wind and thunder (*see* Photograph 23).

(6) The Hozu-gawa rapids. The Japanese archipelago is extraordinary rich in water, and hence in vegetation. Sometimes three of nature's most impressive features, river, rock, and forest, combine at a single spot with tremendous effect. Famous are the Tenryu river (Photograph 26); the Kuro-be, in the Japanese Alps, which is accessible only after a stiff rock-climb; the Doro-hacchō, in the Kii peninsula, along which you travel silently in boats on motionless, emerald-coloured water between dazzling walls of weather-beaten rock, among which vegetation grows; the walls are crowned with twisted pine-trees. The Hozu river, with its marvellously clear waters, winds its way regally through a deep valley near Kyoto. In the fine season you can go down it in long, flat-bottomed, skilfully navigated boats.

II

Signature of the Tokugawa

Climatic Contrasts

WINTER had now descended on Japan; I looked out of the train window at the dry, brown, resting rice-fields which spread out around us in the plains. Here and there women in *mompe* (blue linen trousers) were working in the fields, or a man was leading a beast along a path, perhaps on his way to one of the country markets that are frequent towards the end of the year. In the distance the first snow-covered peaks were to be seen—Mount Ibuki, for instance, between Biwa lake and Nagoya—and I was reminded of ski excursions of long ago. Winter comes later than with us, but is more severe and lasts longer.

The monsoon system, which causes the winds to blow from the south in summer and from the north in winter, makes the Japanese climate almost tropical in the former and sub-arctic in the latter. The map on the next page shows a curious fact; the greater part of Japan lies farther south than Italy, but it enjoys no winter mildness corresponding to that of the Mediterranean. Kyoto is nearer the equator than Tunis, but its winter climate is similar to that of Florence. The latitude of Tuscany is that of Hokkaido, where the winter is colder than in Finland.

After completing my business in Tokyo, I left for a quick visit to Nikko, a three-hour train journey. Nikko is one of the most famous places in Japan and, though my enthusiasm for it is tepid, I must say something about it.

355

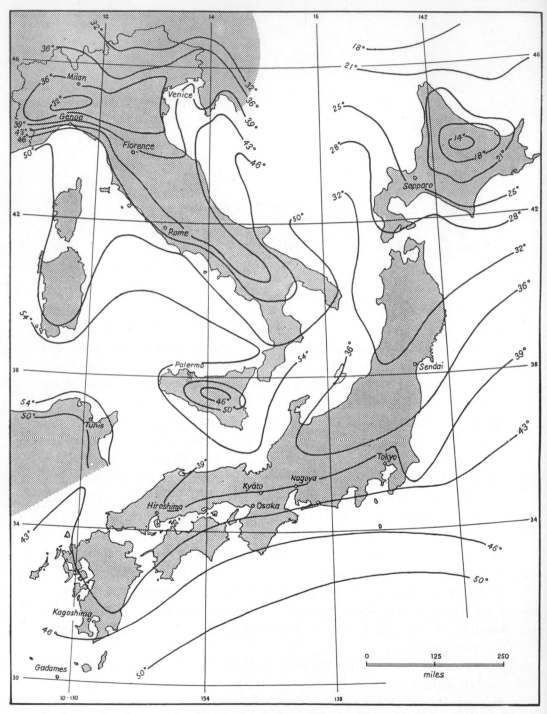

Isotherms for the month of January in Italy and Japan. The cold winter climate of north Japan is due to the proximity of Siberia

The name of Nikko stands for a tremendous symphony of rocks, water-falls, mountains, lakes, flower-covered marshes, shady gorges, impressive volcanoes which provide the background for many works of man. Some of these, if they were built to achieve the most clamorous notoriety, have certainly attained that aim. From the artistic point of view, however, they miss the mark. I refer to the mausoleums built for themselves by the Tokugawa shoguns, in particular Iyeyasu (1542–1616), the founder of the line.

The spot was chosen with a sagacious eye; there are few sites in Japan where water, rock, and forest combine to provide such an extraordinary assembly of natural show-pieces. But times were not what they were. The Japanese of earlier centuries—the Nara and Heian, and perhaps also the Kamakura and Muromachi centuries—would certainly have understood these valleys, peaks, and forests, and expressed the awe aroused in them in architecture worthy of its surroundings. But by the time the seventeenth century was well under way (most of the buildings here were completed between 1634 and 1636) minds had grown soft, servile, complicated; it was a time of repression and fear, for the shadow of the Tokugawa lay heavily over everything; outward display was combined with an inner meanness of spirit, and the tyrants made the old mistake of confusing pomp, luxury, magnificence, with art.

In the train I made the acquaintance of two young women who were also on the way to see the celebrated sights of Nikko; they came from Kyoto, and we immediately agreed in pooh-poohing the fame of these gigantic hearses glittering with gold which were scattered about the mountains. We were like Florentines visiting St. Peter's and finding everything crude and inflated. But there comes a point when such people, if they are intelligent, realize that that attitude can become a pose and, faced with Bernini's colonnades in St. Peter's Square, give way to astonishment and enthusiasm. At Nikko we, too, were sometimes forced to capitulate.

The great avenue, flanked by huge cypresses, that leads to the Tōshōgu shrine is truly solemn and impressive, for instance. It ends with some steps called the Sennin-ishidan ('of the thousand people'), because in Tokugawa times ordinary people had to stop at this point;

only samurai and *daimyo* were allowed to pass beyond. We continued along a broad platform between pagodas, gateways, walls covered with moss and fern, stables for the sacred horses, storehouses and armouries, stone and bronze lanterns, chapels, bell towers, reliquaries, all lacquered and decorated with coloured reliefs representing plants and animals, among them the famous three monkeys with covered ears, eyes, and mouth ('I hear no evil, I see no evil, I speak no evil'). The general atmosphere is one of heaviness, but the huge forest trees dominate the place so majestically as to redeem the less happy details of the work of man (Photograph 86).

At the Yōmei gateway, however—it is also known as Higurashi-mon, 'evening gate', implying that the visitor would wish to remain until sunset to enjoy its infinite beauties—nature is unable to swallow up the horror. True, you are put on your guard in advance by various structures of dubious taste—the small Covered Well, for instance—and are consequently prepared for the worst. Nevertheless you are taken aback; you ask yourself whether it is a joke, or a nightmare, or a huge wedding cake, a masterpiece of sugar-icing made for some extravagant prince with a perverse, rococo taste, who wished to alarm and entertain his guests. But no, it is real architecture, carried out in earnest by people whose ideal was Technicolor or Vistavision. The eye sets out on its painful journey up the white columns, the gilded columns, the lacquered columns; it mounts to heavy, complicated roofs and decorations, loses its way among giraffes, dragons, clouds, lions, Chinese children, peonies, kings and princes, sages and immortals, birds, serpents, flowers, tigers, pines, bamboos, medlars, peacocks, pheasants, all carved with cold and diabolical skill, coloured with visionary fury, polished and plastered for the everlasting delight of *nouveaux riches*. A moment comes when you can stand it no longer and turn away.

A bespectacled little professor who somehow managed to attach himself to us was, however, full of enthusiasm for it all, and we responded with vague, non-committal smiles. As masterpieces of Tokugawa propaganda it must be admitted that the Nikko mausoleums have done their work. Only the most cultured Japanese, those who live in contact with the great traditions of Kyoto, Nara, Kamakura, regard these works as flagrant exhibitions of bad taste and abysmal vulgarity; for the majority they represent the supreme example of terrestrial beauty.

A popular saying is 'Nikko wo minai uchi wa, kekkō to iu na' (if you have not seen Nikko, do not speak of splendour)—rather like 'See Naples and die'.

Unfortunately, the organizers of the Japanese tourist industry, those who have tried to present their country and its history to the west, said to themselves that this was the sort of thing which foreigners could understand and appreciate. Considering the things which the great majority of westerners in the east pick out and pay expensive prices for, no excessive blame should be attached to the Japanese; it was only too natural that they should play what they were bound to consider a safe card. Twenty-three pages of the *Official Guide to Japan,* for instance, are devoted to Nikko and only nineteen to Nara, which is as absurd as it would be to devote the same proportions to the Victor Emmanuel monument in Rome and to Siena. The same guide, though its criticisms are sometimes severe, goes into ecstasies over Nikko. 'The mausoleums of Nikko show us the finest works produced by the hand of man . . .' it says, and 'Nikko is rightly considered by foreigners by far the most interesting thing in the whole of Japan', etc., etc. (pages 406–7).

The fact that Nikko was built only a few years after the Katsura villa gives an idea of the heights and depths between which Japanese art has been capable of moving during the centuries. There is the same distance between the Kyoto villa and the Nikko mausoleums as there is between Brunelleschi and Antoni Gaudì. However, that does a grave injustice to Gaudì; for the Spanish architect is life, striving for something, and therefore forgivable if it goes astray. But Nikko is old age. weariness, feebleness, bad aesthetics, trying to redeem itself with money, gold, size. Nikko, in other words, stinks of death.

In this book I have expressed a great deal of enthusiasm about that pole of Japanese art and taste the ideals of which are simplicity, purity, nature, of which there are so many superb examples at Ise, Nara, Kyoto, and elsewhere. But it should not be forgotten that there is an opposite pole, that Ise, Nara, Kyoto, represent only one aspect of Japan; there is another, which is attracted by the opposite polar force—wealth and display, silver and gold. Nikko is the embodiment of this second pole. Detestable though it is, it is necessary to bear it in mind, because it has occupied an important place in the total picture of Japanese civilization from the seventeenth century to the present day.

It would, however, be a mistake to condemn the Tokugawa centuries out of hand. In spite of the oppressive dictatorship, there were many things that flourished. The country did not easily surrender itself into its hands, and never did so completely. It was a period of striking contrasts, and without some knowledge of the Tokugawa period neither the best nor the worst aspects of modern Japan can be properly understood.

We left the country reunited into a single state by Tokugawa Iyeyasu in the seventeenth century. As soon as he had bent Japan to his will, his supreme aim was the maintenance of absolute power for himself and his descendants; and the institutions that he devised were so well adapted to their purpose that they survived for two centuries and a half. Japanese historians describe him as humane, magnanimous, just, and affable, but a closer examination of his actions and policies leads to the conclusion that this is an idealized portrait, the result of his extraordinary skill in the manipulation of men. His success was outstanding —Machiavelli would have acknowledged him as the supreme Prince— but there is little about him to attract sympathy. If on the one hand he was frugal, patient, perfectionist, on the other he was false, mean, unscrupulous, and, when necessary, cruel. His pitiless extermination of the family of Hideyoshi, his one-time great friend and ally, with whom he was doubly bound by ties of marriage, is celebrated in Japanese history. In short, the *bakufu* (camp government) embodied, not only his will, but the colour and flavour of his personality.

The Tokugawa centuries, looked at in broad outline, fall into three phases. The first, which may be called that of crystallization (about 1600–1680), was followed by a short period of equilibrium, which in turn gave way to a long period of decline and disintegration, culminating in the handing back of the supreme power to the Emperor (about 1710 to 1868).

The process of crystallization, which continued under Hidetada (1616–1622), Iyemitsu (1622–1651), and Iyetsuna (1651–1680) and brought to fruition all the political, economic, and social potentialities that the system possessed, was particularly vigorous at the outset, under Iyeyasu. After the victory of Sekigahara (1600), when he crushed a powerful alliance of hostile lords, he clearly and brutally settled his position with respect to the Emperor and the court. The Emperor's fuctions were limited to ceremonial; the only real act of government left in the hands of the descendant of the gods was that of confirming each of Iyeyasu's descendants in office on his predecessor's death. In future shoguns were to reside at Yedo, far from the intrigues of Kyoto. The imperial family and the court nobles were granted modest allowances but, apart from certain villas and small estates, were forbidden to possess land. Iyeyasu succeeded in confining in a golden cage those who represented a potential threat to him because of their age-long moral ascendancy over the people.

Another direction from which Iyeyasu and his descendants—and with good reason—scented potential danger was that of the great feudal lords; tying the Emperor's hands would have served little purpose had the political and economic power of the *daimyo* not been held firmly in check. Iyeyasu started by dividing them into two broad categories: *fudai* and *tozama*. The *fudai daimyo* ('hereditary lords') were those who had declared their loyalty to the Tokugawa before the battle of Sekigahara; the *tozama daimyo* ('outside lords') were the rest. In the general redistribution that took place at the beginning of the seventeenth century all the best land was given to the *fudai daimyo*; the *tozama* were granted, or permitted to retain, the rest. The consequence was that sixty-four per cent of the national production of rice, the economic foundation of the country, was in the hands of the Tokugawa and their followers. However, a number of *tozama daimyo* (the Shimazu of Satsuma, the Daté in the north, the Maeda at Kanazawa, the Tosa in the island of Shikoku) were very powerful, had been established in their territories for a long time, and considered the Tokugawa as usurpers, having no better title to power than force; and in the second half of the nineteenth century it was these or their followers who worked with the greatest obstinacy and the greatest success to bring about the downfall of the whole system. Thus the fears of the *bakufu* were well founded.

Iyeyasu used a variety of methods to clip the wings of the *daimyo* who were hostile to him. I have already mentioned[1] the *sankin-kōtai* ('alternate attendance') system by which a *daimyo* had either to be at Yedo himself or leave his family there as a guarantee of good behaviour.

[1] P. 114.

True, in 1603 he had made them all sign an oath of loyalty to the régime, but it was as well to be on the safe side. Moreover, all their activities were regulated by a flood of decrees. They were allowed to build castles, for instance, but no alterations were permitted once they were built, and all repairs had to be authorized; marriages, or important journeys, had to be authorized by the *bakufu;* agreements, troop movements, and even trade between them, were prohibited. True, they were exempt from taxation, but the *bakufu* had ways and means of exacting gifts and services from them that effectively kept their coffers empty; the Nikko mausoleums, for instance, kept the most eminent *daimyo* out of mischief for many years. Finally, they were forbidden access to the Emperor.

The Tokugawa system was in fact a provisional military government system extended indefinitely into times of peace. The term *bakufu* shows that no attempt was made to conceal the fact, and the names given to the principal offices of state almost ostentatiously smacked of the backwoods. The state council, for instance, consisted of four or five *toshiyori* ('old men, seniors'), presided over by the *o-doshiyori* ('the great old man'). There was a repetition of what had happened in the times of the Minamoto; the principles that had served to regulate the affairs of a small feudal estate, the principles applied by the house of Tokugawa in their original seat of Mikawa, became the law and constitution of Japan. The position was the reverse of that which followed the Taikwa reforms of 645 or the Meiji reforms of 1868, when political theories, systems, usages and customs of a foreign civilization—the Chinese in the first case and the European-American in the second—were taken over wholesale. Legislation—which was often kept secret, with the result that people kept a respectful distance between themselves and all danger areas—accumulated in an empirical, casual, and often contradictory manner, and its general trend was minatory and repressive. The government, in accordance with an ancient and still not completely forgotten oriental tendency, always preferred an ethical precept to a definite law; and these were displayed on appropriate notice-boards (*fuda*) at every cross-roads.

An inevitable consequence of such a system was the legal sanction given to a number of monstrous class privileges; samurai, for instance, enjoyed the right of *kirisute gomen* ('killing and going away'), of which they sometimes took advantage at the expense of wretched peasants or artisans who failed to bow to them with sufficient respect. Another inevitable consequence was the proliferation of the notorious *metsuké*, who were originally 'censors', but quickly developed into spies. By means of them the government was kept secretly informed of what both *daimyo* and people were thinking, doing, and saying, and this with an efficiency which has not been exceeded elsewhere even in our own day.

The people were no more than a uniform, passive mass, the least dangerous of the forces exploited by the *bakufu* for its own advantage; but the Tokugawa applied to them too their mania for organizing everything, casting everything into an immutable, easily governable, mould. I have already mentioned (p. 72) the four basic classes in which society was organized; samurai (warriors); *hyakushō* (peasants; *shokunin* (artisans); and *shōnin* (merchants, traders). These were intended to be as permanent as the various kinds of ants in an ant-heap. The samurai, who are estimated to have numbered about 350,000,[1] were forbidden to work, and above all to engage in commerce; to prevent them from turning into a class of unemployed, the *bakufu* encouraged them to devote themselves to arts and letters, with the curious result that, for a time at any rate, the military class was the cultivated class. Samurai received a government allowance of from twenty to ten thousand *koku*[2] of rice a year, depending on their grades, of which there were several. The whole burden thus fell upon the peasants, and this, as we shall see later, was one of the greatest weaknesses of the system.

The fourth source from which Iyeyasu and his descendants feared a potential threat to the established order was the outside world. Foreigners, as we have already seen (page 173), had been received with open arms from their first appearance in the little island of Tane in 1542. The Momoyama period (end of the sixteenth century) was, in spite of disputes and misunderstandings, a period of lively exchanges of all kinds; not only did many Europeans land in Japan and live there, preaching or trading, but Japanese ships continually visited the great ports of eastern Asia, and flourishing Japanese colonies were established in China, the Philippines, Formosa. Christian missionary work was remarkably successful, both in the south (Kyushu) and at Meaco

---

[1] Including family and servants, about two millions (Asakawa).

[2] A *koku* (about forty gallons) was the amount considered sufficient to feed a man for a year. *Daimyo*, from the point of view of the Tokugawa bureaucracy, were simply samurai whose annual allowance exceeded 10,000 *koku*. At the head of the list came the Maeda, with more than a million *koku*.

(Kyoto); at the end of the sixteenth or beginning of the seventeenth century there seem to have been about half a million converts. Acting on the advice of the Italian Jesuit Valignani, some southern Japanese *daimyo* sent an embassy to Rome (1592–91), and another followed a few years later (1615–20). Thus the Japanese cannot be said to have been inhospitable, or lacking in a desire to unite their destiny with that of the world.

However, circumstances conspired to persuade the rulers of Japan to revise their attitude to the 'southern barbarians' and the doctrines which they spread. It should, of course, be recalled that the Roman Catholicism of the period, which was that of the Counter-Reformation, desirous of compensating by new conquests oversea for the painful defeats it had suffered in Europe, presented itself in a guise in which the most extraordinary heroism and the most ardent love of humanity were mingled with the most bigoted and aggressive intolerance. Such a faith was extraordinarily well adapted to fire the Japanese mind, which is always ready to respond with enthusiasm to doctrines which promise glory and require total adherence, undisputed obedience, extreme sacrifices. There were some (like the *daimyo* of Bungo) who adopted the worst characteristics of the new doctrine and started hunting Buddhist priests as if they were hares or wild boar; but there were also many men and women, and even children, who faced horrible deaths singing hymns and praying for their executioners.

Phenomena of this sort were bound to make the rulers of Japan shake their heads. Christianity, whichever way it was looked at, was a cause of ferment, which might easily assume forms dangerous to the established order. Besides, it undermined the very foundations of the state by introducing another loyalty, all the more dangerous because of the acts of heroism which it was capable of inspiring. To that there must be added the bitter rivalry between the various religious orders (Jesuits, Franciscans, Augustinians, Dominicans), whose zeal and ambition ended by revealing some unedifying aspects of the character of the men 'with red hair'; to say nothing of the rivalries and intrigues of the various nationalities (Portuguese, Spanish, British, Dutch) to secure special commercial privileges for themselves. Finally, there was the unfortunate mixture of religious propaganda and commercial expansion.

It is therefore not in the least surprising that Hideyoshi, once

convinced that there was a secret link between the preaching of the
missionaries and political penetration, should have taken severe measures to restrict the complicated and often obscure activities of these
foreigners, which can hardly have been intelligible to him. The first
decree proscribing them was issued in 1587. Perhaps in the years that
followed it might have been possible to come to terms had not two
unyielding forces quickly been brought into conflict—Iyeyasu on the
one hand and the *bateren*[1] on the other. If it is true that the bad relations
between Japanese and westerners, and the religious persecutions in
particular, must be attributed chiefly to European errors and blindness,
it is also true that the personality of the Tokugawa shogun, with its
paradoxical combination of vigour, intelligence, narrow-mindedness,
and selfishness, laid its icy grip on the final outcome of events. There is
always one effective, if absurd, solution to all human problems. The
problem of indigestion, for instance, could be solved by not eating, or
of road accidents by banning motor-cars. Similarly, the 'southern
barbarians' could be prevented from causing more trouble by closing
the gates of Japan to them, breaking the bridges between Japan and the
outside world. This was Iyeyasu's famous policy of exclusion (*sakoku*),
which was faithfully and inflexibly followed by Hidetada, Iyemitsu, and
all the other shoguns of his line until 1854.

The closure took place in stages; even the persecution of Christians
became severe only when previous measures turned out to be ineffective.
What should we do if Buddhist monks persisted in making clandestine
landings on our shores, to preach a faith that we considered subversive?
Today we should deport them, but three centuries ago we should have
used more drastic measures of discouragement. It is sufficient to recall
the fate of Savonarola, Giordano Bruno, and others who came into
conflict with western orthodoxy.

Between 1615 and 1637 the Japanese persecution reached a pitch of
horrible intensity; during this period, one of the blackest pages in human
history, men showed both the most revolting cruelty and the most
sublime heroism of which they are capable. The tragedy reached its
climax in the Shimabara revolt, when of 37,000 Christian peasants only
105 survived. In 1630 the importation of any book which mentioned

---

[1] From the Portuguese for 'fathers'. Many Italian preachers died a martyr's death during this
period.

Christianity or was written by a Jesuit was forbidden. In 1639 Japan cut the last links and shut herself off from the world. Any foreigner who landed in Japan was liable to the death penalty, as was any Japanese who left the country, or, having left it, returned. The only tenuous thread that was permitted to survive was a small Dutch trading station at Nagasaki, to which one ship a year was permitted to sail from Macao.

By shutting out the world in this way the Japanese threw away the great economic and political advantages of a position in the Pacific similar to that of Britain in the Atlantic; and not only that, they restricted themselves to a mental and physical strait-jacket at the very moment when the west was setting out on the meteoric advance of the modern age. As, however, any policy, any line of conduct, persisted in to its logical conclusion yields positive results, and as in the last years of the seventeenth and the earliest years of the eighteenth century many forces that were later to diverge with grave ill effects were working harmoniously together, Japan enjoyed a brief summer of wealth and splendour. This more or less corresponds with what the Japanese call the Genroku period (1688–1703),[1] or the shogunate of Tsunayoshi (1680–1709), a complex figure—a magnificent patron of the arts, a man of extreme superstition, and a bad financier.

During these years Japan enjoyed the benefit of long and uninterrupted peace. After four centuries of warfare, arms at last served only for the splendid processions and ceremonies which accompanied every important event at the courts of the shogun or the *daimyo*. During the seventeenth century there was a slow but steady increase in population; according to a census held in 1721, there were 26 million inhabitants of Japan. Trade and commerce, though often hampered by the short-sighted policy of the *bakufu*, flourished; for the first time in Japanese history the despised class of artisans and traders became an important factor with the growth of big towns—Yedo, Osaka, Sakai, Nagasaki, Kyoto.

---

[1] The Japanese, following an ancient Chinese custom, do not date their history as we do, but subdivide it into successive eras of five or six years. In the past these eras were often changed for astrological reasons, or simply to bring good fortune. After 1868, however, it was decided that every era should correspond with the reign of an emperor. Thus the Meiji era (1868–1912) was followed by the Taisho era (1912–1926) and the Showa, the present era, from 1926 onwards. In Japan the year 1958 is Showa XXXIII. It is a picturesque but inconvenient system, and in modern history books a start is now being made in the use of the western system.

It was at the turn of the seventeenth century that Japanese civilization assumed the social, artistic, literary forms so well known to the west; it may be as well, therefore, that we should have a look at these, bearing in mind that many of the phenomena concerned do not correspond in time to the true Genroku period.

One feature was a return to China for the fundamental sources of inspiration. Both Christianity and Buddhism had appeared as disintegrating elements in relation to the state; the former was ferociously persecuted and rigorously excluded;[1] the latter was circumscribed and restricted, lost its driving force, became cold and formal, an empty shell. The best Japanese minds, partly spontaneously, partly encouraged by the *bakufu*, applied themselves to the version of Confucianism developed by the famous Chinese thinker Chu Hsi (1130–1200). Here the Japanese found a philosophy of life which, having been profoundly influenced by Ch'an (Zen) Buddhism and religious Taoism, was less rationalist and rigid than the original; in western terms it might be described as a kind of stoicism. What appealed to the Japanese was the fact that at the core of a grandiose metaphysical system lay the ancient principles of loyalty and harmony between ruler and ruled, father and son, husband and wife, etc., etc. The Five Relationships reflected the fundamental order of the universe.[2]

It would be interesting to deal more extensively with the philosophical background of the period, particularly because Confucianism often assumed the characteristics of a religion, influencing men and their conduct, not only by the force of ideas, but by the far more powerful driving force of myths. During the Tokugawa period Confucianism invaded every sphere of Japanese life; the age-old natural tendency of this people to organize themselves pyramidally found expression in a philosophy of life which had the impressiveness and beauty of a temple. At the same time there was brought to perfection the closely knitted fabric of mutual obligations which still permeates the whole of Japanese

[1] Some groups of Christians succeeded in surviving in secret near Nagasaki; they were rediscovered in 1866.

[2] 'In the history of Japanese thought little part is played by the personal sense of sin, which in western men has engendered puritanical complexes and driven them to extremes of restless inquiry and despair. The Japanese have cared little for abstract ideas of good and evil, but they have always been concerned with problems of behaviour, as questions of a man's duty not so much to himself as to the society of which he is a member.'—G. B. SANSOM, *Japan, a Short Cultural History*, London, 1931, p. 472.

society, and the position of mothers, sons, fathers, the aged, the dependent, girls, artists, geishas, leaders, beggars, prostitutes, hermits, rich men, saints, the Emperor, the pariah, master and pupil, master and servant, were defined in all their innumerable aspects.

In literature, in spite of the depressive atmosphere created by the official tyranny, there was intense activity in the most varied fields. The production comprised 'history, biography, poetry, the drama, essays, sermons, a multitude of political and religious treatises, fiction of various kinds and travels, with a huge mass of *biblia abiblia,* such as dictionaries, grammars and other philological works, bibliographies, medical works, treatises on botany, law, the art of war, commentaries on the Chinese classics (in themselves a host), expositions of Buddhist doctrine, encyclopaedias, antiquarian and metaphysical works, guide-books, and so on'.[1] From the times of Iyeyasu onwards the shoguns kept as counsellor, as a kind of living moral conscience, a *kangakusha,* or 'master of the Chinese sciences'. One of these, notable for the wide range of his interests, was Arai Hakuseki (1657–1725), who wrote with great fluency and learning on history, economics and finance, philology, travel, art criticism, law, and strategy.

For us his most interesting work is the *Seiyō Kibun,* the record of a long interview with Father John Baptist Sidotti, of Palermo, who succeeded in entering Japan in 1708 and was promptly arrested and taken to the Kirishitan Yashiki at Yedo, where the rare missionaries who succeeded in breaking the ban on entry into Japan were kept in isolation. Sidotti was the last missionary who set foot in the forbidden land until the second half of the nineteenth century; and Arai's work was the first sign of a renewal of the Japanese interest in the west. Almost insurmountable language difficulties made it hard for the two to understand each other. Arai, while he professed the greatest admiration for the father's knowledge and erudition, regarded his religion as utterly incomprehensible and strange. 'Suddenly folly takes the place of wisdom,' he wrote, 'and it is like listening to the talk of two different persons.' Sidotti died wretchedly in 1715, after baptizing the two old gaolers who looked after him.

So much for what might be described as the orthodox attitude of the ruling class. The Tokugawa period was, however, characterized by the birth and rapid growth of a bourgeoisie which, if it enjoyed no

[1] W. G. ASTON, *A History of Japanese Literature,* London, 1899.

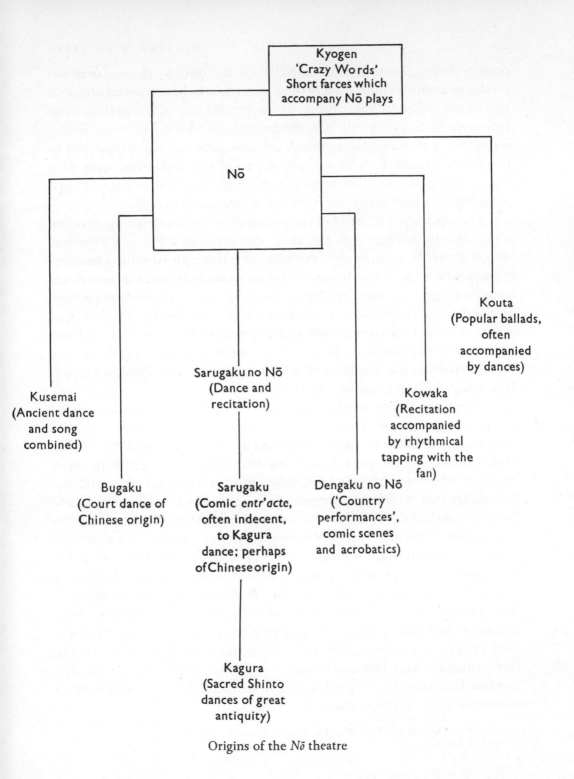

Origins of the *Nō* theatre

prestige, being preceded in the social scale, not only by the samurai, but by the peasants, acquired increasing wealth, and hence social strength and importance. A characteristic of the second half of the period, from the Genroku era onwards, was the struggle conducted in every field—economic, political, philosophical, artistic—between the supporters of the aristocratic ideal, who were both proud and noble but were now slowly dying of conformism and immobility, and those who felt the pulsation of a new life rising from below, from the people.

The academic literature of the period is, generally speaking, erudite, stale, and dry-as-dust, but the true, spontaneous literature expresses a vivid joy in life, an unbridled taste for everything pleasurable, amusing, extravagant, sensational. It was the classic period of novels of adventure and eroticism, whose characters move in the perfumed and sinful atmosphere of the big towns 'where night never falls'. Ibara Saikaku, of whom a critic of a later period said contemptuously that 'he had not a single Chinese character in his belly',[1] went on producing books for decade after decade, the titles of which, according to a Puritan English historian,[2] are 'too gross for quotation'.

One of the things in which the Yedo period showed special originality was the theatre. Here, too, the characteristic dualism made its appearance. On the one hand there was the *Nō* theatre, with its dancing and symbolism and poetry, and on the other the *Bunraku* (puppet theatre), which was born and flourished most notably at Osaka, and the Kabuki theatre, which was primarily a Yedo product. I should properly have mentioned the *Nō* theatre in connection with Yoshimitsu and the civilization of Kyoto in the Muromachi period (fourteenth–fifteenth centuries), but thought it better to say the little that I have to say about the Japanese theatre in one place, and to save it until now, because it was in the Tokugawa period that the *Nō* theatre assumed its place in Japanese society. The *bakufu* included it in its ceremonial for great occasions, and the enthusiasm for it reached a high pitch, particularly in the times of the Shogun Tsunayoshi; it was not for nothing that the stern moralist Arai Hakuseki denounced these performances on the ground that they led to perdition, and persuaded the government to substitute ancient Shinto music for them.

[1] The seat of knowledge, according to Chinese medicine and psychology.
[2] W. G. ASTON.

A *Nō* play is essentially a short sequence of dialogue, dance, and song, with the occasional accompaniment of musical instruments; it is less a drama than a scenic opera, intended to bring to life a poetic moment, using symbolic and often almost abstract means. Both its form and its repertory, which survive to this day, were the creation of the brief and brilliant dynasty established by Kannami Kiyotsugu and his son Seami Motokiyo, which flourished between 1350 and 1450, *i.e.,* the period of Yoshimitsu, of the Golden Pavilion, and of the Sung influence of Kyoto. The *Nō* drama was a happy combination of many pre-existing elements (*see* illustration on page 369). Kannami supplied definite, but not rigid, models which authors of later times have always respected. The language is the court language of the fourteenth century, allusive, elegant, effective. The actors wear masks for many of their parts; their long training starts at the age of about seven, and they are not considered fully trained until they are nearly thirty. This extraordinary seriousness of the theatrical profession has been handed down from ancient times, and the results are evident in the Japanese cinema.[1]

The popular theatre, though it existed in various forms from the earliest times, owes its true birth to the genius of Chikamatsu Monzaemon (1653–1724). Many of the fifty and more plays that he wrote are still played today. He wrote his *jōruri*[2] for the puppet theatre, as first actresses and then actors had been banned from the stage as immoral in one of the *bakufu's* numerous outbursts of Puritanism.

As for lyric poetry, it is sufficient to recall that Bashō (1643–1694) belongs to the earlier phase of the Tokugawa period, and that the names of his major pupils fill the period until our own times with perhaps greater continuity than in any other department of literature.

In the arts the panorama is vast, full of vitality and conflicting forces; here, too, what is most significant is the product of the new bourgeois and popular world. I refer particularly (but not exclusively) to the *ukiyo-e,* which towards the end of the seventeenth century assumed the form well known to everybody as Japanese prints.

For a substantial part of the Yokugawa period painting was officially

---

[1] The ordinary *Nō* repertory consists of about two hundred and fifty plays; more than a hundred —and the best—of them bear the names of Seami or his father Kenami.

[2] From the name of a twelfth-century princess; a play in which she was a character was the *pièce de résistance* of the popular stage.

represented by the Kano dynasty, in which, in accordance with the custom, descent was from father to son or adopted son. As often happens in such cases, particularly when the artists enjoy the favour of a powerful government, they were skilful, learned, decorative, often precious, but they lost in sincerity, freshness, *élan*. *Bakufu* taste was dominated by the ethical principles of Confucianism; the Zen lyricism of earlier times was regarded with suspicion. The object of art was 'to ennoble man, to illustrate models of conduct, to serve in the purpose of good government and to suggest virtues symbolically';[1] and we, observing contemporary examples, are only too well aware of how damaging such restrictions are to artistic spontaneity. These were also eclectic times; the two great traditional schools of Tosa and Kano often produced works difficult to distinguish from each other's and from those of the pupils of Tōhaku, Tōgan, and Yushō.

The only outstanding figure is Kano Tanyū (1602–1674). During his life-time he was exalted as a master without rival by the *bakufu* and the most eminent *daimyo*, high honours in the Buddhist hierarchy were conferred on him, and on all matters connected with art his word was considered final. It is impossible to cast doubt on his immense technical skill, the mastery of line that he exhibits in his many celebrated paintings, 'the noble, ample, breath' by which his work is invariably distinguished, but we are a long way from the fire and ecstasy of Eitoku or Sanraku.

In a certain formal sense the painters of *bunjin-ga* ('paintings by literary men') were related to the Kano dynasty, inasmuch as they followed in the path of Chinese inspiration. They did not constitute a proper school, but consisted of a great many men, for the most part modest samurai, or members of the new bourgeoisie, who were united by a desire to express themselves in painting and poetry and shared a certain contempt for technique and professional polish. The *bunjin-ga* (or *nan-ga*, 'pictures from the south', because their inspiration was drawn from southern Chinese artists) are ruminations in familiar themes, woods, huts, mountains, flowers, hermitages, sages meditating or cheerfully feasting under a tree; in their moments of happiest inspiration they are convincing for a certain clean and serene sincerity.

[1] R. T. PAINE, in *The Art and Architecture of Japan*, London, 1957, p. 107.

Another group of important artists close to the traditional schools of Kano and Tosa, both because of their approach to their art and their personal circumstances, consists of Koetsu, Sotatsu, and, above all, Ogata Korin (1658–1716). Korin was one of those outstanding personalities who are bound to make a deep impression wherever they appear, and the supreme Japanese virtues of purity, simplicity, and a poetic sense of the oneness of man and the universe shine in him in splendid brightness. The *fusuma*,[1] the lacquered boxes, the screens, on which he left the evidence of his harmoniously unsymmetrical genius, combine the most intense sensitivity to the miracle of life with an aristocratic disdain for pedantic detail.

The cult of detail, redeemed by a loving humility, characterizes, and, in the differing context, not adversely, the work of Maruyama Okyo (1733–1795). This painter, who was of peasant origin, ignored the classic (Chinese) literary inspiration and opened his eyes directly on nature—plants, flowers, landscapes, animals—and immersed himself in it. But China, thrown out by the door, came in again by the window; for in the last analysis Okyo drew his inspiration from a great Chinese artist, Ch'ien Hsüan (1235–1290).

Many Japanese of the period, particularly those who favoured the 'literary men' style, and those of the Kano school, looked down on Okyo and his disciples as copiers of nature, men who felt neither the need nor the desirability of rooting their inspiration in an ideal world.

Similarly looked down on, not just by some, but by everybody, were the artists of the period who in our own day enjoy the greatest fame; that is to say the painters of *ukiyo-e*, 'pictures of the ephemeral world'. This form of Japanese art is so well known that a critic (Professor T. Sagara) has said: 'For many westerners Japanese painting is probably represented solely by coloured prints.' Few episodes in the history of art are more extraordinary than the spontaneous growth in isolation of this art form of striking originality and vitality which developed, matured, and decayed in the course of two centuries. It should be noted, however, as the reader will have realized, that it was only one of a number of voices of its time.

It would take us too far afield to trace the numerous remote threads

[1] Sliding screens.

that connect the *ukiyo-e* to the main body of Japanese artistic production; in any case, the work that has been done in this field has been admirably summarized by Paine.[1] It is interesting to note in the first place that *ukiyo-e* as a genre developed very slowly, and that only when it had firmly established itself did it find its happiest expression in the form of prints. What exactly is an *ukiyo-e*? I have already mentioned (page 56) the meaning of this typically oriental term; *ukiyo* is the 'floating world', that is to say this earthly life, and more particularly the ephemeral lives of actors and courtesans, of the pleasures of the moment, of brief loves, of the fascinating, evanescent things the pleasurability of which is over-shadowed by impermanence; *e* means picture, image. For centuries, side by side with the 'official' art nurtured on Chinese traditions by the Kano school or on native traditions by the Tosa (or Yamato) school, there had been artists who had pained scenes of everyday life. These sometimes appeared on scrolls that illustrated the events and festivals of the year (*nenju gyoji*), and sometimes illustrated people's trades, or (a special case, confined to the sixteenth and seventeenth centuries) the strange ways of 'southern barbarians'—Portuguese and Spaniards, Catholic missionaries, Dutch traders. With the *pax Tokugawa* and the development of a class of wealthy townsmen, the new popularity of the theatre, and the widespread softening of customs, a demand arose for illustrations of the things and scenes of everyday life. In view of the rigid stratification of Japanese society, the painters of *ukiyo-e* ignored all learned references, paid no attention to the cultivated traditions of the samurai or the aristocracy, and wholeheartedly devoted themselves to painting anything that was immediately pleasing, desirable, exciting. Their favourite themes were geishas, courtesans and their life, actors playing their parts, legendary warriors and ancient heroes, a few classical personages, often parodies, as when Shunshō made his amusing series of prints called *The Seven Women in the Bamboo Grove,* in which he poked fun at the well-known theme of the *Seven Sages in the Bamboo Grove*, so popular with the severe Confucians. Finally, there were the frankly erotic *haru-e,* 'spring figures', to which even the greatest painters devoted themselves with pristine innocence.

The history of *ukiyo-e,* in the narrower sense of the word, is generally considered to have begun in 1658, with the publication of Moronobu's

---

[1] R. T. PAINE, *loc. cit.* Chapter 15.

famous book of illustrations. These were simply woodcuts in black and white, but hand-painted colours were soon added. The 'primitive' period is generally considered to have ended with the invention of two-colour and then three-colour printing towards the middle of the eighteenth century; finally, in 1765, all technical difficulties were over-come, and twelve colours or more were printed on the same sheet. The years that followed, up to the beginning of the nineteenth century, were the golden age of the *ukiyo-e ;* the level remained high for a few years longer, and then it suddenly declined, and its glory departed for ever; and today, perhaps, no trace of it would remain but for the fact that first the Dutch and then the French fell in love with these ephemeral works, which in Japan were considered superficial, negligible, and plebeian.

The *ukiyo-e* are delightful at every point of their technical and artistic parabola. The tender, innocent, tremulous girls of Harunobu (1725–1770), the plump, sinuous, enchanted creatures of Koryusai (*floruit* 1764–1788), the noble, sometimes proud and marvellously elegant, half-divine creatures of Kiyonaga (1752–1815), and finally the passionate, fragile women of Utamaro (1753–1806) are a permanent enrichment of the human imagination.

The last of the masters were the two wizards of landscape, the dramatic and inexhaustible Hokusai (1760–1849) and the gentle, elegiac Hiroshige, with his humility in the face of light and clouds and the things of his country.

In architecture the Tokugawa period, apart from the limited field of the *suki-ya* (tea pavilion) and the quiet development of the ordinary house in village, town, and country, was frigidly academic. We have already spoken of Nikko, and many other civil or religious buildings of the time reflect the formal, erudite, often pretentious spirit of the régime. The only exception is the Katsura villa, which has the serene glow of an earlier age, though chronologically it comes just within the limits of the Tokugawa period.

Japanese sculpture, after the glories of Nara and Kamakura (eighth to fourteenth centuries), declined completely. This is a curious pheno-menon, for which it is hard to find an explanation. Even today, though in Japanese painting there is vitality and creative talent, sculpture is groping painfully in the dark. During the Tokugawa period manual ability survived and was perfected; in fact the famous Hidari Jingoro

(1594–1634) belongs to the period; he was a prodigious craftsman, who left many specimens of his work at Nikko, Nagoya, and elsewhere. Most of them are decorative panels in which animals, flowers, branches of trees are woven into patterns; you do not know whether to admire the brilliant technique shown in overcoming every limitation imposed by the material or to feel sad that so much skill should reveal a spiritual content of such disconcerting poverty.

The same skill, often enlivened, however, by subtle poetic symbolism, or playful commentary on life, is to be found in many well-known examples of what in western terminology we should call the minor arts; in *netsuké,* for instance, tiny sculptures mostly used as buttons; *inro* (lacquered medicine boxes); *fubako* (boxes for writing materials); *tsuba* (sword hilts), and in weaving, iron-work, lacquer, porcelain, earthenware; in short, in all the numerous products of artisans who were perhaps without equal in the world.

After the Genroku period the economic, political, and intellectual forces which tended to undermine the Tokugawa régime grew more and more threatening. Some shoguns, like Tsunayoshi, sought salvation in inflation; others, like the stern Yoshimune (1716–1745), succeeded in temporarily arresting the decline. But inexorable laws, then not understood, resumed their shaping of men and events. The population, which reached a level of between twenty-eight and thirty million, for a long time remained stationary.[1]

The Tokugawa system, enclosed in its own little world, might perhaps have been able to achieve a satisfactory equilibrium had it not been burdened from the outset by the weight of an unproductive army of samurai, useful in time of war, but a ruinous luxury for ten consecutive generations of peace. With the growth of the towns economic power gradually passed from the warlike nobility to the merchants. Rice had a regrettable tendency to pass out of the hands of the *daimyo* and the samurai and to find its way into those of merchants, brokers, bankers, where it was transformed into something new, of which few suspected the extraordinary power, namely money. When the barons and their followers tried to find a way out, they did not tax the bourgeoisie, whom they needed, but the peasants, who were already op-

[1] For the extent to which periods of famine, the practice of abortion and infanticide, and other factors contributed to this *see* G. B. SANSOM, *loc. cit.,* p. 508.

pressed to the extreme limits of tolerance. Thus the only truly pro-
ductive class in the country found itself with its backs to the wall, and
desperate rebellions became only too frequent. Agriculture suffered,
and the very foundations of the system threatened to collapse. With the
first decades of the nineteenth century a mercantile economy can be
said to have painfully overcome the preceding agricultural phase, but
for that very reason the isolation of Japan could no longer be maintained. The *bakufu,* tied to its traditional policies, was like a gnarled old
tree-trunk, still impressive to look at, but hollow inside and ready to
collapse at the first severe shock.

So much for economic events; equally important was the ferment
of new ideas. When the Tokugawa encouraged the samurai to busy
themselves with literature and philosophy, they certainly did not think
that they were digging their own grave; but that was the final result.
Interest in ancient history, which was pursued in particular at the court
of the princes of Mito, research into the origins of Japanese poetry and
the Japanese language to which the *wagakusha* ('students of Japanese
affairs') devoted themselves, ended by making it clearer and clearer that
the shoguns were usurpers of the imperial privileges. The learned
researches of Kamo Mabuchi (1697–1769) into the *Manyōshū* and the
Norito, those of Motoori Norinaga (1730–1801) into the *Kojiki,* and those of
Hirata Atsutane (1776–1843) into the Shinto religion, and similar work by
their pupils, provided the intellectual content for the movement which
culminated in the restoration, the handing back of power to the
Emperor (1867–68).

Another factor was the growing influence of western science.
During the sixteenth century and the beginning of the seventeenth the
Japanese had met only one face of European civilization. But with the
passage of time faint echoes of the new, original, and vitally important
developments with which the mind of man was being enriched in the
west reached the outposts of Asia through the Dutch warehouse at
Nagasaki. Even the suspicious *bakufu* was forced somewhat to relax the
boycott, and as early as 1719 permitted the importation of certain Dutch
books on medicine, astronomy, and other scientific matters, though
only a few trusted scholars were permitted to read them. The experiences of a few men who, overcoming the most incredible difficulties,
succeeded in taking advantage of this exiguous means to form a vague

378 MEETING WITH JAPAN

and confused idea of foreign lands, and discovered a fabulous, unexplored world of ideas, art, and powerful magic—namely Europe—beyond the known and revered China and the mythical India of Shaka (the Buddha), provide one of the most fascinating pages of Japanese history.[1]

Towards the middle of the nineteenth century the situation in the Pacific, in view of the competition of British, Russian, and American interests, was such that Japan, if she were not to resign herself to becoming a colony, was bound to take an active part in the international game; and the strong external pressure was reinforced by powerful domestic factors, both economic and in the field of ideas. The question was whether Japan was to be opened up by explosion from within or by siege from without; and, in the event of the latter, whether the invisible walls would crumble at the hands of the British, the Russians, or the Americans. In the end it was the Americans who pushed them over. In 1853, and again in 1854, Commodore Perry appeared with his 'black ships' in the Bay of Yedo, within cannon-shot of the seat of the *bakufu*, and a long period of history was over. The old order succeeded in hanging on for another fourteen years of great confusion, but in 1867 Tokugawa Keiki, the last of the shoguns, handed back power into the Emperor's hands, and a year later the Meiji ('Enlightened Government') period began. The mean centuries were over and the century of great adventure had begun.

That brings us to our own day. The history of subsequent events is too well known for me to need repeat it here. Yedo was transformed into Tokyo, and once more became the Emperor's residence, and the feudal order was abolished in 1871; western techniques, the western calendar, and many western customs were adopted; religious liberty was proclaimed; the Kuriles and the Ryu-Kyu islands (Okinawa) were annexed; the first political parties and the first newspapers were founded; a constitution and parliament were established (1889–1890); a victorious war was fought with China (1895) and Formosa was annexed; the treaties were revised and Japan granted absolute parity with other nations; a victorious war with Russia was fought in 1904–5, and the island of Sakhalin was added to the Japanese possessions; Korea was annexed in 1910; Japan took part in the world war of 1914, and in 1918 was granted

[1] *See* D. KEENE, *The Japanese Discovery of Europe*, London, 1952.

a mandate in the Pacific; next came the penetration of Manchuria and war with China; all these were big and little steps in the short but fateful path that led to Pearl Harbour, and then to the most significant date in 2,000 years of Japanese history, the defeat of 1945.

The consequences of this last are so profound and extensive that much time will have to pass before they can be correctly evaluated.

Sketches from a world in transition (about 1870)

12

Red Skies Over Nagoya

The Tempaku

ON THE way from Kyoto to Nagoya we avoided the main road that goes direct to Otsu and instead took a side road, unfamiliar to most people, which winds its way pleasantly through the woods and valleys on the outskirts of the city. Years ago, when we lived in Kyoto, we used to cycle this way, and that made this a sentimental journey. First of all you go through a shady gorge beside a rushing stream, gradually climbing to the quiet little village of Yamanaka ('Among the Mountains'), where the old houses are half-hidden in gardens and stacks of timber. A little farther on there is a pass, not more than 1,500 feet above sea level, with a magnificent view towards Biwa lake and the plain of Omi—the distant villages scattered about the latter look like toys.[1]

We reached Nagoya at about ten o'clock. The weather had gradually deteriorated; the sky was dull grey. As if drawn by a magnetic force, I took the Yagoto road. After passing the last suburban houses, we went down a short stretch of road, or rather track, across a bare, rocky, deserted stretch of country. There, on a hill, was a building that looked vaguely like a chalet; it was the Tempaku-ryo, where I was interned with my family during the war. It was originally a rest and recreation centre for the staff of a big firm, and as such it must have been agreeable

---

[1] The eight beauties of the lake of Biwa are famous; they have been catalogued by Japanese poets in emulation of the similar catalogue of the beauties of Tung-ting lake drawn up by Chinese men of letters. They are: the snow on Mount Hira at sunset; wild ducks in flight at Katata; rain at night at Karasaki; the sound of the Mii temple bell at evening; sun and wind at Awazu; the last light at Seta; the autumn moon at Ishiyama; and sailing boats returning at Yabase.

enough. But it was not suitable for living in all the year round, particularly in a country where the winter is long and hard. But there it was. When we rounded a bend and I saw the well-known outline of the roof, my heart missed a beat.

We left the car at the entrance. A cold wind had arisen, a reminder of some of the worst hours of our stay here; it had grown darker, and perhaps it was going to rain. The place seemed deserted. After much calling, an unattractive, unkempt, badly dressed girl opened the door, and silently let us in, as if she had been expecting us. The place had obviously not been repaired or put back into use since the war. Nothing had changed; I recognized all the innumerable familiar little things which tie us to a place where we have lived for a long time; damp patches on the walls, knots in the wood, cracks in the fittings which I could describe inch by inch. The damage done by the earthquake of December, 1944, was still discernible. The small space all round the house was covered with weeds.

If all that vegetation had been there in our time, we should have eaten it; but then there was nothing but stones. But let me tell the story in order.

From September 8, 1943 (the date of the Italian armistice), the police confined us to our house; we were forbidden to communicate with anyone, or to use the telephone. We had been vaguely informed that we should get ready, but for what? Presumably for internment, but uncertainty, as always, was worse than any positive bad news. After some days our 'arrest' was formally communicated to us; I have described this incident elsewhere,[1] and therefore shall not do so again. In fact we ceased to 'depend' on the Italian Embassy (the Japanese always regard foreigners as 'dependent' on their embassies; one's country is a big family, society a closely knit, hierarchical texture of *mibun* and *giri*), and henceforward we were 'dependent' on the Japanese Minister of the Interior. On the last day but one before our departure my wife was allowed to take the children to the doctor, escorted by a policeman. Two days later the journey began. It was one of those marvellous autumn days on which Kyoto is more beautiful than ever. The light, the colour, the sky stifled Miki's tears and those of the children; it was impossible to be sad. Even the police, who had known us for years, were

[1] *Secret Tibet*, Hutchinson, London, and The Viking Press, New York, 1952, Chapter VIII.

friendly; they escorted us as unobtrusively as possible. We went in two taxis, and we might have been on a Sunday outing. In the train, however, the restrictions began to be perceptible. We were forbidden to speak to people, to look out of the window, to get out. As Toni, aged two, attracted the attention of the Japanese women in the same compartment, the police opened a brakeman's box and put the child and me in it, with a big bottle of milk. Two hours later we reached Nagoya; in the distance we could see the castle, which was later to be destroyed by bombs, with Tokugawa Iyeyasu's famous golden dolphins shining in the sun.

At the station the Kyoto police handed us over to the Nagoya police; their surly faces and dry orders formed a sharp contrast to the behaviour of the *junsa* of Kyoto, who were at heart a quiet, decent lot, principally concerned with keeping out of trouble with their superiors. We were taken to Yagoto by tram, and then on foot, across the stony hills that we saw again this morning, to the Tempaku. There we met other Italians in the same condition as ourselves, including Giorgio and Somi, to our great pleasure. There were also some other old acquaintances. After nearly a month in isolation, it was a great pleasure to be in company, and to be able to exchange news and conjecture. We liked the place; the magnificent autumn sun made everything a little more tolerable.

The first few days passed peacefully, while we settled down into a routine that was to remain unchanged for many months. The Nagoya chief of police came and talked to us. He told us in effect that we were in his hands, and that if we behaved things would be all right. Then he introduced us to our four guards, who were to live at the Tempaku and be on duty two at a time. The senior of these also made a speech, repeating the same points and adding that we should have to live entirely in Japanese fashion; this implied that the womenfolk would enjoy no privileges, that we should have respectfully to greet our superiors morning and evening, that food would be sparse, and that we should show *gaman, i.e.,* patience and fortitude, in facing what lay ahead of us.

This beginning, apart from some minor details, did not seem to be too bad; and the small group of Italians, thrown together by chance at the extreme confines of Asia, set out on what was to be a long and painful experience with high morale. It turned out that we were all there for anti-Fascism, either suspected or openly declared. Giorgio told us that at Tokyo there had been a solemn ceremony at which every Italian citizen had had to declare on oath whether he was with Mussolini or Badoglio. Apart from Somi and Giorgio, there was a stout old diplomatist of Jewish origin who for intelligible reasons had left the service some years previously and had been living in retirement in Tokyo with his Japanese wife; there was a missionary and his lay assistant, and a variety of others who had been caught in the net. The police appointed as *incho* ('head of the community') an old resident of Yokohama who was born in Japan and therefore spoke excellent Japanese.

Our friends from Tokyo told us that nearly all the members of the embassy staff had been summarily deprived of diplomatic privileges and confined in a house near the capital. The only representative of Italy to whom the Japanese granted recognition was a certain Colonel Principini, a Fascist transferred from Manchuria. The Imperial Government appeared to be particularly incensed against the dissident Italians because the crews of some of our ships in the Far East had tried to scuttle them. Our behaviour, from the Japanese point of view, stank of treachery, *i.e.,* the lowest depth of moral turpitude. Contempt was implicit in every word and gesture of the only Japanese whom we saw— that is to say, our four policemen. Our only redeeming feature was that we could be considered 'loyal to our King'; we were therefore not entirely without *chugi* ('a sense of loyalty'). Those who tried explaining our position to the police took advantage of this argument. Would they not follow their Emperor in every conceivable circumstance? The argument, however, did not make much of an impression, and it had its dangers, for it was based on the heretical assumption that the Japanese Emperor and ordinary crowned heads belonged to the same category, but at any rate it was formally accepted as reasonable.

Our initial optimism was also favoured by the fact that we considered ourselves friends of Japan, not in any political or partisan sense, but because we were bound to it by strong ties of affection; nearly all of us, in fact, spoke Japanese. It seemed reasonable to expect at least humane treatment.

My wife's diary during those first few days had optimistic entries. She noted that the house was clean and in a beautiful spot, that there were *tatami* on the floor, that the police here were stricter but not impolite, and that, having got used to being called 'you, Maraini!' they had that day actually called her *okusan* (Mrs.), and that they seemed to be becoming more humane, seeing that we all behaved marvellously, never complained, and never asked for anything. Only the men had asked permission to shave every day, and that had been granted. The food was meagre, but it was said that it would improve after the beginning of November. The children were allowed everything. She noted that Japanese kindness to children was extraordinary, that she was given milk for them, and that they were allowed in the garden whenever they liked.

That entry gives some clue to what our life was like. A necessity of the Japanese character, to which I alluded in the chapter on the Tokugawa, is that of regulating every collective function in the most minute detail. Imagine sixteen Latins put at the mercy of the most bureaucratic police in the world. But they had to obey silently, and to say *hai*, yes, to every new restriction. Every half-hour of the day was regulated. Those like Giorgio, Somi, and myself who had looked forward to using our internment for reading and study were quickly disillusioned; reading was permitted only for a short time in the afternoon. We had to get up at six, wash, and clean the house. Breakfast was at seven, followed by half an hour's rest; and so on, until ten o'clock at night. Moreover, space was regulated as well as time. Here you were allowed between seven and half-past, but not between ten and twelve; there you could sit but not read, here you could walk but not speak, and so on and so forth, in an infinity of meticulous rules laid down with exasperating impassivity. Sleeping during the daytime was absolutely forbidden.

The fire to heat the bath was lit once a week. It was a handsome, wooden bath, and the water was really hot. But Japanese rules of precedence prevailed. First of all the police took their bath, followed by the housekeepers (an old couple whom we rarely saw), then the oldest internees, followed by myself, my wife, and children. On the first occasion there was a general protest at this imposition; we asked that at least the children might be allowed to have their bath when the police had finished. But a question of principle was at stake, and we had to give in. A few weeks later we had other things to worry about than precedence in the bathroom.

On November 21 my wife noted in her diary that after a month of

120

After the hurricane. Nagoya, 1945.

*Mid-twentieth-century Japan; mingling and clash of clothing, customs, styles.
(121) Men and women students on an outing; (122) the Picasso amusement arcade;
(123) photography as a hobby; (124) geisha and an ageing motor-car;
(125-130) street scenes in town and country.*

125

126

127

128

129

131

Tools, books, ideas of east and west; the perpetual thirst for knowledge (128, 129, 131, 132).

Lion dance and gasometer (133); truckload of Samurai (134).

132

133

134

139

The new hegemony, on land, sea, and in the air; and in sex. Nudity crosses the Pacific (139, 140).

The sleepless city of Yoshiwara (141). In the best houses racial discrimination is practised in reverse; westerners are not admitted.

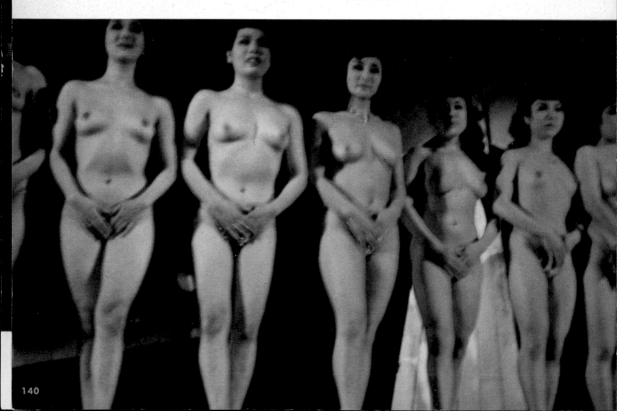

Tradition and style. (143) *Spring in the Meiji park in Tokyo;* (144) *The little* maiko *of Kyoto;* (145) *farewell to the departing boss;* (146) *welcome to the arriving teacher.*

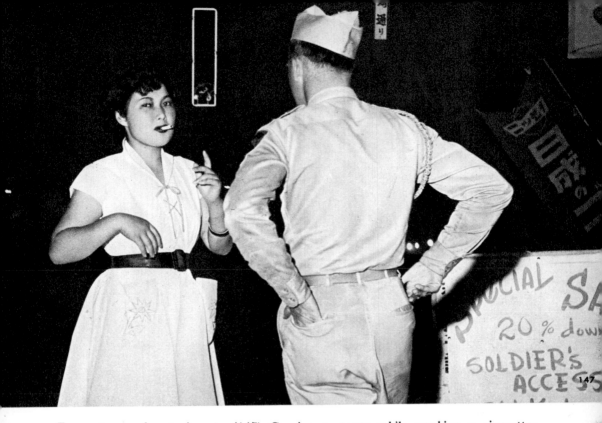

Encounters and experiments. (147) *Coming to terms while smoking a cigarette;* (148) *bar and exotic drinks;* (149, 150) *Asian-American friendship;* (151) *skirt, trousers, and* yukata.

Victors.

153

Vanquished.

this she felt that she was reaching the end of her tether. During the first few weeks we supplemented our meagre rations with tinned food which we had brought with us, but then we went on short commons. After some initial variations, our rations were stabilized at twenty-eight *go* of rice a day for sixteen persons,[1] plus a few spoonfuls of *miso* (bean paste), *shoyu* (soya sauce), and some vegetables. Every now and then we would be given some small fish (half each); we saw meat perhaps once a month, a few grammes each. This diet was sufficient to sustain life on the borderline between survival and disintegration.

Every link with the outside world was cut. The Tempaku house is isolated in the middle of a bare heath. The old professor and the diplomatist among us received short visits once a month from their wives, the missionary was visited about once a month by a German father, but these were exceptions. We were not allowed to receive parcels, gifts, help of any kind. Our mail was, of course, censored, and delayed for long periods before we received it.

With the end of November it started getting cold; there was no means of heating, and our sensitivity to cold was increased by undernourishment. All of us, at any rate the men, started suffering from incontinence of urine; I was among the more fortunate, having to get out of bed only two or three times a night; others had to do so five, six, sometimes eight times. The lavatory was a long way from the room where we slept; you had to go down a staircase, and then down a long, barely lit corridor, the wooden boards of which echoed hollowly. I shall never forget the encounters with my fellow-internees in this corridor in the middle of the night; we all tried to wake ourselves up as little as possible, and we crept past one another without speaking, wrapped in a blanket or shawl, or cloak. In the morning the less fortunate were exhausted, but it was forbidden to remain in bed even for five minutes extra. A medical examination would have been desirable, but this, in the absence of fever or any more obvious symptom, was difficult to obtain.

After engaging in a few conversations during the first few days, our warders withdrew into the most complete reserve. They never raised their voices, they appeared rarely and always unexpectedly, checked that everything was in order, said nothing, and vanished again. We soon discovered what their method was if they wished to punish us; they

[1] *I.e.*, about 130 grammes of rice each; a *go* is about 180 cubic centimetres.

Half-melted and twisted by the atomic bomb.

simply decreased our rations. Gradually every detail of our lives was regulated in a fashion from which it was not permissible to depart by a hair's breadth. After our evening meal, which consisted of a plate of rice and a cup of Japanese tea without sugar or milk, the two of us whose turn it was to work in the kitchen next day went to the police to fetch the *bun*, the rations. This was the supreme moment of the day; we were reduced to a state in which one *go* more than usual was enough to make us jump for joy like children, and one less enough to plunge us into the blackest despair. We would sit waiting in anxious silence in the little so-called dining-room, and we could tell what the situation was like from the sound of the footsteps of the men coming back. Sometimes one of them would come running in. 'Boys! there are two eggs!' he would exclaim (the two eggs were for sixteen persons, of course), or: 'We've got twenty-eight *go*!' Such occasions were rare, however. More often the footsteps in the corridor would be dragging and depressed, and the 'cooks' would open the door and deposit the *bun* box on the table, announcing in lugubrious tones: 'Only twenty-four *go*.' You felt as if you were being very slowly strangled, and that your life was ebbing away.

At first we tried protesting, but soon discovered that it made matters worse; they were determined to bend us to their will, reduce us to dying with a smile on our lips, saying thank you; then, perhaps, they would grant us the small supplementary ration that would keep us going for a few more hours.

The four policemen formed a compact, unanimous, unassailable and incorruptible block. The senior of the first couple was named Kasuya; he was a meticulously groomed, thin little man of about thirty, who never raised his voice and hardly ever smiled; I shall always remember his slender, nervous, intellectual's hands. He spoke a little English, and may have understood Italian. We immediately christened him Valentino, because he looked like a film star. He was the most feared and hated of the four, because he was the most intelligent. During the early days his companion, Nishimura, gave us some extra vegetables and some extra *go* of rice, but one day Kasuya caught him at it, and that was the end of him so far as we were concerned; our contact with him ceased to exist.

The senior of the other two was Aoto, a short, rough, crafty individual of about fifty, who had obviously made his way up in the world, quite the reverse of Kasuya; his unpleasantness lacked the cold and calculated quality of Kasuya's, and was more direct and plebeian. He sometimes raised his voice and lost his temper, and sometimes had moods in which he behaved like a crude but kind patriarch taking pity on the poor devils whom chance had delivered into his hands. When you asked Aoto for anything, there was always a chance that you might find him in a good mood, but with Kasuya never. The fourth man was named Fujita; he was young, ferocious, stupid, and had an overweening sense of his own importance. He was the most obviously militarist of the four. He strutted about with his chest stuck out, bawled at us like a sergeant-major, and took every opportunity of making us speeches about the greatness of Japan and the sublime majesty of the divine Emperor. We used to call him Radetzky, but he was the least to be feared of the four, because he was the most stupid.

We naturally tried as far as possible to follow events in the outside world. After a time we were allowed two newspapers, the *Mainichi* and the English-language *Osaka Mainichi*. Events seemed to move with exasperating slowness; the spectacular Japanese advances southward had been stopped, but there was nothing in sight that seemed to bring any promise of peace. How long might it last? Two, three, five years? It is, I am afraid, impossible to communicate to the reader the sense of total isolation, total abandonment, in which we lived. Vast distances separated us from the nearest friendly persons; to attempt escape was unthinkable in a country where a westerner is identifiable half a mile away. We might have been buried alive. Sometimes black despair seized hold of us, and we privately resigned ourselves to death.

As can well be imagined, furious arguments arose among us about almost everything under the sun; hunger sharpens both the intelligence and the temper. How would the Japanese react when they started losing? Whole life-times of experience and torrents of learning, the sciences human and divine, St. Thomas, Aristotle, Hegel, Vico, Spengler, Gobineau, Buddhist philosophy, were marshalled in the course of heated debates about this question, which was of such vital concern to us. Some, including myself, argued that they would be worse than ever; *certa morte ferociores*. The fiery, brilliant, and cultivated old diplomatist, however, maintained that they would be as gentle as any cooing dove.

The argument continued evening after evening, and many months later he was proved to be right.

These discussions were our only pastime (games were not allowed), and they sometimes acted like a drug, an anaesthetic. After squabbling about religion, politics, archaeology, health, the literature of I do not know how many different periods and civilizations, science, fashion, the east, law, and I do not know what else, we would suddenly notice that two hours had passed like a flash. 'Two hours nearer to liberty! X hours minus two!' somebody would exclaim. Then suddenly, having heard our raised voices, the silent shadow of Kasuya in slippers would appear behind the glass door, reminding us that we were impotent, useless, forgotten men, perhaps near a sudden, silent end.

The characters of the members of our little group revealed themselves in innumerable ways, and there was little about ourselves that we were able to conceal from each other. The four old gentlemen all resented each other. The diplomatist, a courageous, highly intelligent man of the world, full of an extraordinarily youthful vigour, who had enjoyed by no means inconsiderable successes in life, could not stand the *incho*, who had spent his days behind an office desk in Yokohama. The white-haired professor of languages always remained apart from everybody else; he was the only one who did not seem to fit in. He used to have private conversations with the police, and we never understood what was really going on in his mind. After six months he suddenly disappeared one day; he had been released. He left us almost without saying good-bye, taking with him every tin of food in his possession. Equally unsociable, on the whole, was the missionary, a hard Piedmontese, who was difficult to understand.

A second group consisted of what I might call the 'strong' men, the seven who took turns in doing the 'fatigues'—kitchen duty, sweeping and cleaning, the odd jobs that always turn up in an old house full of people. It consisted of a chemist from Naples, an engineer from Milan, a Fiat representative, a peasant from Friuli, a student from Rome, Giorgio, Somi, and myself. The Roman student was often gloomy and silent, though he sometimes unexpectedly raised his voice; he seemed to get on well enough with the missionary; the two in fact formed a sub-group by themselves.

Naturally, after the first few days, squabbles arose, as was inevitable among persons confined for a long time in a limited space. During the first period, however, the storms were confined to the upper layer of the atmosphere; they did not yet touch the deepest, darkest roots of the personality. We were educated, twentieth-century Europeans, arguing about politics, religion, aesthetics, confronting a hostile environment in a compact, dignified manner, determined to overcome every obstacle with the aid of reason and good sense.

When Christmas approached, my wife and children spent their time making little presents, dolls, etc., out of odds and ends. A letter arrived from the Uriu saying they had sent us some *mochi,* the traditional Japanese rice-sweet made for the New Year; but by the time the police handed them over they had become mouldy and uneatable. By economizing with the rations we managed to set aside enough flour and sugar to make a sweet for Christmas Eve. The cooking and distribution of this famous dish was a matter of earnest discussion for days on end, but it was eaten in a minute. However, that night we slept better; it seemed warmer, and there were fewer of those ghostly walks along the corridor.

Plenty of ordeals and humiliations lay ahead of us. Shortly before Christmas a military commission had appeared at the Tempaku and interrogated us one by one about our attitude to events in Italy, which, of course, we knew about only in general outline. It must have decided that we were beyond redemption, and that the authorities had been quite right to lock us up, and that locked up we should remain. That, at any rate, was the assumption. All we knew for certain was that from the New Year onwards there was a new turn of the screw every day, whether in the absurd disciplinary regulations or the gradual reduction of rations, calculated in such a manner as to keep us just alive. We were reduced to twenty-six, and often twenty-five or twenty-four, *go* of rice a day, and we lived in fear of a still greater reduction. The chemist and the engineer put their heads together and calculated that we might perhaps be getting 800 calories a day; an inactive adult requires at least 2,000.

When the human organism is subjected to this treatment it reacts by using up its reserves. We all got incredibly thin. The unfortunate Neapolitan chemist aged in an alarming manner. His eyes grew sunken, his skin hung in folds round his neck. On Saturdays, the day of the weekly bath, we amused ourselves by studying each other's skeletons;

only the three old men and the priest to some extent maintained their physical condition, for their rations were supplemented from outside; the extra that the laymen received from their wives, the priest from a colleague, was little enough, heaven knows, some fish or dry bread, or a bottle of oil; but it served to combat the extreme limit of starvation. For all of us hunger had previously been something we had read about in books, in Canto XXXIII of the *Inferno*, for instance; we had little thought that we should ever become experts in this, one of the most terrible of human ordeals.

Three times a day, in the morning after our few spoonfuls of rice and our hot cup of *miso*, and at midday and in the evening, after our single meagre plateful of rice, over-cooked to increase the volume, we had half an hour of peace and tranquillity; after that hunger began its gnawing again, sometimes in the form of pain, a sensation of void in the stomach, sometimes in the form of extreme weakness, which was far worse. Those who managed to hide themselves from the eyes of Kasuya would then lie down somewhere to save their failing breath. Those who amused themselves by taking their pulse found that the rate was fifty or less a minute; life was just ebbing away. At night the torment was dreadful. Though exhausted, we could not sleep. Getting up for the usual pilgrimages down the corridor required an enormous effort.

Meanwhile the cold had grown intense. The only place where there was any warmth was the kitchen, at any rate during the few hours when the fire was alight to boil the *kama*, the rice pot. But the police forbade the kitchen to anyone not working there. The result was that a kind of black market arose; a few spoonfuls of soup would be bartered for a spell of kitchen duty. At night we slept fully dressed under our *futon*; it was like camping in the high mountains. Saturday, bath day, was the only occasion on which we had a two-hour respite from continual shivering.

January passed and February came, a truly terrible month. More and more often rice was replaced by less nutritive or less digestible substitutes, such as soya beans or a coarse kind of macaroni, flour, bread, or, worst of all, dried sliced sweet potatoes which when cooked produced a black brew containing a minimum of nourishment. Meanwhile we saw boxes of sugar, baskets of eggs, bags of rice, packets of *miso*, bottles of *shoyu* arriving at the camp and mysteriously disappearing. Only after the war, from information received from Tokyo, were we able to confirm our suspicions; our warders were a collection of racketeers. The whole Nagoya police force was trafficking at our expense. The Minister of the Interior had laid down very generous rations for us. The ordinary Japanese ration was 2.3 *go* of rice daily, with small quantities of other foods depending on their availability; in addition to the ordinary rice ration, we should have received supplementary rations of eggs, fat, meat, beans, and bread. But the Nagoya police saw their opportunity; the Italians, being enemies and traitors into the bargain, would receive just enough to keep them alive; the rest would go to their own benefit. The full rations arrived at the camp, but quietly disappeared again in small parcels on Kasuya's or Aoto's bicycle, or in the suitcases of their superiors, who every now and again paid us unexpected, ceremonious, or even cheerful afternoon visits. It was this that enabled us to understand the loathing for the police, the heir of the hated *metsuké* under the Tokugawa, felt by all decent Japanese.

During that February we all, I think, passed through a profound crisis; we were so near death that the only choice seemed to be between giving in and dying and fighting tooth and claw for whatever chance of survival there might be. The Milanese engineer grew so weak that Kasuya had to allow him to stay in bed; he spent the days motionless, his eyes covered by a black carnival mask, a relic of happier days that had been left in one of his suitcases. The old diplomatist had a long illness of the respiratory passages, and some evenings we thought he might be going to die from one minute to the next. Somi and others had the first symptoms of beri-beri—swollen legs, bleeding gums, irregular heartbeat. Everyone felt at the extreme limit of his resources. There seemed no choice but revolt or death.

My wife and children no longer moved from their room. On January 10 she noted that the temperature of the room was at freezing point, and that the children were lying down.

'January 19. For some days past great perspiration during the night, very tired during the daytime. Hunger from morning to night and from night to morning. The doctor came, said I was suffering from *kakke* (beri-beri) and malnutrition (what a discovery!). I hope it will move them. . . . January 20. Stayed in bed because of pain in the legs; very discouraged yesterday. . . . January 28. Felt ill at lunchtime and feeling of nausea. Could not see, hands insensible, feeling of being unable to breathe, and then intense cold. Dreadful. They carried me upstairs. Kasuya-san came too. How angry I am that he saw me in that state! Look at that weak European woman, he must have said to himself, who faints and trembles and weeps (I couldn't repress a few sobs), and her weak husband embrac- and kissing and holding her hands. . . . He sent me up an egg and three mandarines and a little sugar. For several days past they have been giving me mandarines that I hate eating by myself. . . . February 15. Time passes, but our situation does not change. . . . I feel dreadful, weaker than ever. I was up for four days, but one evening I again felt oppression, shortness of breath, and nearly fainted. Since then I have been in bed, and if I get up for more than ten minutes I feel ill. . . . Hunger, hunger, emptiness, weakness; it is impossible to think of anything else. . . . February 19. It snowed. Zero or at most four degrees in the room in the evening, cold.'

Food became a mania with us all. From morning to night we were like stray dogs looking for a bone. We had long since ceased talking about anything else. Every day someone or other would think of some idea, on which we would work feverishly, only to be defeated in the end. The chemist thought of straw, of which there was a quantity about the house. But how were we to free it from its cellulose, make it edible? We tried pounding, kneading, boiling, roasting it, all in secret, like conspirators making bombs. I suggested acorns, and we carried out all sorts of experiments with them, but it was impossible to rid them of the tannin. After a heavy fall of rain we tried the mushrooms which sprang up under the trees. Somi ate one, saying: 'If I die, all right; if not, we shall be able to fill our bellies.' Unfortunately these mushrooms were a powerful emetic; one was harmless, but the big plateful which we all ate, satisfying our appetites for the first time in months, had the effect of castor oil.

This incident ended in laughter, and even the grim Kasuya was amused when we told him about it, as we had to, in view of the effects and the colour of our faces. Other incidents, however, ended in tears or scenes. Every evening, after the swift emptying of the wretched plates of over-cooked rice, we started indulging in daydreams, talking about our favourite dishes back in Italy, until someone, more nervous or more sensitive than the rest, jumped to his feet, told us to shut up, walked out and slammed the door. Food formed the background of all the children's games. They used a box of paints to mark stones the colour of bread, vegetables, meat, fruit.

We had long since left politeness behind; nothing was left but the imperious need to survive. Under the tension personalities started to disintegrate; every night we receded a few more centuries. One morning we were Merovingians, another Scythians and Huns; we reached the Neanderthal stage, and finally one day we became wild animals. The bone of contention, needless to say, was rations. Theoretically we should have received 36.8 *go* of rice a day, which would have kept us going. Instead the police (apart from deductions made as punishments and out of pure robbery) gave us food 'for fourteen', which meant that the little community as a whole had to deprive itself to provide food for the youngest children. Until we reached the Palaeolithic stage the question remained dormant; but then the day came when people started counting spoonfuls, and saying it wasn't right for adults to be deprived for the sake of children, or that it was the parents who ought to make the sacrifice, that three spoonfuls were all right, but four, no. It was a problem to which no satisfactory solution was possible, but it remained a continual source of trouble until we managed to an extent to side-step it by means of the stratagems which I shall shortly describe. I do not wish to imply that our companions were mean or selfish; we were reduced to a level at which we fought tooth and nail to survive.

'We ought to be able to console ourselves'—I read in my wife's diary—'by the thought of the thousands (or millions) of persons in the world who are as badly or worse off than we are . . . but when you have hunger-cramps, and your head aches, and you go and look for food in the dustbin, it is impossible to console yourself with anything!' Nothing, unfortunately, grew in the grounds of the house (except, rarely, the emetic mushrooms; nothing grew on the stony soil even beyond the barbed wire except junipers and some dried-up bushes, vegetation which a botanist would immediately identify as xerophilous, adapted to dry conditions. Thus the day came when we started taking an interest in the police refuse-bin. The passage from the habits and values of civilized life to the habits of moles was painful but, once we had accepted the new order of ideas, we felt, or at any rate I felt, a kind of revitalizing slap in the face. First we acted secretly, unknown to each other. I remember making a list when going to sleep in the evening of what I had scavenged in the course of the day: a bit of cabbage picked up during the morning while sweeping (excellent); some mandarine peel picked up at eleven o'clock near the door (delicious); some potato peelings retrieved from the dustbin (divine); a fish-tail found at six o'clock just after dark, unfortunately with hair on it (disgusting but nourishing). . . . On one of these days the chemist from Naples caught me with my hands in the dustbin. 'Fosco, you ought to be ashamed of yourself!' he exclaimed. 'What a thing for a lecturer of the Imperial University to do!' I think I blushed; I certainly withdrew. But five minutes later, going by chance to the kitchen window, I saw him doing exactly what I had done. Looking back on it now, it is laughable; at the time these things assumed the proportion of tragedies.

Another private crisis for everybody was the first theft. I shall never forget mine. I stole a carrot. Vegetables were stored in a place which could be reached by climbing a wall; as a mountain climber, I noticed this, and decided to make the attempt. The vegetables were part of the police ration, and I was therefore not robbing my companions. I climbed up, went in, and fell on a heap of carrots; to me they were riches, diamonds, gold, rubies, uranium, the most fabulous riches in the world. I filled my shirt with them to take them to the children; outside, by the light of the stars, I ate one. Heaven forgive me, I said to myself, eating this most exquisite carrot, which was still all earthy.

Gradually these 'salvaging' expeditions became the normal thing. We lost our sense of shame, and organized them in gangs of two or three. One man acted as look-out, or distracted the attention of the police, while his companions got to work. One day the engineer made a sensational discovery: the key of one of his trunks fitted the padlock of the room under the staircase which the police used as their larder. The discussions that followed this electrifying discovery were long, and as vitriolic as the atmosphere of conspiracy in which they took place permitted. The old men, whose rations were supplemented from outside, were opposed to any 'salvaging'. The diplomatist pointed out that if we were discovered we should suffer severely, and they would all have to pay for it. Several others were doubtful. Somi observed philosophically that it was a magnificent idea, but excitement caused hunger, hunger made more food necessary, and to get it more stealing would be required; it was a vicious circle. That left three of us: the engineer, the man from Friuli, and myself.

Every detail of the *coup* was worked out. We decided that the amount that we would steal would be a minimum, to be carefully worked out, and that it was essential to keep the police under constant observation, both before and afterwards. We decided that it was possible that for a time they might pretend not to notice, in order the better to catch us out later. We agreed that the best time would be in the evening, preferably on a windy day, just after the new shift had come on duty, while the news was being broadcast. This had two advantages: (i) the attention of the police would be monopolized by the loudspeaker, and (ii), if it were subsequently noticed that anything was missing, it would most probably be assumed that the previous shift had been helping themselves. In great secrecy we made small bags to put the booty in, and waited for zero hour. Because of my knowledge of Japanese, it was only too obvious that I should have to act as look-out; I should have much preferred to be 'on the job' with the others, though the task assigned to me could turn out to be both difficult and dangerous. Knowing that the police were much worried by mice which haunted the Tempaku and helped themselves to an unauthorized share of the rations, I armed myself with a stick and a big, empty tin. If Kasuya or one of his colleagues appeared, I was noisily to drop the tin to warn the others and fling myself under a table shouting: 'A mouse! A mouse!' and, as an additional security measure, I should try if possible to trip up the policeman.

I shall never forget our first raid on the store-cupboard. We approached it from opposite directions and I stopped outside the police door. As soon as the news had started, I made a sign to my companions, and they disappeared. My heart thumped; the time seemed to pass at a snail's pace. Every noise was like a shriek; the police stood still. From down the corridor I heard the sound of the cupboard door being quietly opened. Suddenly I saw a shadow on the glass door of the police room. It was Kasuya; I recognized his unmistakable silhouette, his odious, elegant, feline gestures. He stood there for a moment, listening, and then turned away and sat down. Had he suspected something? Seven or eight minutes later, when I heard the door of the store-cupboard gently closing again, and realized that I could go away, I was exhausted by the tension.

A few minutes later we were in the luggage-room on the first floor. We were forbidden to go there without permission, but in winter the police never went up there because of the cold.

'You should have seen it!' the engineer exclaimed. 'Rice, rice, whole boxes of rice! What a sight! I wanted to take pounds and pounds. We took only a few *go*; it was much wiser. . . . And then beans, noodles, eggs, just think of it, eggs and sugar! What a sight!'

Our attitude to food at that time was tender, mystical, religious, ready to become lyrical at the slightest excuse. It was then that I came to understand many aspects of primitive life that normally seem strange and incomprehensible—the divinity of corn, bread, the harvest.

Henceforward, and practically until the end of our internment, these salvaging operations occupied a good part of our time and a great deal of our thoughts; perhaps it was thanks to them that we managed to survive in reasonable condition. Some minor deity (Mercury? Ebisu?) must have kept watch over us, for we had the good fortune never to be caught, though we had some narrow shaves. The actual robbery was only the principal link in quite a long chain. We scientifically divided the whole thing into nine phases: (i) preparation of kit; (ii) making the haul; (iii) removing it to prearranged place; (iv) organization of communal store; (v) dividing the haul; (vi) taking own share to private hiding-place; (vii) removing own share from hiding-place to kitchen; (viii) cooking it; (ix) eating it. A single mistake in any of the nine phases would have blown the whole thing sky-high.

Taking the stuff from hiding-place to store, and from store to kitchen, was exceedingly dangerous, for if a policeman had stopped us and noticed an over-full pocket, it would have been the end. The same applied to the cooking. There was no end to the stratagems to which we resorted. We hid tins with a handful of rice under the communal pot; flat tins of beans went up the chimney; and onions were concealed in the ashes. To hide the onion smell, we pretended to be repairing a hot-water bottle; the smell of burning rubber smothered that of the onion. Finally there came the eating; this was done rapidly, standing in some hiding-place, while somebody else stood guard; it would have been a fatal mistake to be seen with one's mouth full out of hours. For me there was a tenth phase—taking the cooked food from the kitchen to the room where my wife and children were.

Thus by thieving and ingenuity we managed to get through the winter. On March 5 we were visited by Colonel Principini, the representative of Mussolini's short-lived puppet Italian Social Republic, with some of his aides. We were allowed to speak to him only in Japanese, and were not allowed to approach him closely. We were too terrified to tell him that we were hungry. Besides, for those who have never been hungry, what does hunger mean? A word in a dictionary, not a torment in your inside.

Even more absurd was the visit of a Red Cross delegate on March 19. The evening before Giorgio, who was always the first to smell anything new in the wind, said: 'Something's going to happen, you'll see.' The slightest prospect of 'something happening' was always sufficient to put us in a state of hysterical excitement. On this occasion the real surprise occurred when double the usual rations were handed out, besides eight eggs, and various other things. Someone suggested that they wanted to feed us up before letting us out; or before sending us to prison, someone else suggested. Finally Kasuya arrived, all smiles, told us how we were to cook the next day's rations, and how we were to eat them; above all, before sitting down to table we were to await his signal. We spent the morning in a state of feverish excitement; the slightest, most insignificant incidents were sufficient to plunge us into the wildest expectancy or the deepest gloom. At last the meal was ready—a magnificent meal, with portions actually sufficient to fill our plates. At a signal from Kasuya we took our places and started eating. A few moments later the door opened, and a distinguished-looking European gentleman of Nordic appearance looked in at us and smiled. Before we had a chance to pull ourselves together and start explaining to him that he was the victim of a gross deception, Kasuya, with an elaborate display of bows and smiles, led him away. We subsequently learnt that this gentleman was a representative of the Red Cross; that he went back to Tokyo and reported that all was well with us; and that his name was Angst ('fear').

During our long internment the only visit that resulted in anything was that of Monsignor Marella, the Apostolic Delegate in Japan.

His diplomacy even succeeded in getting the better of Kasuya, with the result that he managed to talk to us and listen to our complaints. He left us a supply of tins which saved us from the necessity of 'salvaging' for two whole months.

None of these visits, however, made any fundamental difference to our position. My wife noted in her diary:

'April 2. Everybody down in the depths—high hope has given way to deep pessimism. We were all certain we should be let out in March; now we're convinced that we shall be here for years. And we are like a lot of squabbling children. One wants tea before nine o'clock and another after; one wants his carrots cut in cubes and another in slices, and people accuse each other of having moved their slippers, or gone out without shutting the door—or, still worse, they start personal discussions or insulting each other.'

In such circumstances people's sense of property is exasperated, becomes pathological. One of the older men had a small saucepan, another had a small bottle, the chemist had a pocket knife, I had an earthenware lighter, Somi an ashtray, etc., etc., and each one of us concentrated on these commonplace objects all the loving care, the feeling that they were vital extensions of our personality, that in normal circumstances is diffused and diluted over a whole wealth of things. These objects were like fetishes; woe to anyone who dared touch or move them! and if they were lost or broken, there would be high words and threats of violence. But violence there was none. Though we sometimes felt like fighting, we hardly had the strength to stand erect.

Winter gradually faded into spring, and spring faded into the long, silent rains of early summer. In May the bread incident occurred. The police must have made a profitable exchange of rice for bread, for one day we saw what Somi christened 'the cubic yard of bread' arriving at the Tempaku. The police, having little experience of this exotic food, were not aware that, unlike rice, it quickly grows mouldy in a damp climate like the Japanese. A fortnight later we saw Kasuya and his men anxiously working in the open store-cupboard. After a few moments of anxiety (had they discovered our depredations?) we realized that they were taking the 'cubic yard of bread', which by this time was green with mould, out into the garden to bury it; perhaps they thought it would help to manure the small vegetable plot which they sometimes amused themselves by digging. In any case, after they had finished burying it, we saw to our horror that they started pouring liquid from the cess-pool over it.

The sequel was a measure of the state to which we were reduced. As soon as it was dark we went into the garden, dug up the bread, and took it into the kitchen, where the chemist, the engineer and other specialists first roasted the damp, earthy, mouldy fragments and then boiled them with some *shoyu*. That night there was an extra plateful for everybody; it was a wonderful occasion, and we went to sleep happily, like cave-dwellers in a famine who had feasted on a putrefying hyena.

With the spring we discovered other ways of supplementing our diet—ferns, snails, and an occasional snake. Wild chicory leaves were a great delicacy, and so were some kinds of roots. We had become experts; we could smell out food a mile away. We never succeeded in satisfying our appetites, but we were so emaciated, the arrears to be made up were so huge, that sudden abundance might have been dangerous to us.

High summer came, and heat had never been so welcome. It was the equivalent of a certain amount of food; the body, not losing so much heat, needed less fuel. We learned to sleep sitting in the most uncomfortable positions; the extent of human adaptability is incredible; you discover it only under the pressure of circumstances. The war, so far as we could tell, seemed to have got bogged down, and the attitude of the police never changed in its methodical hostility. Perhaps I may be mistaken, but I do not believe that with us the police would have had sufficient self-control to be able to persist so steadily, consistently, and single-mindedly in a deliberate programme of minute vexations; there would have been days when they became vulnerable, weakened a little, let slip a kind word, showed a spirit of accommodation in some minor matter, accepted a bribe for some petty favour. Nothing of the sort happened with our Japanese. We might have been dealing with members of a religious order; they were, and they remained, unapproachable, incorruptible, always in the breach.

After the rainy season, which ends in July, for some mysterious reason —perhaps a new and harsher chief of police—a new period in our lives began. Our wretchedness, our malnutrition, reached such a pitch that we decided on a hunger strike. It was a sudden decision; somebody suggested it, and everybody immediately agreed. 'At least the fact that we exist will be brought to somebody's notice,' remarked one of the old gentlemen, who had now been forbidden to receive food parcels. Now, the last thing that the Nagoya police wanted—though this was a fact that we were able to deduce only after the war—was that our existence should be brought to anybody's notice. An inquiry from Tokyo would have spoilt their little game.

When, therefore, on the morning of July 18, 1944, we calmly said to Kasuya, who had immediately noticed that the kitchen fire had not been lit: 'Thank you for your courteous and honourable interest, but we have decided not to eat today, and we shall not do so until we have had an opportunity to speak personally to the chief of police, and until our conditions are at least slightly improved,' we realized that we were being taken seriously, very seriously indeed. I still remember distinctly the slight and sinister smile into which Kayusa's thin lips curled as he replied: '*Yoshi*' (all right), '*ima-ni kōkai suru zo*' (but you'll be sorry for it). Not two hours later a party of officers and non-commissioned officers arrived in a kind of jeep. We were called together outside the kitchen and addressed violently in a speech in which the forms of maximum contempt of which the Japanese language is capable were used. We were told that we ought to be ashamed of asking anything whatever, that we had absolutely no rights, that it was a great concession that we had been left alive, and that the Italians were liars and traitors.

'At that'—I quote from my wife's diary—'Fosco picked up the [kitchen] chopper, chopped off the little finger of his left hand, picked it up and offered it to the terrified Kasuya.[1] "*Itarya-jin uso-tsuki de wa nai!*" (Italians are not liars!) he shouted. There was general consternation. I saw everything from behind. At first I did not realize what was happening, then I saw from Kasuya's face. The

---

[1] Actually I threw it at him.

400

children saw, and started screaming. I ran forward with Toni in my
arms, but fainted, and B. carried me upstairs. Let them learn that
we have character too. The police very shaken and pale.'

I, too, still have a clear picture in my mind of Kasuya's white uniform spattered with blood. This detail had a considerable degree of
magic importance. By my action I had imposed upon him the necessity
of purification, transferring all responsibility for the incident to him.
Violence against oneself, shedding one's own blood, in extreme cases
sacrificing one's life, is a demonstration to a superior of one's sincerity,
and must be carried out with certain formalities—like duelling with us
—if it is to carry conviction. Fortunately it had all passed off very well.

I also remember distinctly the scientific detachment with which
later in the afternoon I watched the purification being punctiliously
carried out with salt wherever there was the slightest bloodstain. But let
me tell the story in order. After the *yubikiri* ('the cutting off of the finger')
I was taken to hospital for treatment. The chopper had cut across
a phalanx, and a piece of broken bone had to be removed. When I got
back to the camp I found my wife and children locked in a room while
the men waited to be interrogated by the chief of police.

None of us yet knew that a few days earlier the Americans had
captured the island of Saipan, and that on that very day, July 18, General
Tojo's government had fallen. Perhaps our warders suspected some
secret link between our actions and these events. The interrogation was
severe. The police wanted to know who the 'ringleader' was. But there
was no ringleader; it was a spontaneous action by a group of starving
people who wanted to survive. When my turn came, Azumi, one of the
most villainous of the police officers, immediately asked where the
finger was. Now, Giorgio, who never loses his head, even in moments
of the greatest confusion, had picked it up and carefully put it in a
bottle of spirit from the medicine-chest. The valuable relic was now
solemnly presented to the board of interrogators; in handing it to them
I said jokingly: 'Here is a present; you can make a *sukiyaki* of it.' Alas! this
was another unfortunate coincidence, for just at that time the Japanese
had been accused of cannibalism in the allied press. No sooner had
I made my unfortunate remark than Azumi leapt from his seat and
started striking me in the face, shouting '*Ayamaré!*' (Apologize!) I

laughed, pretended to be vastly amused, and went on laughing while tears and blood ran down my cheeks. *'Jodan datta yo,'* I kept on saying, *'jodan datta yo,'* and he went on hitting me; but I do not think that I bent my head. In the end he got tired of it, or accepted my statement that it was a joke, and returned to his seat.

Late that afternoon the police officers left, taking Giorgio and Somi with them. We were left in the dark, terrified, hungrier than usual, with the obscure threats made by the police still ringing in our ears. 'Weakness and headache,' my wife noted in her diary. 'Electricity in the air; two meals missed; everyone very excited.' Yuki came tip-toeing towards me, and brought me a toffee, her 'great treasure', which she had kept hidden in a little box for who knows how many months. We ended by meticulously dividing it into five parts.

In the succeeding days there followed the inevitable reaction of tyranny to a weak attempt at rebellion. 'The hunger is terrible,' I find in my wife's diary. 'We now get half a *kin* (300 grammes) of bread in the morning with a cup of *miso,* less than a *go* (180 cc.) of flour at midday, with pieces of onion, and half a *go* of rice in the evening, with a handful of vegetables for everybody.' Such a diet is tolerable for a few days if one is in good physical condition (and many people would, indeed, benefit by it); but with many months of starvation behind you, it makes you either half-conscious from sheer weakness, or liable to sudden outbursts of rage and violence. The daily time-table, with all its absurd prohibitions, was re-imposed with all the old severity, and newspapers, the wireless, in short all communication with the outside world was totally cut off.

My wife's diary speaks of 'physical weakness'; it recalls spots in front of her eyes when reading or sewing; it adds that her hair was falling out, and it says this:

'I remember in the first few weeks of our imprisonment, when we were still *ourselves,* the discussions after meals, the reading of verse in the kitchen, the philosophical duels with ladle in hand. Now it is as if a grey cloak were suffocating everything, mentally and physically.'

We hardly spoke, we no longer thought about anything, we wandered about like caged beasts, we made absurd experiments with the bark of trees, the rare snails that we found, with grass, even with earth (someone remembered having read that during famines in China peasants ate clay for the sake of the sensation of a full belly). We had even dropped our 'salvaging', thinking it too dangerous to tempt fate in the present circumstances.

After a few days Giorgio was brought back, thinner than ever, dirty and with a long beard. He had been interrogated for hours and hours, and in the end the police must have been convinced that there had been no revolt. But there was no sign of Somi, about whom we were left in anxiety. A fortnight later he reappeared. I shall never forget it. I was sitting outside when suddenly I saw what looked like a ghost appear at the bathroom window. It was Somi. His eyes were hollow, his cheeks sunken, his beard long, his shirt bloodstained and filthy.

No, he explained, he had not been beaten; it had been the bugs—the quantity of them! The place must have been a breeding-ground And how he had envied them. He had had nothing to eat, but they had had him.

Unlike Giorgio, he had not been harassed with interrogations; the police had merely punished him by putting him in a cell which was particularly popular with bugs. For food they had given him a potato a day and a little water. He said that he had resigned himself to death, and that he had passed the time, which had seemed to go more and more quickly, in a kind of stupor. After a certain point, he said, you went into a kind of daze which was almost pleasing. He had wondered whether he still existed. The obvious answer was no, and then for two or three hours he had not existed. It was a matter of consolidating all those little fragments of non-existence into one big, definite non-existence. A most interesting experience.

In honour of Somi's return somebody produced some tinned meat which he had been hoarding for a special occasion. It was characteristic of Somi that he insisted on washing, shaving and changing from head to foot. Only then, looking terrifyingly thin and pale, red-eyed, but in immaculate shirt and trousers, did he come down and ceremoniously eat his tin of meat, together with a little rice which had been set aside. He continually interrupted his meal to philosophize about life in general and life in prison in particular, and interpolated learned references to the customs and habits of bugs.

The old diplomatist's forecasts invariably turned out to be correct. The period of reprisals which he foresaw as the consequence of our 'revolt' duly set in. But then a gradual improvement in our treatment began, particularly in regard to the children, whose bottle of milk now appeared daily. Slowly our rice ration crept up to the minimum of thirty-two *go*, which was the absolute minimum to which we had a right. As I have already several times indicated, the concept of 'right' in the east is entirely different from that with which we are familiar; a right is not a right in our sense, something to which you are inherently entitled by virtue of your existence, but a concession granted from outside and above, and therefore liable at any time to be revoked. The first time we dared to speak of our 'rights' *(kenri)*[1] in regard to our rations, the police laughed in our faces. But it was easy to see that, whether because of the course that the war was taking or as a consequence of our 'revolt', our position was noticeably stronger. Our warders laughed in our faces (thus saving theirs), but we got practically the whole of our rations. That was still little enough, but at least it served to raise us somewhat above the bestial state to which we had been reduced for about a year.

Once more autumn approached, beautiful as always in Japan. The days ripened serenely, the afternoon haze filled the landscape with a charming melancholy, the trees dotted about the countryside turned rust-colour. We actually succeeded at last in reading and working a little. The senseless discipline was a thing of the past; no one came and chased you away angrily if you dared to sit and think under a tree. Our library was small but substantial. I have often seen the question asked in newspapers: if you were allowed to take one, three, or ten books with you to a desert island which would you choose? That was a question with which we were all more or less confronted on the day we were told to pack our things and make ready for internment. My own small collection, gathered more or less haphazardly in the last few days, included Flaubert's novels, Frazer's *Golden Bough*, James Joyce's *Ulysses*, Weber's history of philosophy, a French medical dictionary, Sansom's history of Japan, the *Oxford Book of English Verse*, the *Divina Commedia* and

[1] Word coined in 1868 (*See* G. B. SANSOM, *The Western World and Japan*, London, 1950, pp. 471–2.

a few others that I can no longer recall. Giorgio and Somi had their own little libraries, ranging from the *Bhagavad Gita* to McGovern's *Ancient Empires of Central Asia,* from Rabelais to Leopardi. Eventually the Red Cross, if it did nothing for our starving bellies, sent us a whole shelf full of novels and thrillers which served admirably to fill in the empty hours. Without news, without mail, alone with our thoughts, with our hunger slightly assuaged, we lived in a strange limbo out of the world.

Soon great changes were to take place. But in the meantime the cold returned, and hunger started tormenting us again. Then there came the famous month of December, 1944, with the first serious air-raid (on December 13), and a period of restlessness on the part of the big fish which holds up the world, and the consequent earthquakes; and finally a period of extreme nervousness and intractability on the part of our guards, we did not know why.

It was a remarkable experience on that grey, clear, December afternoon when for the first time we saw dozens of aircraft in formation appearing in the sky. They approached at such a height that at first we could not see them; there was nothing but the deep roar of the engines and the white vapour trails that spread from an invisible point in the sky and grew and grew like colossal flowers in space. We certainly were somewhat alarmed to note that they seemed to be making straight towards us, but at the same time we were fascinated. Then we heard the sinister whistle of the bombs, followed by innumerable explosions; the Americans were demolishing the Mitsubishi works near the harbour.

The first raid was, I think, a lyrical experience for all of us. The vastness of the spectacle, which was on a scale which we had hitherto associated only with natural events, storms, earthquakes; the sense of the physical nearness of men with whom our fate was bound up; the demonstration that at last things were on the move, freeing us from our limbo and plunging us into the midst of immense historical events, were all profoundly moving. But after the poetry came the prose. The first raid was followed by a second and a third, and then many more; often isolated aircraft came at night, dropping a bomb here and there as if by chance, or there were air-raid warnings which obliged us to carry our children on our backs in the cold and the snow down to the damp shelter, where a few inches of earth offered protection against splinters only.

Air-raids were soon supplemented by earthquakes. For some time the earth seemed obsessed. There were continual tremors, by day and particularly by night, and there were frequent rumblings of the kind which seismologists describe. The epicentre must have been shallow, and pretty near us. At night you would feel a sharp shock under your pillow, and then you had to get up and take the whimpering children outside; the poor things could not understand why the world was conspiring against them in this fashion. One night was worse than all the others. At ten o'clock the air-raid warning came and we went down to the *boku-go,* the shelter, and waited until midnight, but there was no raid. As soon as we got back to our room and fell asleep there was a pretty strong earthquake. Once more we had to go downstairs and wait. Eventually we went back into the house, because it was freezing and blowing hard. A little before dawn there was another warning, followed by a raid almost immediately, and another hurried descent to the shelter with the children and our goods and chattels while the bombs fell. That day the police insisted on the normal time-table; sleeping during the day-time was strictly forbidden.

One morning, while we were all at breakfast, the earth started quaking with a violence and an obvious determination to wreak evil that we had not previously experienced. After a moment's hesitation, while the window-panes broke and the plaster fell from the walls, I seized the children and we dashed out. Fortunately there was little danger of being buried alive even if the house collapsed, because there was an outside staircase; but going down it was like negotiating a companion-way of a ship in a violent storm, and Toni slid most of the way. At that moment the earthquake must have reached its height. The earth was undulating just as if it were a liquid; it was impossible to stand on one's feet; it was a sight I shall never forget. Then it suddenly stopped, and it was all over. Our house, which was well pegged down against the high winds that blew on the hillside, was still standing, though the walls had peeled. We all started laughing; we felt as if we had fallen a hundred yards and miraculously remained unhurt.

I have no memory of Christmas and the New Year of 1945. My wife had given up keeping her diary. We were so surrounded with trials and tribulations—cold, earthquakes, air-raids, lack of news, total isolation, to say nothing of the police, who were nervous, tired, and irritable—that

I expect we just awoke one morning and said to each other: Good gracious! Today's Christmas!' The only good side of the situation was that we now all formed a united front; there was no longer time for squabbling among ourselves.

We organized an efficient system for getting the news. Sometimes we found bits of old newspapers in the dustbin, but that was a chancy and primitive business. More effective, though more risky, was the system we devised of borrowing the newspaper from the police office, either shortly before we were roused in the morning or during the period of about ten minutes when the office was deserted while the police took their bath. As soon as the newspaper was in our hands it was quickly scanned by the missionary or by Somi, the essential news was translated by them or by others, written down on a piece of paper by Giorgio, and finally commented on by the old diplomatist before the assembled community. Thus we were able to follow the progress of the war in east and west.

One morning in October I remember being taken to hospital to have my finger attended to (because of malnutrition it would not heal). On the way back—I remember the exact spot, I saw it again this morning —I suddenly heard my mother's voice calling me. I turned, with tears in my eyes; I had understood. A year later I learnt that at that moment she had died in distant Italy.

When January came the earthquakes diminished; the earth seemed tired and exhausted. But the raids went on, and some bombs fell pretty close. Later we discovered that a military establishment was hidden in a valley a few hundred yards away from us, and it was this that the Americans were trying to hit. But human beings get used to anything; I even have some striking memories of that terrible winter of 1945. One of them is of going back to my room after a raid and seeing what looked like a strange red moon descending over the horizon; it seemed not a terrestrial spectacle at all. I might have been a visitor to another planet, watching some entirely unfamiliar phenomenon in the skies; and I think of some excursions into the Yagoto woods with the children; the sudden sense of liberty; hunting for food like wild animals—a berry, ferns, or wild *tampopo* (chicory) leaves. Once we actually picked up a potato; it was like finding a gold nugget. Who could have dropped it there? For a long time we talked about the potato miracle.

At last March came; our supreme ordeal, and the supreme ordeal for Japan. The Americans had established themselves in a number of islands near the Japanese archipelago, among them Iwojima, and now air-raids could be expected in earnest. In fact, as soon as the offensive started, the big towns of Japan were totally destroyed in the space of a few weeks; all that was left of Tokyo, Osaka, Kobe, Nagoya, Yokohama, was plains of green stones.

Nagoya was systematically destroyed by fire in three raids on March 11, 18, and 25. Each time the warning came at 9 p.m. In the silence, the total darkness of country and town, we could hear the announcements coming from the loudspeakers in the distance: 'Many hundreds of aircraft expected. . . . Prepare for a heavy raid.' The police put on their 'war paint' as the children, who were very much impressed, put it—complete with steel helmets and big samurai swords, and we went down to the shelter with all the *futon* we could collect, hoping that a stray bomb would not fall on us now, so near the inevitable end. Towards midnight the air was filled with a powerful throbbing ('the great breath of the world', as Somi said, manicuring his nails and walking up and down in the garden, defiantly smoking a cigarette), and soon the first waves of B29s arrived.

They no longer flew at a great height; the defence must by now have been so weak that they could afford the luxury of coming in at about 3,000 feet or even less. Every wave dropped a shower of incendiaries, which landed with a sharp crackle, in strong contrast to the deep roar of high explosive. Meanwhile the city burnt, and the flames rose to the sky. Acres, square miles, of houses and huts, hundreds upon hundreds of tons of timber, blazed in one enormous bonfire, which lasted all night. For us cowering in our shelter the night passed with exasperating slowness. The minutes seemed centuries. When so many aircraft had passed that it seemed no more could be left in the world, as many more approached, flying still lower in the smoky sky, lit up from below by the red glow of the burning town. At last a horrible silence descended, and a ghostly, bluish light appeared—the dawn.

For us the worst of these raids was the last, when the part of Nagoya where the Tempaku stood—it was surrounded by suburbs on three sides—was destroyed. The first aircraft bombed one of the quarters immediately to the south; each wave dropped its bombs a little nearer.

At one point we thought our turn had come; we held our breath; my wife and I nearly suffocated the poor children under the *futon*; but the wave passed over without dropping its bombs. The destruction was resumed on the other side of the hills. Several stray bombs fell near us, destroying houses and setting light to stretches of woodland.

At dawn, when we went up to our rooms, once more we saw the extraordinary bluish light, the first effect of dawn on the night lit up by the orange reflection of the fires. The air was laden with smoke, and the horrible smell of burnt flesh (about 10,000 persons lost their lives in these raids). At the window, from which there was an excellent view of the blazing city, Dacia was standing and looking out; she had gone upstairs ahead of us. She was gazing at the tremendous spectacle as if turned to stone. *'Doshite, papa-chan, doshite?'* she kept saying. (Why, father, Why?)

One last big raid took place at the beginning of April in daylight. Nagoya as a town was now dead, but there must have been something left to justify the effort. This time the aircraft flew low and went about their task in leisurely fashion, as if they were on a tourist flight, and took aim with infinite care. It was then that we saw some black dots in the sky which looked like insects because of the huge mass of the American bombers; these, we at once realized, were the suicide pilots in their death-machines. Immediately overhead, perhaps 3,000 feet up, we saw one of these insects making straight for a B29. The distance between them narrowed, disappeared, and they crashed. A red flame burst out in the sky, and the big bomber, a wing of which fell off and plunged to earth, started coming down, burning and exploding. While bombs, bodies, fragments of aircraft, fell earthward with what seemed tragic slowness, we heard a loud shout coming from the town, I imagine from thousands of throats: *'Banzai!'* they shouted. *'Banzai!'*

Nagoya was now really reduced to cinders, and the raids ceased. Even Iyeyasu's famous castle had been destroyed. One day the police told us that they were taking us into the country, 'beyond Koromo'. We could not see the reason for this, now that everything was over, but the news gave us much pleasure. We had decided, among other things, that it would not be advisable to be near a big town if the Americans landed; we did not know that orders had been given that in the event of an allied landing all prisoners, internees, and citizens of hostile countries should be killed without exception.

It is strange that returning, whether physically or in one's imagination, to a place where you have suffered severely fills you with a profound and far from disagreeable emotion, which you can describe only as religious; a feeling, that is to say, that here you were close to the great mystery; that here you were significantly in touch with the essence of things, with good and evil, time and non-time, life and death, love and hate; that here the thick veil of conventions and soft living which in ordinary times obscure them was torn away.

Thus, when I left the Tempaku, I was too moved to be able to speak. Then, driving away from Nagoya, the sky cleared, and the country was so beautiful that the present came uppermost again; for quite a distance we sang as we drove. We were making towards the mountains beyond Korome, to the Kosai-ji, the temple to which we were evacuated in April, 1945, where we remained until the war ended in September.

At one point we noticed some curious sculpture at the roadside, near a farmhouse. This was so unusual that we stopped to look. A child came towards us and said: 'There are more inside, come in.' Thus we found ourselves in the house of a charming old peasant of about seventy, who received us with fresh and innocent hospitality.

'The idea of sculpting came into my head one day when I was fifty-seven,' he told us.

'Indeed it did,' his wife interrupted with a sigh.

'I did not know how to set about it, but fortunately I had some cement and some pieces of iron, so I started by sculpting in reinforced concrete.'

His wife brought us green tea and biscuits, and kept up a grumbling running commentary on her husband's account of his absurd passion for art.

'Come,' he insisted, 'let me show you my masterpiece!'

He took us into the tiny garden behind the house where there was a tall statue of Kwannon, again in reinforced concrete, modelled with freedom, intelligence, and gaiety. However, we preferred his self-portrait, with bowler hat and *haori* (Photograph 31), because of its liveliness and the skill with which he handled the intractable material.

Beyond Koromo, an ugly village in the middle of a big valley, the road grew more rural again, and we drove alongside a river, with a dyke and artificial lake, and soon caught sight of the Kosai-ji ('Temple of the Vast Salvation') at the foot of a wooded hill.

The Kosai-ji constitutes one of the happiest memories of my life. Not that things changed suddenly, or that we passed straight from the horrors of the Tempaku to an earthly paradise. We still suffered from hunger, cold, humiliations, but we felt that things were on the move; it was easier to supplement our rations, and above all we were at an extraordinarily beautiful spot.

The road degenerated into a track, and the track into a path and, after passing the last houses of the village, we had to leave the car and walk. All the most delightful features of the Japanese countryside were concentrated in this valley. The rice-fields, which certainly yielded less than the rich, regular fields on the plain below, were laid out on irregular terraces—some were only pocket-handkerchief size—on the surrounding slopes, which were crowded by wooded hills. Dotted about were farmhouses with thatched roofs (like those in Photograph 20), connected by paths which wound their way casually and unhurriedly through the countryside.

On one side, where the slope was too steep for rice-fields, there was a group of ancient, twisted, vigorous, tall pines at the edge of a wood, in which clumps of cypresses (sugi) alternated with denser, less tidy, deciduous trees. There were some stone funerary pillars, ancient walls, and an arched gateway that marked the beginning of the long stairway that led to the temple. Nothing had changed. The wind sang in the pines. Nobody was about. Our footsteps re-echoed on the stone steps.

We went down a short avenue flanked by momiji; the last red leaves still hung from the boughs. We reached the second gate, taller, more elegant, better cared for than the first, and went through it into a courtyard, or rather cloister, bounded on three sides by various low buildings, and on the fourth, at the end facing us, by the temple itself. This was built essentially like a big farmhouse, with heavy, imposing, thatched roof (Photograph 18). The sun suddenly came out and flooded the courtyard which, then as now, was half-cloister and half-farmyard; oats and liturgical instruments, agricultural implements and ecclesiastical vestments, immediately struck the eye; the smell of earth mingled with the odour of incense.

'*Ará, Fuosuko-san!*' a voice called from the entrance to the kitchen; the son of the former abbot had recognized me, and came over to greet us. He apologized for being dressed as a peasant; he explained that they had been ruined by the agrarian reform, and they had to work like horses to survive. We were invited inside to take tea with him.

The temple belongs to the Soto branch of Zen, a more accommodating variety than the Rinzai, the acquaintance of which we made at Kyoto (Chapter 9). Priests are allowed to marry, and in the country they live a life not unlike that of an English farmer. In 1945 the *hōjō* (abbot) of the Kosai-ji was an old man of about eighty, of magnificent appearance but somewhat irritable nature. His family consisted of his wife, an old lady of whom we saw little; their daughter; her husband, who was the old man's adopted son; and their children.

From the first day of our arrival we naturally tried to establish friendly relations with the *hōjō's* family, hoping that we might be able to earn some extra food by working in the fields, chopping wood, etc. However, the police must have terrorized the old man, and for a long time all our attempted overtures were rebuffed. Also, for at least two months, we failed to find out who was really in charge of farm and temple; we were confronted with yet another example of delegation and re-delegation of power. At first we thought that the person in charge must be the old *hōjō*, whom we used to see walking about, looking as impressive as a Chinese sage of the Ming dynasty, with his Greek philosopher's head, his dry and decisive orders, his voice, which suggested a patriarch in full enjoyment of his powers. However, many small signs showed us that this was a mistake. The *hōjō*, for instance, would say, with a slight inclination of his head, like a sovereign interrupted in his meditations: 'Yes, you can sit here to read.' But then the chief policeman would come up to us in a rage and ask us if we did not know that this spot was forbidden to us, because the temple people objected. Next we decided that the person who really mattered must be his son, who bore the family name and, though his job was teaching at the village school, often took the old gentleman's place at important religious services. But this, too, turned out to be a beautiful theory spoilt by inconvenient facts.

Eventually, however, we hit on the truth. Every now and then we noticed in the fields, or in the various yards behind the temple, where farm carts were drawn up and wood was stacked, but rarely in the temple courtyard itself and practically never in the temple proper, an unprepossessing, middle-aged woman who—an unusual thing in Japan —was dirty into the bargain. Always she was carrying a heavy load, a bundle of twigs under her arm or a sack of cereals on her back, or a load of fresh leaves in her apron. She always wore *mompe,* the blue trousers which Japanese women have worn since time immemorial for working in the fields, and a tattered old handkerchief over her dirty, untidy hair. She never spoke to us or, I think, to the police, but occasionally she was to be heard shouting hoarsely from the kitchen. She was the *hōjō's* daughter; her husband was a *yoshi,* her father's adopted son who had been given to her in marriage and, as the old *hōjō* had retired, it was she who held the legal, moral, and material keys to this little kingdom. Who knows what psychological twist had reduced her to this state? Perhaps, aware of her unprepossessing appearance, she took masochistic pleasure in making herself repulsive; or perhaps she enjoyed the contrast between the power she exercised over so many persons and her own beggarly appearance.

Her domains were certainly well populated at that time. There were her parents, husband, and children, of whom there were four or five, the labourers who worked in the fields, the four policemen, and finally ourselves. In regard to the police, Kasuya disappeared with the move to Nagoya; his place was taken by a colleague who had the manners and appearance of a rather crude sergeant. Every now and then he gave us to understand that he was not to be trifled with, but in fact he spent most of the day asleep, and in the evening went down to the village to enjoy himself. He was succeeded by other *junsa,* who came, remained for a short time, and disappeared in their turn.

We followed the *sensei,* the schoolmaster, as we always called him, into the temple kitchen; I shall not describe it; it was like that at Hanase (page 298), but even more legendary and barbaric. The rafters that supported the high roof were lost in a darkness pregnant with mystery and soot. They were of fabulous size, whole tree-trunks roughly squared up with a giant's axe. Here we found his old mother of eighty squatting by the fire, trying to boil a pot full of water over a few cinders.

She exclaimed with delight when she saw me, and said she had been expecting me; she had always known that I would come back before she died. The poor *hōjō* had died last year; he had always talked about us a great deal. She had been told that she would survive him by three years, so she still had two more left. How were the children? Had not *okusan* (the lady) come with me? And how were Somi-san and Jyorujyo-san? And why did they never come and see them? Were they so far away? She remembered how we used to steal the rice placed as an offering before the *Hotoke-sama* (the Buddhas). Ha! Ha! She had always replaced it immediately, so that the old man shouldn't notice. In fact nobody had ever noticed, because she had known we were hungry and wanted to help us. . . . She had the loveliest chrysanthemums; she had tended them hoping I would come back and see them, and she would like to show them to me. Come, let us go and see the chrysanthemums! We would have tea afterwards. 'Make the tea for Fuosuko-san and his friends in the drawing-room, not here in the kitchen!'

We went and looked at the chrysanthemums. It had not occurred to me before that the incursion of a group of foreigners into the life of this remote, ancient, and solitary place, the appearance of fifteen Italians (in addition to twenty Dutchmen who were lodged in a little temple 200 yards lower down), was a major historical event, a revolution, in the life of this village, where the only news was the passing of the seasons; perhaps we had already ascended into legend.

While we admired the chrysanthemums the old lady gave us news of every member of the family and the sun beat down warmly on the cloister. What a peaceful, dreamlike place it was against the background of cypresses! The sound of the wind in the trees reached us like a caress.

The temple, or at any rate its foundation, dates back to the fourteenth century, to the time of the great Emperor Go-Daigo[1] (page 301). The present building seems to have been built at the beginning of the eighteenth century, though the date is uncertain. When we lived here ten years ago it was a perpetual delight to look at this simple, modest old building which, with its big irregular thatched roof and its massive wooden walls, covered with lichen, somehow possessed a beauty born of the earth, like that of trees or growing crops.

Over the principal door there was a big *gaku* (wooden board) which in ancient times must have been framed and gilded, but now had few

[1] It is also famous for its many associations with Kojima Takanori, a legendary warrior figure of the fourteenth century.

traces left of its ancient splendour, and displayed only the ideograms standing for the name of the temple, the 'Vast Salvation'. The school-master and his mother took us round the place which I knew so well. The interior consisted of a big nave with a number of recesses. The altar was in the middle. Here and there the old *tatami* showed signs of wear and tear. Here, too, the basic agricultural-monastic motif was repeated. In front of the altar was a silk red-and-green cushion on which the abbot sat during services; a reading desk with a number of sacred books; two wooden drums (*moku-gyo*); two bells (*kane*), one big and one small. Over all this was a gilded palanquin with hangings similarly gilded; but not far away were buckets, pails, boxes, agricultural implements, and sacks of cereals.

Many memories crowded back into my mind as I walked up and down bare-foot on the temple *tatami*. The interior of the temple was one big nave, but on one side *shoji* which slid to and fro on wooden rails could be used to divide off two small rooms. It was in these that we lived; we were somewhat cramped, to be sure, but not too uncomfortable. At night we could hear the croaking of the frogs in the rice-fields; in the morning we often listened to the beautiful voice of the *hōjō* conducting an exceedingly long service, emphasizing the important points with rhythmical blows on his metal or wooden instruments.

As soon as we arrived at the Kosai-ji the police made us a long speech to the effect that we were utterly forbidden to move so much as a hundred yards from the temple; but we were old gaol-birds by now, and this was like talking to the wind. We promptly organized a complicated system of look-outs, etc., which made it easy, when necessary, to distract the attention of the police or explain a suddenly noticed absence. We discovered that the peasants, though afraid of the police, were friendly enough, and willing to do deals with us. A shirt, for instance, turned out to be worth fifteen *go* of rice. Moreover, my family and I had an excuse that justified almost any amount of absence from the temple.

One of our new warders explained to us that, being unable to provide the three small bottles of milk to which the children were entitled, the Nagoya authorities had decided to provide us with a nanny-goat. He reminded us that this animal was the property of the Imperial Japanese Government; we must therefore treat it with great care, for

it had its exact market value. The goat was thin and exceedingly tem-
peramental; she had long, bristly white hair, a beard like a bad-tempered
old aristocrat, and reddish eyes. We immediately took a great liking to
her; for the children in particular she became almost a member of the
family. Whether the honourable she-goat of the honourable Japanese
Government returned our affection I do not know; she was a difficult
creature to understand.

The excuse of taking her out to graze enabled us to explore the
whole neighbourhood, and make friends with several peasant families.
She had her own decided likes and dislikes. Sometimes she pulled like
a maniac, wanting to go down to the village, where we dared not be
seen, and if we wanted to go uphill we had to carry her on our shoulders;
she weighed as much as a sack of stones. But once at the top she grazed
like mad and would not come down again.

After a month we could claim to have settled down very nicely.
My wife worked mornings and afternoons making sheets into shirts for
the peasants, with the result that every now and then we started seeing
eggs, packets of *miso*, small parcels of rice. I used to get up before dawn
to uproot mulberry trees for a peasant who wanted to make a kitchen
garden; he used to leave me the agreed fee in kind at daybreak before the
police were about. Dacia became the Benjamin of a peasant family; she
helped them to look after the silk-worms, and in return was given
a bowl of rice. Everybody else in one way or another succeeded in
engaging in some form of profitable traffic. We were gradually remount-
ing the scale of civilization; perhaps we had returned to the Neolithic
age; soon, no doubt, we should be discovering money, writing, laws.

Moreover, day by day we were recovering physically, too—not just
because we were getting more to eat, but because we were overcoming
the isolation which is so terribly bad for human beings and from which
we had suffered for so long; to say nothing of the fact that we had re-
established contact with nature, could wander in the wood, and enjoy
at any rate a limited sense of freedom.

'This is where they used to come and eat the rice from the offerings,'
the old lady said to my Japanese friends, showing us the small cups
which were always kept full of rice. This, though always rather dusty,
I am afraid, was no less welcome for that during the early months.
Behind the great altar there was a small room where Somi, Giorgio, and

I often used to work in the afternoon (if only I could remember all the ideograms that I then learnt, I should be a *gengokaku hakase*, a professor of philology). A little way beyond we came to a small chapel containing many statues, some of which, though lacking artistic value, are of considerable historical interest. One of them is of the founder of the temple, the Abbot Kaisan, and another of the thirteenth abbot, Gessen Tanko, who had it rebuilt. The place is chiefly notable, however, for its ceiling, which is divided into seventy-two squares in each of which there is a painting of a plant or a flower. These are probably contemporaneous with the rebuilding of the temple, and were painted with delightful innocence by an extraordinarily loving and competent hand.

White Lice for Blue Blood

While the *sensei,* the schoolmaster, went to change (he wanted to be photographed in his best clothes), the old lady accompanied us up the hill behind the temple.

'Look how the cherry you planted has grown!' she exclaimed, stopping for a breather, because the path was steep.

Just beyond the cherry-trees, where the wood began, were the sepulchral pillars *(sotoba)* recording the titular abbots of the temple. They were stone structures rather resembling Tibetan *chorten* (the pagoda motif again, the symbolic model of the universe), and there were twenty-nine of them; from the time-worn ones dating back to the fourteenth century down to the newest bearing the name of the patriarch whom we had known ten years ago. It was a moving spot, dedicated to twenty-nine men who had succeeded each other in the course of the centuries; all around was the unchanging wood, exactly as it had been a hundred, a thousand, years ago.

We stopped at the 'tomb' of the old *hōjō,* and his face returned to my mind with extraordinary vividness. I recalled, for example, the morning when we planted the cherry-tree. On such rustic occasions, which he enjoyed with juvenile ardour, he appeared in a grey and patched, but spotless, *yukata,* which he tied high round his body, leaving his muscular, athlete's legs bare; he wore *waraji* (straw sandals) and a huge *kasa* (cone-shaped straw hat) such as peasants wear in the rice-fields, The air of the wood, the sunshine, the smell of the earth, seemed to go

2D

slightly to his head; he would jump about like a fawn, sing, hold spade or hoe caressingly in his strong, lined hands; but two hours later he would reappear in his splendid abbot's robes, making his way solemnly towards the high altar to read the Buddhist scriptures. All of him that was visible was the superb white beard, the shining philosopher's pate, the solemn bearing of a personage venerated in a court of angels and bodhisattvas. Wise and adorable *hōjō*!

Opposite to him in nearly every possible respect was the decrepit Baron Sato. Everything about the three Sato was strange and grotesque. Not long after our arrival at the Kosai-ji three more persons were added to the company: Baron Sato, an old gentleman who looked like an epicurean in the final stages of decay; his sister, a horribly thin, bent, nervous, strident, and toothless old woman; and an idiot nephew of theirs, aged about thirty. These nightmarish individuals were lodged in the lower wing of the building on the valley side of the courtyard. We were informed that they belonged to an important family, that the baron had squandered the greater part of his fortune, and that his family had ended by repudiating him; his responsibilities and title had been transferred to a more respectable brother. In Japan, where, particularly before the war, the family enjoyed extraordinarily wide powers, which were recognized and sanctified by law, being repudiated by one's family was no joke. The old baron and his sister lived in total indigence. The nephew had apparently been sent to complete the trio as an undesirable disgrace to the human species.

The degree of squalor to which a person who was born and bred to a life of luxury can succumb when he finds himself impoverished sometimes passes belief. Being totally untrained to look after himself, and having no servants to look after him, the descent is only too easy. The three Sato were so dirty that the smell used to reach us when the wind was in the right direction. They always wore kimonos. Elegant as the kimono is when it is properly looked after, admirably though it sets off the human form, both male and female, when it is neglected it is highly objectionable; it hangs everywhere, picks up every scrap of dirt, catches in everything, and gets torn to tatters. The physical ruin of the three Sato was matched by their nervous ruin. Not a day passed without horrible, crazy screams coming from their direction. The old woman made the most noise, but the baron not infrequently added his hoarse voice to the uproar, which was invariably accompanied by the whine of the idiot nephew.

After a few days, one of us discovered that the baron used to receive a newspaper. The police had strictly forbidden all contact between them and us, but we decided that it must be possible to persuade the baron to pass us the newspaper when he had finished with it, so as to supplement our chronic lack of news about the progress of the war. The Sato, like us, were hungry; but, unlike us, they had no way of supplementing their rations, so that, if necessary, we could offer them rice or sweet potatoes in exchange for the newspaper. One evening, when our chief warder had gone down to the village to toast with the locals the victories which the wireless still continued to promise, the diplomatist decided to pay the baron a clandestine but formal visit. I accompanied him as look-out.

The sun had just set behind the rice-fields. We found the baron seated squalidly in front of a pretence of a *tokonoma,* while his sister and nephew busied themselves with a pot perched over some glowing cinders. The baron, as it happened, was reading the newspaper, and he looked up at us in a rather sinister fashion, with a strange mixture of fear and contempt; but then, when we addressed him in respectful language, his manner changed. It was pathetic to note how he immediately assumed the gestures and language of a man of the world, though he was dressed like a beggar and was living in a room that had been u ed for years as a dump for unwanted tools, and the ceiling was falling to pieces, the walls were peeling, and there were cobwebs in all the corners.

After the usual preliminaries and circumlocutions, the old diplomatist raised the matter we had come about, and suggested that, instead of destroying the newspaper when he had finished with it, the baron should pass it to us, surreptitiously, of course. This seemed to rouse in him his native pride, his hidalgo's nature; the idea of doing anything surreptitious *(naishō)* was obviously entirely against the grain. Perhaps we had made a mistake in treating him so respectfully. All his gestures were invested with dignity and pride. The movements of his thin, filthy fingers with their long, grimy finger-nails suggested a nobleman of high degree discussing a matter of deep moment with a distinguished friend of slightly lower degree.

The old diplomatist, however, conducted the conversation with skill, and it became clear that the baron's resistance would shortly collapse. It was curious to watch these two men, each used to a very different kind of life, at grips with one another, negotiating the surreptitious passing of a newspaper with the circumstance and formality of two secretaries of state, though both looked like beggars in a thieves' kitchen. Not that the two, except on a most superficial level, really had anything in common. They shared a certain veneer resulting from the sufferings they had undergone and the poverty to which they were reduced; but the baron was a wreck, was done for, finished, and inspired nothing but revulsion and pity, while the diplomatist was a tough old root, temporarily under the weather, to be sure, but ready to send forth new shoots as soon as conditions were favourable.

While the conversation proceeded ceremoniously towards its inevitable end, I looked carefully all round. There was some pathetic evidence of the circumstances in which these people had once lived; a burnished iron teapot, for instance, and some extraordinarily delicate lacquered wooden cups, which were in a dirty old cardboard box full of rubbish and scraps of food, and a box for letters (*fubako*) lacquered and gilded with the bold elegance of the Korin school. All of a sudden the nephew, while stirring the fire, upset the pot and spilt a good part of the food, filling the room with a cloud of steam. His aunt leapt at him, screaming like one possessed, and we became eye-witnesses of one of the horrible scenes which we heard so often. The old woman, still screaming, picked up a piece of wood and started chasing her idiot nephew round the room, trampling in the overturned food each time she came to it. Finally the baron's voice joined in the chorus, vainly trying to reimpose calm. We took to flight, taking a pile of newspapers with us.

In July the baron suddenly died. His nephew came and told us, laughing horribly; you could not tell whether he was pleased or not, or whether he understood what death meant. The old woman, however, completely lost her head, not so much from grief, it seemed, as in the general confusion. She wandered about, picking up things and putting them down again, and made none of the preparations necessary for the funeral. So revolting was the heap of rags and bones that had been her brother that, among all the Japanese, Italians, and Dutch present, no one felt inclined to go to her assistance. Fortunately two young Japanese came up from the village during the afternoon with the coffin. In Japan coffins are not oblong, but broad and stumpy, and bodies are not laid out in them, but curled up, like a foetus in the womb. The old woman succeeded in persuading the two young men to put the body in the coffin, but *rigor mortis* had set in, and it was a difficult task.... It was thus, after returning from an expedition with the goat to an isolated cottage on the other side of the hill, that I found the whole population of the Kosai-ji and the neighbourhood—the Italian internees, some of the Dutch, the temple children, and many people from the village—-watching, half-amused and half-horrified, the two sturdy young peasants dancing like bears on the coffin-lid, trying to close it; the baron obstinately refused to curl up in the proper manner. At one point one of the young men let out a shriek and jumped off the coffin, promptly followed by his companion. 'Lice!' he shouted. 'Lice!' It seemed that the lice had decided to abandon the corpse. There was naturally a great commotion. Then the *hōjō* arrived, dressed in his peasant's clothes, with a big tin of disinfectant, which he proceeded to sprinkle all over the courtyard.

The funeral took place next day. The baron belonged to a rich and well-known family, and the *hōjō* had evidently received orders to conduct a really impressive service. Buddhist priests started gathering at the Kosai-ji from early morning, accompanied by young assistants carrying the sacred vestments in big parcels, and the place was full of voices and people. At about eleven o'clock the ceremony began. The temple had been opened and decorated for the occasion; the *hōjō* and the *sensei* appeared, dressed in magnificent silk cloaks (*kesa*), coloured purple, yellow, and orange; their colleagues wore the same. There was also a nun, with shaven head shining like a fruit. Extracts from the sacred books were read, and incense was burnt. But no one managed to be really serious; the story of the baron's vermin was now known to everybody; there were fresh alarms at every moment, which led to smiles imperfectly concealed behind kimono sleeves.

Expressions grew more serious and respectful when the brother of the deceased, the true Baron Sato, appeared for a moment at the entrance to the cloister, together with some other gentlemen, who followed him at a respectful distance; he was a corpulent, oldish man, funereal both in appearance and clothing, and wore spats. The little group stood for a few moments in silence, without showing any emotion, and then left. This was indeed fortunate, for a few minutes later the second exodus of lice began. The monk who was standing nearest to the coffin noticed the army of big, white parasites emerging from the bier and advancing aggressively towards the chapter of chanting priests. There were cries of alarm and a general flight into the court-yard, to the irreverent laughter of the small international crowd of onlookers. The service was resumed outside.

At this point someone remarked that the coffin was still in the temple, where we slept, after all, and that it would be as well to make sure that the lice did not reach our rooms. It was thus that Somi, always ready to do disagreeable jobs at which others baulked, went to fetch the coffin outside. He could not do so alone, of course, so I gave him a hand, together with a local peasant, and we quickly carried the coffin out into the middle of the courtyard, where the purifying midsummer sun was shining. But by now the funeral had turned to a farce; everyone was laughing, including even the *hōjō* in the gilded shadow of his big, yellow, ceremonial umbrella.

Shoe Tree

August came, and it was clear that the end was near. The police hardly showed themselves, and we even went down into the village, where everyone knew us and greeted us as friends. When it was hot we went and bathed in the river. Thus the return to liberty, to normal life, took place in stages, a very fortunate thing. I do not know whether it was on the seventh or the eighth that we read about Hiroshima, but for the first few days the newspapers were unable to give a satisfactory explanation of the disaster. Nagasaki followed. Some aircraft passed low overhead and machine-gunned people in the fields. On the fifteenth a boy came running along to tell us that the Emperor was going to broadcast; this was the first time in history that such a thing had happened, and it caused a great sensation. 'Perhaps he will tell us to fight on to the death,' one of the policemen suggested half-heartedly, but he obviously said so only to make a good impression.

Then a curious thing happened. The Emperor delivered his broad-cast, in which he in fact announced the surrender, but none of the Japanese around us was able to understand him. The speech was written in court language so remote from ordinary speech that you needed to be a philologist to grasp its meaning. The result was that until the evening, when the newspapers arrived with explanations, the police refused to allow us to go out. But then, by moonlight, we at last heard the news that we were free.

For the time being we remained at the temple. We went out when we felt like it, went down to the village, paid visits. The *hōjō* and his family invited us successively in little groups to a meal in the hall of honour behind the temple, and offered us pink rice (*o-sekihan*), which is served on auspicious occasions.

About a week after the surrender some news was broadcast which was of immediate interest to us. Allied aircraft were to fly over all prisoner-of-war and civilian internment camps, and signals were to be laid out on the ground in prominent positions, where they could be seen from the air. . . . Was it really possible that anybody still remembered us? It seemed too good to be true. Naturally, we laid out the prescribed signals in a clearing in the wood on the hill behind the temple. spreading towels and sheets on the ground. Then we waited.

A day passed and nothing happened, and then another. We took turns of an hour each to wait on the hilltop, ready to call the others if an aircraft appeared. One grey, cloudy afternoon (was it August 26?) we made out a big aircraft flying low over the hills on the horizon. It seemed to be almost touching the tree-tops and to be flying very slowly. Then it vanished. We had given up all hope when it appeared again. It turned, and turned again, and for an hour or more it kept disappearing and reappearing over the hills. Then it came straight towards us. Twice it passed overhead, flying lower each time. It was a huge, four-engined aircraft of a size we had never seen before. It passed over a third time, its belly opened, and what looked like a lot of tiny packages started floating down, suspended from little parachutes. When they landed near us they turned out to be big containers a yard-and-a-half high. Some of the parachutes failed to open, and the containers came crashing down to earth, putting both Italians and Dutch to flight.

The aircraft passed overhead once more, as if in final greeting, before it disappeared, and we were left with a hillside and a wood covered with boxes, clothes, shoes, cigarettes, parcels and packages of all kinds; a whole supermarket was scattered among the bushes, on the grass, on the trees. After two years of starvation, of counting grains of rice and hoarding single beans like precious stones, here was the land of Cockaigne, all the fabulous wealth of America, here was generosity and magnificence on a legendary scale. We did not know where to begin, what to pick up first; whether to stop and open a tin of pineapple now or patiently to collect all these riches and take them back first. The children danced about, crazy with joy, holding bars of chocolate in their hands, and asking: 'What's this black stuff? Can you eat it?' They had never seen chocolate before.

We found a tree in the wood covered all over with shoes, as if it had suddenly produced some strange tropical fruit. The dry bed of a rocky little stream was full of cigarettes, Lucky Strike, Camels, Philip Morris; there were thousands of packets of them. One container, the parachute of which had not opened, must have been filled with packets of sugar, tins of milk, and bags of powdered chocolate. It had crashed, turning the contents into a superb, nourishing brew, which we took away by the bucketful. On my way back to the temple, bent under the weight of booty, I found Somi sitting in a clump of bushes, surrounded by tins of every kind: meat, fruit, fish, Russian salad, sweets. He was opening them at random, eating the contents, and passing on to the next.

When at last we gathered in the temple that evening, among mountains of Cornflakes, tinned milk, K rations, avalanches of cigarettes, and enough clothes for a whole army, we all had to confess to a slight feeling of revulsion. The feast had been so vast, so unexpected, so unbounded, that all we wanted to do was to lie down and wait for the surfeit to pass. We were like a snake that had made a meal of a whole kid and retired into a hole to digest it. Next day, when we took stock of the riches that had descended on us, we found ourselves very well provided for. There were about thirty of us all told, including the Dutch. The minimum number catered for by the Americans was a hundred, and we had been given supplies for that number. That meant three pairs of shoes each, three jackets, six shirts, piles of tins and cigarettes. . . . We could begin free life with a certain tranquillity, at any rate for the first few weeks. Thank you, Uncle Sam!

The local peasants behaved excellently. Perhaps they did pick up one or two pairs of shoes lost in the wood, but, if they wanted anything, they came and offered rice or other food in exchange. We were well aware that solid possessions were the only thing that made one really independent; we were just about to re-emerge from a long period of barter into a money economy; we were about half-way through the Tokugawa period.

The police, however, were disgusting, particularly Fujita (whom we called Radetzky), who used to shout at us so much at the Tempaku. He reappeared during the last few days, after disappearing for several months. I ran into him near the temple; looking anxiously all round to make sure that nobody could see, he spoke to me in the manner perfectly described by the Japanese expression *osoru-osoru*, that is to say with extreme servility, and asked me in the most grovelling manner if I would kindly give him a pair of shoes, a jacket, some cigarettes. 'Take them,' I said, flinging him some stuff, 'and never let me set eyes on you again!'

August drew to an end, and the time came to leave the Kosai-ji and the companions with whom for two years we had shared a great deal of suffering and few joys. The Nagoya prefecture sent a lorry for us, and the police hovered round like obsequious valets to see what more they could do for us. They were terribly afraid that we would avenge ourselves by reporting them to the Americans. But the war was over, and all we wanted was to return to ordinary life. Perhaps we should have liked to punch Kasuya's head, but he did not show himself.

The *sensei* reappeared in his best clothes, and I took some photographs of him, and his mother called us to the temple reception-room, where tea was ready. We remained talking for a time, exchanging memories of 'when the *hojo* was alive, when the wise and patient Buddhas shut one eye when you helped yourselves to their offerings'. The *sensei* showed us two famous ancient Chinese paintings of the Sung period, signed by Keisō, which were the principal items in the temple treasure; one of them, showing ducks and cranes, was of remarkable beauty. At the last moment the *sensei's* wife, the *hojo's* daughter, the true mistress of the place, appeared, removing her dirty handkerchief from her head. She was quite unchanged. We greeted her cordially, but a few moments later she vanished again, explaining that she must light the fire for the evening meal. We rose, the old lady gripped my hand. '*Sayonara Fuosuko-san*' (Good-bye, good-bye), remember me to everybody. Two big tears were in her eyes. It was late, and the sun was setting rapidly.

13

Tokyo Farewells

The Golden Demon

JANE left suddenly yesterday. I called at the Imperial Hotel, where all foreigners stay in Tokyo, to buy some European and American papers, and found her in the entrance-hall, surrounded by her luggage, giving orders to a crowd of solicitous porters.

She was nervously cheerful, showed me her air ticket—Tokyo, Honolulu, San Francisco, Dallas—to convince me that she was really going, and she overwhelmed me with a torrent of conversation to prevent me from asking any questions; she talked about everything under the sun except about Giorgio, and I refrained from asking. I realized that everything was over between them. Giorgio had been in a particularly black mood lately.

Tama, too, had disappeared from circulation, as well as Somi. Thinking about the events of the past month or so, perhaps that evening a few weeks ago when we went to see a recent colour film, *Konjiki Yasha* ('The Golden Demon'), had been a turning point in the lives of several of us.

It was a fascinating film for anybody interested in observing how the acts of men are governed by obscure ancient forces, and no less obscure new ones. The story is taken from a well-known novel written at the end of the nineteenth century by Ozaki Kōyō, a famous author of the realist school. It tells the story of the love affair between the student Kanichi, who is intelligent, ambitious, full of ardour for the ideals of progress and liberty which must have inspired young people at that time,

426

and the sweet, charming, and submissive Miya, who has been brought up entirely in the traditional atmosphere of old Japan. Their approaching marriage is brought to nothing when the girl's parents suddenly accept the formal proposal made by a rich banker's family on behalf of one of its young members, who is fat, selfish, and vulgar. Kanichi, defeated in love, refuses to be defeated in practical life; he throws up his promising career as a medical student, if I am not mistaken, and becomes a money-lender; and, after many minor incidents, the film ends violently in an orgy of money and wickedness.

The story, whether in the novel or the film, reveals to the observer more plainly than any analytical study two emotional, almost sensual, attitudes which are so often to be met with below the surface of Japanese life and strongly colour events in times of crisis; the first concerns money and the second violence. Money is not merely a means of facilitating economic exchange, an element in the life of society to be dealt with as the engineer deals with falling water, the architect with gravity, or the gardener with the growth of seeds and bulbs; to many Japanese it has the fascination that liquor must have for Muslims, or that the nude and sex have for westerners. For centuries the samurai cultivated a total contempt for 'filthy lucre', and such attitudes leave profound traces; it is still, for instance, considered unpardonable among persons of traditional customs to give a tip without wrapping the money in a piece of paper or, better, putting it in a special envelope with an *awabi* printed on the back. In *Konjiki Yasha* money rouses emotions similar to the great passions (as, indeed, it does in *Eugénie Grandet*, for example), and surrounds it with an atmosphere of supreme, delightful, horrible sinfulness. There is such a thing as virginity in relation to money, which contaminates, makes you fall in love, has magic, secret, irresistible powers. It is now enchanting, now disgusting; now delightful, now rejected with scorn and horror.

As for violence, that is another theme which I should like to have developed at greater length. But this book is long enough already, and I shall refrain from writing a chapter about pre-war Japan and the war in the Pacific, and trying to explain how it came about that the Japanese, who in many respects are so civilized, behaved in such a brutal and savage manner under the supreme test of war. It is a difficult problem, which should be approached dispassionately and without prejudice.

There are points here which they share with the Germans, though some of the resemblances, in my opinion, are accidental. Here I shall say only that for those who have eyes to see sado-masochistic elements are evident at every step in the life and history of the Japanese.

Even a superficial glance at Japanese literature and the Japanese theatre shows that it is full of the most ferocious battles and combats. I shall not stop to quote examples from the *Romance of the Heike* (thirteenth century), all the plays dealing with the adventures of the forty-seven *ronin* and their joint suicide, all the films of our own age, for instance the moving and terrible *Himeyuri no To,* which tells the story of the adventures, sufferings, and end of a handful of schoolgirls who turn themselves into nurses in Okinawa during the last months of the war. Throughout there runs a constant thread of sublime sacrifice and horrid bloodshed. Interesting in this respect is the so-called *Kirishitan* (Christian) literature of the sixteenth and seventeenth centuries, in which the theme of martyrdom is treated with fascinated attention.[1] An Italian missionary, Father Gnecchi-Soldi (1530–1609), observed how necessary it was to keep the new Japanese converts in check in times of persecution, because they offered themselves for death as if it were a festival. The Japanese persecution of Christians, both because of the atrocities committed by the persecutors and the heroism displayed by the converts, was one of the most terrible ordeals to which the Church has ever been subjected.

The figurative arts are less explicit in the matter. But a clear light is thrown by erotic fantasies. Besides a whole literature and traditional iconography there still exists, among other things, a particular kind of magazine (the *Fuzoku Zasshi,* for instance) which, under the mask of anthropological research, supply their numerous and loyal readers with accounts of bloodshed, violence, and torture sufficient to make one shudder, and always spiced with sex.

The most typically Japanese feature of all this, however, is the strong emphasis on the passive pole of suffering, the strong attraction of the masochistic rather than of the sadistic pole. In the light of this it is easy to understand why there are so many suicides in Japan, and why the most difficult methods of committing suicide are so often chosen. When such impulses are ennobled, become a ritual, we have *seppuku*

[1] *See*, for example, M. ANESAKI, *Writings on Martyrdom in Kirishitan Literature*, Tokyo, 1931.

(*hara-kiri*); at the top of the scale passive violence is sublimated in self-sacrifice. I think it was Nitobe who remarked that the samurai must consider himself the 'dier, not the killer'. The attitude of stoic serenity in life and of obstinate contempt for death is illustrated with extraordinary frequency in Japanese history; the reader will recall examples quoted in this book.

There is no doubt that the best Japanese soldiers confronted the last war in this spirit. But it was absurd of their leaders to imagine that in a mass army of conscripts instincts of such terrible power, associated with archaic levels of the human personality, could be regulated with the rigour of a rite, of an etiquette of death, as they had been among small groups of samurai brought up from childhood to an extremely rigorous code. Hence the blots that disfigure the most recent pages of Japanese history; the atrocities of Manila, Nanking, and other places of unhappy memory.

Konjiki Yasha, like all self-respecting Japanese films, has its scene of violence; Kanichi, disgusted at Miya's failure to revolt against her family, her willingness to leave the man she loves to marry a man whom she at heart despises, attacks the girl, and strikes and kicks her on the beach at Atami.

At this point literature, cinema, psychology, personal relationships, all combined into one of those chance situations which often decide the whole course of people's lives.

The scene of Kanichi's outburst of rage and violence, acted with the usual consummate brilliance of Japanese actors, was nearly over when Jane, who was seated between us, turned to Giorgio and exclaimed: 'Oh, these Japs, sometimes I hate them!' Afterwards, when the lights went up, I noticed that Giorgio looked extraordinarily grim. But then, catching sight of Tamako and Lanzetti at the other end of the hall, the incident passed from my mind. Tamako looked grim too, you could tell in spite of her cascade of smiles; she had seen Jane and Giorgio together, so her suspicions were confirmed. What an evening!

Thinking about it afterwards, it all seemed perfectly clear. The Jane incident, though negligible to me, had certainly not been negligible to Giorgio. Devoted as he was to his son, what she said must have been like a stab to the heart. So she, too, at the bottom of her heart, and in spite of all her enthusiasm for Japan, in spite of all the intelligence with which she was reacting to her experience of the east, was still capable of detaching herself, retiring to a pedestal of we and they, Japs and non-Japs. Supposing one day she grew impatient with little Enrico and called him: 'You little Jap!' Giorgio, torn between love and paternal affection, did not hesitate; I know him too well for that. In any case, Jane left.

And Tamako? There was no more news of her, she simply disappeared without trace.

Young Woman Ends Her Days

Everybody left; it was the fashion at the moment; I, too, was leaving for the north, for Hokkaido. During the last few days I was too busy even to have five minutes alone with Giorgio. Perhaps in a month's time, when I came back, there would be a chance of seeing him alone and talking. One evening, while we were drinking *saké* with friends, perhaps I should ask: By the way, what happened to Jane? Or perhaps I should not. Perhaps Giorgio would be counting on my having understood without asking.

Somi came to see me off at the station; I had not seen him for a long time either. But now I understood many things. It was not women, but the Church, that had called him back, for he appeared on the platform wearing a clerical collar, as Roman Catholic priests do in countries where theirs is a minority faith. I am used to my friends' mental earthquakes, but this latest step of Somi's was one which I should have liked to reconstruct step by step. But it was useless to try to talk about it now with the train just about to leave. I merely alluded jokingly to his clerical collar. He laughed.

'My dear chap, there comes a point where you have to make up your mind,' he said. 'Either we are right or they are right. I have been thinking about it for ten years. I have come to the conclusion that we are right.'

The train started moving. I jumped in, opened the window, and we said good-bye.

Some time later the train was passing between rice-fields, brown in their winter sleep. Every now and then a wisp of smoke licked the outside of the window.

Gradually everything concerning Tokyo became strangely remote.

I was going north, to Hokkaido, the isle of snow, of the Ainu, of bears. The people beside me suggested northern climes; sturdy, rather stolid, red-cheeked young countrymen; women the edges of whose wooden *geta* were covered with waxed cloth trimmed with fur, as is the custom where it is really cold; old men with beards so thick that they suggested descent from the mysterious inhabitants of the ancient forests of Dewa and Mutsu. On the seat beside me I noticed a newspaper. To pass the time I picked it up and read it, spelling out the news with a polite old peasant fellow-traveller. Last of all a small item at the bottom of the pages attracted our attention. 'Another suicide at the Mihara volcano,' it said. 'Young woman ends her days because of tiredness with life *(ense).*' Some vague, stereotyped details followed, and then came the name—Kiyama Tamako.

Another puff of smoke lightly touched the outside of the window. More rice-fields passed, and then a *torii*. Then we suddenly entered a tunnel. It was dark, and there was a metallic roar and rattle.

Appendix

THAT peoples differ profoundly from one another is a fact that strikes human sensibility in the raw.

All the best-known European languages make possible a clear distinction between the foreign and exotic. 'Foreign' means belonging to another nation, *i.e.*, province of a civilization; 'exotic' means (in the present context) what does not belong to the west. For Italians a Rolls-Royce or a Volkswagen is a foreign car, as is an Alfa-Romeo or a Ferrari for an Englishman or a Belgian. But Buddhism, like Indonesian *gamelan* music, is exotic to us all.

There are two categories into which the human phenomena with which we are concerned can be divided. The first and more important is that of civilizations, supreme entities which are incommensurable with one another. The second, more restricted category, is that of nations. On the one hand, then, we have the exotic, the logical opposite of which we may therefore describe as endotic.

How many and what civilizations are there? Where do the endotic and the exotic begin and end? At first sight it would appear easy to draw a demarcation line; in reality, because of reciprocal influences, contacts, conquests, superpositions, infiltrations, cross-fertilizations between civilizations, nations, and empires in the course of history, it is extremely difficult. Nevertheless, every civilization, like every individual, is unique. It will be recalled that Professor Toynbee distinguishes twenty-six civilizations in history, whether complete or interrupted, as well as three abortive civilizations. The number may be too many or too few, but that is immaterial. What matters is the principle. The better definition of boundaries, areas, successions, links, will be the work of generations.

The various sub-units of our own civilizations have for many years fought and denounced each other. Dante calls the Germans gluttonous,

and Baudelaire calls the Belgians dunces. Albion is traditionally per-
fidious and Italy a turncoat. But nobody doubts the profound links that
connect all the members of what used to be called the Christian world
and is now called the west.

When you cross the age-old borders of a civilization, you find yourself confronted by the strange, the mysterious, the incomprehensible,
often by a puzzling combination of the fascinating and the repulsive.
Thus the west builds up a picture of a 'wild and barbarous east, rich in
gold, marble and purple, but also in blood and corruption and iniquity
side by side with delicious perfumes' (Mario Praz); while Asia thinks of
Europe and America as full of 'vanity and pride' (Taha Huasain[1]), of
'sensuality' (Nakahama Manjiro[2]), of 'superstition' (Tomomatsu Entai[3]),
a collection of peoples who, in spite of all their progress, have learnt only
four principles of conduct, namely 'to be selfish, to kill others, to have
little integrity, and to feel little shame' (Yen Fu, 1854–1921).[4]

How do men react to the great problems with which their experiences and emotions confront them? Two ways are open to them. On
the one hand, ignoring the fact that all men eat, work, make love, are
fond of children, and sleep soundly after hard drinking, the conclusion
is drawn that resemblances are only apparent, and that the mind, the
heart, the essential something hidden in the interior are fundamentally
different ('East is east and west is west . . .'). The alternative view is that
differences in thought and custom are superficial, and that we are all
united by a common humanity.

Neither of these two attitudes can be said to be more ancient and
primitive, or more modern and more apposite, than the other; and both
have been held by men of intellectual distinction who have had long
experience of different civilizations. Normally the attitude adopted
depends more on the writer's fundamental outlook on life than on
a dispassionate analysis of the facts. Roman Catholics (and hence missionaries) have always been strong supporters of the 'common humanity'
school, and are followed and supported in this, as often happens, by the
Communists, and, incidentally, all who think in terms of universals.

[1] 'The vanity and pride of the west, which thinks its own civilization and culture the only
possible civilization and culture.'—*Oriente Moderno*, Rome, Year 35 (1955), p. 395.

[2] *See* ISHII KENDO, *Ikoku Hyoryu Kidanshu*, Tokyo, 1927, pp. 429–47.

[3] E. TOMOMATSU, *Le Bouddhisme*, Paris, 1935.

[4] Quoted by H. G. CREEL, *Chinese Thought from Confucius to the Present Day*, London, 1954.

The few who have gone deeply into these problems without being bound *a priori* to ideas the verification of which is sought in facts have had to admit that the picture is far more complex than it might seem at first sight.[1] There is no doubt that we must accept as our starting-point the common humanity shared by African pygmies, professors of the Sorbonne, delicate Nepalese princesses, and robber-nomads in the Arabian desert. 'Man constitutes a single zoological species.' Everyone, as we have already said, laughs, feels pain, enjoys himself, buys, sells, and uses his wits to procure food, money, and affection. Not only is this an extremely low human common denominator, not only does it suggest a kind of glorified anthropoid ape, distinguished at most by a certain inventive capacity, but it looks at man exclusively from the outside, as a zoological specimen.

Besides—and this is the important point—'common humanity' stands for an enumeration of impulses, points of departure, not of results, destinations reached. There are the more complex but equally important necessities of making some sort of a figure in the world, establishing oneself among one's kind, regulating one's affections, solemnizing death, managing public affairs, etc., etc. Common humanity exists as an objective entity and not just as a theoretical classification, but only on condition that you observe it through the keyhole, or under the microscope as if it were a curious species of insect, to be described rather than understood.

But what happens if instead we look at men who belong to different civilizations from the inside? If we substitute words for actions, which may look identical but are often only similar? If we say to man and woman: Speak! Speech is the magic key that opens up the panorama of the mind. We shall then discover that every phrase, from the simplest to the most complex, is pregnant with implicit assumptions. Every single manifestation of thought yields unexpected flashes of insight, disclosing the mental dominions, principalities, and powers which denote the mind's grasp of the outer world, by that very act enriching itself by the creation of an inner world.

I do not wish to indulge in paradoxes and argue that simple phrases like 'Go!' or 'Give me a piece of wood', or 'We shall see each other later'

[1] For instance A. TOYNBEE, *The World and the West*, Oxford, 1953; L. Abegg, *The Mind of East Asia*, London, 1952; F. S. C. NORTHROP, *The Meeting of East and West*, New York, 1946.

contain a wealth of implicit assumptions, though it would not be impossible to demonstrate such a thing. 'Go!', for instance, has certain grammatical peculiarities common to all the Indo–European languages, and grammar is an important repository of implicit assumptions. In other civilizations, as we have seen (page 246 *et seq.*), instead of distin- guishing logical categories such as person and time ('Go!' *i.e.,* you, now) ceremonial categories are distinguished, *i.e.,* the relations between the speaker and the person addressed.

If implicit assumptions thus threateningly raise their head in the most innocent manifestations of language, it is easy to imagine how they proliferate and oppress us on all sides when we enter the field of really complex thought. It is worth while recalling a phenomenon familiar to all translators of works belonging to non-western civiliza- tions. The further you depart from everyday actions, the further you enter into the domain of the mind, the harder does it become to find satisfactory equivalents; a clear demonstration that humanity is united at the point of departure but divided and differentiated at the point of arrival. Let us take an example, opening an anthology at random:

> *Dice di lei Amor; Cosa mortale*
> *come esser po' si adorna e si pura?*[1]—Dante

If we try to translate this into Chinese or Japanese, we shall find our way blocked at the outset by an enormous difficulty. How shall we render the word—and the concept—of love into the languages of a civili- zation which has reconstructed the universe in a manner entirely different from ours, and has assembled the elements of its experience in a totally different manner? A rough translation is, of course, always possible. The figure 3.14 for the relationship between the circumference and diameter of a circle is good enough for a carpenter; it would hardly satisfy a mathematician. Nor will it satisfy us if we wish to think in rigorous terms. The word 'love' is one of the great pillars of the western interior universe, a concept charged with thousands of years of history —from Empedocles to Stendhal, from Plato to Christ, from Venus to St. Theresa, from Marsilio Ficino to Descartes, Spinoza, Schopenhauer, to say nothing of Petrarch, Sappho, Baudelaire, Walt Whitman, St. John and St. Francis, St. Thomas and Dante. It is a concept laden with fire,

---

[1] Love says of her: How is it possible that mortal thing can be so beautiful, so pure?

one of the vital nuclei at which men and gods meet, one of the hinges on which the western conception of the universe rests. Even in the simplest and most matter-of-fact use of the term it always carries with it this tremendous, highly charged load.

In the Far East thought, internally reconstructing the universe in different patterns, has taken other roads, the various elements of experience have been organized into different geometries or remained dispersed, and the vast domain covered by the word 'love' is only partially covered by any of the various concepts that can be said to resemble it. There is *jin, nin,*[1] for instance, which the dictionaries translate as 'virtue, benevolence, humanity, compassion', but this covers different emotional territory; it is more philosophical and serene; it has none of the incandescence which the word love draws from its secret and earthly roots, from the fact that it implies both the infinity of the stars and the force which unites lovers, with the result that, as Aldous Huxley remarked, it is difficult to tell whether the ardours of the mystics are directed towards God or to an earthly being of flesh, blood, and senses. *'Jen,'* Confucius says, 'is a characteristic element of man, and is exercised above all in affection shown to parents.'[2] We are dealing here with the loftiest feelings, but are dangerously near the area where generic, pleasing, 'official' feelings begin.[3]

Japanese *Jin, Nin*
Chinese *Jen*

仁

Then there is the word *ai*, a word with a long history, used by lovers in their declaratons of affection, by sons thinking of their mother, brothers of their sisters, citizens of their country. But it always remains in the strictly human sphere. While in relation to *jin* love is too incandescent, too passionate, in relation to *ai* it has a higher, more cosmic sweep. We say of Christ that He is love, divine love, the embodiment of love. But in the east *ai* is only rarely applicable to the divine;

---

[1] In Chinese *jen*.

[2] *Doctrine of the Mean*, XX, 5.

[3] S. LOKUANG, *La Sapienza dei Cinesi, Il Conjucianesimo*, Rome, 1945, observes: 'The translators of the *Lungnu* of Confucius are confronted with the gravest difficulty in finding a word corresponding to the Chinese word *jen*. In reality no word exists in the European languages which expresses exactly and exhaustively the content of the word *jen*.' He adds in a footnote about thirty different translations which have been used. These range from the *pietas* of the Latin version by Noel (1711) to the *virtuous manners* of Legge's English version (1861). Others include: *cordis rectitudo, virtus, probitas, benevolentia, concordia, cordis perfectio, humanitas, la pratique de toutes les vertus, la vertu d'humanité, probité, vertu sincère, art of virtue, beneficence, etc., etc.*

its territory is bounded by this world. Nor could we satis-
factorily use as an equivalent the term *ji-ai*, which is used
by Catholics when they speak of God's love of man; the
term in general applies to love of parents for children, of
a superior for his inferior.

Japanese *Ai*
Chinese *Ai*

Other terms (apart from the many compounds
formed from the above roots) take us straight into the
erotic field and miss the mark completely; all those, for
instance, which begin with the ideograms *ren,* or *jo.*

Japanese *Ji-ai*
Chinese *Tsu-ai*

Love, then, is not a universal reality, but a magnificent western creation, as, for that matter, are beauty,
truth, right, soul, God, all the fundamental pillars of our
world. Every civilization constructs its own inner world
like a cathedral round those remarkable stalagmites
which embody its dreams, fantasies, revelations, its
boldest flights of thought, the cumulative life of the
mind throughout the ages. These stalagmites are incommensurable in relation to one another.

Japanese *Ren*
Chinese *Lien*

Let us now adopt the opposite procedure and
pick a passage at random from Confucius: 'The philosopher Yu said: In practising the rules of ceremonial (*li*)
a certain naturalness is desirable."[1]

Just as in the passage from Dante we were immediately brought up against an obstacle in the form of the
word love, so now we are brought up by the word *li,*
a concept of primary importance in the inner world
of the Far East. A concept is intelligible only when you
know its history; the history of a concept is the concept

Japanese *Jo*
Chinese *Ch'ing*

itself. A whole volume would be necessary to do full justice to all the
meanings and overtones that the ages have concentrated into the
word 'love'; the same applies to the word *li,* which is the age-old
child of Confucius. It bristles with philosophy, history, and poetry,
and carries in its blood whole dynasties of thinkers from the
Chinese Mencius to the Japanese Motoori, whole philosophies of
different periods and different nations, the intellectual ferment of
whole civilizations. Translating it by 'ceremonial' is setting foot

[1] *Analects,* I, 12.

Japanese *Rei*
Chinese *Li*

barely on the periphery of the vast territory which it includes.

Li originally had the restricted meaning of 'sacrifice', which it still partially retains in modern Chinese.

'It was extended to denote the ritual used in sacrifice and then to every sort of ceremony and the 'courtesy' that characterized the conduct of those who made up a ruler's court.'[1] But this was only the beginning of a process by which the concept was enriched until it became one of the foundations of the interior universe of the Far East. Just as with us the concept of love has absorbed, merged, ennobled, elements which in other civilizations remained scattered or were gathered into other constellations, so the remarkable depth of meanings, the wealth of intellectual and emotional echoes, which survive in the word *li* with us are scattered elsewhere or exist in a different area of the mind with different associations.

The greatness of the teaching of Confucius lies in the extraordinary equilibrium which he maintains in his conception of human nature between the two poles of individual and society; and the concept of *li* is the keystone of the arch that connects the two, the foundation of the whole vast edifice. *Li* stands for all the profound links which tie men to each other, both outwardly (courtesy, manners, rites) and inwardly (ethics, morals). 'Not knowing *li* means not being able to take one's position.'[2] The west has never integrated the implications that it contains into a similar fundamental concept, and its various elements have remained remote, often exceedingly remote, from one another, or have been integrated into other constellations. For us courtesy, ceremonial, rites, are something very distinct from morals and ethics, and belong to orders of thought which are often mutually suspect. We like to attribute a somewhat rude, naked, genuine quality to ethics, and with us courtesy enjoys a modest place among the virtues, and can be said to verge perilously on hypocrisy. From some points of view, and in some of its aspects, *li* could be translated by 'right', but that again touches only part of its patrimony without fully exhausting the wealth of meaning of the

---

[1] H. G. CREEL, *Chinese Thought from Confucius to the Present Day*, London, 1954, pp. 43–6.

[2] CONFUCIUS, *Analects*, XX, 3. *See also* FUNG YU-LAN, *A History of Chinese Philosophy*, London, 1952. It should be noted that another very important word *li* is used by the neo-Confucian schools; but this has a different meaning, is represented by a different ideogram, and is pronounced in a different tone.

western word.[1] Just as our word 'love' has a strength, flavour, a high voltage, because it carries within itself a whole conglomeration of human realities, ranging from the voluptuousness of the senses and the tenderness of the affections to mystical ecstasy and divine solicitude, so in the Far East the word *li* implies both minor rules of daily conduct, the harmony of human intercourse, the harmony of the universe. Both these aggregates' really exist only within the borders of the civilization which created them; they are difficult to translate because they are not meant to be, and should not be, translated; if they are mentioned, they should be quoted in their original phonetic shape and then explained.

How is it that men, setting out on a basis of common impulses, should gradually have come to think in such profoundly different ways—in other words, have become so different from each other? The question is not difficult to answer. As soon as man becomes man he ardently desires to understand the things around him and how they work, to discover the reason for birth, disease, and death, for storms and the season, for love and hate. That is his most universal characteristic. He sees himself naked, ephemeral, minute, in the midst of an unlimited and incomprehensible outer world; he needs the warmth and protection of a mental order, or a mental house of his own, in which his mind can take refuge. He starts rudely and confusedly, with a medley of myths, fears, wishes, superstitions. The work begun with the first human stammerings continues tirelessly, heroically, sometimes with marvellously swift advances, sometimes with long pauses, and each generation takes up the process, revising, amplifying, penetrating deeper, adding enrichment with new facts or intellectual conquests. The results are embodied in the language; and here aggregations take place round certain vital, magnetic nuclei. Prophets, seers, legislators, oracles, poets, philosophers, scientists add, adorn, and refine; the discourse becomes ever more agile, bold, precise; and the whole of its fibre is impregnated with the fundamental assumptions of the civilization of which it is the voice. In other words, civilizations are organic complexes of implicit assumptions crystallized in the mother-rock of language; or, put in another way, grandiose systems by means of which men display in different fashion their fundamental similarity.

Let me add a comparison from the field of zoology. If we observe

[1] J. NEEDHAM, *Human Law and the Laws of Nature in China and the West,* London, 1951, p. 12.

the forms of life which covered, or still cover, the earth, at one point we observe a kind of division in the great evolutionary stream. On the one hand are all the increasingly complex creatures (chordata, fish, amphibians, mammals) culminating in man; on the other there are those culminating in insects. Insects and man are thus, as it were, like two huge civilizations looking at each other across an abyss; like a Matterhorn and a Mont Blanc on either side of an imaginary Valley of Aosta. Now, men and mammals were studied and their parts and organs were distinguished and given names first. When the study of insects began it seemed natural to use the terminology which had been adequate hitherto, and terms such as abdomen, heart, blood, brain, etc., were used accordingly. But when things were looked at more closely it turned out that, as applied to insects, they were approximations only, and did not really apply unless their meanings were extended in a fashion which would make them vague and imprecise. In fact in modern works a new and complicated terminology is used. The 'blood' of insects, for example, has as much in common with human blood as an Italian dictionary has with a Basque dictionary. It is generally bluish rather than red, because it contains haemocyanin instead of haemoglobin, and this, instead of being contained in the corpuscles, is dissolved in the plasma; it plays only a minor part in the respiratory function; it circulates only partially in blood vessels; and generally it moves by negative instead of by positive pressure; also it acts as a lymph, etc., etc. In other words, it is not really blood at all. Thus the organs of mammals and insects are incommensurable with one another, just like the key concepts of different civilizations.

Now that the world is growing smaller and smaller and more and more highly populated, involving frequent contacts where previously none existed, and continuous contacts where only irregular contacts prevailed, it is important to have accurate, clear, realistic ideas about the human species as a whole and of the various civilizations in which and by which it lives. It will be much easier to understand each other if we realize clearly where the endotic ends and the exotic begins; if we realize that within the borders of the exotic we shall meet profound differences, it is true, but that these can be overcome, not by translating thought, which is a waste of time or at best a crude approximation, but by re-living from the inside mental universes which were built up from the foundations entirely independently of each other.

Bibliography

More than 20,000 books about Japan have been written in the major European languages. The reader should not be intimidated, however; in all that mass of printed paper there are few works of significance. I have tried to assemble below a number of titles which seem essential at the present day, ignoring many which were important in their time but are out-of-date. I had several times to choose between a number of titles for the sake of brevity; in such cases the choice was inevitably personal, and I ask the reader's pardon for involuntary omissions. With one or two exceptions, I have not quoted articles in periodicals, though some are of capital importance.

GENERAL INFORMATION

Bibliographies: for specialists that of Wenckstern and Nachod, followed by the American *Far Eastern Bibliographies* by Gaskill and his collaborators. Extremely useful and handy is *A Selected List of Books and Articles on Japan in English, French and German,* compiled by H. Borton and others, Harvard, 1954 (one volume, about 2,000 titles).

Japan Year Book, annual (with interruptions), rich in facts, statistics, and economic, political, social, and cultural information. Published by the Foreign Affairs Association of Japan.
The Japan Annual (Institute of World Economy, Tokyo).
Nippon, A Charted Survey of Japan (Tsuneta Yano Memorial Society, Tokyo); essentially economic.
A Guide to Japanese Studies (Kokusai Bunka Shinkokai, Tokyo, 1939).
PAPINOT, E., *Dictionnaire d'histoire et de géographie du Japon,* Tokyo, 1906. (Old, and to be used with caution, but important; there is an English translation.)
BORTON, H., *Japan,* Ithaca, 1951. (Extract from the *Encyclopedia Americana;* a good summary.)
KAGAMI, BUSH, and LEWIS, *Japanalia,* London, 1938. (Small alphabetical reference book, very well done.)
TSUSHIHASHI, Y., *Japanese Chronological Tables,* Tokyo, 1952.
Tourist Library; collection published by the Japan Travel Bureau, Tokyo. Pre-war series of forty booklets, each dedicated to an aspect of Japanese life, history, culture, written by well-known specialists. Of the new post-war series 22 volumes have been published (1956).
Iwanami (Tokyo), collection of photographic manuals; so far about 200 booklets have been published on every conceivable aspect of Japanese life; brief explanatory matter in Japanese.

Periodicals devoted wholly or partly to Japan provide an inexhaustible mine of information. I shall mention only:
Transactions of the Asiatic Society of Japan, Tokyo (about 70 volumes, from 1872 to the present day).
Bulletin de la Maison Franco-Japonaise, Tokyo (from 1927).
Mitteilungen der Deutschen Gesellschaft für Natur und Völkerkunde Ostasiens, Tokyo (from 1873).
Monumenta Nipponica, Tokyo (from 1938).

Also:
Contemporary Japan, Tokyo (from 1932); official publication, quarterly.
Japan Quarterly (from 1954); published by the *Asahi* newspaper; livelier than the preceding.

GEOGRAPHY; GUIDES; PHOTOGRAPHIC ALBUMS

TREWARTHA, G. T., *Japan, a Physical, Cultural, and Regional Geography*, University of Wisconsin, 1945.
Japan, the Official Guide (Japan Travel Bureau), Tokyo, 1952.
Le Japon, Odé, Paris, 1954. (Not a real guide, but an excellent introduction for the traveller.)
Art Guide of Nippon, Tokyo, 1943. (Only Vol. I, *Nara, Mie, Wakayama*.)
BISCHOF, W., *Giappone* (109 photographs), Milan, 1954. (Delightful photographic interpretation by a great artist recently dead.)

HISTORY

BORTON, H., *Japan's Modern Century*, New York, 1955. (Clear and well-documented summary; from the opening up of Japan in 1854 to the present post-war reconstruction.)
BRINKLEY, F., *A History of the Japanese People from the Earliest Times to the End of the Meiji Era*, New York, 1915. (Hardly critical.)
GROOT, G. J., *The Prehistory of Japan*, 1951.
HAGUENAUER, C., *Origines de la Civilization Japonaise*, Paris, 1956.
MUNRO, N. G., *Prehistoric Japan*, Yokohama, 1908. (Still the best general study of the subject.)
MURDOCH, J., *A History of Japan* (3 vols.), Kobe, 1903 and 1910, London, 1926. (Rich in detail about political events.)
NACHOD, O., *Geschichte von Japan* (2 vols.), Leipzig, 1906–1930. (From the beginning to A.D. 850. Very detailed.)
REISCHAUER, E. O., *Japan, Past and Present*, New York, 1953. (Concise and pithy.)
REISCHAUER, O., *Ennin's Travels in T'ang China*, New York, 1955.
REISCHAUER, R. K., *Early Japanese History* (up to 1167), 2 vols. Princeton, 1937. (Important; based on contemporary Japanese documents.)
SANSOM, G. B., *Japan, a Short Cultural History*, London, 1931. (First-rate.)
SANSOM, G. B., *The Western World and Japan*, New York, 1950. (A lucid and learned study of the relations between the west and Asia, particularly China and Japan.)
YANAGA, C., *Japan since Perry*, New York, 1949. (A mine of information about modern Japan.)

ECONOMICS; POLITICS; CONTEMPORARY EVENTS

ACKERMAN, E. A., *Japan's Natural Resources and their Relation to Japan's Economic Future*, Chicago, 1953.
ALLEN, G. C., *A Short Economic History of Modern Japan* (1867–1937), London, 1946.
ALLEN, G. C., *Japan's Economic Recovery*, London, 1957.
BROWN, D. M., *Nationalism in Japan; an Introductory Historical Analysis*, Berkeley, 1955.
COHEN, J. B., *Japan's Economy in War and Reconstruction*, Minneapolis, 1949.
COLBERT, E. S., *The Left Wing in Japanese Politics*, New York, 1952.
FEARY, R. A., *The Occupation of Japan—Second Phase: 1948–1950*, New York, 1950.
FEIS, H., *The Road to Pearl Harbour*, Princeton, 1950.
GUILLAIN, R., *Le peuple japonnais et la guerre; choses vues 1939-1946*, Paris, 1947.
INOGUCHI, NAKAJIMA, PINEAU, *The Divine Wind.*, U.S. Naval Institute, 1958.
JONES, F. C., *Japan's New Order in East Asia: its Rise and Fall, 1937–1945*, London, 1954.
JONES, F. C., *Hokkaido*, London, 1958.
LOCKWOOD, W. W., *The Economic Development of Japan: Growth and Structural Change, 1868–1938*, Princeton, 1954.

NORMAN, E. H., *Japan's Emergence as a Modern State*, New York, 1940.
SHIGEMITSU, M., *Japan and her Destiny*, London, 1958.
STOETZEL, J., *Jeunesse sans Chrysanthème ni Sabre*, Paris, 1954.
STORRY, R., *The Double Patriots*, London, 1957.
SWEARINGEN, R.; LANGES, P., *Red Flag in Japan*, Harvard, 1952.
YANAGA, C., *Japanese People and Politics*, New York, 1956.

RELIGIONS AND PHILOSOPHY

ABEGG, L., *The Mind of East Asia*, London, 1952.
ANESAKI, M., *History of Japanese Religion, with Special Reference to the Social and Moral Life of the Nation*, London, 1930.
ANESAKI, M., *Religious Life of the Japanese People*, Tokyo, 1938. (Two excellent and lucid summaries by a writer with a profound knowledge of the subject.)
BUNCE, W. K., *Religions in Japan*, Rutland and Tokyo, 1955.
ELISSÉEV, S., *Mythologie du Japon* (in *Mythologie Asiatique Illustrée*), Paris, 1928.
NITOBE, I., *Bushido*, New York (many editions).

RELIGIONS: SHINTO

ASTON, W. G., *Shinto, the Way of the Gods*, London, 1905. (Basic work by a pioneer.)
HOLTOM, D. C., *Modern Japan and Shinto Nationalism: a Study of Present-Day Trends in Japanese Religions*, Chicago 1947 (second edition).
KATO, G., *A Study of Shinto, the Religion of the Japanese Nation*, Tokyo, 1926.
PETTAZZONI, R., *La mitologia giapponese*, Bologna, 1929.
PETTAZZONI, R., *Lo shintoismo*, Bologna, 1929.
PETTAZZONI, R., *Religione e politica religiosa del Giappone moderno*, Rome, 1934.

RELIGIONS: BUDDHISM

BLYTH, R. H., *Zen in English Literature and Oriental Classics*, Tokyo, 1948.
ELIOT, SIR C., *Japanese Buddhism*, London, 1935. (Still essential reading on the subject.)
HERRIGEL, E., *Zen in the Art of Archery*, New York, 1953.
STEINILBER-OBERLIN, E., *The Buddhist Sects of Japan*, London, 1958 (new edition).
SUZUKI, D. T., *Essays in Zen Buddhism* (3 vols., 1927, 1933, 1934), London.
SUZUKI, D. T., *An Introduction to Zen Buddhism*, London, 1949.
SUZUKI, D. T., *Living by Zen*, London, 1950.
SUZUKI, D. T., *Manual of Zen Buddhism*, London, 1950.
SUZUKI, D. T., *Zen Buddhism and Japanese Culture*, London, 1959.
SUZUKI, D. T., *The Training of the Zen Buddhist Monk*, Kyoto, 1934. (The works of this author are particularly valuable for obtaining an understanding of Zen Buddhism.)
TAKAKUSU, J., *The Essentials of Buddhist Philosophy*, Honolulu, 1947.

RELIGIONS: CONFUCIANISM

ARMSTRONG, R. C., *Light from the East, Studies in Japanese Confucianism*, Toronto, 1914. (Old, but the only general study of the subject.)

RELIGIONS: CHRISTIANITY

BOXER, C. R., *The Christian Century in Japan, 1549–1650*, Berkeley, 1951.

CARY, O., *A History of Christianity in Japan*, New York and London, 1909.

HAAS, H., *Geschichte des Christentums in Japan* (2 vols.), Tokyo, 1902–4. (Essential for the sixteenth and seventeenth centuries.)

LAURES, J., *The Catholic Church in Japan*, a Short History, Tokyo, 1954. (Good recent summary.)

RELIGIONS: OTHER ASPECTS

STRAELEN, H. VAN, *The Religion of Divine Wisdom*, Tokyo, 1954. (Interesting study of the Tenri-kyo religion.)

LANGUAGE: GENERAL

ELISSÉEV, S., *La Langue Japonaise* (in *Les Langues du Monde*), Paris, 1924.

SANSOM, G. B., *An Historical Grammar of Japanese*, Oxford, 1928.

LANGUAGE: GRAMMARS

CHAMBERLAIN, B. H., *Japanese Grammar* (new edition revised by J. C. McIlroy), Chicago, 1944.

ROSE-INNES, A., *Conversational Japanese for Beginners*, Yokohama, 1933.

VACCARI, O. and VACCARI, E. E., *Complete Course of Japanese Conversation Grammar*, New York, 1942.

YAMAGIWA, J. K., *The Modern Japanese Written Language*, Ann Arbour, 1945.

Cards for learning ideograms have been published by Vaccari and by Naganuma (both in Tokyo).

LANGUAGE: DICTIONARIES

KIMURA, K., *Grosses japanisch-deutsches Wörterbuch*, Tokyo, 1942.

OKAKURA, Y., *Kenkyusha's New English-Japanese Dictionary*, Tokyo (various editions).

ROSE-INNES, A., *Beginners' Dictionary of Chinese-Japanese Characters*, Tokyo (various editions). (The handiest dictionary of ideograms in current use.)

SATOW, E. M., ISHIBASHI, M., *An English-Japanese Dictionary of the Spoken Language*, Tokyo (various editions).

TAKENOBU, Y., *Kenkyushu's New Japanese-English Dictionary*, Tokyo (various editions). (An essential tool for studying the language.)

VACCARI, O., and VACCARI, E. E., *Japanese-English Conversation Dictionary*, Tokyo, 1954. (The Vaccari have also published a big dictionary of ideograms, as well as a whole series of books useful for students of Japanese.)

LITERATURE: LITERARY HISTORIES

ASTON, W. G., *A History of Japanese Literature*, New York, 1903. (Old and often prejudiced in its judgments, but still useful today; new edition, 1933.)

BONNEAU, G., *Histoire de la Littérature Japonaise Contemporaine* (1868–1938), Paris, 1940.

GUNDERT, W., *Die Japanische Literatur*, Potsdam, 1929.

KEENE, D., *Japanese Literature, an Introduction for Western Readers*, London, 1953. (Clear, concise, up-to-date.)

OKAZAKI, Y., *Japanese Literature in the Meiji Era* (translated and adapted by V. H. Viglielmo), Tokyo, 1955.

LITERATURE: ANTHOLOGIES

BLYTH, R. H., *Haiku* (4 vols.), Tokyo, 1952.

BONNEAU, G., *Anthologie de la poésie japonaise*, Paris, 1935.

BONNEAU, G., *La sensibilité japonaise*, Paris, 1935. (Prose and verse of unequal value.)

BONNEAU, G., *Yoshino; collection japonaise pour le présentation de textes poétiques* (11 vols.), Paris, 1933 *et seq.* (Important work by a well-known man of letters.)

KEENE, D.; *Anthology of Japanese Literature*, London, 1956. (Concise; texts carefully selected and lovingly translated.)

KEENE, D., *Modern Japanese Literature*, London, 1957.

KOKUSAI BUNKA SHINKOKAI, *Introduction to Classical Japanese Literature*, Tokyo, 1948. (Brief summaries of more than seventy important works, from the *Kojiki* to the Meiji period.)

MATSUBARA, I., *Minyo, Folk-Songs of Japan*, Tokyo, 1928. (Good collection of popular songs.)

MIYAMORI, A., *An Anthology of Haiku, Ancient and Modern*, Tokyo, 1932.

MIYAMORI, A., *Masterpieces of Japanese Poetry, Ancient and Modern* (2 vols.), Tokyo, 1936. (Text in ideograms and Latin alphabet, with translation.)

REVON, M., *Anthologie de la littérature japonaise dès origines au XXième siècle*, Paris, 1928. (The best work of its kind.)

LITERATURE: TRANSLATIONS: (only some of the most important)

Kojiki. English translation by B. H. Chamberlain (Kobe, 1932).

Nihongi (or *Nihon-Shoki*). English translation by W. G. Aston (new edition, London, 1956).

Manyōshū, English translation by the Nippon Gakujutsu, Shinkokai, Tokyo, 1941.

SEI SHONAGON, *Makura no Sōshi* (Notes from a Pillow-Book). English translation by Arthur Waley, Boston, 1929.

Diaries of Court Ladies of Old Japan (Heian period). English translation by A. S. Omori and K. Doi, Tokyo, 1935.

MURASAKI SHIKIBU, *Genji Monogatari* (The Tale of Genji). English translation by Arthur Waley (various editions from 1925).

Kokinshū (Poems Ancient and Modern), English translation by T. Wakameda, Tokyo, 1929.

Tsure-zure gusa (The Miscellany of a Japanese Priest), English translation by W. N. Porter, London, 1914.

BASHŌ, *Oku no Hosomichi*. English translation by Y. Isobe, Tokyo, 1933.

UEDA, A., *Contes de pluie et de lune*, (translation of *Ugetsu Monogatari*) Paris, 1956.

IKKU JIPPENSHA, *Hizakurige*. English translation by T. Satchell, Kobe, 1929.

DAZAI, O., *The Setting Sun*, London, 1957.

OOKA, S., *Fires on the Plain*, London, 1957.

TANIZAKI, J., *Some prefer Nettles*, London, 1956.

TANIZAKI, J., *The Makioka Sisters*, London, 1957.

LITERATURE: THEATRE

BOWERS, F., *Japanese Theatre*, New York, 1952.

MIYAMORI, A., *Masterpieces of Chikamatsu*, the Japanese Shakespeare, New York, 1926.

MIYAMORI, A., *Tales from Old Japanese Dramas*, New York, London, 1915.

PERI, N., *Le Nō*, Tokyo, 1944.

PIPER, M., *Das japanische Theater*, Frankfurt-on-Main, 1937.

RENONDEAU, G., *Le Nō*, Tokyo, 1954.

RENONDEAU, G., *Le bouddhisme dans les Nō*, Tokyo, 1950.
SCOTT, A. C., *The Kabuki Theatre of Japan*, London, 1955.
WALEY, A., *The Nō Plays of Japan*, London (new edition), 1950.

CINEMA

GIUGLARIS, S. and M., *Le Cinéma Japonais (1896–1955)*, Paris, 1956.
Special number of the magazine *Bianco e Nero* devoted to the Japanese cinema, Rome, 1954.

ART: GENERAL

ANESAKI, M., *Buddhist Art in its Relation to Buddhist Ideals*, London, 1956. (Important for an understanding
    of the religious background of Japanese art.)
BINYON, L., *The Spirit of Man in Ancient Art*, Harvard, 1935. (Asian thought presented to the reader by
    a delightful humanist; an excellent introduction.)
BUHOT, J., *Histoire des Arts du Japon*, vol. I (up to 1350), Paris, 1949. (Standard work, but for specialists.)
EDMUNDS, W. H., *Pointers and Clues to Subjects of Chinese and Japanese Art*, London, 1934.
ELISSÉEFF, S., *L'art du Japon* (in *Histoire Universelle des Arts*, edited by L. Réau), Paris, 1939. (Excellent short
    summary.)
FISCHER, O., *Die Kunst Indiens, Chinas und Japans*, Berlin, 1928.
GROUSSET, R., *Les Civilisations de l'Orient*, Vol. IV, *le Japon*, Paris, 1930. (Brilliant exposition, perhaps the
    best introductory reading for the reader of general education.)
PAINE, T. R.; SOPER, A., *The Art and Architecture of Japan*, London, 1955. (Excellent; makes wide use of
    Japanese sources.)
SWANN, P. C., *An Introduction to the Arts of Japan*, Oxford, 1958.
TSUDA, N., *Handbook of Japanese Art*, Tokyo, 1935.
TUCCI, G., *Il Giappone, tradizione storica e tradizione artistica*, Milan, 1943. (Brief introduction by a great
    orientalist.)
WARNER, L., *The Enduring Art of Japan*, Harvard, 1952.
Pageant of Japanese Art (6 vols.), Tokyo National Museum, Tokyo, 1952.
YASHIRO, Y., *2000 Years of Japanese Art*, London, 1958.

ART: ARCHITECTURE

BLASER, W., *Temples et Jardins au Japon*, Paris, 1956.
DREXLER, A., *The Architecture of Japan*, New York, 1955.
SADLER, A. L., *A Short History of Japanese Architecture*, Sydney, 1941.
TAUT, B., *Houses and Peoples of Japan*, Tokyo (new edition), 1958.
YOSHIDA, T., *Japanische Architektur*, Tübingen, 1952.
YOSHIDA, T., *The Japanese House and Garden*, London, 1955.
    (As will be seen, interest in Japanese architecture is very much alive; nearly all these works are
admirably illustrated.)

ART: SCULPTURE

WARNER, L., *The Craft of the Japanese Sculptor*, New York, 1936.
WARNER, L., *Japanese Sculpture of the Suiko Period*, New Haven, 1923.

ART: PAINTING

BINYON, L., *Painting in the Far East*, London (4th edition), 1949.
ELISSÉEV, S., *La peinture contemporaine au Japon*, Paris, 1923.
GROSSE, E., *Die ostasiatische Tuschmalerei*, Berlin, 1923.
MORIYA, K., *Die Japanische Malerei*, Zeisbaden, 1953.
TODA, K., *Japanese Scroll Paintings*, Chicago, 1935.
YASHIRO, Y., *Einführung in die japanische Malerei*, Tokyo, 1935.
(YASHIRO, Y.), *Index of Japanese Painters*, Tokyo, 1941.

ART: PRINTS (*Ukiyo-e*)

BINYON, L., *Japanese Colour Prints*, New York, 1923.
HILLIER, J., *Japanese Masters of the Colour Print, a Great Heritage of Oriental Art*, London, 1954.
HIRANO, C., *Kiyonaga*, Harvard, 1939.
KURTH, J., *Die Geschichte des japanischen Holzschnitts* (3 vols.), Leipzig, 1925–29.
NOGUCHI, Y., *Hiroshige*, London, 1940, and other editions.
NOGUCHI, Y., *Harunobu*, London, 1940.
MICHENER, J. A., *The Floating World*, New York, 1954.

ART: MINOR ASPECTS AND POPULAR ARTS

BLACKER, J. F., *The ABC of Japanese Art*, London, 1929. (Useful manual for collectors.)
GORHAM, H. H., *Japanese and Oriental Pottery*, Yokohama (no date).
JOLY, H. L., *Japanese Sword Guards*, London, 1910.
KUMMEL, O., *Das Kunstgewerbe in Japan, Handbuch für Sammler und Liebhaber*, Berlin, 1922.
MEINERTZHAGEN, F., *The Art of the Netsuke Carver*, London, 1956.
MITSUOKA, T., *Ceramic Art of Japan*, Tokyo, 1949.
MUNSTERBERG, H., *The Folk Arts of Japan*, Rutland, 1957.
ROBINSON, B. W., *A Primer of Japanese Sword Blades*, London, 1956.
RYERSON, E., *The Netsuke of Japan*, London, 1957.
YANAGI, S., *Folk-Crafts in Japan*, Tokyo, 1936.

ART: GARDENS

HARADA, J., *The Gardens of Japan*, London, 1928.
KUCK, L., *The Art of Japanese Gardens*, New York, 1940.
NEWSOM, S., *Japanese Garden Construction*, Tokyo, 1939.

ART: FLOWERS, DWARF TREES

CONDER, J., *The Theory of Japanese Flower Arrangements*, Kobe, 1935.
HERRIGEL, G. L., *Zen in the Art of Flower Arrangement*, London, 1958.
KOBAYASHI, N., *Bonsai, Miniature Potted Trees*, Tourist Library, XIII, 1951.
OHCHI, H., *Ikebana* (in German and English), Teufen, 1957.
PREININGER, M., *Japanese Flower Arrangements for Modern Homes*, Boston, 1936.
SADLER, A. L., *The Art of Flower Arrangement in Japan*, New York, 1933.
TESHIGAHARA, S., *Ikebana; Japanese Flower Arrangement*, New York, 1958.

ART: THE TEA CEREMONY

OKAKURA, K., *The Book of Tea*, Sydney, 1932. (Many editions.)
SADLER, A. L., *Cha-no-yu, the Japanese Tea Ceremony*, Kobe, 1934.

ART: CALLIGRAPHY

CHIANG YEE, *Chinese Calligraphy*, Harvard, 1955.

MUSIC

HARADA, J., *Japanese Music* (from *Encyclopaedia Britannica*), 1946.
HATTORI and MATSUBARA, *Melodies of Japanese Folk-Songs*, Tokyo, 1951.
HATTORI and MATSUBARA, *Thirty-one Japanese Folk-Songs*, Tokyo, 1954.
PERI, N., *Essai sur les gammes japonaises*, Paris, 1934.
PIGGOTT, SIR F. T., *The Music and Musical Instruments of Japan*, London, 1909.
For recordings of Japanese music *see* Vol. XI of *World Library of Folk and Primitive Music*, edited by A. Lomax (Columbia).

DANCE

UEMOTO, R., and ISHIKAWA, Y., *Introduction to the Classic Dances of Japan*, Tokyo, 1935.

SOCIOLOGY, ANTHROPOLOGY

BEARDSLEY, R. K., WARD, R. E., HALL, J. W., *Village Japan*, Chicago, 1958.
BECKER, J. E. DE, *The Nightless City, or the History of the Yoshiwara Yukwaku*, Yokohama, 1899.
BENEDICT, R., *The Chrysanthemum and the Sword, Patterns of Japanese Culture*, Boston, 1946.
CHAMBERLAIN, B. H., *Things Japanese* (various editions), Kobe and London. (Invaluable collection of information by a distinguished student of Japan.)
CORNELL, J. B., and SMITH, R. J., *Two Japanese Villages*, Ann Arbor, 1956.
EMBREE, J. F., *Suye Mura*, a Japanese Village, Chicago, 1939. (Important sociological study of Japanese rural life.)
ERSKINE, W. H., *Japanese Festival and Calendar Lore*, Tokyo, 1933.
GARIS, F. DE (and YAMAGUCHI, K.), *We Japanese*, Yokohama, 1934 *et seq*. (Useful collection of information about usages and customs.)
HEARN, L., *Japan, an Attempt at Interpretation*, New York, 1904. (The classic introduction of Japan to the west.)
JOYA, M., *Quaint Customs and Manners of Japan* (4 vols.), Tokyo, 1951–5.
MAREGA, M., *Il Giappone nei racconti e nelle leggende*, Bari, 1939.
RUMPF, F., *Japanische Volksmärchen*, Jena, 1938.
TAEUBER, I. B., *The Population of Japan*, Princeton, 1958.
UENODA, S., *Calendar of Annual Events in Japan*, Tokyo, 1951.

In regard to the enormous impressionistic literature about Japan, which ranges from Pierre Loti to Michener, from Lafcadio Hearn to Tracy, I agree with those who hold that one work stands head and shoulders above the rest, namely T. Raucat's *L'honorable partie de campagne* Paris, (1924; published in English as *The Honorable Picnic*, New York, 1927; London, 1928). The distortions of farce conceal a profoundly true portrait.

Notes on Photographs

1. Fujiyama (12,389 feet) seen from the banks of the Izu peninsula, near Mito. The volcano last erupted in 1707, since when it has seemed to be extinct. The wooded islet in the left foreground is Awa-shima. The photograph was taken in February; in summer the snowcap disappears.

2. Matsushima ('Pine Island'), near Sendai, in north Japan. This broad gulf, scattered with rocks on which pines strike root, is traditionally one of the three great natural beauties of Japan. The other two are Ama no Ashidate on the Sea of Japan and the small island of Miyajima, not far from Hiroshima. At Miyajima the natural beauty of the place is enhanced by an ancient Shinto shrine, with a magnificent *torii* made of camphor wood; at high tide this rises straight from the blue sea (Photographs 45, 52, 121).

3. Another beautiful but less well-known stretch of coast is that at Iwami ('Beautiful Rocks'), near Tottori, on the Sea of Japan.

4. The fabulous snowfalls of north Japan are due to the combination of great cold and great humidity. The photograph shows the forest of the Sapporo Dake (4,100 feet), near Sapporo, in Hokkaido. The snow usually lies down to sea level, so that a 3,000-feet mountain provides excellent ski runs. Ski-ing is very popular in Japan; it is more of the Swiss-Austrian than of the French-Italian type, the emphasis being on excursions from hut to hut rather than on running downhill.

5. The peak of Asahi-dake (7,644 feet), the highest in Hokkaido; it is a semi-extinct volcano in a long chain of volcanic mountains (Tokachi-Daisetsuzan).

6. The peak of Hodaka (10,466 feet) in the Japanese Alps, seen from the north. These mountains resemble the Maritime Alps, or the Gran Sasso in the Abruzzi. It is well provided with huts, and climbing there is very popular; it provides excellent scope for the Japanese love of nature and open-air exercise.

7. The wealth of water in Japan is a result of the abundant rainfall.

8. The Kegon waterfall is notorious for continually returning to fashion as a place for suicide, especially *shinjū* (double suicide) as the only way out for lovers who come into conflict with the Confucian code or belong to different social classes; these obstacles still survive powerfully in spite of all appearances to the contrary.

9–10. The rice is sown in seed-beds, planted out in June and July, gathered in October and November. Note the straight lines of seedlings; agriculture done in gardening style. The procession is part of the annual samurai festival *(Soma Noma oi)* at Haramachi in north Japan. On this occasion descendants of the samurai, who nowadays are for the most part farmers, discard the plough and the spade for their ancestral armour and compete in spectacular displays of horsemanship.

11. Fabrics laid out to dry along the Katsura-gawa, not far from the Katsura villa. Washing fabrics in the river *(nuno-sarashi)* is a characteristic activity in the neighbourhood of Kyoto.

12. Gathering in the rice near Hanase (Kyoto). Note the handsome traditional printed cotton dresses worn by the women. After the rice is cut, it is laid out to dry on special wooden frames such as are to be seen in the background; these have different shapes in different districts.

13. In autumn the leaves of the *momiji* (*Acer japonicum, Acer miyabei,* and numerous other species) redden with an extraordinary richness of colour. No Japanese family fails to make at least one excursion to admire the *momiji* 'in bloom'; the newspapers (at Kyoto, for instance) always publish information about the places in the neighbourhood where the leaves are at their best (which lasts for only a few days).

14. Takao (Kyoto), a mountain pass with temples and hermitages scattered about, famous for its *momiji*. At Takao there are also some important art treasures. The Kozan-ji ('High Mountain Temple'), for instance, possesses a series of eleventh- and twelfth-century drawings on scrolls *(emakimono)*; notable among these are the drawings of Toba Sōjō (1053–1140), delightfully parodying the life and customs of Buddhist priests in the form of animals (it should be noted that in view of the unity of the whole world of living things this is not offensive, only playful). Some important and vigorous portraits of the Kamakura period (thirteenth century) are to be found among the pictures in the treasure of the Jingo-ji; the portrait of Minamoto Yoritomo (1147–1199), the founder of the line of Kamakura shoguns, is rightly famous.

15. The temple has recently been rebuilt, faithfully following the ancient design; the fire which destroyed the earlier building can be seen in Photograph 28.

16. Farmhouse in the country near Izumo, which is among the best cared for in Japan. Note the attention which is paid to hedges, roof, rice-field, trees in the garden.

17. Country near Hiroshima; same remarks as above.

18. A corner of the Kosai-ji (Chapter 12); the temple building, with thatched roof, seen from the little balcony by the entrance gate. On the right is the roof of the abbot's house.

19. The biggest farmhouses in Japan, the only ones with three or sometimes four storeys, in the Shirakawa valley (Hida). In this area a patriarchal system used to prevail (it is now disappearing) by which all the members of the same family lived together *(dai kazoku-sei,* 'big family system').

20. Country between Izumo and Hiroshima.

21. Average winter temperatures at Sapporo do not differ greatly from those of Leningrad, though the latitude is that of Elba. The photograph was taken on a stormy day *(fubuki)* in December; little snow was lying yet; in February or March it is deep.

22. Typhoon, hot wind from the south. A sudden gust shook the photographer's hand, causing strange patterns of light on the film.

23. *Rai-jin,* the *kami* of thunder, in the Sanjusangen-do temple at Kyoto. National treasure *(koku-hō)* of the third category.

24. Crater of the Aso volcano (Kyushu). When the author reached the summit he saw a girl at the crater's edge about to throw herself in; her father and brother came hurrying towards her and dragged her away. She had placed a flower among the stones at the crater's edge and traced in the ashes *gomen-kudasai,* 'forgive me'.

25. The pool of boiling mud at Noboribetsu (Hokkaido); this is another place popular with suicides. The boiling mud is said to swallow up everything, even bones; disappearance from this world is immediate and complete. In the same area there is the biggest thermal bathing station in Japan, frequented by those who love life and all its pleasures.

26. The Tenryu ('Holy Dragon') river in flood. On the rocky cliffs on either side above are some enchanting hotel-hermitages, suspended like nests over the waters among ancient pines and ferns.

27. Ruins of a village destroyed by floods scattered over rice-fields buried in mud; a disaster frequent in Japan (at Uji, between Kyoto and Nara).

28. Fire at the great Izumo shrine (1953). Recent fires in which important Japanese artistic monuments have been destroyed include:
    1944—Horinji pagoda, near Nara (one of the three pagodas that had survived from the seventh century; due to lightning).
    1947—Chishaku-in, Kyoto (important pictures by Kano Eitoku and Kano Sanraku destroyed).
    1949—Horyu-ji, near Nara (nearly total loss of famous seventh-century frescoes; the result of negligence).
    1950—Kinkaku-ji, Kyoto (complete destruction of the Golden Pavilion, dating from 1397; arson apparently).
    1953—Taisha, at Izumo.
    1953—Ko-gosho, part of the Imperial Palace at Kyoto.

29. The Ambo pass in the Japanese Alps.

30. Concrete road after an earthquake; between Kobe and Okayama.

31. Self-portrait by peasant-sculptor of the Nagoya neighbourhood (*see* p. 410).

32. *Ukiyo-e,* by Utamaro, belonging to a series of prints called *Ten Portraits of Women*.

33. For *haniwa see* p. 139. That photographed here is in the National Museum in Tokyo.

34, 35. Magnificent old man of typically Mongolian type (rudimentary beard); another magnificent old man of typical Ainu type (strong beard, European-like features). As a result of the continual crossing of the two races few pure Ainu survive.

36. Young and old members of the Japanese *interi* (intelligentzia).

37. Japanese worker. The Chiba steelworks, Tokyo.

38. Peasant girl of Ohara (Kyoto).

39. Girl from Akana, between Izumo and Hiroshima.

40. Girl at Kinosaki (province of Hyogo) with her little brother on her back. This is the normal manner *(ombu)* of carrying a child; it leaves the hands free for house-work, or even work in the fields.

41. Children are held in their mother's arms *(dakko)* only for feeding. Fisherman's wife at Tottori, a village on the Iwami coast.

42, 43. Two of the powerful girl swimmers who fish for *awabi* (a highly appreciated sea delicacy) off the island of Hekura, in the Sea of Japan. Provided only with goggles, they dive to a depth of sixty feet and more; the piece of metal is to remove the shells from the rocks. The fishing season is from July to September. There are several hundred of these *ama* ('sea women') in this neighbourhood; there are other *ama* villages elsewhere along the Japanese coast.

44, 45. Religious music *(gagaku)* and dancing at the Shinto shrine of Miyajima.

46. The chief priest of the Shinto shrine of Izumo in his ceremonial dress. On his head he wears the *kammuri,* in his hand he carries the *shaku* (symbol of authority); his silk robe is called a *shōzoku.*

47. Procession of *uneme* ('ancient court ladies') at Nara.

48. The long covered ascent that leads to the Hase temple, near Nara.

49. Meditation *(zazen)* in a chapel reserved for the purpose in the Shokoku temple (Kyoto).

50. Lanterns lit, house open, ready to welcome the spirits of the dead during the *o-bon* festival in August; at Onjuku, in the Bōsō peninsula.

51. Religious service *(kuyō)* for the dead at the Gokoku temple (Tokyo). The eclectic Japanese generally celebrate marriages and births with Shinto ceremonies; in the case of death, however, recourse is had almost exclusively to Buddhist ceremonial.

52. Miyajima, near Hiroshima.

53. Country near Hamamatsu.

54. A delegation of industrialists pays homage to the *kami* Inari (Kyoto). Typical interior of a Shinto shrine, characterized by extreme cleanliness and simplicity; the only ornaments are certain ritual pieces of paper called *gohei* (they are to be seen on the left, and high up on the right) which stand for offerings of cloth made to the god in ancient times. In the course of time these have turned into symbols for the *kami.*

55. At prayer outside the Tōji gate at Kyoto. The pagoda in the background, of which only part is to be seen, is the highest in Japan (206 feet).

56. Typical of Shinto ceremonial are the purity of the colours and the absence of ornament.

57. Preparations for the Kanda Myojin procession (Tokyo); two *kannushi* (Shinto priests) with flabellae. In the background groups of palanquin bearers, wearing their characteristic skirts *(happi).* In the foreground box for offerings, decorated with *gohei.*

58. Crowd on its way to the Shinto shrine of Kurama.

59. Samurai festival at Haramachi. *See* note to Photographs 9, 10.

60, 61. *Iyomande*, the 'sacred despatch' of the bear, the great annual Ainu festival in Hokkaido, at Kotan, on the banks of Lake Kuccharo (Akan). Old people pray outside the bear's cage, offering drops of millet beer with libation sticks *(iku-bashui)*. The red coats *(jimbaori)* are of Japanese origin. Women dance round the cage singing prayers and refrains. Note the sacred poles called *inao* on the cage, which resemble certain Shinto *gohei*. The women's costumes *(attush)* show the characteristic Ainu decorative motifs. Photograph taken in March.

62–66. Types and faces at a popular festival in Tokyo, that of the Three Guardians, which takes place at the end of spring and is held in commemoration of three fishermen who in the seventh century A.D. fished up a golden statuette of the *bodhisattva* Kwannon in their nets and founded the celebrated Asakusa temple. The festival, with its mixture of Shinto and Buddhist elements, is a normal manifestation of Japanese religious eclecticism.

67. The town of Kurashiki (55,000 population, prefecture of Okayama) was a great centre of the rice trade in the time of the Tokugawa shoguns. Many of the ancient warehouses (of architectural interest) have been preserved, thanks to the munificence of the industrialist and patron of the arts Ohara. At Kurashiki there is also the only good collection of western art in Japan (particularly French nineteenth century, Renoir, Matisse, Toulouse Lautrec, Van Gogh, Monet; also a valuable El Greco). The two peasants to be seen in the photograph came from Shikoku and, like the author, were visiting the Ohara museum of popular arts.

68. Not all houses in the Japanese countryside have thatched roofs; in many areas the roofs are made of wooden shingles, held in place by stones. The trousers *(mompé)* that women wear for work in the country are traditional, not a modern importation.

69. Typical peasant kitchen, with open hearth *(irori)* in the middle of the room; near Wadayama (province of Kyoto).

70. Kitchen of an old and wealthy country house, near Kyoto.

71. Note the Buddhist altar and the wireless set, ancestors' portraits (old photographs), grandmother and grandchildren. The floor is covered with *tatami*; behind there are *fusuma* (opaque sliding doors) and *shōji* (sliding doors with light paper panels).

71, 72. The presence of a small Shinto altar *(kami-dana)* does not exclude that of a small Buddhist shrine *(butsu-dan)* in another room in the same house. The altar always contains tablets bearing the names of the family's ancestors, as well as a statue, which may be of Shaka, *i.e.,* Sakyamuni, the Buddha of history, or of Amida, or some other celestial personage, depending on the sect to which the household belongs. The Shinto altar generally includes a small metal mirror (standing for the sun, *i.e.,* Amaterasu Omikami), or some other sacred object from the shrine with which the family is traditionally connected. Note in the photograph the branches of *sakaki (Cleyera japonca)*, the piece of rice-straw rope *(shimenawa)* with paper ornaments *(nigite, gohei)*, and various talismans.

73, 74. Lessons in classical matters at Kyoto. Flower arrangement and the tea ceremony were and still are considered important elements in the education of girls of good family. Note how the best traditional taste harmonizes naturally with the most modern western taste; the ideal of both is simplicity, avoidance of the superfluous. The male Japanese dress is perhaps the most elegant, dignified, and practical means of covering the human form that has yet been devised, in contrast to our irrational and hideous western dress, which constricts the limbs and the neck as if they were sausages. It should be remembered that our style of clothing is basically derived from the clothing of nomadic barbarians who lived by hunting, and was intended in the first place for riding; that is why it binds and constricts. In the case of women the Japanese kimono is less practical than the western blouse and skirt; the *obi*, the big sash round the waist, is difficult to keep in place, and sometimes restricts the breathing.

75. This Kyoto craftsman is finishing a lantern with the word *sushi* (croquettes of rice with raw fish) on it, no doubt for some small restaurant. The gaiety of the lanterns by day and their enchantment by night is largely responsible for the attractiveness of Japanese popular and entertainment quarters.

76. Entrance to the Heihachi restaurant in the neighbourhood of Kyoto, an ancient establishment, dating back to the times of the samurai, where everything is of solid and sober country taste. The two waitresses are wearing peasant dress.

77. Interior of one of the best-known shops at which tea is sold at Kyoto. This establishment too is several centuries old. Some of the innumerable varieties of tea sold here are contained in the earthenware vessels on the shelves. The ideograms above read *Ryuō-en* ('Cherry and Willow Garden'); they recall the name of a famous tea-garden at Uji, between Nara and Kyoto.

78. Meeting of peasants to read announcements about the latest findings in regard to chemical fertilizers. The picture was taken when the author stopped by chance in the country and was offered tea in the house shown here. Note *(a)* the typical Japanese interior; the *tatami* on the floor; the sliding doors of wood and paper *(shōji)* in the background; in the middle rails which can be used to support sliding wall-doors *(fusuma)*; what is now in use as a big room able to contain a number of people is probably normally divided into two; *(b)* the three men on the right are seated in the formal position, the position of respect *(suwaru)*, i.e., practically on their knees; the fourth is sitting in the position of familiarity or rest *(agura wo kaku)*. Each has a cup of tea in front of him; there is the usual plate of biscuits; and there are several braziers (*hibachi*), which are used to warm your hands in winter and serve as ash-trays all the year round. The clothes are those normally worn during the warm season and for work, that is to say, trousers and short-sleeved shirt; the Japanese, used to kimono or *yukata*, sensibly decline the irrational servitude of long sleeves fastened at the wrist. The scene is an interesting example of the Japanese tendency to do everything in groups or parties, and of their lively interest in every novelty, particularly technical novelty, aimed at solving the practical problems of life.

79, 80. A big steelworks on the outskirts of Tokyo. Recording bargains in the Osaka stock exchange.

81. The Naiku at Ise *(see pp. 132–6)*. Note the following details: the construction on tall piles; weight borne by the pillars, the walls being partitions only; the meticulous thatching of the roof, attention being paid both to line and surface; the ornamental prolongation of the four beams *(chigi)* at the extremities of the roof; the ornamental development of the timbers *(katsuogi)* which keep the top of the roof in place (in this case there are an even number of these; in an ordinary Japanese house the number is always uneven) as well as of the beam which runs along the top of the roof; the clean *hinoki* (cypress) wood; the lack of ornamentation or paint. The building is rebuilt in the *shimmei* style every twenty years in accordance with plans which have remained unchanged since A.D. 685 (the next rebuilding is due in 1974). It is closely related to the typical south-east Asian house (Indo-China, Malaya, East Indies). It contains the *yata no kagami* (the sacred mirror, one of the Three Treasures and token of the imperial power).

82. This fine piece of sculpture is mentioned on pp. 189–90.

83. Photograph taken during repairs to the temple in September, 1953; steel scaffolding can be seen in the background. Normally it is impossible to take a photograph so close to the Buddha's head; the statue is about twelve feet high, including the base; it is one of the finest examples of Fujiwara sculpture, and bears the signature of Jōchō. (*Kokuhō*, national treasure.)

84. This small temple contains the tombs of a number of Fujiwara princes who in the twelfth century tried to introduce some of the splendour and refinement of the capital (Kyoto) to their cold territories in the far north. A number of temples in a big park near Hiraizumi still bear witness to the flourishing of a brief dynasty; they contain some of the most notable examples of twelfth-century Japanese sculpture.

85. The pagoda, one of the most elegant in Japan, was rebuilt in 1426, its predecessor having been destroyed by fire. It forms part of the Kōfuki-ji, a huge temple built at Nara by the Fujiwara family. The pinnacle *(sōrin)* is the part of the structure in which the metaphysical symbolism culminates (pp. 163 *et seq.*).

86. In the background, behind the *torii,* is the sacred library *(rinzō)*; on the right is the so-called Drum Tower. Overhanging everything is the marvellous *sugi* foliage, fading into the mist.

87–90. Tokyo, at Marunouchi, outside the Central Station; Osaka, seen from the Shinsai bridge; Kyoto, view from the Eastern Hills (Higashi-yama); Himeji, dating originally from about 1350, but rebuilt and expanded by Hideyoshi in 1581. This is the biggest Japanese castle, dating back to the Momoyama period (sixteenth century); dozens were built during that agitated period, but as a result of wars, fires, earthquakes, neglect, only the memory of most of them remains.

91. Another view of the pagoda seen in Photograph 85 (Kōfuki-ji at Nara), at sunset, from the top of one of the trees in the park.

92. The garden of the Temple of the Celestial Dragon at Kyoto is described on pp. 279 *et seq.*

93. The path is indicated by big, irregular-shaped stones *(tobi-ishi)*; and mosses are used to merge them with their surroundings (private garden at Kyoto).

94. Not a branch is left to its own caprice; on the other hand no trace of man's hand must be visible. The result is subtle fusion of house and nature (private garden at Kyoto).

95. Note the flower-vase made out of a hollowed-out old tree-trunk; the wealth of harmonics that are born when rough, corroded surfaces (corroded by the sea? driftwood found on the beach?) are placed next to flowers in the full glory of scent, colour, sap (Ryoan-ji, Kyoto).

96. Fusion of house and garden; edge of veranda *(engawa)*, cushion, book, irregular stones, *geta* (wooden sandals), lawn (private house, Atami).

97, 98. On the tables, left: *hashi* (chopsticks) on tiny porcelain supports; on the left-hand plate some kinds of *tsukidashi* (hors-d'œuvre); in the square dish *sashimi* (raw fish) and seaweed; then a vessel containing sauce and a *saké* cup. Right: cup with lid, containing soup; red, leaf-shaped plate with various hors-d'œuvres; small *saké* cup, *hashi*. Below in both pictures *tatami*, with the regular lines of the smooth, woven straw (restaurant, Tokyo).

99. Kimono, with pattern inspired by the sixteen-petalled imperial chrysanthemum, worn by Yachigusa Kaoru, a well-known actress. Photograph taken in Rome, on the steps of Santa Trinità dei Monti, with azaleas in bloom.

100. *Obi* (sash) of a fashionable type *(fukura-suzume)* which harmonizes with a particularly loose and light kimono. In the infinite variety of movements the *tamoto* (wing of the sleeve) becomes an element in the plastic composition. The girl is standing on one of the 'anti-demon' bridges often to be found in Japanese gardens. According to an ancient and amusing belief, demons (like rhinoceroses) are able to charge only in a straight line; a suitably constructed bridge will therefore inevitably make them fall into the water.

101. *Maiko* (pupil geisha) at Kyoto. Her hair is done in the *momoware style*: the big hairpins decorated with flowers are called *kanzashi*. In the background *momiji* 'in bloom'.

102. The sash worn by *maiko* is of a special shape *(darari no obi)* and reaches down nearly to the ankles. The high sandals *(pokkuri)* are made of specially light wood.

103. The colour of a kimono is always adapted to the age of its wearer. Red is worn by girls, blue by young women, purple by older women, and grey by the aged.

104. *See* p. 343.

105. Inscription on a *tsuitate* (screen placed outside the entrance to a house) at the Sambō-in temple at Kyoto.

106. *Fusuma* (sliding doors) with paintings in the Tenkyu-in temple (part of the Myoshin-ji) at Kyoto. Momoyama period, traditionally attributed to Kano Sanraku (1561–1635).

107. Late windy afternoon on the Japanese coast, in Tsuruga bay.

108. Pine tree shuts off a walk in the Katsura villa.

109. At certain times of the year this 'lion dance' is danced in the street as a cheerful way of exorcizing evil spirits. Note the drum in the foreground. The dancer's boots and muddy trousers show the spontaneous nature of the performance. Photograph taken not far from Kanazawa.

110. The celebrated actor Kita Minoru; the mask is that of Hannya, the female spirit in its fierce, vindictive, jealous aspect.

111. Scene for the *Tale of Genji* at a *kabuki* theatre. This is not a typical play in the *kabuki* repertory, but a recent adaptation.

112. View from the 'murmur of the pines' kiosk in the gardens of the Katsura villa.

113. Cat and peonies on an ancient door of bare wood in the Myoshin-ji (Kyoto), attributed to Kano Motonobu (1476–1559).

114. Materials, interior and exterior, clothes, man; aesthetic equilibrium of a civilization that has achieved fullness of expression. Izumo, at the residence of the Taisha priests.

115. Another detail of the Katsura villa (Kyoto). Note the decorative value of the stone lantern *(ishi-doro)*.

116. Gesture of a fleeting moment fits naturally into the clear geometry of the Japanese room and background. Photograph taken in an ancient Buddhist monks' home, looking towards the Yasaka pagoda (1618) at Kyoto.

117. Eating with chopsticks *(hashi)*. The rice bowl is held in the left hand.

118. Bed made of *futon* (quilts) laid on the *tatami* for the night. During the day the *futon* are put away in wall cupboards, and the room is without encumbrances. Note the telephone in the *tokonoma* (alcove for objects of beauty), together with an arrangement of flowers and a painting. Certain elements of modern life have not yet found their place in the Japanese aesthetic and functional pattern but, in view of what has happened in the past, it is safe to foresee that eventually the arrangements that are reached will be ingenious, tasteful, and intelligent.

119. Small bath at a hot spring. For domestic baths perfumed wood is generally preferred to tiles. (Yumoto *onsen*, between Tokyo and Sendai.)

120. What remained of Nagoya (a town of a million inhabitants) after the raids of March–April, 1945. In the foreground, the author's wife and three daughters. Photograph taken soon after release from internment. (Chapter 12.)

121. Student couples visiting the Miyajima shrine; in the background the celebrated *torii*. Students of different sex who go out together still have to face strong prejudices.

122. A small *pachinko* establishment the name of which speaks of the clash of civilizations (Kinosaki hot springs, on the Sea of Japan).

123. In the background, eighth-century temples at Nara, the oldest wooden buildings in the world and remarkable examples of building technique. In the foreground, enthusiastic twentieth-century photographers testing the latest long-distance lens produced by the Japanese industry. (The same craftsmen's and engineers' eyes and fingers applied with equal skill and assurance to new problems.)

124. The car has the ordinary Tokyo number plate (p. 100).

125. The old man has put his ticket in the band of his bowler-hat; the rest of his clothing consists of kimono and coat *(haori)*; he is carrying a closed fan and some personal effects wrapped in a big handkerchief *(furoshiki)*; and he is wearing velvet socks *(tabi)* and wooden sandals *(geta)*. In the background is an ordinary third-class railway carriage. Small country station in Kyushu.

126. Peasant with baby tied to his back *(ombu)* enjoying himself taking photographs in the street (Sendai).

127. The art of carrying children on one's back raised to perfection. Note also umbrella and *geta* (Tokyo).

128. Publicity (for mass-produced clothing) and reading. Probably a student supplementing his meagre allowance from home by *arbaito* (German *Arbeit,* work).

129. Reading matter for children is abundant; here there is to be seen a medley of illustrated song-books, fairy stories, descriptions of the wonders of modern technique, ancient Japanese legends, translations of Walt Disney, translations from the French *(Le Petit Oiseau Vert).*

130. Street in modern Kurashiki.

131. Everybody reads in the train (the man facing is reading baseball reports).

132. Tokyo bookshop. Provided you do not sit down, there is nothing to prevent you from reading a book from cover to cover. There are impoverished young men who succeed in educating themselves in this way.

133. Popular festival *(matsuri)* at Shinagawa, near Tokyo. Note the elegance of the costume on the left, with its black and white triangles. This photograph, with the gasometer in the background, reveals the Japanese loyalty to their traditions, which is one of the most important factors in the country's spiritual strength.

134. Some samurai whose horses were lamed at the Haramachi festival *(see* Photographs 9 and 10) go home by lorry. The big samurai on the left does not seem pleased at the scene's being photographed. The three ideograms on the lorry door say *Jika-yo* ('private carrier').

135. Lights of the Ginza, the commercial centre of Tokyo; it should be borne in mind that they are in continuous movement.

136. The *pachinko* craze.

137. The inscription on the lantern is *go-sairei* ('honourable festival'); it was one of those hung in the street for the Three Guardians festival (Tokyo).

138. The sign on the right bears the two ideograms for 'Fuji', the name of the *o-chaya* (p. 348) of which it marks the entrance.

139. At the top the words 'Terrific, terrific' can be seen. The signs shows the names of the artists; one of them announces a parody of *The Seven Samurai.* The Americans are wearing silk shirts embroidered with maps and dragons. (Tokyo, Asakusa quarter.)

140. Tourist publicity speaks of 'Tokyo, the Paris of the Orient', but there is something homely and domesticated about the nude here; it seems to lack the naughty touch it would like to have borrowed from the Folies Bergère (theatre at Shinjuku, Tokyo).

141, 142. Yoshiwara, the famous red light district in Tokyo, dating back to the seventeenth century. It has recently been closed.

143–146. The refinements of Japanese life form a brief interruption to the bustle of modern life.

147. Near the American camp at Chitose, in Hokkaido (now done away with).

148, 149. Tokyo.

150. Nikko.

151. Chitose (Hokkaido).

152. Chitose (Hokkaido). Note 'Beer Holl' *(sic)* in the background.

153. The inscription on the box says: 'Wounded soldier trying to re-establish himself respectfully seeks honourable co-operation' (Sendai).

154. The heat generated by the atomic bomb melted and twisted the bottle without destroying it. A mouthful of beer remains inside, imprisoned and immortal.

General Index